CHRISTIANITY

IN

JEWISH TERMS

RADICAL TRADITIONS

THEOLOGY IN A POSTCRITICAL KEY

Series Editors: Stanley M. Hauerwas, Duke University, and Peter Ochs, University of Virginia

BOOKS IN THE SERIES

FORTHCOMING

Radical Traditions cuts new lines of inquiry across a confused array of debates concerning the place of theology in modernity and, more generally, the status and role of scriptural faith in contemporary life. Charged with a rejuvenated confidence, spawned in part by the rediscovery of reason as inescapably tradition constituted, a new generation of theologians and religious scholars is returning to scriptural traditions with the hope of retrieving resources long ignored, depreciated, and in many cases ideologically suppressed by modern habits of thought. *Radical Traditions* assembles a promising matrix of strategies, disciplines, and lines of thought that invites Jewish, Christian, and Islamic theologians back to the word, recovering and articulating modes of scriptural reasoning as that which always underlies modernist reasoning and therefore has the capacity—and authority—to correct it.

Far from despairing over modernity's failings, postcritical theologies rediscover resources for renewal and self-correction within the disciplines of academic study themselves. Postcritical theologies open up the possibility of participating once again in the living relationship that binds together God, text, and community of interpretation. *Radical Traditions* thus advocates a "return to the text," which means a commitment to displaying the richness and wisdom of traditions that are at once text based, hermeneutical, and oriented to communal practice.

Books in this series offer the opportunity to speak openly with practitioners of other faiths or even with those who profess no (or limited) faith, both academics and nonacademics, about the ways religious traditions address pivotal issues of the day. Unfettered by foundationalist preoccupations, these books represent a call for new paradigms of reason—a thinking and rationality that is more responsive than originative. By embracing a postcritical posture, they are able to speak unapologetically out of scriptural traditions manifest in the practices of believing communities (Jewish, Christian, and others); articulate those practices through disciplines of philosophic, textual, and cultural criticism; and engage intellectual, social, and political practices that for too long have been insulated from theological evaluation. *Radical Traditions* is radical not only in its confidence in nonapologetic theological speech but also in how the practice of such speech challenges the current social and political arrangements of modernity.

CHRISTIANITY
IN
JEWISH TERMS

EDITORS

Tikva Frymer-Kensky

David Novak

Peter Ochs

David Fox Sandmel

Michael A. Signer

Westview Press

A Member of the Perseus Books Group

Published in 2000 in the United States of America by Westview Press, 5500 Central Avenue, Boulder, Colorado 80301-2877, and in the United Kingdom by Westview Press, 12 Hid's Copse Road, Cumnor Hill, Oxford OX2 9JJ

Find us on the World Wide Web at www.westviewpress.com

Library of Congress Cataloging-in-Publication Data
Christianity in Jewish terms / edited by Tikva Frymer-Kensky ... [et al.].
     p.   cm.
   Includes bibliographical references and index.
   ISBN 0-8133-3780-1
   1. Judaism—Relations—Christianity.   2. Christianity and other religions—
Judaism.   3. Judaism (Christian theology).   4. Christianity in rabbinical literature.
I. Frymer-Kensky, Tikva Simone.

BM535 C5775   2000
296.3'96—dc21
                                                                    00-044773

The paper used in this publication meets the requirements of the American National Standard for Permanence of Paper for Printed Library Materials Z39.48-1984.

10   9   8   7   6   5   4   3   2   1

CONTENTS

PREFACE

Over the past few decades there has been a dramatic and unprecedented shift in Jewish and Christian relations. Throughout the nearly two millennia of Jewish exile, Christian theologians and clerics have tended to characterize Judaism as a failed religion or, at best, a religion that prepared the way for Christianity and that is completed in and replaced by Christianity. In the four decades since the Holocaust, however, Christianity has changed dramatically. Both individual theologians and, then, an increasing number of official church bodies, both Catholic and Protestant, have made public statements of their remorse about Christian mistreatment of Jews and Judaism over the last two millennia. These statements have declared, furthermore, that Christian theologies, liturgies, and Bible teachings can and must be reformed so that they acknowledge God's enduring covenant with the Jewish people and celebrate the contribution of Judaism to world civilization and to Christian faith itself.

Most Jews have experienced the profound social consequences of this change in Christian beliefs, but few Jews are aware of the religious sources of the change, and even fewer seek to assess its impact on Jewish life today and in the future. The Jewish authors and editors of this book believe it is high time to acknowledge these recent changes in Christianity and to examine their implications for Jewish life in the Western world. In this volume, we begin the process of examination by taking a careful second look at Christian religious belief—as it has been since the early centuries of the Christian era and as it has become in the last few decades.

We believe that living as a minority in a still largely Christian America—and Christian West—Jews need to learn the languages and beliefs of their neighbors. They need to understand the meaning of what their Christian neighbors are saying: about what modern society should become, and about the place of the Jewish people itself in that society. Jews need to learn ways of judging what forms of Christianity are friendly to them and what forms are not, and what forms of Christian belief merit their public support, and what forms do not. They need, as well, to acknowledge the efforts of those Christians who have sacrificed aspects of their work and of their lives to combat Christian anti-Judaism and to promote forms of Christian practice that are friendly to Jewish life and belief. Jews need to know enough about Christian belief to be able to explain their own Jewish goals and ideals for society in terms their Christian neighbors will understand.

For the past hundreds of years, when Jews have been taught about Christian belief, it has been primarily in non-Jewish terms. During the years of their residence in Christian Europe, Jews learned about Christianity only through the untranslated terms of a Christianity that separated itself from its Jewish roots. Then, during the years that followed Emancipation, Jews learned about Christianity through the equally non-Jewish terms of secular European thought. This was often the most difficult kind of learning, since secular European thought often treated Christianity as a universal religion, as opposed to the particularity or "tribalism" of Judaism. We believe it is time for Jews to learn about Christianity in Jewish terms: to rediscover the basic categories of rabbinic Judaism and to hear what the basic categories of Christian belief sound like when they are taught in terms of this rabbinic Judaism. To hear Christianity in our terms is truly to understand it, perhaps for the first time.

If Christianity is changing in these years after the Holocaust, Judaism is changing as well. During the past two hundred years, Judaism has suffered from an increasing inner division that has separated the realms of science and reason on the one hand from those of faith and tradition on the other. It is as if the Jewish religion itself spoke of an unbridgeable gulf between the human and the divine. The editors of this volume, however, are animated by a different vision. The Judaism of the Bible, Talmud, and other classical Jewish sources has always emphasized the partnership of humanity and God. In this volume, the editors have therefore gathered together essays that help rediscover the power of the classical sources of Judaism to heal the divisions from which we suffer today: between human reason and Jewish faith, as well as between Judaism and Christianity.

The central ten chapters of this volume address our two main concerns: how to renew our understanding of Judaism today from out of the sacred texts and, then, how to understand Christianity in terms of this Judaism. Each chapter, consisting of three essays, treats a key theological concept in Judaism and Christianity. In the first essay, a Jewish scholar teaches about a particular area of Jewish theological tradition and then offers ways for Jews to understand a corresponding set of Christian beliefs. In the second essay, another Jewish thinker describes from his or her own perspective another way to understand both the Jewish and the Christian beliefs. In the third essay, a Christian scholar responds to the first essay and answers the questions: "Do I recognize my Christianity in what has been written? What is the significance of Judaism for my understanding of Christianity?"

This is a bold undertaking: to be open to thinking seriously about Christianity, let alone about God and religion in a new way! How do we avoid the pitfalls that have characterized efforts at Jewish and Christian understanding in the past? In Chapter 1, one of our editors offers lessons in "what to seek and what to avoid in Jewish–Christian dialogue." In light of the tragic history of Jewish–Christian relations in the past, why should we risk this endeavor at all? In Chapter 2, a Jewish historian notes both the negative and positive aspects of Jewish and Christian interaction from the first century through modern times. In Chapter 3, a Jewish and a Christian theologian offer responses to the most challenging question of all: "And *now*, after the Shoah, do we still dare to promote such a dialogue? How can Jews and Christians speak about each other's religion and about God?" While creating this volume, the authors and editors themselves have wrestled with these same questions, and in the process have gained new understanding and insight. In the Epilogue, one Christian scholar evaluates the impact of Judaism on Christian belief today, and the book's editors then reflect on the impact of this project on their own expectations of the future of Judaism and of Jewish–Christian relations.

The publication of this book marks only the beginning of an effort that may engage us for years to come, an effort to encourage Jews to rediscover the revered place of Judaism among the great religions of the world. This is also an effort to help Jews relearn the vocabulary of their own faith and then, within this vocabulary, to help them recognize and understand the main tenets of their neighbors' faiths. At the same time, our goal is to acknowledge and aid the complementary efforts of Christian scholars and leaders to teach Christians the main tenets of Judaism and, thereby, to rediscover the significance of Judaism as both a source of Christianity and a dialogue partner in the ultimate work of redeeming a troubled world.

In September 2000, we published a public statement in the *New York Times* and other newspapers. The statement is a brief explanation of how we believe Jews should begin to learn about Christianity and to understand Christianity in Jewish terms. This volume of essays is a scholarly extension of that statement, which appears here just after the acknowledgments. This volume has also stimulated the preparation of a study guide, which is being prepared by the Institute for Christian & Jewish Studies for the use of synagogue, church, and student groups who would like to make the issues addressed in this book the subject of ongoing discussion.

The Jewish and Christian scholars and theologians who have contributed to this project are among the most revered and influential contributors to religious thought today. We are profoundly grateful to them. They have taken considerable time from demanding work schedules to meet this volume's exacting publication requirements—the first of which was to enter boldly into a form of theological exchange that may have no precedent! The energy, efficiency, and depth of their responses are testimony both to their generosity and, we believe, to the urgency of this endeavor.

Tikva Frymer-Kensky
David Novak
Peter Ochs
David Fox Sandmel
Michael A. Signer

ACKNOWLEDGMENTS

For years, the Institute for Christian & Jewish Studies (ICJS) has played a leading role in fostering Jewish–Christian understanding. We are deeply grateful to the ICJS for helping sponsor this book project and the activities of publication and discussion that accompany it. We are indebted, in particular, to Charles Obrecht, board chairman of ICJS; Rev. Dr. Christopher Leighton, executive director of the ICJS; Dr. Rosann Catalano, ICJS Roman Catholic scholar; and Rabbi Joel Zaiman, ICJS board member and spiritual leader of Congregation Chizuk Amuno. We wish to thank the Stella and Charles Guttman Foundation, Inc.; the David and Barbara B. Hirschhorn Foundation, Inc.; the Hoffberger Family Fund; the Harvey M. Meyerhoff Fund; and the Harry and Jeanette Weinberg Foundation for their ongoing support of this project. This book was also made possible, in part, by funds granted by the Charles H. Revson Foundation. The statements made and the views expressed, however, are solely the responsibility of the authors. Finally, we want to thank all of our editors and support staff at Westview Press, in particular Sarah Warner, the editor for this book. We owe a particular debt of gratitude to David Toole, whose editorial work was above and beyond the call of duty.

T. F.-K.
D. N.
P. O.
D. F. S.
M. A. S.

A JEWISH STATEMENT
ON CHRISTIANS AND
CHRISTIANITY

In recent years, there has been a dramatic and unprecedented shift in Jewish and Christian relations. Throughout the nearly two millennia of Jewish exile, Christians have tended to characterize Judaism as a failed religion or, at best, a religion that prepared the way for, and is completed in, Christianity. In the decades since the Holocaust, however, Christianity has changed dramatically. An increasing number of official church bodies, both Roman Catholic and Protestant, have made public statements of their remorse about Christian mistreatment of Jews and Judaism. These statements have declared, furthermore, that Christian teaching and preaching can and must be reformed so that they acknowledge God's enduring covenant with the Jewish people and celebrate the contribution of Judaism to world civilization and to Christian faith itself.

We believe these changes merit a thoughtful Jewish response. Speaking only for ourselves—an interdenominational group of Jewish scholars—we believe it is time for Jews to learn about the efforts of Christians to honor Judaism. We believe it is time for Jews to reflect on what Judaism may now say about Christianity. As a first step, we offer eight brief statements about how Jews and Christians may relate to one another.

Jews and Christians worship the same God.

Before the rise of Christianity, Jews were the only worshippers of the God of Israel. But Christians also worship the God of Abraham, Isaac, and Jacob, creator of heaven and earth. Although Christian worship is not a viable religious choice for Jews, as Jewish theologians we rejoice that through Christianity hundreds of millions of people have entered into relationship with the God of Israel.

Jews and Christians seek authority from the same book—the Bible (what Jews call "Tanakh" and Christians call the "Old Testament").

Turning to the Bible for religious orientation, spiritual enrichment, and communal education, we each take away similar lessons: God created and sustains the universe; God established a covenant with the people Israel; God's revealed word guides Israel to a life of righteousness; and God will ultimately redeem Israel and the whole world. Yet, Jews and Christians interpret the Bible differently on many points. Such differences must always be respected.

Christians can respect the claim of the Jewish people upon the land of Israel.

The most important event for Jews since the Holocaust has been the reestablishment of a Jewish state in the Promised Land. As members of a biblically based religion, Christians appreciate that Israel was promised—and given—to Jews as the physical center of the covenant between them and God. Many Christians support the State of Israel for reasons far more profound than mere politics. As Jews, we applaud this support. We also recognize that Jewish tradition mandates justice for all non-Jews who reside in a Jewish state.

Jews and Christians accept the moral principles of Torah.

Central to the moral principles of Torah are the inalienable sanctity and dignity of every human being. All of us were created in the image of God. This shared moral emphasis can be the basis of an improved relationship between our two communities. It can also be the basis of a powerful witness to all humanity for improving the lives of our fellow human beings and for standing against the immoralities and idolatries that harm and degrade us. Such witness is especially needed after the unprecedented horrors of the past century.

Nazism was not a Christian phenomenon.

Without the long history of Christian anti-Judaism and Christian violence against Jews, Nazi ideology could not have taken hold nor could it have been carried out. Too many Christians participated in, or were sympathetic to, Nazi atrocities against Jews. Other Christians did not protest sufficiently against these atrocities. But Nazism itself was not an inevitable outcome of Christianity. If the Nazi extermination of the Jews had been fully successful, it would have turned its murderous rage more directly to Christians. We recognize with gratitude those Christians who risked or sacrificed their lives to save Jews during the Nazi regime. With that in mind, we encourage the continuation of recent efforts in Christian theology to repudiate unequivocally contempt of Judaism and the Jewish people. We applaud those Christians who reject this teaching of contempt, and we do not blame them for the sins committed by their ancestors.

The humanly irreconcilable difference between Jews and Christians will not be settled until God redeems the entire world as promised in Scripture.

Christians know and serve God through Jesus Christ and the Christian tradition. Jews know and serve God through Torah and the Jewish tradition. That difference will not be settled by one community insisting that it has interpreted Scripture more accurately than the other, nor by one community exercising political power over the other. Jews can respect Christians' faithfulness to their revelation just as we expect Christians to respect our faithfulness to our revelation. Neither Jew nor Christian should be pressed into affirming the teaching of the other community.

A new relationship between Jews and Christians will not weaken Jewish practice.

An improved relationship will not accelerate the cultural and religious assimilation that Jews rightly fear. It will not change traditional Jewish forms of worship, nor increase intermarriage between Jews and non-Jews, nor persuade more Jews to convert to Christianity, nor create a false blending of Judaism and Christianity. We respect Christianity as a faith that originated within Judaism and that still has significant contacts with it. We do not see it as an extension of Judaism. Only if we cherish our own traditions can we pursue this relationship with integrity.

Jews and Christians must work together for justice and peace.

Jews and Christians, each in their own way, recognize the unredeemed state of the world as reflected in the persistence of persecution, poverty, and human degradation and misery. Although justice and peace are finally God's, our joint efforts, together with those of other faith communities, will help bring the kingdom of God for which we hope and long. Separately and together, we must work to bring justice and peace to our world. In this enterprise, we are guided by the vision of the prophets of Israel:

> It shall come to pass in the end of days that the mountain of the Lord's house shall be established at the top of the mountains and be exalted above the hills, and the nations shall flow unto it . . . and many peoples shall go and say, "Come ye and let us go up to the mountain of the Lord to the house of the God of Jacob and He will teach us of His ways and we will walk in his paths. (Isaiah 2:2–3)

ABBREVIATIONS

Tanach

Gen.	Genesis
Ex.	Exodus
Lev.	Leviticus
Num.	Numbers
Deut.	Deuteronomy
Jos.	Joshua
Jud.	Judges
1 Sam.	1 Samuel
2 Sam.	2 Samuel
1 Kgs.	1 Kings
2 Kgs.	2 Kings
Is.	Isaiah
Jer.	Jeremiah
Ezek.	Ezekiel
Hos.	Hosea
Obad.	Obadiah
Jon.	Jonah
Mic.	Micah
Nah.	Nahum
Hag.	Haggai
Zech.	Zechariah
Hab.	Habakkuk
Zeph.	Zephaniah
Mal.	Malachi
Ps.	Psalms
Prov.	Proverbs
Qoh.	Qohelet
Lam.	Lamentations
Est.	Esther
Dan.	Daniel
Neh.	Nehemiah
1 Chr.	1 Chronicles
2 Chr.	2 Chronicles

New Testament

Mt.	Matthew
Mk.	Mark
Lk.	Luke
Jn.	John
Rom.	Romans
1 Cor.	1 Corinthians
2 Cor.	2 Corinthians
Gal.	Galatians
Eph.	Ephesians
Col.	Colossians
1 Thes.	1 Thessalonians
2 Thes.	2 Thessalonians
1 Tim.	1 Timothy
2 Tim.	2 Timothy
Tit.	Titus
Heb.	Hebrews
Jam.	James
1 Pet.	1 Peter
2 Pet.	2 Peter
1 Jn.	1 John
2 Jn.	2 John
3 Jn.	3 John
Rev.	Revelation

Rabbinic Sources

M.	Mishnah
T.	Tosefta
B.	Babylonian Talmud
TJ	Palestinian Talmud
R.	Rabba (e.g., Gen. R., Ex. R., etc.)

Tractates

Ar.	Arachin	Mak.	Makkot
AZ	Avodah Zarah	Meg.	Megillah
BB	Baba Batra	Men.	Menachot
Bech.	Bechorot	Mid.	Middot
Ber.	Berachot	Mik.	Mikva'ot
BM	Baba Metsi'a	MK	Mo'ed Katan
BK	Baba Kamma	M. Sh.	Ma'aser Sheni
Dem.	Demai	Naz.	Nazir
Eduy.	Eduyot	Ned.	Nedarim
Er.	Eruvin	Neg.	Nega'im
Git.	Gittin	Nid.	Niddah
Hag.	Heagigah	Ohol.	Oholot
Hor.	Horayot	Pes.	Pesachim
Hul.	Heullin	RH	Rosh Hashanah
Kel.	Kelim	Sanh.	Sanhedrin
Ker.	Keritot	Sem.	Semachot
Ket.	Ketubot	Shab.	Shabbat
Kid.	Kiddushin	Shev.	Shevuot
		Shek.	Shekalim
		Sof.	Soferim
		Sot.	Sota
		Suk.	Sukkah
		Tam.	Tamid
		Ta'an	Ta'anit
		Tem.	Temurah
		Ter.	Terumot
		Yev. (Yeb.)	Yevamot
		Yom.	Yoma
		Zev.	Zevachim

1

INTRODUCTION

What to Seek and What to Avoid in Jewish–Christian Dialogue

DAVID NOVAK

Then shall all those who fear the Lord speak, each to his neighbor, and the Lord shall listen and hear. It shall be written in a book of remembrance before Him, for those who fear the Lord and contemplate His name. (Mal. 3:16)

In this text, the prophet speaks of a time when the worshipers of God will communicate in a new way. From an earlier verse, it is clear that the worship of God, which is the basis of this new conversation, is not confined to the Jews: "For from the rising to the setting of the sun My name is great among the nations" (Mal. 1:11). Since Jews and Christians have the most to say to each other about God and his ways with humankind, perhaps the prophet is pointing toward the new conversation that is now taking place between serious Jews and serious Christians.

The new conversation between Jews and Christians may avoid the anger and suspicion that have characterized most of our past conversations. Due to this new sense of trust between us, deeper understanding each of the other is slowly emerging. Now it is important to reflect on why this new conversation has been so hopeful and why it has led to such new understanding, not only a new Christian understanding of Jews and Judaism and a new Jewish understanding of Christians and Christianity, but perhaps even a new Christian understanding of Christianity and a new Jewish understanding of Judaism. As such, this

new conversation, called by many "the dialogue," has already had profound ramifications both externally and internally.

   We are now at a stage in the dialogue where we have enough experience of what has already happened between us to reflect on the conditions that have made it possible. These are methodological issues, but
they have practical import since our successful continuation of the dialogue, even its improvement, requires that we know how it has been
sustained as something much more than a historical accident.

What to Seek

Underlying the dialogue are two positive preconditions. First, each
side must be willing to see the other side in the best possible light
from within its own tradition. Second, that vision must not lead to any
distortion of what each tradition, itself separately, teaches as the
truth.[1] True dialogue requires the adherents of each tradition to find
justification for the other tradition from within his or her own tradition. One cannot use understanding of the other as any kind of escape
from full commitment to the authority of Judaism for Jews or of
Christianity for Christians.

What to Avoid

Participants in Jewish–Christian dialogue must be careful to avoid five
negative conditions, all of which are dangerous theological stumbling
blocks: disputation, proselytization, syncretism, relativism, and triumphalism. The very recognition of these dangers makes a valuable
contribution to the dialogue. By carefully separating the dialogue
from these five dangers, we infer the positive from the negative, which
has long been a feature of rabbinic thinking.[2] From what ought not be
done we can learn what ought to be done.

1. Avoiding Disputation

Dialogue takes the form of a disputation when the adherents of each
tradition assume that everything the other tradition asserts is denied
by their own tradition. This is what occurred in those public debates
in the Middle Ages, when Jews and Christians faced each other as ad-
versaries, even as enemies. In this type of hostile atmosphere, the goal
is for there to be a winner and a loser. The memory of these disputa-

tions, which were always instigated by the Christian rulers who had political power over the Jews, has made many Jews wary of the new dialogue with Christians. There are still many Jews who believe that if Christianity asserts something, Judaism therefore denies it. Indeed, for some Jews, Judaism means nothing more than not being Christian. Jews must understand that there are many commonalities between Judaism and Christianity and that to deny them is as much a distortion of Judaism as it is a distortion of Christianity. Jews need to understand that those Christians who have entered the dialogue with Jews in good faith do not seek the defeat of Judaism. Jews entering the dialogue must also not seek the defeat of Christianity, even in situations where we now might have political or emotional power over Christians.

2. Avoiding Proselytization

The dialogue takes the form of proselytization when the adherents of one tradition seek to persuade the adherents of the other tradition that they truly have what the others have been seeking all along. Proselytization is rooted in the hope that the others will become converted to one's own faith by their contact with members of one's own tradition. Proselytization has been a greater danger for Jews than for Christians because Christianity can claim that it includes all of Judaism and then carries it beyond the level now maintained by the Jewish people. Judaism cannot make a similar claim any more than parents can claim to have succeeded their children. Even if Christians generally hope that all humankind will come to the church, they should not use dialogue with Jews as a specific occasion for realizing that hope. The dialogue must respectfully recognize that the differences between Jews and Christians here and now are of greater importance than the commonalities that the dialogue acknowledges and develops. The dialogue must be justified as an end in and of itself and not used as a means for some other agenda.[3]

3. Avoiding Syncretism

Syncretism is the attempt to construct a new religious reality out of elements of Judaism and Christianity. But no religious tradition, least of all Judaism or Christianity, could accept the replacement of its ultimate claims by a new religion.[4] Indeed, both Judaism and Christianity would have to see the construction of such a new religious reality as a form of idolatry. In Judaism and Christianity, it is God who reveals to the covenanted community *how* God is to be worshiped and not just *that* God is to be worshiped. In fact, according to some Jewish and Christian teaching, that no other god is to be worshiped is something humans can know even before any specific revelation.[5] Idolatry is the worship of "a strange god" (*el zar*).[6] The wrong worship of the right God is called "strange service" (*avodah zarah*), which means the worship of God by humanly constructed rather than by divinely revealed means.[7] Judaism and Christianity are grounded in revelation. Syncretism denies the ultimate character of either Jewish revelation or Christian revelation by substituting something else for both of them. It can thus turn an authentic religious dialogue into an ideological monologue. The integrity of this dialogue cannot stand syncretism in any form.

4. Avoiding Relativism

In the atmosphere of modern secularism, which we can also call "relativism," in which most Jews and Christians now live, religion is taken to be a matter of private preference at best. Relativism is especially dangerous to the dialogue because it denies that some things are true all the time everywhere for everyone. But Judaism and Christianity make such claims. Indeed, these claims, like "God elects Israel" or "God is incarnate in Jesus," are what Judaism and Christianity are all about. In fact, Judaism requires Jews to die as martyrs rather than exchange Judaism for anything else, even something as similar to Judaism as Christianity.[8] Christianity makes a similar claim on Christians. Martyrs are willing to die for what they believe to be the highest truth one could possibly know in this world, because without a commitment to the existence of truth, one cannot affirm the truth of God. Martyrdom is therefore the ultimate expression of belief and represents the personal affirmation of public, universal, and perpetual truth. But with relativism, which sees all beliefs as simply private preferences, the martyr is the biggest fool.

The willingness of Christians to accept Jewish converts and the willingness of Jews to accept Christian converts shows that both religions reject relativism. Even though Jewish–Christian dialogue must not be an occasion for the conversion of either side, Jews and Christians recognize that conversion is always a possibility within the larger covenantal realities in which Jews and Christians participate. Jews know very well that Christianity is open to converts. But Christians must understand that even though Jews have not engaged in the type of active proselytizing that many Christians have engaged in, we have always accepted converts.[9] Indeed, most of those converts have been former Christians. Religious conversion is an impossibility for a relativist, since for the relativist there is no essential, intelligible difference between one religion and another.

There are good political and moral reasons why Jews have not engaged in proselytization. Politically, proselytization has frequently been dangerous for Jews. In the past, Christian societies even outlawed it, and it also involves the danger that too many persons of questionable commitment to the full authority of Jewish law might dilute the religious integrity of the Jewish community.[10] Morally, since Jews have been the objects of so much proselytization on the part of Christians, something we have deeply resented, most of us have been loathe to do the same thing to others, especially since proselytization inevitably involves the denigration of the religion of the person being proselytized. Yet, despite these serious reservations, Jewish tradition has never actually ruled proselytization out.[11]

The reason that proselytization and conversion remain issues for both Jews and Christians is that truth is not relative, and thus the ultimate truth claims of Judaism and Christianity are not only different but mutually exclusive. The highest form of worship of the Lord God of Israel is *either* by the Torah and the tradition of the Jewish people *or* by Christ and the tradition of the church. That the choice is framed in just this way is the result of the historical origins of Judaism and Christianity: both traditions originate in the history of Israel presented in the Hebrew Bible. Accordingly, our differences are over the same God who first appeared in that same history. One cannot live as a Jew and as a Christian simultaneously. One could well say that the greatest temptation for a Jew is Christianity and that the greatest temptation for a Christian is Judaism. That this is so explains why Jews and Christians have so much to talk about and, also, why the stakes in the Jewish–Christian relationship are so high.

5. Avoiding Triumphalism

Triumphalism is the insistence that not only the highest truth but the final truth has already been given to my community alone. Triumphalism poisons the dialogue before it begins. Jews are triumphalists when we assume that Christianity is nothing more than a deviant form of Judaism; Christians are triumphalists when they assume that Judaism is but a precursor to Christianity. Triumphalists believe that there is no commonality to discover between the two religions, and that therefore there is nothing to learn from dialogue. This claim, however, is historically false. It is also dangerous, as it prevents us from building areas of peace between us.

Jewish and Christian anticipations of the end of days contradict the triumphalists' assumption that our differences are final. For Jews, there is a time called "the Days of the Messiah"; for Christians it is called "the Second Coming."[12] In anticipation of this time, when human history will come to an end and the kingdom of God will be established on earth, Jews and Christians look forward to an everlasting divine redemption of Israel, of all humankind, indeed of the whole universe.[13] The end of days will be a time when, unlike the present, "the kingdom will be the Lord's" (Obad. 1:21). What, however, of those Jews who assert that it is precisely at the end of days that the triumph of Judaism will be manifest, and what of those Christians who assert that at the Second Coming Christianity will triumph? We must answer that the final judgment of all human history is not yet in. "No eye has seen but yours O God what will be done for those who wait for you" (Is. 64:3).[14] The world-yet-to-come *(olam ha-ba)*, this coming-future *(l'atid la-vo)*, is mysterious; it lies on the other side of our present horizon. Therefore Jews and Christians cannot see their past traditions or their present efforts and differences as the last word. The different claims of Judaism and Christianity are only tentative. Surely what God will do at the end of history will be radical enough to surprise everyone—Jews, Christians, and all others who wait for that time here and now.

2

CHRISTIAN–JEWISH INTERACTIONS OVER THE AGES

ROBERT CHAZEN

For much of the past millennium, the world's Jewish population has been concentrated in the Christian areas of the globe. As a result, Christian attitudes and behaviors toward Jews have been paramount in conditioning Jewish fate. Jews have had to contend regularly with a Christian environment—its dangers, its pressures, and its stimulation. Christian impact on the Jewish minority was particularly strong during the Middle Ages, when the powerful Roman Catholic Church exercised considerable control over key aspects of societal existence and when Christian imagery pervaded every facet of individual life. With the movement from the Middle Ages to modernity and the waning of the power of the Roman Catholic Church, widely held Christian attitudes and perceptions have maintained their hold on majority thinking and have continued to affect the Jewish minority.

Christians, over the ages, have been far less exposed to the influence of Jews. The major instance of Jewish power exercised over Christians was brief, but because it occurred during the formative period in Christian history, impressions of negative Jewish impact upon Christianity have been embedded in Christian consciousness. Also, during the Middle Ages, Jews constituted the only non-Christian element in many areas of western Christendom, thus presenting useful—although hardly appreciated—stimulation to the Christian majority.

Over the past few centuries, Jews in the predominantly Christian sectors of the world have continued to have a circumscribed but significant influence on Christian culture.

In differing ways, then, these two faith communities have deeply affected each other, often negatively. As the two faith communities have ranged against each other, Christians and Jews have tended to perceive and highlight the negative interplay. Less obvious and less noted have been the fruitful interactions between the two communities, interactions enriching to both sides.

Negative Interactions

The First Century: Crucifixion

Negative interactions between Christianity and Judaism can be traced back to the very origins of Christianity. At the earliest juncture in Christian history, Jesus and his followers were part and parcel of the fractious Jewish community in first-century Palestine. Palestinian Jewry was divided politically into Jews who favored accommodation to the Romans and those who favored rebellion against them; it was divided spiritually into Pharisees, Sadducees, Essenes, and a number of other religious subgroups. Although the earliest stages of Christian history are shrouded in obscurity, it seems safe enough to say that Jesus and his followers ranged themselves—along with others—in opposition to the Jewish authorities in first-century Palestine and may well have suffered some adverse consequences as a result of their oppositional stance.

The Book of Acts is replete with stories of Christians suffering persecution at the hands of the Jewish authorities. However, all these stories of the persecution of Jesus' followers pale in comparison to the tale of the crucifixion of Jesus himself, which is key to the New Testament portrait of the Christian Messiah and Savior and stands at the very core of the Christian faith. Once again, the historical reality is blurred. We possess detailed Gospel accounts of Jewish culpability for the crucifixion but have no way of judging the accuracy of these reports. In any case, the reality of Jesus' crucifixion combined with the authoritative Gospel accounts of it have served to create a lasting perception of Jews and their faith. In the most central drama of Christianity—the crucifixion and resurrection—Jews play the role of persecuting villains, inflicting incalculable damage on Christianity and its hero.

Christianity and Christians remained susceptible to Jewish influence for only a brief period of time. Quickly, the young faith showed signs of wide-ranging appeal, first to Greek-speaking Diaspora Jews and then increasingly to Gentiles. Christianity rapidly spread beyond the confines of Palestinian Jewry, indeed beyond the confines of Palestine. As Christianity distanced itself from its Jewish moorings and attracted a large following throughout the Roman Empire, it escaped any shred of control by the Palestinian Jewish authorities. Nonetheless, the early stories of persecution, in particular the purported Jewish role in the crucifixion, served to establish an image of Judaism and Jews that would exert profound influence on Christian thinking over the ages.

The reality of a Gentile majority within the Christian community necessitated a number of adjustments. On the theoretical level, the issue of Gentile Christianity, Judaism, and the world order had to be faced. What emerged was an important and complex theory of historical progression. According to this view, the Jews had indeed been the chosen people, intended for an ongoing covenant with the one God whom they had brought into the world. The Jews had regularly stumbled in their appointed vocation, as indicated eloquently by the prophets of Israel, who had attempted recurrently to bring their people back to fulfillment of the covenant. As a result of the advent of Jesus as promised Messiah, the Jewish failure to acknowledge him as such, and the breathtaking act of occasioning his death, the Jewish people—again as warned by its own prophets—forfeited forever its role in divine history. The place once occupied by the Jewish people had of necessity to be ceded to a different group, the Gentile Christian community, which thereby fell heir to the responsibilities, the promises, and the glory once the portion of the Jews. Blindness to divine truth became, for Christians, the hallmark of Jews. Ongoing Jewish commitment to Judaism, which Christians saw as erroneous, was readily explained by this blindness. At the same time, this theory of historical progression served to deepen the significance of the alleged Jewish role in the crucifixion. As noted, Christian theory posited that role as the decisive factor in the disruption of the divine covenant with the Jews and the transmission of that covenant to Christians, the successor people.

The Second to Fourth Centuries:
Christian Ascendancy

Through the second and third centuries, Christianity continued to attract a multitude of followers. Christianity now constituted a major problem for the leadership of the Roman Empire in its entirety. A critical juncture in Christian–Jewish interaction was reached early in the fourth century, when the rulers of the Roman Empire abandoned their persecution of Christianity and instead embraced it. This shift, so momentous for the subsequent history of the Western world, raised for the first time the question of the place of Judaism and Jews in a society ruled by Christians and committed to the advancement of the Christian worldview. What developed was a position of moderate toleration. Judaism was seen as error-ridden and displaced; it was, however, sufficiently important and valued as to necessitate its legitimization. Jews were to live a tolerated, albeit limited, existence within the Christian commonwealth. The limitations to be imposed on Jewish life were aimed at obviating potential harm that Jews might inflict on their Christian hosts and at maintaining Jewish inferiority in ways that would highlight their error and punishment.

This position of moderate toleration, forged during the heady times of Christian ascendancy in the Roman Empire, required theological grounding, which was advanced by a number of major thinkers, perhaps most strikingly by Augustine. These thinkers rooted the toleration of Judaism in the pedagogical value Jews might provide, once more highlighting alleged Jewish shortcomings. As noted, Christianity had recognized an early Jewish role as the people of God's covenant. This Christian acknowledgment was tempered by the claim that the Jews had capped their long history of recalcitrance by committing a sin—the crucifixion—so dastardly as to occasion the rupture of the covenant God had struck with the Jews and their replacement with a new covenant people, the Christians. God had responded to this sin with immediate punishment, exile, and degradation of the Jews. In this view, the Jews as a degraded people served a most useful pedagogic role, attesting to the working of sin and punishment in God's universe and—in the process—to the truth of the Christian faith as well.

Slightly less demeaning to the Jews was a second rationale for maintaining Jewish presence in Christian society. In this view, Jews played a useful function by attesting to the authenticity of prophetic prediction. Jews proclaimed regularly to the world that the visions of Isaiah, Jeremiah, Ezekiel, and the other prophets of biblical Israel were divinely inspired and true. From the Christian perspective, Jewish understanding of these prophets was deficient, a function of the blindness already cited. Nonetheless, the Jewish insistence on the truth of the prophetic visions played a useful role in the Christian case for Jesus' mission. If those who stood outside the Jewish and Christian camps could be convinced of the divine inspiration and truth of the prophetic words—with the help of disinterested Jewish testimony—then a simple and direct reading of those prophetic words would, it was presumed, lead inevitably to Christian conclusions.

The Middle Ages:
Increasing Contact

While Christianity emerged as the dominant religion in much of the Western world, Jewish life was in fact centered to the east, in areas that lay outside Christian hegemony. With the great Muslim conquests of the seventh century, the bulk of world Jewry found itself living under the rule of yet another competing monotheism. For treatment of both Jews and Christians living within Islamic domain, the Muslims adopted much of the stance that Christianity had developed toward its Jewish minority. However, Islam lacked the potent sense of Jewish (or Christian) roots and Jewish (or Christian) malevolence that is so prominent in the Christian–Jewish interaction. Radically different historical development, in which Jews (and Christians) played a relatively inconspicuous role, accounts for the relative mildness of the Muslim–Jewish (and Muslim–Christian) interface.

For the first half of the Middle Ages, Christendom was much on the defensive against the new and vigorous forces of Islam. During the tenth and eleventh centuries, the balance of power in the Western world began to shift slowly but decisively in the direction of Christendom. This shift held profound implications for the history of the West and for the history of Christian–Jewish interaction. Increasing numbers of Jews came under Christian rule, partly as a result of Christian conquest of Muslim territory and partly through Jewish migration in the direction of vital and rapidly developing societies. These increasing numbers had important ramifications. Jews, always a theoretical issue for Christianity because of its Jewish roots, now presented practical problems and concerns as well. And from the Jewish perspective,

Christianity now became the faith that most affected—in both negative and positive ways—the realities of Jewish life.

As Jewish presence in western Christendom expanded, the moderate toleration designed during the fourth century as the framework for Jewish existence in Christian society remained very much in effect. The notions of precluding Jewish harm and maintaining Jewish inferiority lent themselves to considerable adaptation and intensification. In particular, western Christendom, from the late twelfth century on, became increasingly concerned with a variety of minority groupings in society and sought to counter the dangers these dissident groups allegedly posed. In the case of the Jews, the Roman Catholic Church augmented the regime of limitations under which they lived, often to the point of drastically constricting Jewish life. The leadership of the church identified a series of important limitations intended to curb alleged Jewish harm—social segregation, rigorous censorship of Jewish literature, and restrictions on Jewish economic activity.

From their earliest days of power in the fourth century, Christian authorities were concerned to minimize the influence Jews might exert on their Christian neighbors. Early church enactments addressed relationships in which Jews were perceived to wield authority and hence influence. Jews were forbidden to own Christian slaves, occupy positions of political authority, or take Christian spouses. By the twelfth and thirteenth centuries, when Jews had become increasingly concentrated in the Christian sphere and no longer held slaves, occupied positions of political power, or took Christian spouses, the church became concerned with and attempted to mitigate all relations that might have allowed Jewish influence on Christian neighbors: Christians working in Jewish homes, Jews living in small towns where social relations were inescapable, Jews living alongside Christians in larger towns. The most extreme measure adopted by the church was the call for distinguishing garb, intended to single out the Jew at all times.

Yet another type of damage feared by the church over the ages was the possibility of Jewish blasphemy. Obviously, Jews were deeply opposed to Christianity and expressed their opposition vigorously among themselves. Public expression of such opposition was, however, prohibited. Again, during the thirteenth century, this old prohibition was intensified. Nicholas Donin, a convert from Judaism to Christianity, brought purportedly anti-Christian statements in the Talmud to the attention of the papal court. Donin's allegations sparked careful investigation of the charges, condemnation and burning of the Talmud in

Paris in 1242, prohibition of the Talmud in certain sectors of western Christendom, and censorship of the Talmud in others.

During the twelfth and thirteenth centuries, an entirely new area of church concern with potential Jewish harm emerged. After the church had inadvertently opened up new business opportunities for the Jews of western Christendom through its efforts to wipe out usury among the Christian population, perceptions of the harm inflicted by Jewish moneylenders intensified. Once more, the demand that Jews live in Christian society without inflicting damage was sounded, this time to warrant a series of moves intended to limit Jewish moneylending and the ill effects it allegedly caused. In some instances, such Jewish business was prohibited entirely.

The foregoing Christian stances toward Jews and Judaism were essentially defensive—moves initiated by the church and executed by the secular authorities in order to protect Christianity and Christians. One set of further initiatives was aggressive. Missionizing has been a major Christian preoccupation over the ages. Successful proselytizing turned Christianity from a small subgroup in Palestinian Jewry into a serious threat to the Roman Empire and then into the dominant force in that vast empire. Historically, the Christian commitment to missionizing always included an effort to bring Jews into the faith. In some periods, the commitment to proselytizing among Jews took on heightened significance, turning into a genuine preoccupation among certain church leaders.

During the middle decades of the thirteenth century, the effort to convert Jews intensified. The church allocated resources to train expert missionizing personnel, made an effort to convince the secular authorities to support the proselytizing campaign, and took care to cultivate new lines of argumentation. The church's commitment to missionizing among the Jews remained strong throughout the concluding centuries of the Middle Ages, with considerable success. Especially on the Iberian peninsula, large numbers of Jews were brought to the baptismal fount, often as a result of the argumentation with which they were ceaselessly confronted. Many of the conversions, however, were effected through the illegitimate imposition of force.

Escalating Violence

All the measures discussed thus far have involved Christian anti-Jewish initiatives that were legitimate within the framework established by the church, but illegitimate violence was yet another dimension of negative Christian–Jewish interaction during the Middle Ages. Anti-Jewish violence resulted from a variety of damaging stereotypes of Jews and Judaism. In medieval western Christendom, the realities of Jewish life itself conditioned some of these stereotypes. Thus, Jews were often perceived—particularly in northern sectors—as newcomers, which they in fact were. As a result, Jews suffered many of the stigmas normally associated with recent arrivals. The further realities of limited economic outlets often put these Jewish immigrants at the cutting and unpopular edge of the economy and in a potent alliance with the political authorities. This new status affected the imagery of Jews in western Christendom, but it was the negative legacy from antiquity that most shaped medieval Christian perceptions of the Jews.

The church insisted that the alleged Jewish role in the death of Jesus and the persecution of his followers was not to serve as a ground for acts of revenge. Christians were not to avenge Jesus, largely because God himself had taken care to do so, by stripping the Jews of their role in covenantal history and consigning them to exile. Christians were to treat Jews with the charity that might hopefully open the eyes of the latter to Christian truth. Not surprisingly, the niceties of this theory could readily be lost in times of tension.

In western Christendom, the First Crusade served in many ways as a point of considerable transition. On the material level, the great expedition called forth by Pope Urban II in 1095 reflected the growing power and militancy of western Christendom. A century earlier, such a western initiative would have been unthinkable; a century later, it was commonplace. Spiritually, the sacralization of battle and bloodshed represented a significant innovation for Christian thinking. Surprisingly and unsurprisingly, the call to arms against the forces of Islam had a disastrous impact on some of northern Europe's leading Jewish communities.

This turn of events was surprising in that, so far as we know, Pope Urban II, his ecclesiastical advisers, and the barons who played a leading role in the enterprise took no note whatsoever of Jews. The military venture called for and undertaken was projected as a war against the armies of Islam, an effort to reach the holiest sites of Christendom and liberate them from Muslim rule. However, given the legacy of negative Christian imagery of Jews and Judaism, the unforeseen anti-Jewish violence is not all that difficult to fathom.

Along the Rhine River, German crusaders and local burghers assaulted a number of Jewish communities, sometimes with devastating results. The most frightful slaughter was committed by one particular crusading force, a ragtag army that coalesced around the little-known figure of a Count Emicho, probably of Flonheim. For the costly assaults on the Jewish communities of Worms, Mainz, and Cologne, we possess a number of sources—both Christian and Jewish—that corroborate one another rather fully. Christian and Jewish sources are in accord about the following crusader slogan, here offered in the version found in the oldest and most trustworthy Hebrew narrative of the events of 1096: "Behold we travel to distant land to do battle with the kings of that land. We take our lives in our hands in order to kill and to subjugate all those kingdoms that do not believe in the Crucified. How much more so [should we kill and subjugate] the Jews, who killed and crucified him." Explicit here is the view that of all the enemies of Christendom, the Jews are surely the most loathsome, the most deserving of vengeance at the hands of Christian warriors.

In the wake of the limited but costly anti-Jewish violence associated with the First Crusade, ecclesiastical leadership was deeply concerned to obviate repetition of such illegitimate anti-Jewish behavior. The spiritual leader of the Second Crusade, Bernard of Clairvaux, went to considerable lengths to denounce the thinking that had led to the 1096 massacres and to oppose incipient manifestations of anti-Jewish zeal. He wrote extensively on behalf of the endangered Jews and imposed himself in person to put down danger when it threatened. The major Jewish chronicler of the Second Crusade and its impact on northern Europe's Jews, Ephraim of Bonn, knew well of Bernard's interventions and appreciated them deeply. Still, Bernard's case for Jewish safety began with the traditional assumptions of Jewish sin and of God's punishment of the Jews through exile and the rupture of the prior covenant. Bernard of Clairvaux thus simultaneously fostered Jewish safety and reinforced the negative stereotypes that jeopardized the Jews.

Intensified Anti-Jewish Imagery

The stances of Bernard of Clairvaux, subsequent ecclesiastical leaders, and the major secular figures associated with the later crusades succeeded in obviating repetition of the violence that marred the First

Crusade. However, during the middle decades of the twelfth century, the traditionally negative Christian imagery that gave rise to the bloodshed of 1096 underwent significant evolution. Bernard's great contemporary, Peter the Venerable, abbot of Cluny, gave eloquent voice to the intensified anti-Jewish imagery. Whereas Bernard had spoken of Jewish acceptance of secondary status and subjugation, Peter claimed that—quite to the contrary—the Jews of his day were involved in an ongoing effort to inflict harm upon Christians and Christianity. In effect, Peter claimed that the Jews of the twelfth century regularly expressed the selfsame hostility, albeit in a different form, that had led their ancestors to call for Jesus' crucifixion. Peter singled out two patterns of purportedly hostile Jewish behavior—their incessant blasphemy of the Christian faith and their harmful economic practices. For Peter the Venerable, Jews constituted a present and unremitting threat to the well-being of Christian society.

Peter the Venerable did not create this new sense of the Jews as people steeped in hostility and malevolence; he merely provided articulate expression for a broadly held view. Evidence of this new and damaging perception of Jews can be found in many quarters. During the middle decades of the twelfth century, the most striking reflection of this new perception can be found in the dangerous stereotype of Jews as murderers of Christians, particularly Christian youngsters. It is of course significant that the Christian victims are identified as youngsters. Besides highlighting the defenselessness of the victims, this perception suggested groundless hatred on the part of the Jews, hatred of these youngsters simply for their Christian faith. In an age noted for its imagination, this broad notion of groundless murder by Jews was embellished with the claim that these murders took place in ritualistic fashion, as a reenactment of Jesus' crucifixion. This claim was articulated for the first time in the middle of the twelfth century by Thomas of Monmouth, chronicler of the life and death of the young Saint William of Norwich.

The thirteenth century saw further embellishments of the theme articulated by Peter the Venerable and expressed in the ritual-murder allegation. A widely known and damaging embellishment involved the charge that Jews ritually abused the host wafer. The descendants of those who allegedly murdered Jesus purportedly continued to express their ongoing hatred through maltreatment of the wafer that is the enshrinement of his body. From the middle of the thirteenth century down into the twentieth century, many Christians accepted yet another variation on this theme: the ritualized Jewish use of Christian blood as an expression of Jewish hatred of Christians.

Just as such leaders as Bernard of Clairvaux had opposed vigorously the radical crusading notion of human vengeance against Jews for the crucifixion of Jesus, so, too, did ecclesiastical authorities generally reject the ritual murder allegation, the host desecration charge, the blood libel, and the anti-Jewish violence they spawned. However, by the end of the thirteenth century, these imaginative embellishments of traditional Christian notions of Jewish enmity and malevolence began to take a considerable toll of Jewish life. Waves of anti-Jewish violence swept northern Europe in the 1290s, the 1330s, and the 1340s. By 1391, the violence reached Spain as well, costing tens of thousands of Jewish lives and forcing large numbers of Jews to the baptismal fount. In the wake of the First Crusade, Bernard of Clairvaux had embraced the stereotype (Jewish responsibility for the crucifixion) but condemned the actions of the rampaging crusaders; now church leadership decried both the stereotypes (for example, the blood libel) and, even more strongly, the assaults.

Through most of antiquity and all through the Middle Ages, the balance of power in the Christian–Jewish relationship was heavily skewed in favor of Christians. As noted, Jews exercised power only briefly in the long history of Christian–Jewish relations. However, the legacy of that brief period was indelibly inscribed in Christian consciousness. Jews were seen as the killers of Christ and as intent upon expressing their hatred of and harming his followers. Thus, Christians and Jews were heavily focused on mutual perceptions of animosity and harm.

Positive Interactions

Although Christians and Jews over the ages have left largely unexplored the positive interactions between their communities, such positive interactions did in fact take place. Christians have benefited from the presence of Jews in the Christian world, and Jews have been attracted to the Christian world because of the advantages they perceived it to offer.

What Christians Gained from Jews

Given its power, Christianity has regularly posed the question of whether Jews should be tolerated in a Christian society and has regularly responded in the affirmative. As we have seen, these affirmations of Jewish rights have been based on notions of the useful purposes Jews serve and have almost always been couched in demeaning terms. But sometimes views of Jewish utility did not have such negative overtones.

Although Bernard's demand for Jewish safety during the Second Crusade began with the notion of divine punishment of the Jews for the crucifixion, he proceeded to add other elements to his case, including genuine Jewish docility under Christian rule. At the end of his complex set of arguments for Jewish safety, Bernard demanded security "for those from whom we have a law and a promise, from whom we have a forefather, and from whom we have Christ of the flesh." This is a direct statement of the positive role Jews and Judaism had played in the evolution of Christianity. And there is no reason to stop with such overt articulations. Christendom of late antiquity and the Middle Ages in fact benefited in diverse ways from Jewish presence.

On many occasions, Jews served a useful pioneering role in Christian culture, bringing the advantages of a more advanced milieu to an area in the process of development. For example, as a mobile people, Jews were attracted to the rapidly developing areas of northwestern Europe during the tenth through twelfth centuries and brought useful skills and techniques from their Mediterranean places of origin. German Jews who moved eastward into the rapidly emerging Kingdom of Poland during the thirteenth and fourteenth centuries played the same role. In both cases, progressive Christian rulers were unabashed in their support for Jewish settlers who would improve the general economy of the areas over which they ruled.

In addition to their contribution to rapidly developing geographic areas, Jews were also a cornerstone of the emergent sectors of the medieval economy. Again, as a minority with limited economic outlets, Jews were willing to move into risky sectors of the economy and make a pioneering contribution. The outstanding example of such a contribution involves the important, dangerous, and reviled economic activity of moneylending and banking. Medieval western Christendom required a flow of capital, but the church impeded this flow with its policy on usury. Modern historians of the European economy note that Jews made a significant contribution to the economic maturation of European society through their lending activities. Nonetheless, these activities were highly unpopular and reinforced the dominant Christian perception of Jews as ranged in harmful opposition to Christianity and Christians.

Jews likewise made notable contributions to the spiritual life of medieval Christendom. The easiest contribution to document is the Jewish command of the Hebrew language, the language of almost all the corpus that Christianity had absorbed into its sacred literature as the Old Testament. Medieval Christians generally read their Old Testament in the accepted Latin translation and accorded sanctity to that version. From time to time, however, awareness of the Hebrew original and a desire to penetrate it led Christian savants to seek enlightenment among their Jewish neighbors. The same twelfth and thirteenth centuries that saw deepening Christian mistrust of the Jewish minority also saw protracted efforts in certain intellectual circles to enhance Christian understanding of the Hebrew Bible by encountering it in its original. To that end, Christian scholars, such as the well-known school of St. Victor, were comfortable in approaching Jewish contemporaries and enjoying the benefit of their facility with Hebrew.

The final benefit derived by medieval Christendom from its Jews reflects a distinctly modern perspective. For the medieval world, homogeneity was the ideal, with the regnant worldview unchallenged by alternatives. From this perspective, medieval Jews were thus a disruptive and negative influence, to be tolerated but rigorously controlled. Moderns have come to view religious and intellectual life in radically different terms. For moderns, creativity is in fact dampened by homogeneity and enhanced by difference. According to modern observers, the challenge of difference, more than anything else, has stimulated human creativity over the ages. And indeed, the Jewish presence in western Christendom provided an important goad to Christian reflection and spiritual growth.

Precisely because of the intertwined roots of the two faith communities, the Jewish challenge to Christianity moved Christian thinkers all through the Middle Ages to ponder, to reconsider, and to reformulate old insights. Judaism and the recovered legacy of ancient Greco-Roman thought provided the two major stimuli to creative Christian reflection, and again the twelfth and thirteenth centuries stand out as the centuries of the most notable activity.

What Jews Gained from Christians

Discussion of the benefits derived by Jews from the medieval Christian–Jewish encounter must begin with a simple observation. Just as the Jewish minority suffered more from that encounter than did the Christian majority, so, too, did the Jewish minority benefit more from a rich, complex, and dynamic majority civilization.

Although medieval Christians spoke, usually in a demeaning way, of the benefits of having the Jews in their midst, medieval Jews speculated little on the benefits conferred by Christianity. There was occasionally a sense that the Christian and Muslim religions served the valuable purpose of spreading religious truth among the nations. But if these two daughter faiths were successful, it was only because they provided useful popularizations of genuine Jewish truth. Despite these occasional reflections, Jews were not deeply concerned with validating the Christian presence, since that presence was such an overwhelming reality. Jewish efforts were far more fully focused on combating the challenges the Christian majority and its faith presented.

The simplest index of Jewish benefit from medieval Christian society is the demographic reality of Jewish life. Despite the disastrous results of the influx of Jews into western Christendom in the twelfth and thirteenth centuries, it is striking to note that at no point did a majority of Jews turn their back on western Christendom and relocate or return to the Islamic world. Even after the expulsions from the more advanced sectors of the Christian world at the end of the thirteenth and beginning of the fourteenth centuries, the northern European (Ashkenazic) Jews opted for the less developed Christian sectors of northern Europe, rather than moving in numbers back into the (steadily declining) Muslim lands. Obviously, these Jews sensed something about the balance of power in the Western world and opted to stay in the hostile Christian sphere, out of a sense of the advantages it offered. When Jews did leave western Christendom to move back into adjacent Muslim territory in large numbers, it was at the end of the fifteenth century, when the Spanish (Sephardic) Jews were expelled from the Iberian peninsula and almost no contiguous Christian lands were open to them. But even after this mass exodus, the imbalance between Jewish population in the Christian and Muslim spheres reasserted itself, once more a tribute to the advantages of the Christian West.

These advantages were, first of all, material. From the tenth through the twelfth centuries, the Christian sector of the Western world caught up with and surpassed the previously more prosperous Muslim sector. For Jews, as a mobile minority community, there was obvious advantage in locating within the geographic area that was enjoying the most impressive economic gains, rather than remaining in an arena of steady economic decline.

The advantages Jews enjoyed were surely more than material, as well. Western Christendom flourished in a variety of ways, all of which had meaning for both the Christian majority and the Jewish minority. Cities grew continuously in medieval western Christendom, and Jews were overwhelmingly city dwellers. Patterns of governance matured, in ways advantageous to both the majority and the minority. Literacy expanded, and culture developed in a number of fruitful directions, with advantages again to both the majority and the minority.

As was the case for medieval Christianity, medieval Jews gained something else from their encounter with Christianity: the creativity that arises from difference. Jews were, of course, far more cognizant of the religion of the Christian majority than were Christians of the religion of the Jewish minority. Everyday life was suffused with Christian monuments, symbols, and celebrations. Jews were deeply aware of medieval Christianity and, as a minority, profoundly challenged by it. Once again, medievals did not usually see such challenges in a positive light, but moderns do. Modern observers would comfortably suggest that medieval Judaism was very much invigorated by its ongoing encounter with Christianity. That encounter regularly stimulated consideration of the essentials of the Jewish faith and the ritual and moral precepts through which that truth was expressed. That there was so much conscious reflection on parallels and contrasts with Christianity attests to the challenge of majority culture and to its role in advancing the clarification of Jewish ideas and ideals.

Modernity

With modernity has come the dissolution of the world order introduced into the West by the Christian conquest of the Roman Empire. The fragmentation of the Roman Catholic Church opened the way for this dissolution. The fragmentation itself occasioned no real change in Christian attitudes toward Judaism and Jews. The case of Martin Luther is instructive. Like so many reforming predecessors, Luther saw prior policy toward the Jews as error-ridden and as an opportunity to show the superiority of his new vision. In his early essay, "That Jesus Was Born a Jew," Luther castigated the Roman Catholic Church for its harsh treatment of Jews. His own milder and more loving stance would, he believed, bring the Jews to Christian truth. Disappointed in the Jewish response to his overtures, Luther turned angry and vicious in his denunciation of the Jews. In his later "On the

Jews and Their Lies," he leveled harsh charges against the Jews and incited Christians to anti-Jewish violence.

With respect to the Jews, it was not the content of the Reformation thinking that was decisive, it was simply the breakup of the monolithic character of western Christendom. So long as there was one dominant church in western Christendom, the intimate linkage of church and state that typified the medieval order could be maintained. With the proliferation of Christian churches, the linkage could lead only to persecution, warfare, and carnage. Fairly quickly, voices began to call for a new order that would be founded on toleration of diversity. Although such diversity was initially seen in Christian terms—toleration of a variety of Christian groupings—it was soon extended to Jews and others. The position of the Jews in the West was irrevocably altered.

Much of the negative interaction described above came to an end. The secular authorities in the West no longer enforced the onerous restrictions or the aggressive missionizing that had been so prominent in the Middle Ages. To be sure, this change did little to efface the negative imagery that had developed over the centuries. Once again, Jews were in many instances recent immigrants, found niches in developing but unpopular sectors of the economy, and were perceived as locked into a limited political stance. These real characteristics were interpreted against the backdrop of the New Testament and the medieval imagery of the malevolent and harmful Jew, now simply adapted to the new circumstances of modernity. Despite Jewish hopes for greater acceptance and tranquillity, the tendency toward anti-Jewish violence was maintained and in some cases intensified. Indeed, the restraining voice of ecclesiastical leadership that had combated some of the most obnoxious anti-Jewish stereotypes was very much weakened with the advent of modernity.

The kinds of mutual benefit outlined above have also been maintained and reinforced in the modern period. Jews have continued to play a catalytic, albeit often unappreciated, role in the development of the modern economy. With the advent of modernity, Jews, again unable to find their place in the well-established sectors of the economy, made their way to the new, the exciting, the risky, and the often despised. Jewish contributions to modern civilization moved into entirely new domains. The universities of the West, which had been church institutions during the Middle Ages, began to break their ecclesiastical bonds and slowly opened themselves to Jewish presence and contribution. Newly developing areas of cultural creativity likewise felt the impress of Jewish presence and creativity.

Jewish appreciation of the vitality of western Christendom was obviously enhanced by the new opportunities that flowed from the sundering of the tight relationship between church and state. Once freed of medieval constraints, Jews rapidly located themselves in the great cities of the West. As the Americas in general and the United States in particular began to emerge as a magnet for migration, Jews joined that migration, expressing their hopes in a younger and seemingly freer society and casting their lot with the vision that animated that society. By the beginning of the twentieth century, the overwhelming majority of world Jewry was located in lands that housed a Christian majority.

The one obvious exception to the Jewish preference for the Christian sphere has been the establishment of the State of Israel in the heart of the Muslim world. This development has resulted from the ideological significance of the Land of Israel to the Zionist movement, which rejected resolutely all alternative sites for the Jewish homeland/state. Yet even this exception points up the close identification of modern Jewry with the Christian West. It is precisely the sense of the Jewish state as an outpost of the Christian West that has occasioned a good part of the Muslim resistance to Zionism and the State of Israel.

Over the past century, as Jews have suffered some of the most horrific disasters in their long history, new stimuli to Christian–Jewish cooperation have emerged. As the magnitude and horror of the Holocaust became obvious, observers both Jewish and Christian sought to identify the wellsprings of the hatred that moved one part of European society to undertake the systematic annihilation of Jews while the other part sat passively as the killing was carried out. Attention in many quarters fastened on the legacy of Christian anti-Jewish thinking, moving many Christians to search for new relationships to Jews and Judaism. How successful these innovative efforts might prove will be known only during the course of the next century.

At the same time, both majority Christians and minority Jews have slowly begun to see that the old relationship of antagonism is in many ways outdated. Many Christians and Jews have concluded that all religious communities must unite in the face of powerful forces that seek to destroy these traditional religious communities and their belief systems altogether. In the face of modern anti-religious tendencies and movements, interreligious disputes have become a luxury that many

view as no longer affordable. This perception of the deteriorating circumstances of the religious communities has resulted in new modes of
cooperation and new mutual respect. Again, how long-lived these tendencies might prove will be known only with the passage of time.
There does seem to be a real possibility that some of the negative interactions of the past (which were in any case never the whole of the
story) may give way to more positive relations between two faith communities that have sprung out of common ground.

3

THE SHOAH AND THE
LEGACY OF
ANTI-SEMITISM

Judaism, Christianity, and Partnership
After the Twentieth Century

IRVING GREENBERG

The Challenges of the Holocaust

Judaism and Christianity tell of God's love for man and stand or fall on their fundamental claim that the human being is, therefore, of ultimate and absolute value ("He who saves one life it is as if he saved an entire world" [B. Sanh. 37a]; "God so loved the world that He gave His only begotten son" [Jn. 3:16]). The cruelty and the killing in the Holocaust raise the question of whether those who believe after the

---

This essay was edited and compiled by Tikva Frymer-Kensky from various essays on the relationship of Judaism and Christianity written by Irving Greenberg over the past several decades.

Holocaust dare talk about a God who loves and cares without making a mockery of those who suffered.

The Christian "Teaching of Contempt" about Jews and Judaism furnished stereotypes that enabled Nazis to focus on the Jews as scapegoat and created a climate of anti-Semitism in Europe. This climate enabled some Christians to feel they were doing God's duty when they either helped kill Jews or did not stop the killing. Even the great Christians who recognized the danger of idolatry and resisted the Nazi government's takeover of the German Evangelical Church at great personal sacrifice and risk did not speak out on the Jewish question. Christianity may be hopelessly and fatally compromised; the penumbra of Christian complicity challenges the credibility of Christianity as a gospel of love.

More generally, the Holocaust challenges the credibility of modern culture. Limits were broken, restraints shattered. Science and technology—the accepted flower and glory of modernity—climaxed in the factories of death. The humanistic revolt for the "liberation" of humankind from centuries of dependence upon God and nature has been shown to sustain a capacity for demonic evil. Twentieth-century Western civilization, in part the product of the Enlightenment and liberal culture, was a Frankenstein that authored the German monster's being. Liberalism and internationalism served as cover beliefs—designed to weaken the victims' perception that they were threatened and to block the kind of action needed to save their lives. The human and moral failure that made such cruel slaughter possible has deeply tarnished the validity of all modern values. Moreover, the fact of the Holocaust and the failure to confront it make a repetition more

---

The composite essay was then edited further by David Toole. For those who seek a fuller understanding of Greenberg's views, the original essays are: "Cloud of Smoke, Pillar of Fire: Judaism, Christianity, and Modernity After the Holocaust," in *Auschwitz: Beginning of a New Era?* ed. Eva Fleischner (New York: KTAV, 1977), 7–55, 441–446; "New Revelation and New Patterns in the Relationship Between Judaism and Christianity," *Journal of Ecumenical Studies* 16, no. 2 (spring 1979): 249–267; "The Relationship of Judaism and Christianity: Toward a New Organic Model," in *Twenty Years of Jewish/Catholic Relations,* ed. Eugene Fisher, James Rudin, and Marc Tanenbaum (New York: Paulist Press, 1986), 191–211; "Judaism and Christianity: Their Respective Roles in the Divine Strategy of Redemption," in *Visions of the Other, Jewish and Christian Theologians Assess the Dialogue,* ed. Eugene J. Fisher (Mahwah: Paulist Press, 1994), 7–27; "Covenantal Pluralism," in *Journal of Ecumenical Studies* 34, no. 3 (summer 1997): 425–436. See also: "Pluralism and Partnership," in *Unity Without Uniformity: The Challenge of Pluralism,* International Council of Christians and Jews: Martin Buber House publication no. 26 (spring 1999): 68–81.

likely—a limit was broken, a control or awe is gone—and the murder procedure is now better laid out and understood.

The Holocaust's moral challenge also confronts Jews. Organized Jewry felt bound by the principles of national loyalty and national interest and feared to protest when those principles were used to justify the restricted efforts by the national governments to save Jews. Moreover, those Jews who feel no guilt for the Holocaust are tempted to moral apathy, and religious Jews who use the Holocaust to morally impugn every other religious group but their own are tempted thereby into indifference at the Holocaust of others.

Responses to the Holocaust

The Holocaust confronts us with unanswerable questions. But let us agree to one principle: no statement, theological or otherwise, should be made that would not be credible in the presence of the burning children.

There are two polar ways in which theologians have correctly grasped the centrality of the Holocaust to Jewish thought and faith. One upholds the God of History, the other affirms the death of God and the loss of all hope. Neither is credible alone, in the presence of the burning children. After Auschwitz, faith means that there are times when faith is overcome. Since faith is a response to the Presence in life and history, this response ebbs and flows. The difference between the skeptic and the believer is frequency of faith, and not certitude of position. The ability to live with what I call "moment faith" is the ability to live with pluralism and without the self-flattering, ethnocentric solutions that warp religion or make it a source of hatred for the other.

There are reasons to keep the life of faith: in the light of Auschwitz, secular twentieth-century civilization is not worthy of ultimate loyalty. The victims ask that we not jump to a conclusion that retrospectively makes the covenant they lived an illusion and their death a gigantic travesty. After the Holocaust it is all the more urgent to resist this absolutization of the secular. The Holocaust experience insists that we best err on the side of the moral necessity of a God who called this people to a sacred, albeit dangerous, mission of testimony rather than surrender to the immediate logic of nonbelief. The moral light shed by the Holocaust validates skepticism toward contemporary claims. To follow this orientation is to be opened again to the possibilities of

Exodus and immortality. The capacity to resist and criticize contemporary models is a test of the Holocaust as the new orienting experience of Jews and an indication that a new era of Jewish civilization is under way. This new era will not turn its back on modernity; rather, it will reject some of its elements and take from the past (and future) much more fully. Recognizing that ultimate claims and absolute forces are the seedbed of unlimited Holocausts, this era's religious thinking will seek to live with dialectical theological affirmations, with all claims subject to and tested by contradictions.

There are several theological models for living in contradiction. One such model is that of Job and involves the rejection of easy pieties or denials and the expectation of further revelations of the Presence. Another is the model of the Suffering Servant; here Israel, by focusing on the abuse of the servant, testifies to the suffering God who shares in pain and pleads for ultimate redemption. The treatment of the Suffering Servant is an early warning of the sins intrinsic in the culture but often not seen until later, just as the Holocaust was an advance warning of the demonic potential in modern culture: the pollution is in the liberating technology; the uniformity in the powerful communication and cultural explosion; the mass murder in the efficient bureaucracy. These lurking forces must be checked by God and humanity alike.

Christians and Jews are called upon to preserve their inner community. They are also called by the Holocaust to participate in the new, open civilization. The Holocaust suggests a fundamental skepticism about all human movements, left and right, political and religious—even as we participate in them. Nothing dare evoke our absolute, unquestioning loyalty, not even our God.

In a third theological model for a life of contradiction, that of Lamentations 3, there is only anger and pain checked by the flickering memory of past goodness. But the lamenter does not offer a pious prayer about the Holocaust. Rather, we seek a prayer on the Holocaust that expresses the anger, that blames God. Anger is more compatible with love and involvement than are pleasant niceties and old compliments. The religious task is to justify human beings, not God, a task that requires a total and thoroughgoing self-criticism that purges the emotional dependency and self-abasement of traditional religion and its false crutch of certainty and security. This task involves a willingness to confess and clear up the violations of the image of God (including women, Jews, Blacks, others) in our values, as well as a willingness to overcome the institutionalism that sacrifices God to self-interest. Even the word of God must be held to account for nourishing hatred and for culpability in, or being an accessory to, the fact of genocide. Justifying people means the fullest willingness, in both Judaism and Christianity, to defend the revolt against God and the faith that grows out of the desire to liberate humanity. Yet here, too, the Holocaust demands a dialectical capacity from us. Rebels are not usually good at conserving; if we simply validate the contemporary, we fall into idolatry and prepare the legitimization of another Holocaust.

Extraordinary catastrophes are not mastered by routine treatment or evasion. Only extraordinary outbursts of life or creativity can overcome them. In the silence of God and of theology, there is one fundamental testimony that can still be given: the testimony of human life itself.

The Holocaust as Revelation

The Holocaust is itself a revelation. It is a model and pedagogy for future generations; it bears the lesson that genocide can be carried out with impunity: evil ones need fear neither God nor man. This revelation has several consequences.

1. There is one supreme response to such overwhelming tragedy: the reaffirmation of meaningfulness, worth, and life through acts of love and life-giving. The act of creating a life or enhancing its dignity is the countertestimony to Auschwitz. This is a critical religious act. Only millions or billions of such acts can begin to right the balance of testimony so drastically shifted by the mass weight of six million dead. To speak of the image of God, which points beyond itself to transcendence, is the only statement about God that one can make. And it is human life itself that makes the statement—words will not help.

It takes enormous faith in ultimate redemption and meaningfulness to choose to create or even enhance life again. In fact, this choice reveals faith as an ontological life force that reaffirms creation and life in the teeth of overwhelming death; having the child makes the statement of redemption. The reborn State of Israel is the fundamental act of life and meaning of the Jewish people after Auschwitz. To fail to grasp that inextricable connection and response is to fail utterly to comprehend the theological significance of Israel.

2. This revelation summons humankind to create and rehabilitate the divine image in a human community. This rehabilitation of the di-

vine image is the ultimate testimony, perhaps the only credible one that can speak of God in a world of burning children. And it is a task that summons humans to co-responsibility with God in an attempt to preserve and nourish this fragile redemption.

We face the challenge of creating the conditions under which human beings will grow as an image of God, of building a world in which wealth and resources are created and distributed to provide the matrix for existence as an image of the divine. We face the urgent call to eliminate every stereotype that reduces—and denies—this image in the other. A vigorous self-critical review of every cultural or religious framework that may sustain denial of the absolute and equal dignity of the other is the overriding command of religious existence. Without this self-critical review, the act of the religious enterprise simply lacks credibility. Religion that justifies evil becomes the devil's testimony. Whoever joins in the work of creating and rehabilitating the image of God participates in "restoring to God his scepter and crown." These must be seen as the central religious acts. The command to create and rehabilitate the divine image sheds a pitiless light on popes who deny birth control to starving millions to uphold the authority of the magisterium, or on rabbis who deny women's dignity out of loyalty to divinely given traditions.

3. The Holocaust teaches that the meaning of "chosenness" in Jewish faith is a "forced option." A Jew's life is on the line, and therefore every kind of Jew gives testimony at all times. When times are difficult, Christians can choose to be merely Gentiles; Jews remain Jews. Were Christians to be like Jews in this way, they would have to surrender the self-deceiving universalist rhetoric of the church and adopt a conception of themselves as people of God. Christianity could then live and testify in a truly pluralist world while preserving the ultimacy of its message.

4. Jews have a vested interest in Christianity's existence. Modern values created a milieu as dangerous as—more dangerous than—Christianity at its worst. In pure secularity, humans appoint themselves God and thereby become the devil. Glorification of human autonomy contains the potential for mass killing. When Jews and Christians realize this fact, they are liberated to be in tension with, as well as to celebrate, the secular city.

5. There must be a fundamental shift in the ethics of power. We must have a fundamental reorientation away from the traditional Christian and medieval Jewish glorification of suffering passivity. Never again should anyone be exposed to such one-sided power on

the side of evil. There must be a demand for the redistribution of power. Only the transfer of power to potential victims—power enough to defend themselves—can create a new balance of power. But one should not romanticize the moral stature of the victims. With the balance of power restored, victims can all too easily become perpetrators. Thus one must support not only a balance of power but also the unceasing reconciliation and resolution of conflicts. The need for a restoration of the balance of power accounts for the urgency with which Jews proclaimed the State of Israel after the Holocaust and for the overwhelming worldwide shift of Jewry toward Zionism. It equally accounts for the push within a strengthened Israel to make peace with the Palestinians and to assure a balance of power that protects, without endangering, Jewish survival.

6. Governments have obligations to protect people; they cannot do this without some involvement with power. But how can religion meet the challenge of calling for this involvement without blessing bloody arms or supporting an exploitive status quo? Each religion will need the other's norms, strengths, and criticism to save it from failing this challenge and to correct its behavior along the way.

Israel as Revelation

Jerusalem symbolizes that God's promises are being fulfilled and that His people live on, that human dreams are more real than force and facts. Israel's faith in the God of History demands that an unprecedented event of destruction be matched by an unprecedented act of redemption, and this has happened. The whole Jewish people is caught between immersion in nihilism and immersion in redemption—both are present in immediate experience, and not just historical memory. The reestablishment of the physical community of Israel in a physical and political state may inspire new reflection on the religious significance of a physical people and their actual existence.

Faith is a "moment truth," but there are moments when it is not true, and invoking the truth at the wrong moment is a lie. The sense of Presence gives strength to go on living in contradiction. The recreation of Israel is the classic covenantal symbol. The flaws, the difficulties, are part of the fundamental proof that here we have a revelation of the hidden Presence. Judaism's ongoing life and new harvest of revelation undercut the whole Teaching of Contempt in Christianity, if Christianity finds the strength to admit the reappearance of revelation in our time. The bringing forth of new revelation truly affirms that God does not repent of giving gifts. The acknowledgment of persistent Jewish vitality restores God's gift of Christ to Christian Gentiles as an act of love; it represents a broadening of the covenant, which contradicts the notion that the new revelation in Jesus constituted an act of cruelty that spiritually and physically destroyed the original chosen people. The recognition of revelation in our time removes the shelter of legitimated hatred and allows Christianity to confront the evil in human hearts with the unqualified challenge of the command of love. This recognition does not undercut the validity of the gospel; rather, further revelation clarifies Paul's affirmation that Jewish rejection of Christ paves the way for Gentile acceptance into the covenant: thus later revelations illuminate earlier ones, giving us a new interpretive key to God's unbroken promises.

The reappearance of revelation is an enormous gift in an age when secularism and scientism have all but undercut the sources and credibility of covenant faith, when Holocaust and history have all but overcome hope. The most powerful confirmation of religious hope is that crucifixion and resurrection have occurred in this generation—in the flesh of the covenanted people. This revelation liberates us from the tyranny of modern categories and restores the old religious role of fighting idolatry. Understanding this revelation releases Christianity from timeless spirituality to find its word incarnate in the temporal lives of humans.

If Judaism finds the strength and feeling to admit revelation in this time, then it, too, has the prospect of renewed hope and divine Presence. Paradoxically enough, the security of its own confirmation—the restoration of the land, the covenantal sign—releases Judaism to ponder anew the significance of Christianity. Confirmed now in its resumed redemption and responding to the Holocaust's challenge not to put down others, Judaism must explore the possibility that through the covenant, nurtured and given birth through its body, God has called the Gentiles. By displaying the power of love and concern for Jews and the embattled beginnings of Jewish redemption, the State of Israel can give Jews a new and serious sense of Christianity's own perception that Israel is a vehicle of divine Presence and redemption in the world.

The unqualified Jewish renewed encounter with Christianity is a painful prospect. For Jews to accept the revelation of the Holocaust and Israel leads them to challenge existing denominational lines and to open up to fellow Jews and the world in a new, painful, risky, yet exhilarating, way. The acknowledgment of the Holocaust and Israel as revelation brings with it many gifts: an end to easy Jewish identification of liberation with secularity and liberalism; a much greater Jewish sense of pluralism; an appreciation of Christianity as a moral/religious balance wheel; a recognition of the need to preserve and husband the resources and values of particular traditions in a fast homogenizing world.

If Jews take the risk, later generations will tell of how 4,000 years after the Exodus and 2,000 years after Calvary, Jews and Christians renounced the guarantees and triumphalism. They faced ultimate death, worked together, and overcame that death with renewed life; they overcame extreme hatred with love—which summons the divine Presence in our midst. Truly, if Jews and Christians can accomplish such feats, then Judaism and Christianity are again models for the world, and this is a messianic moment.

A New Relationship Between Judaism and Christianity

The relationship of antagonism between Judaism and Christianity is rooted in the dynamics of the fact that they have grown out of the same covenant and sought to be faithful to differing experiences of messianism, fulfilled and unfulfilled. If this antagonism is to be overcome, Judaism and Christianity must change the inner coherence of their classic relationship. As I have indicated, the Holocaust and the rebirth of the State of Israel as revelatory events in Judaism are the key to a new relationship. These events are both the further unfolding of and commentary on a changed self-understanding that includes a new conception of the pluralism of God's choosing. New patterns of understanding are possible alongside the finality of Christ or the absoluteness of the Jewish covenant. After the Holocaust, the relationship of Judaism and Christianity should enable one to affirm the fullness of the faith claims of the other, to affirm the profound inner relationship between the two, and to recognize and admit how much closer they are to each other than either has been able to say.

One instructive example of a changed self-understanding on the part of both traditions has to do with the other-worldly character of redemption. In the past, both Jewish and Christian conceptions of redemption, in differing ways, have been accompanied by the temptation to abandon this world.

Judaism insists that redemption is going to happen in this world and that this achievement of total perfection of the world will take place as the result of the efforts of both partners, divine and human. In spite of its insistence on this model of redemption, there have been times when Judaism has been tempted to step away from this worldly view. After the Holocaust, this temptation has no place. Rather, the covenant is Israel's commitment to achieve perfection step by step. The model of perfection itself unfolds in history. When evil reigns supreme, the true balance and direction of history have been disturbed. The only event that can correct such imbalance is a major redemptive move on the other side.

From the beginning, the situation was different for Christianity. Christians responded to an event they had not anticipated, the messiah's death, by concluding that true redemption is not in this world. The kingdom of God is within you, and faith leads to a world of spiritual perfection: even though I am a slave, I am free in Christ. Christians responded faithfully to what had transpired, but later history suggests that they made a hermeneutical error when they explained the crucifixion as an indication that redemption is beyond history. Because of this error, Christianity is continually tempted to say: "This vale of tears is not the real world. The world of suffering and oppression does not matter."

Christians went on to make a second error, an error that, in a way, strengthened Judaism's own temptation with other-worldly redemption. In retrospect, a key moment of the division between the two traditions came in their differing responses to the destruction of the Second Temple. The Christians reacted to the destruction as the best proof that the Jews had forfeited their covenant. The Christians were wrong. Judaism did not disappear. And yet at least in part because of Christian claims of triumph, Jews were tempted to step out of history because in that arena, Christianity had won. To reduce the impact of Christianity's triumph among Gentiles, Jews dismissed the significance of this world and of politics and military power. Instead, the rabbis placed emphasis upon a different arena—the arena of the internalized, participatory faith that characterized the rabbinic period. The rabbis responded to the destruction of the Temple with faith in the covenant and trust in God and the goal. God had "pulled back." God was calling the people of Israel to participate more fully in the covenant, but not in history.

To Christian claims that the destruction of the Temple was a sign that God had rejected Jews who did not accept Jesus, the rabbis had another response, as well. The rabbis concluded that Christianity was an alien growth developed by those who followed a false messiah. Perhaps the rabbis erred. Out of defensiveness, the rabbis confused a "failed" messiah and a false messiah. A failed messiah is one who has the right values but did not attain the final goal. The Bar Kochba rebellion was crushed. It turned out that he was a failed messiah. But Akiva did not repudiate him. Moses and Jeremiah were "failures." These "failures" are at the heart of divine and Jewish achievements. The Christian concept of the "second coming" is, in a way, also a tacit admission that if at first you don't succeed, try, try again. The danger, however, as aspects of both Judaism and Christianity attest in different ways, is that such "failures" will be taken as a sign that redemption lies somewhere beyond history. Indeed, as a result of their differing errors, both the rabbis and the early Christians tended to abandon the world to Caesar or to mammon.

After the Holocaust, such abandonment is no longer an option. In our time, both Judaism and Christianity have been forced to confront their own places in history. Through the Holocaust, Jews discovered that without power, they were dead; in response the Jewish people took responsibility for their fate and reestablished the State of Israel. Christians, for their part, discovered that they had to become more involved with the world, lest evil triumph as they stood by and watched. In short, the Holocaust forced Jews and Christians to see that the attempt to protect faith against history was an error and that both religions can have no credibility in a world in which evil can triumph totally. The overwhelming call for both religions is to stop the crucifixion, not to glorify it. Christians are called to purge themselves of the hatred that made them indifferent to others.

After the destruction of the Second Temple, God became more hidden, about that the rabbis were right. By this logic, after the Holocaust God is even more hidden. Therefore, the sacred is even more present in every "secular" area. When God is hidden after Auschwitz, one must find God in the street, in the hospital, in the bar. The responsibility of holy secularity is the responsibility of all human beings.

The final question for the believer is not: where was God in the Holocaust? The manifest answer is that God was present, being tortured, gassed, shot down relentlessly amidst God's people. Rather the question is: what was God's message when God did not stop the Holocaust? Let us venture to say that God was calling humans to take full responsibility for the achievement of the covenant. Judaism is entering a third stage; the Judaism of both biblical Israel (in which God initiated events) and of the rabbis (in which humans met God halfway) has now led to the understanding that the ultimate logic of covenant is for humans to take full responsibility. As humans take power, they must develop their antenna to perceive God as the Presence everywhere. This perception will moderate the use of power. Still, without taking power, without getting involved in history, one is religiously irresponsible. To pray to God as a substitute for taking power is blasphemous. If there is anything in our own traditions that demeans, or denies, or degrades somebody else, then one cannot answer "it is the Word of God," and so be it. One must answer, "it is my responsibility." We are living in an age of the Jewish reacceptance of the covenant. The religious message is not to accept inequality but to demand its correction. Jews must reaccept the covenant without making God into the convenient one who says what one wants to hear. This is a renewal that will demand that Jews and Christians remain open to each other, that we learn from each other, and that we have respect for the distinctiveness and the ongoing validity of each other's traditions. Such openness puts no religious claim beyond possibility but places the completion of total redemption at the center of the agenda. Nor does this affirmation undercut the belief of each group that it is an elected people of God. There is enough love in God to choose again and again.

Christian Theology After the Shoah

CHRISTOPHER M. LEIGHTON

Christians walk a path that repeatedly crosses Jewish boundaries. There is no way around this stubborn fact. Christians cannot enter into relationship with the God of Israel without simultaneously becoming entangled with God's covenantal partner, Israel. Whenever Christians have ignored the ongoing interplay between God and Israel or attempted to sever their own ties to the Jews, the churches have undermined their own spiritual and moral integrity and simultaneously imperiled the physical and spiritual vitality of the Jewish people.

The imperative to disarm those dynamics of Christian thought and practice that threaten the Jewish people has in large measure arisen out of the encounter with the Shoah. Yet, the necessity of reconfiguring the churches' relationship to the Jewish people is not simply an act of theological reparation. The credibility and coherence of the Christian narrative demand a radical recasting of its foundational story. In this essay, I sketch some prominent examples of Christian efforts to gather the sacred fragments of a long and anguished history and to recast them into a Christian theology that invites partnership with the Jewish people.

Jews in the Christian Story

At both the beginning and the end of the Christian story, Jews figure prominently. Jesus and his earliest followers were Jewish, and however ambivalent Christians have been in their interpretation of this fact, the doctrine of the Incarnation compels them to regard this "historical detail" as theologically significant. Yet Jews not only figure prominently at the beginning of the church's story, they also occupy a conspicuous place in its dreams for the future. Christians have long imagined an ending when the ancient ruptures are healed and all of God's people find their place at the messianic table. The church has traditionally rested in the hope that God will reintegrate the Jewish people into covenantal partnership with Christians. Whether through gentle suasion or apocalyptic battle, the conclusion of the Christian story is envisioned as a cosmic triumph that overcomes the anguished divisions between Jew and Gentile "so that God may be all in all" (1 Cor. 15:28).

The place and function of Jews in the middle of the Christian drama have remained far more ambiguous. How were the followers of Jesus to make sense of a movement that was rooted in Jewish soil but found its most fertile ground when transplanted among Gentiles? How were Christians to cope with the mounting opposition of rabbinic leadership? How were Christian communities to negotiate their classification as an "illegitimate religion" by the Roman Empire? What pedigree could an upstart religion offer to anchor its truth claims and to authorize its outreach? The narrative formulation that eased the predicament took shape in the first and second centuries of the common era, and the churches have remained in the thrall of this schema for nearly two thousand years. This theological framework goes by the name of Christian supersessionism, and its appeal resides in the relief it offered Christians on two fronts. On the one hand, Christian supersessionism deflected political and religious criticisms threatening the church from outside. On the other hand, it blunted doubts and fears about its own integrity that arose within its ranks. These dynamics reverberate through the New Testament, and they are best understood by turning to some specific examples.

Christian Supersessionism

The contours of Christian supersessionism are displayed in the traditional interpretation of the Parable of the Wicked Tenants in Matthew's Gospel (Mt. 21:33–46). A landowner plants a vineyard and then leases it to tenants. When the harvest comes and the landowner sends his servants to collect the produce, the tenants seize the slaves, beating one, killing another, and stoning a third. The pattern is repeated with another groups of messengers, so the landowner sends his own son in the hope that the tenants will respect the heir. The tenants, however, see an opportunity to claim the inheritance for themselves, and they murder the landowner's son. The parable culminates in an indictment: "Therefore I tell you, the kingdom of God will be taken away from you and given to a people that produces the fruits of the kingdom."

The typological reading of the parable that evolves in the Christian tradition depicts the Jews as the unjust tenants who conspire to possess for themselves alone the fruit of God's kingdom. In response to their murderous betrayal, God hands over the kingdom to another people, namely, the church. This narrative pattern constitutes the main plot of Christian supersessionism. The "new" people of God, the followers of Jesus and subsequently the church, displace the "old" people, the Jews who subsequently comprise the adherents of rabbinic Judaism.

The church displaced the synagogue as God's covenantal partner, and as a consequence halakhic observances defined by rabbinic interpretations of the Torah and the institutions associated with the Temple were either deemed obsolete or were reshaped to articulate Christian understandings of religious sacrifice. The dynamics of this transposition are evident in the Letter to the Hebrews. The author reframes the sacrificial worship of the Temple by casting Jesus in the role of the high priest who gives himself as the perfect and eternal offering. As a consequence, a "new covenant" has displaced "the old." Followers of Jesus need no longer take their bearings in relation to the religious practices of the people Israel, for "what is obsolete and growing old will soon disappear" (Heb. 8.13). The rejection of Torah observance increasingly became integral to the process of defining the terms of a covenantal partnership patterned on Jesus Christ. The result was a fracture in understanding between Christians and Jews over the content and character of their "deep religious symbols."

The New Testament harbors multiple, often conflicted, views of the Jewish people and Judaism. But the supersessionist rendering of the New Testament became the standard strategy by which the church fathers maintained the tradition. The dominance of this strategy is established by means of typological readings of the Scriptures: beneath the surface of the "Old Testament" looms the figure of Christ. The church fathers were able to detect hidden correspondences between "the old" and the "new," "the inner" and "the outer" meanings of sacred texts that both revealed and consolidated Christian claims to a venerable antiquity.[1] The church fathers saw the failure of Jews to discern the spiritual depths of their own Scriptures as a sign of the "hardhearted" and "carnal" nature of Judaism. In the most fundamental sense, Christians concluded that Jews no longer understood their own Bible and therefore were no longer worthy of being God's covenantal partner.

Christians found confirmation for these interpretations within salient historical events. The destruction of the Second Temple, the defeat of Bar Kochba, and the emergence of the triumphant church were heralded as irrefutable evidence in support of a displacement theology. The early Christians viewed every catastrophe that befell the Jewish community as just punishment for Jewish complicity in the murder of Jesus Christ.

Although the logic of Christian supersessionism anticipates a contest in which the Jewish people yield to the "new covenant" and are successfully absorbed into the body of Christ, an underlying ambivalence is reflected in the church's refusal to exercise its imperial prerogatives. Christianity did not attempt to eliminate Judaism and the Jewish people in the same terms with which it assailed "paganism." Restraint in a world where falsehood is thought to hold no privileges implies a church deeply divided in its perceptions of the Jewish people. The ambivalence is evident in the position developed by Augustine (354–430 C.E.), a position that informed ecclesiastical policy throughout the Middle Ages and continues to linger in our own times.[2] Augustine sets a limit to the logic of Christian supersessionism. Jews are protected so that their degraded condition provides the world with a "negative witness," giving irrefutable evidence of what happens to those who reject Jesus as the Christ.

At various times and in various places, the protection offered by this formulation collapsed under the strains of political, economic, and religious upheavals. The atrocities visited upon the Jews during the Crusades, the recurrent patterns of expulsions, and the eruption of violent pogroms indicate the precarious condition of the Jewish people, especially after the thirteenth and fourteenth centuries. The church collaborated intimately with the state in the formulation of legal codes that situated Jews on the margins of society. The policies of exclusion were sustained by anti-Jewish caricatures that were etched into the art, literature, music, philosophy, and theology of Western culture's greatest luminaries.

The Christian Critique of Supersessionism

This legacy of Christian contempt is well known within the Jewish community, but only in the wake of the Shoah and the founding of the modern State of Israel has it begun to claim the attention of Christians. Prior to these events, there were few Christian scholars whose work exposed the underbelly of anti-Judaism within the Christian tradition. The passivity, if not the active complicity, of Christians in the face of the Nazi genocidal assault on the Jews has called into question the spiritual and moral credibility of the Christian tradition.

Christians did not respond immediately to the horrors of the Shoah, in large part because the connections between Christian anti-Judaism and modern anti-Semitism were either ignored or denied. The first major ecclesiastical report that alluded to the linkage was presented at the First Assembly of the World Council of Churches in 1948. On the one hand, the document acknowledges "the extermination of six million Jews" and the failure "to fight with all our strength the age-old disorder of man which anti-Semitism represents." The report confesses that "the churches in the past have helped to foster an image of Jews as the sole enemies of Christ," and it insists that "anti-Semitism is sin against God and man" and "absolutely irreconcilable with the profession and practice of the Christian faith." Yet, the cornerstones of Christian supersessionism remained unchallenged. According to this declaration, the Christian evangelical imperative to missionize was first directed to the Jewish people, and Christians today need "to recover the universality of our Lord's commission by including the Jewish people in their evangelistic work." There is no hint in this document of an underlying contradiction between this missionary outreach and the call to combat misunderstanding and prejudice. The statement assumes the eclipse of God's covenant with the Jewish people and so reinforces the age-old negative assessment of Judaism.

At the Third Assembly of the World Council of Churches in 1961, a resolution on anti-Semitism signaled a more radical critique. Not only did the assembly urge its member churches "to do all in their power to resist every form of anti-Semitism," it noted that "the historic events which led to the Crucifixion should not be so presented as to impose upon the Jewish people today responsibilities which must fall on all humanity, not on one race or community." To reject the deicide charge as foundational for the Christian story amounted to a confession of complicity. The task of making restitution for a legacy of contempt began to emerge as an exacting mandate of repentance, one that might require a radical reorientation of the tradition.

The single most important document to advance a dramatic reversal in the supersessionist narrative is a short declaration known as *Nostra Aetate* and was issued at the Roman Catholic Church's Second Vatican Council in 1965. The document teaches that Jews and Christians share a common spiritual ancestry, and it insists that the death of Jesus "cannot be charged against all Jews, without distinction, then alive, nor against the Jews today." Yet, the greatest reordering of the Christian story is the assertion that "Jews should not be presented as rejected or accursed by God, as if this followed from the Holy Scriptures." Despite Jerusalem's failure to recognize "the time of her visitation . . . God holds the Jews most dear for the sake of their Fathers; He does not repent of the gifts He makes or of the calls He issues."

With this declaration, the Roman Catholic Church initiated a shift in thought that is still revolutionizing Christian understandings of the Jewish people and Judaism. By insisting on the enduring character of God's covenantal promises, the document began a process of authorizing a nonsupersessionist reading of the Christian story. Yet, the declaration also preserves an ancient ambiguity and an all-too-resilient triumphalism. "By His cross Christ Our Peace reconciled Jews and Gentiles, making both one in Himself. . . . Therefore, the burden of the Church's preaching is to proclaim the cross of Christ as the sign of God's all-embracing love and as the fountain from which very grace flows." The enduring problem emerges yet again: Jews find themselves cast in a subordinate role within the grand Christian narrative. They are present at the beginning of the Christian story, and they will be claimed in the end. But in the meantime, they are simply an indispensable and eternal witness to somebody else's saving truth, a truth that ultimately they need to recognize as their own.

By the standards that now prevail within the Roman Catholic Church, *Nostra Aetate* may appear timid and flawed. Neither the Holocaust nor the creation of the State of Israel are mentioned, and the need for Christians to embark upon a long process of repentance remains unacknowledged. Yet, what in hindsight might appear as a small turn of the rudder has altered the course of history, and the momentum begun by *Nostra Aetate* has acquired greater force and focus through the publication of a series of landmark documents.[3] Dioceses and national bishops conferences have provided Roman Catholics with the educational resources needed to recognize the enduring place of the Jewish people and Judaism in God's plan. These documents demonstrate an unprecedented theological resolve to reshape the tradition, an undertaking rarely understood or appreciated by those unfamiliar with church history.

Protestant denominations such as the Lutheran World Federation, the United Methodist Church, the Presbyterian Church U.S.A., the United Church of Christ, the Mennonite European Regional Conference, the Synod of the Protestant Church of the Rheinland, and others have also issued statements over recent decades. They decry the evils of anti-Semitism and call their churches to a new and constructive engagement with the Jewish people. Although a growing number of Protestant scholars have made groundbreaking proposals, Protestant denominations are only beginning to redirect congregational life and community practice.

To be sure, the Southern Baptist Convention's call to evangelize the Jewish people, issued in time for the High Holy Days in the fall of 1999, signals the enduring grip of Christian triumphalism among many evangelical Protestants. Yet, even this outreach needs to be read and interpreted as a response to the Baptist Alliance statement, which called fellow Baptists to renounce those Christian teachings that impugn the enduring integrity of Judaism.[4] In the internal struggle to define what it means to be a Christian and to demarcate the boundaries of Christian identity, the Jews are pulled into the middle of the fray.

However inadequate the implementation of Christian declarations on Judaism and the Jewish people, these statements taken together indicate a historic shift that Paul van Buren has claimed will prove as pivotal to the future of Christianity as the Reformation proved to the sixteenth-century church. They reveal a radical reorientation. Yet, they also signal an enduring ambivalence and an unresolved ambiguity. For nearly two thousand years, Christians have approached Jews as a problem to be solved, and they have seen Judaism as a temporary stage in the progressive march to the gospel truth. Only recently have Christians begun to perceive Judaism and the Jewish people as inseparably bound to the mystery of God.

The anguished history that mandates a radical realignment within the Christian tradition also threatens to freeze Christians and Jews into a rigid script that confines Christians to the roles of perpetrators and bystanders and Jews to the backdrop as victims. The guilt that animates many of the churches' official statements not only serves as a painful acknowledgment of past complicity; these pronouncements also disclose an inability to imagine a new and mutually beneficial partnership. As a result, the haunting legacy of the Christian–Jewish encounter may lead both communities to abandon hope that any new project can make a genuine difference. Paradoxically, the Holocaust both impels an unflinching accounting from Christians and constricts the terms for creative engagement with the larger Jewish community. Nowhere are the promises and obstacles to the challenge more evident than in the recent Vatican document *We Remember* and in the debates about Pope Pius XII.

Reforming the Christian Story

Some maintain that everything within the Christian tradition requires rethinking in the aftermath of the Shoah. As a consequence, any and every doctrine, indeed any and every theological affirmation, must undergo rigorous scrutiny, and the tradition must purge itself of those tenets of belief and practice that sanction contempt of the other, most especially the Jewish people. The task of neutralizing supersessionist patterns entails nothing less than the reenvisioning of the Christian narrative—from beginning to end.

The Beginning

When Christians embark upon a process of reformation, they reach into their earliest memories to recover the generative ground from which the tradition derives its sense of direction. Although Christians once regarded the times of the fledgling Christian movement as a golden age, recent scholarship portrays this age as a time when fragile and defensive communities were caught in the midst of intense struggles. These scholarly reappraisals have also stressed the Jewishness of Jesus as well as the Jewish roots of Christianity; thus these reappraisals are loaded with significance for the contemporary church and its understanding of the Jewish people.

Until recently, New Testament scholars have in large measure remained captive to a "classical" education and an anti-Jewish cultural bias that exaggerated the Greco-Roman influences on the emergent church.[5] During the last thirty-five years, New Testament scholars have increasingly shifted their attention to the rich diversity of Palestinian and Diaspora Judaism and to the impact of Judaism on early Christianity.[6] This shift of attention has led to new views about Jesus. Depending on the scholarly filter, Jesus emerges as a quietistic Pharisee, a revolutionary Zealot, a charismatic prophet, a magician, an apocalyptic miracle worker, a messianic figure, or a Jewish version of an itinerant Socrates. These portraits are composed of fragments from the diverse inventory of first-century Judaism. Although the contrasting, indeed conflicting, images indicate that the historical Jesus will remain elusive, the restoration of Jesus to his Jewish context is remarkably consistent across the theological spectrum.

The reclamation of Jesus' Jewishness poses new challenges to Christian and Jewish assumptions about the origins and character of early Christianity. For example, if the teachings and ministry of Jesus fit within the range of the first-century Jewish imagination, wherein lies his distinctiveness? Or, differently stated, how does one get from the Jewish Jesus to the Christ of Christian faith?

This query necessitates a fresh examination of Jesus' early followers, of the Gospel writers, and, most notably, of Paul. In recent years, the notion that Paul, not Jesus, was the founder of Christianity and the architect of Christian anti-Judaism has been largely discredited. Jewish and Christian interpreters alike have increasingly relocated Paul within a Jewish context.[7] The trend to unearth the Jewish substratum of Christianity extends from Paul to other New Testament writers, most of whom are thought to have been Jewish Christians with links to the Palestinian homeland, either directly or through educational experience. The implications of this view lead to a different assessment of the pitched polemical battles within the New Testament.

The rhetoric of slander was a common phenomenon among first-century Hellenists, and the practice spilled into numerous Jewish writings of the time.[8] The defamatory assaults against the Jewish opponents of the Jesus movement need to be read alongside Josephus's attacks on the Zealots (*Jewish War* 4.6.3: § 385, 387, 388), the Dead Sea Scrolls (1QS 2:4–10; 3:19–21; 4:9–14), the Wisdom of Solomon (14:22–28), and Jewish apocalyptic writings such as I Enoch and 4 Ezra. Clearly, the New Testament authors utilized stock literary tropes widely circulated within the culture. And many Christian interpreters insist the intensity of the verbal assaults against the Jewish opponents in the New Testament is indicative of an internal familial conflict—hotly pursued by people who had no intention of launching a new religion. Some scholars argue that this historical and literary analysis of early Christian writings blunts the anti-Jewish edges of the Christian tradition at a decisive juncture, for it suggests that the elevation of the church at the expense of the synagogue is not an essential theological conclusion but a time-bound rhetorical flourish.

Whether this strategy disarms or merely obscures the magnitude of the problem of anti-Judaism demands further scrutiny, but the effort to relocate the New Testament within a Jewish matrix extends well beyond the analysis of polemical discourse. For example, doctrinal affirmations that became constitutive of Christian faith are increasingly traced back to Jewish sources. Scholars have linked Paul's exalted language about the experience of Christ to the vocabulary of Jewish mysticism and apocalypticism. Matthew's Christology transposes Jewish conceptions of Wisdom and applies them to Jesus. Even John's identification of Jesus with the divine Logos has analogies within Palestinian Judaism and the Diaspora.[9]

To be sure, the early followers of Jesus stretched the conceptual boundaries of the Jewish tradition to the breaking point. And yet, their struggle to articulate the meaning and significance of Jesus can be understood only against a Jewish backdrop. Some readers of this volume may want to contest the degree of continuity between Judaism and Christianity, but the emerging picture of our tangled beginnings is far messier and confused than once assumed. And the recovery of our interwoven origins may encourage Christians to begin to affirm their solidarity with the Jewish people.

The Middle

The recovery of Christian origins is a start. But Christians cannot ignore the fact that those origins stand in the shadow of subsequent history. Any attempt to neutralize Christian anti-Judaism by hurdling nearly two thousand years of history is suspect in the wake of the Shoah. Christians and Jews cannot retrieve the lost horizon, a world unscarred by the separation of church and synagogue. An anguished history creates a chasm that divides Christians and Jews. Although the authors of the New Testament may not have intended to promote a supersessionist ideology, modern scholars can never retrieve the intentions of the New Testament authors. More tellingly, the motivations of New Testament authors cannot exorcise the ghosts of interpretations that have dominated the church for centuries. Indeed, the temptation to dwell within the historical reconstructions of the past threatens to deflect Christians and Jews from the present challenges of exploring what it means for a religious community to live in tension with its sacred writings.

Western history discloses the dreadful consequences of a church that reads the people Israel out of its own story. In the aftermath of the Holocaust, Christians are compelled to ask themselves anew what they are making of their Scriptures and what their Scriptures are making of them. They are prompted by the internal logic of their own theological claims as well as by the external urgings of non-Christian neighbors to ask how their traditions—their beliefs, their practices, their pieties—have shaped them and their perceptions of others. After the Shoah, Christians must confront the middle of their story and not find easy comfort in historical reconstructions of the first century.

The End

Even if Christians reframe the beginning of their narrative and come to terms with the ghosts that haunt its middle, their story will remain slanted toward a supersessionist agenda until they critically assess the content and character of their future hopes. Plurality and difference are the inescapable realities of our existence, and any theological attempt to dissolve our diversity through appeals to a higher truth or a totalizing unity are suspect, even when projected against an eschatological horizon. To overcome the deeply ingrained habit of envisioning a future in which the particularity of Judaism and the Jewish people is boiled away in a soteriological melting pot, Christians will need to revisit the biblical conceptions of election or chosenness.

The expectation that in the end everyone, including the Jews, will become one in Christ was articulated by Paul and reinforced by subsequent generations of Christian thinkers. The expectation is formed in large measure by Galatians 3:28: "There is no longer Jew or Greek, there is no longer free or slave, there is no longer male and female; for all of you are one in Christ Jesus." Addressed to an audience composed of Gentiles, Paul's explication of faith among the baptized points to a condition in which the social, political, economic, and even religious rankings are transcended. In the Christian tradition, this description set in motion a view that the categories of Jew and Gentile are transient barriers to be overcome in God's future. The Christian theologian Kendall Soulen has noted that another interpretation is possible. Unlike the social artifice separating slave and free, the categories of Jew and Gentile can no more be dissolved than the distinction between male and female. Galatians 3:28, then, suggests not that in some distant future we will all be alike but that in the present we should not hierarchically arrange our natural endowments; rather, we need to discover the sanctity of our irreducible differences and recognize that they serve as a vital source of blessing. In other words, Christian hope is not to eliminate the distinct ways in which we are embodied, but to live in covenantal partnerships that bring honor to our own and the other's particularity. Paul makes something like this point in his first letter to the Corinthians (1 Cor. 12:14–26).

The construction of the Tower of Babel was animated by the human ambition to annul the divide between heaven and earth, between humanity and divinity. God destroyed the edifice, scattered the people, and confused their languages to punish this misplaced ambition, or so it appears. But a compelling case can be made that God's "punishment" was in fact a great blessing. As scattered people, we have the God-given task of discovering that an expansive and irreducible wisdom resides hidden within difference. In the face of the other, we are challenged to detect the traces of the One who is totally Other.

The distinction between Jew and Christian might become a blessing if we do not try to construct an edifice that loses touch with the biblical ground on which we both stand. The challenge for Christian theology is to accept, perhaps even celebrate, the gaps, the silences, the distances between us Christians and Jews. Only in the recognition of the unbridgeable spaces between our traditions can Christians come to see the Jewish people not as a problem to solve but as a mystery in whose company we may discover our own limits and in whose midst we may also discern new and unsuspected insights into ourselves, the world, and God.

4

GOD

The God of Jews and Christians

PETER OCHS

God and Jewish Tradition

The title of this chapter represents the ultimate reason we have compiled a book like this. We speak and write as members of a people pulled apart from the world and, to a degree, from other peoples only because of our relationship to the One we call Creator of the world *(bore olam)*, Master of the world *(ribono shel olam)*, Almighty *(el shadai)*, Holy One blessed be He *(ha-kadosh baruch hu)*, the Place *(ha-makom)*, the Presence *(ha-shechina)*, Merciful—or "womb-like"—Father *(av ha-rachamim)*, the name YHVH who cannot be spoken, our God *(elohenu)*.

Living still in the shadow of Holocaust, we remember, nevertheless, that we are a people of God, and we write to share with fellow Jews our sense of the meaning, joys, and challenges of being such a people in our day. One of the striking features of contemporary Jewish life is that, outside of the more traditional circles of observant Jews, Jews do not often speak and write openly about their God, even those who privately acknowledge their continued faith. This silence does not appear to be a matter of mere protest against a God who would be God in the awful twentieth century. It seems to be more a sign of unfamiliarity: a consequence of two hundred years of adjusting to the modern habit of relegating "religion" to the sphere of the "private" and "individual" and "confessional." As if speaking to and of God were too immodest a matter to share publicly! Well, I hope readers will not consider the authors of this book to be immodest. I hope, instead, that readers will consider us markedly *ordinary*. Most people in the world, from children to old folks, feel rather comfortable talking about, and even talking to, the one(s) they call "God," or some linguistic equivalent. Speaking of and to God is, most of all, a *traditional* practice. It is something people learn to do from childhood because their parents and grandparents and teachers do it, and because it is the way they speak from the heart in a language that is intimate to them. It may, therefore, require more chutzpah for a human being to claim to have *no* need for such a God than to admit to participating in the everyday faiths and beliefs of ordinary traditional people!

So, then, this book is founded upon a traditional belief: that we creatures are neither alone in the universe nor accompanied by strictly impersonal or malevolent spirits. This Jewish traditional belief has, to be sure, changed over the millennia. The Israelites appear to have once peopled the spirit world with many spirits and gods. During the days of the First Temple, however, belief in the unique power of one God seems to have become commonplace, and this belief, in turn, became a belief in the unique One as the only God: Lord God Creator of heaven and earth. Other beliefs remained, of course, and some of them were in competition with belief in the one God, but what we, rather loosely, call "monotheism" appears to have guided everyday beliefs from the Second Temple period on.

Prayer

The best way to learn about the God of traditional Jewish belief is to examine the language of prayer that is recorded in the Bible and in the literature of the rabbinic sages who canonized the Bible in the first century and who have since interpreted the meaning of the Bible for everyday Jewish life. Traditional prayer may be characterized most simply as the way ordinary Jews open their hearts most deeply; the God of Israel may be characterized most simply as the One to whom ordinary Jews pray.

Of the many kinds of prayer in Jewish tradition, three in particular illustrate vividly how Jews have traditionally opened their hearts to God: what we call prayers of petition, of praise, and of blessing.

Petition *(bakashah* or *techinah)* could be called the open heart's simplest call for help. When his sister Miriam turned ill, Moses prayed simply, *el na refa na lah* (God, please heal her). Elemental prayers of petition are addressed to God as *bore olam* (Creator of the Universe), who is Savior *(moshi'a)* and Redeemer *(go'el)*: "O God, save me by Your name (Ps. 54:3); "May the words of my mouth and the prayer of my heart be acceptable to you, O Lord, my rock and my redeemer" (Ps. 19:15). To learn to pray in the fashion of the psalmist is not to acquire esoteric knowledge and technical skill but to open the heart.

Praise *(hallel)* is the psalmist's most frequently uttered form of prayer: "Praise Him with loud clashing cymbals . . . *Halleluyah!*" The God addressed through prayers of praise is the Creator whose world we inhabit, the Sustainer whose gifts keep us in life, and the Redeemer and Healer who answers our petitions. When the rabbinic sages standardized the *siddur*, or Jewish prayer book, they filled it with biblical psalms and, thus, with many prayers of praise to the One who has the tenderness to hear our petitions and the power to respond to them.

The blessing *(berachah)* is the prayer that makes almost every moment of the day an occasion for addressing God. To utter a *berachah* is neither "to bless God," per se, nor to "be blessed by God." It is, instead, to declare of every event of everyday life that *this* is an occasion in which I sense the direct consequence of God's acting in the world. The most well-known example accompanies the most ordinary daily act, eating a piece of bread. After washing the hands and breaking a morsel of bread, the traditional Jew utters the words, "Blessed are you, YHVH our God, leader of the world, who brings forth bread from the earth." The individual then consumes the bread. The words of the blessing and the taste and substance of the bread are conjoined in the act of eating. One scholar calls this joining an act of "normal mysticism," in which the simple act of eating something from this earth is literally transformed into an experience—and acknowledgment—of that which is not of this earth: the gift of God.[1] This is the God whose words create this world and whose words, or Torah, also bring us to acknowledge and even taste his creative actions. By uttering such blessings, the individual transforms any *thing (davar)* on this earth into a created-word *(dibur)* of God.

Some readers may be uneasy with the anthropomorphism of what I have just reported. Here, in an age of science and technology, I am writing about a God who is not of this earth but whose presence can be experienced through the simple act of eating bread! These readers may be uncomfortable with the rabbinic terms I have used to talk about God and may prefer to encounter the unknown more nakedly, examining our tradition's moments of change, questioning the limits of our knowledge, and speculating imaginatively about what may lie beyond our received systems of language. Others may prefer to approach the challenges of talking about God dressed in as many words of the received tradition as we can acquire, and they may be uncomfortable with the speculations that will come later in this essay. To serve both kinds of reader, I will begin now to address our topic from three different, yet complementary, perspectives. These are the perspectives of received tradition, of new encounters and the questions they raise, and of something in Judaism that always keeps the new and the old in constructive relation.

Received Tradition

In the biblical account, Moses at the burning bush encountered a God who named himself "the God of your ancestors, Abraham, Isaac, and Jacob" (Ex. 3). The God we learn about from our ancestors is not a God whose modes of existence are to be proved or disproved but a God whose name belongs to our natural language. Just as we learn to use the words "please" and "thank you," so we learn to use the words "God created the world" and "God's justice." Although different Jews may picture what these words say in many different ways, the main point of the words is not to deliver a specific picture of something out there. The point is, instead, to provide all Jews with adequate vocabularies for engaging all their ancestors, as it were, in earnest discussions about all the details of everyday life. In the biblical account, Judaism's received tradition begins with the Torah that Moses received on Mt. Sinai. In the rabbis' account, "Moses received the Torah on Mt. Sinai and transmitted it to Joshua, who transmitted it to the elders, who transmitted it to the prophets, who transmitted it to the 'Men of the Great Assembly' [the legislative body in early Second Temple days], who transmitted it to the Pairs [the early, protorabbinic sages]," and on to the rabbinic sages themselves (M. Avot 1:1).

New Encounters

Moses was, however, not just a passive recipient of God's words. In the biblical account, when God appeared to Moses out of the burning bush, his response was to question as well as obey. God said he would send him to Pharaoh; Moses replied, "Who am I that I should go to Pharaoh?" God told him to bring his people out; Moses asked, "When the Israelites ask me, 'What is His name?' what shall I say?" And later, "What if they do not believe me?" (Ex 4:1). Moses asked questions before he enacted God's commands. According to the biblical account, however, when Moses read the tablets to the community of Israel, they declared, "*na'aseh ve-nishmah*" ([what you have commanded] we will faithfully do—Ex. 24:7); in the Talmud's gloss, "they committed themselves to doing *(na'aseh)* before hearing *(ve-nishmah,* or pondering the meaning of what they were to do)."[2] Unlike the people, Moses' response to God is to question and ponder *before* doing. This is the prototype of the *philosopher's* response, rather than the traditionalist's, since the traditionalist receives but the philosopher asks why? what? and how?

Throughout Jewish history, new encounters have framed questions and philosopher-sages have posed them—questions both about the nature of God and God's word and about the justice of God's actions and the ethical meaning of God's word. The Book of Proverbs asked the first kind of question, "Where can Wisdom be found?" Similarly, Philo asked about the relation of God's word to God's own being, and Maimonides asked about the conditions of intellect that are present in prophecy. Examining God's intention to destroy Sodom, Abraham offered a prototype of the second kind of question: "Shall not the judge of all earth act justly?" (Gen. 18:25). In the face of personal and national loss, the psalmist cried, "Why have You forsaken me?" And the rabbinic sages cried, "When Rabbi Akiva was executed [by the Romans] . . . the ministering angels said before the Holy One, blessed be He: 'Such Torah, and such a reward?'"[3] In response to the pogroms in the Ukraine, the Yiddish poet Peretz Markish wrote, "I yearn to merge with you in prayer. And yet my heart, my lips are moved only to blasphemies and curses."[4] The talmudist and Auschwitz survivor David Halivni composed his own midrash: "The sword and the book came down from heaven tied to each other. Said the Almighty, 'If you keep what is written in this book, you will be spared this sword; if not,

you will be consumed by it.'[5] We clung to the book, yet we were consumed by the sword."[6]

Such words, one might suggest, indicate that what Jews encountered in the twentieth century pushed them beyond questions, that
Jews have lost faith in God because of the Shoah. But Eugene
Borowitz argues that modern Jews lost faith in God long before the
Shoah, through the work of Enlightenment, Emancipation, rationalism, and assimilation. What Jews lost in the Shoah, he says, was their
faith in humanity.[7] They lost faith in a utopian humanism that
promised, "Give up your superstitions! Abandon the ethnic and religious traditions that separate us one from the other! Subject all aspects of life to rational scrutiny and the disciplines of science! This is
how we will be saved." It didn't work. Not that science and rationality
are unworthy; what failed was the effort to abstract these from their
setting in the ethics and wisdoms of received tradition.

Between Tradition and New Encounters

If the Jewish scientist contemplates the limits of the universe directly,
without the support of religious tradition, then what can mediate today between this secular enterprise and traditional Jewish inquiries
into the unknown? In the language of rabbinic Judaism, the mediation
comes in the practice of "Oral Torah," but we may now find other
terms useful as well. We may say simply that the questions and doubts
raised in every age change the shape and modify the language of Jewish religious tradition. Judaism's age-old dialogue between the voices
of tradition and of new encounter has always mediated between ancient religious beliefs and everything new. Mediation is simply a matter of bringing the dialogue up to date as new encounters raise both
philosophic questions about the nature of God and ethical questions
about the justice of God's actions.

Consider, for example, how traditions of Jewish philosophy emerge
in response to questions about Moses' dialogue with God. According
to the biblical account, when Moses asked God's name, God replied,
"Tell the people ehyeh [I will be] sent me to you." And further, "Tell
them ehyeh asher ehyeh [I will be what I will be] is My name for everlasting" (Ex. 3:15). When these names entered Israelite religion, they
added something new, deep, and mysterious to traditional language
about God. For the rabbinic sages, these names remained a source of
perennial dialogue, but this dialogue produced no single dogma:

R. Abba b. Mammel said: God said to Moses, "You want to know My Name? Well, I am called according to My work. . . . When I am judging created beings, I am called *elohim* (God). . . . When I suspend judgment . . . , I am called *el shaddai* (God Almighty). . . . And when I am merciful toward my world, I am called YHVH, which refers to the attribute of Mercy. . . . Thus *ehyeh asher ehyeh* in virtue of my deeds."

R. Isaac said: God said to Moses: "Tell them that I am now what I always was and always will be; for this reason, the word *ehyeh* is written three times." . . .

R. Jacob b. Abina in the name of R. Huna of Sepphoris: God said to Moses: "Tell them that I will be with them in this servitude, and in servitude will they always continue, but I will be with them!"[8]

In the context of the philosophic and mystical inquiries of medieval Jewish scholars, Maimonides and Nachmanides opened up yet another level of debate about God's name. Maimonides offered a philosophic interpretation. He read *ehyeh asher ehyeh* as proof of God's essential attribute of necessary being: "God made known [to Moses] the knowledge . . . through which [Israel] would acquire a true notion of the existence of God: . . . There is a necessarily existent thing that has never been or ever will be, non-existent."[9] Nachmanides offered a mystical interpretation. He argued that Maimonides' reading violates the narrative context in Exodus: Moses and Israel needed no rational proofs, for they knew God. "Moses asked only by what divine attribute he was being sent. . . . God told him he was being sent "with the attribute of justice, which is within the attribute of mercy.""[10]

Such discussions of God's being and action tend to be technical; traditions of Jewish philosophy tend therefore to be esoteric. Questions about Israel's suffering, however, engender more general discussions, giving rise to more public traditions of Jewish ethics. After the First Destruction, for example, the latter chapters of the Book of Isaiah characterized Israel as God's "Suffering Servant": one whose suffering did not necessarily reflect her own sins, as in the earlier traditions of Deuteronomy, but the sins of an unrepentant humanity at large. The Second Destruction stimulated even more radical conceptions. The Book of Exodus taught that God is "with Israel," which means, according to the psalmist, that God is "with Israel in her suffering" (Ps. 91:15). After the Destruction, however, the rabbis said of this verse that it means "God is with Israel sufferingly" (*hu be-tsarah*).[11] Later, some esoteric groups taught that God Himself suffered for humanity's

sins,[12] and others taught that God's own name was divided in two at
the creation, and that the end of history will bring not merely the redemption of humanity, but also, through that redemption, the repair
of God's name.[13] Through the years of pogrom, there were poets who
taught that the very words we use to pray are now broken and that
only silence can express our grief. And in the years since the Shoah,
there are philosophers who teach that God can no longer touch us but
shows Himself only through bare traces: our task is not now to look
for Him, but only to seek out the faces of those who suffer and bring
care and consolation. However burdened, these are not mere plaints,
but teachings of religious change.

According to the Jewish theologians who conceived this book, Judaism is now changing in another way as well. From sad experience,
our recent forebears learned to assume that our religion is despised
by its host nations. They grew accustomed to acting on this assumption, either by joining the despisers, or by despising them in turn:
redefining Judaism as a religion that survives only if set entirely
apart. Although compassionate toward our forebears and their suffering, we conclude nevertheless that their assumptions belong to
the past of Judaism, not to its future. Our students gain strength and
confidence from the way Judaism teaches its truths to its neighbors.
And our Judaism has gained the strength and confidence to teach
our students, in Jewish terms, about who these neighbors are and
what they believe. In this book, we begin by teaching about
our Christian neighbors and what they believe about the God of
Israel.

The God of Christian
Religious Tradition

Introducing Christianity the way I have introduced Judaism, I begin
by distinguishing the received traditions of Christianity from the new
encounters that stimulate Christian philosophers and theologians to
reflect in new ways on what they believe. To study Christian belief in
Jewish terms is to ask, first, how Christians *practice* their traditions
and, only then, how their sages speak about God in ways that may
sound more abstract and technical to us. As with Judaism, I assume
that Christianity must ultimately be studied in ways that integrate
these two perspectives.

Christian Practice:
A Brief Illustration

The best place to hear the beliefs and see the practices that are shaping Christian desires is in the local churches, in congregational prayer and in the sermons of local ministers and priests. Stanley Hauerwas writes, "One of the most important questions you can ask theologians is where they go to church. . . . Theology can too easily begin to appear as 'ideas,' rather than the kind of discourse that must, if it is to be truthful, be embedded in the practices of actual lived community."[14] With space for one illustration, let us consider Hauerwas's own description of the Methodist church he attends weekly, Aldersgate United Methodist Church in Chapel Hill, North Carolina. After each part of his description, I will comment on features of traditional Christian belief he has illustrated *and* on how they compare with traditional Jewish beliefs.

> Our worship area is . . . not an attractive sanctuary, but at least its simplicity insures there is no ugliness. . . . Given the simplicity of our space it makes all the difference who is and is not present on any Sunday morning. We need everyone we can get. . . . I assume Aldersgate is a very typical example of a mainline Christian church.

Comment: There is a communal space for communicating with God. The locus of traditional Christian belief in God is the church, embodied in local Christian community, just as the locus of traditional Jewish belief ought to be the people Israel, embodied in the local Jewish community.

> One of the highest points of our liturgy is always the prayers of the people. . . . This person is having an operation, or their mother has just died. . . . Through our prayers, we learn to have our lives lifted up to God and thus to one another.

Comment: Prayer is not just about God, but also about one another. The Christian community, like the Jewish community, is a gathering of people who care about one another, pray for each other's welfare, and receive together the blessings and summons of their tradition's scriptural witness.

> Reverend Allred begins her sermon by citing . . . both Hebrew scripture and New Testament. The God to whom she appeals is the one God of

Israel's scripture reinterpreted now to be also the one God of the scriptures of the early Christian community.

Comment: The God to whom Christians pray at Aldersgate is the God of Israel whose word is made known through Hebrew Scripture.

The God who anointed King David (1 Sam.) is now seen to have anointed the Christian community, as well, by way of baptism. "But you are a chosen race, a royal priesthood, a holy nation, God's own people" (1 Peter); in Rev. Allred's reading, this means that "when God called us Gentiles to be grafted into God's family he made of us a royal nation." The consequence is that the Gentiles, and not only the Jews, are obliged to do God's work in the world: there are also "risks of baptism."[15]

Comment: The church is grafted onto the people Israel and to its covenant with God. To share in the covenant with God is to do God's work in the world, from care for the homeless down to the need to raise money for the church and its missions.

The God of Israel is also the God of Jesus Christ. The title of [Rev. Allred's] sermon, in fact, is "Christ's Body at Aldersgate," and it is offered at Lent, a time of "the church's pilgrimage again to Jerusalem to experience again Christ's death and resurrection."

Comment: Christians know the God of Israel through the life and resurrection of Jesus of Nazareth, whom the church calls the Christ. Christians retrace and reenact the life of Christ the way we Jews retrace and reenact the life of Israel.

The very fact that the Christian story is so close to the Jewish story leads Jews to view Christianity as a misunderstanding of our own religion. Similarly, Christians may claim that the Jews misunderstood the coming of Christ in the person of Jesus. Consequently, Christian traditional belief is a challenge and irritant to Jewish traditional belief at just this point.

Incarnation and Trinity

The claim that God is incarnate in Jesus is the basis of Christianity's Trinitarian doctrine, enunciated in the Nicene Creed, a classical version of which I excerpt here:

> We believe in one God the Father all powerful, maker of all things both
> seen and unseen. And in one Lord Jesus Christ, the Son of God, the
> only-begotten from the Father, that is from the substance of the Father,
> God from God, light from light, true God from true God, begotten not
> made, consubstantial with the Father, through whom all things came to
> be, both those in heaven and those in earth; for us humans and for our
> salvation he came down and became incarnate, became human, suffered
> and rose up on the third day, went up into the heavens, is coming to
> judge the living and the dead.

For the church, the God of Israel is thus also God the Son, the one
who lived as a human, was crucified and resurrected. Furthermore,
God is God the Holy Spirit, the identity of the one who brings Father
to Son and Son to Father: "Being therefore exalted at the right hand
of God, and having received from the Father the promise of the Holy
Spirit, he has poured out this that you both see and hear" (Acts
2:32–33). The one God of Israel is thus known by Christians as the
unity of relationship among these three identities of the one divine
being.

The Christian doctrines of the Incarnation and the Trinity present
two main challenges to traditional Jewish study. One challenge is that
the narrative of God's incarnation in one Jew belongs to a history that
Jews do not share and cannot accept as part of their story. In this case,
the Christian doctrine of the Incarnation appears comprehensible but
simply wrong: the event did not occur. A second challenge is that the
doctrine of God's having three identities appears incomprehensible:
the Jewish biblical record does not speak of God in a way that allows
us to characterize His nature as a relation among Father, Son, and
Holy Spirit. From this perspective, Trinitarian doctrine, like the Kabbalah, appears incomprehensible and alien even before it appears
wrong. The traditional Jewish response is therefore to walk away from
any discussion of such things. For this third epoch of Judaism, however, Jews are called to do more than throw up our hands in the face of
Christian doctrines; we must, instead, find a way to reason Jewishly
about them.

Recommendations for a Jewish Approach to Christian Doctrine

I would recommend that Jews consider four things when faced with
Christian doctrine.

First, we should observe that Jewish and Christian religious traditions tend to overlap in the following doctrines: that the one God of Israel created the universe through His word; makes humans in His image; speaks to humanity through His word, commanding them to imitate him; speaks to each nation through its own language; sends Israel the Torah and makes a special covenant with Israel to serve as light to the nations; will send his Messiah to redeem Israel and the nations in the end of days.

Second, we should note that Christian tradition adds certain claims to Jewish traditions: that the God of Israel is incarnate in one Jew, Jesus of Nazareth, who suffered and died for the sins of all humanity, who was resurrected and appeared again to his disciples, and who is the Messiah in whom Israel and the nations are redeemed.

Third, we should note that Jewish religious tradition does not accept these additions for itself. They belong to a religion other than Judaism and are incompatible with what it means for a Jew to live according to the dictates of Jewish religious tradition. At the same time, these additions derive from and retain recognizable elements of biblical and rabbinic Jewish belief—which are, in fact, the elements examined in the central chapters of this book. To render Christian beliefs about God comprehensible in Jewish terms, Jews need only identify these elemental beliefs and observe how Christian tradition retains and also reinterprets and extends them.

Fourth, we should ask, What is the legitimacy of these additions for non-Jews? In this third epoch of Jewish religious tradition, Jews should learn how to judge specifically Christian beliefs "by their fruits" (to use a phrase of Jesus' from the Gospel of Matthew). Such learning is based on five guidelines:

1. As God's spoken words for Israel, the words of Torah must be clarified anew for each generation, within the life of each community. In themselves, therefore, these spoken words always remain incompletely defined. Like interpretations of the words of Israel's Torah, the Scriptures of the early church are also defined only within the life of each Christian community. We therefore assume that there is no single, clear meaning of the basic doctrines of the Christian Scriptures, such as Incarnation and Trinity.

2. Since they are incompletely defined in themselves, the Christian doctrines would be illegitimate on our terms only if all

possible meanings and behavioral consequences of these doctrines would violate Jewish beliefs or the Noahide laws. This is
not the case: Christian beliefs that the end of days is here and
that God is incarnate in Jesus of Nazareth do not necessarily
lead Christians to act in ways that violate the conduct rabbinic
Judaism expects of non-Jews.[16]

3. One task for Jewish scholars in this third epoch is therefore to
   evaluate, for each specific Christian community, whether or
   not its understandings of basic Christian doctrine violate these
   expectations. Regarding any community that does not violate
   these expectations, a second task is to evaluate how that community's beliefs may enhance or retard Israel's mission to be a
   light to nations. A new obligation for Jews may be to support
   Christian communities that enhance Israel's mission and to
   criticize, or at least withhold explicit support for, communities
   that do not. If these guidelines seem presumptuous, we must
   remember that living still in the shadow of the Shoah, we have
   unusual obligations to work against the corrosive influences of
   supersessionism in the forms of both religious anti-Semitism
   and radical secularism.

4. Only certain methods of evaluation are appropriate. To evaluate Christianity from the perspective of received Jewish tradition, *alone*, would be to offer a reversed form of *Jewish* supersessionism: treating the words of Christian doctrine as if they
   could be understood and judged independently of how they
   are actually lived and interpreted in a given community. On
   the other hand, to evaluate Christianity only from the perspective of some new encounter between Jews and Christians
   would be to abdicate responsibility to offer a specifically Jewish judgment. Christian doctrines must therefore be evaluated
   from a perspective that mediates between such new encounters
   and received Jewish tradition. A new generation of Jewish
   scholars often obtains this perspective by promoting dialogues
   between Jewish skeptics or rationalists and more traditional
   practitioners.

5. This means that the skepticism that so typifies modern Jewish
   life makes a major contribution to Jewish–Christian understanding. Jews trained in their religious traditions may have
   more to say about biblically based Christian teachings, but

more skeptical or rationalist Jews may have more to say about philosophic approaches to Christian belief. This generation of Jewish scholars therefore achieves its understanding of Christianity by bringing an inner dialogue between Jewish tradition and Jewish skepticism into relation with an inner dialogue between Christian tradition and Christian skepticism.[17] In the following section, I offer one illustration of how such a dual dialogue may be undertaken.

Understanding Christianity Through Dialogue

To set a standard for future studies of all forms of Christianity, it is best to begin by examining forms of Christianity that are most compatible with the goals of Judaism in its third epoch. One such form is articulated by the theologian Robert Jenson. Jenson reasons that Trinitarian belief is the Christian belief that God is incarnate in the Jew, Jesus Christ, which is fundamentally the Christian belief that God has no qualities that we know apart from how both the Old and New Testaments say God acts. "God is whoever raised Jesus from the dead, having before raised Israel from Egypt. . . . The doctrine of Trinity only explicates Israel's faith in a situation in which it is believed that the God of Israel has, prior to the general resurrection, raised one of his servants from the dead."[18] Explicitly rooted in the received traditions of both the New and Old Testament, Jenson's theology will speak most clearly to traditional Jews who draw on comparable biblical roots. However, Jenson's Trinitarian doctrine may also prove most challenging to these same, biblically based Jews. Skeptical or philosophic Jews may have a different relation to Jenson's work. Although his biblical allusions may remain opaque to them, they will be much more comfortable with the new encounter he opens between ancient Jewish and Christian traditions. Overall, Jenson's version of Christianity will have the most value for Jews influenced by both of these Jewish perspectives, that is, for Jews who are engaged in the inner dialogue between Jewish tradition and Jewish skepticism that I mentioned above.

The simplest way I have found to engage traditional and skeptical Jews in dialogue with each other is to ask them what they understand by "the Infinite." Ideally, skeptics will permit themselves to speak of the "Infinite" as that which exceeds our various, finite capacities, and traditional Jews will accept the term as another name for God. By engaging both groups in a dialogue about the Infinite, I believe it is possible for skeptics to speculate, in different terms, about God and for traditionalists to encounter Jewish theology in a new form. By way of illustration, let us imagine such a dialogue. It begins when a skeptic and a traditionalist attempt to make a list of their shared beliefs about the relation between human finitude and the Infinite. They agree to take note of biblical sources that appear to illustrate these beliefs. They agree, finally, to invite a Christian, Robert Jenson, into the dialogue, noting whatever beliefs he shares with both of them, as well as the biblical sources he associates with these beliefs. This dialogue might generate something like the following list of beliefs and sources:

Human finitude: Humans are finite creatures. Here, Jewish and Christian theologians share common, biblical source texts, for example, "male and female He created the human being" (Gen. 1).

Reference to the Infinite: Our finitude is judged with respect to the Infinite, which we may name "God." Common biblical sources include Genesis 1 and also the text of Job: "Who then can stand up to Me? Whoever confronts Me I will requite" (Job 41:2–3). From the perspective of the finite creature, God is infinitely distant and unknowable except for the property of being *that* One who is not finite as I am. Infinity is here a negative character: as the One who is utterly *other*, God is *kadosh* (holy; literally, "separate") and thus never known as He is but only through his acts or effects. Jewish mystical literature refers to God as *Ein Sof*, the One "without end," or the Infinite.[19]

Knowledge of the Infinite: We cannot know the Infinite merely by pointing to it. We know the Infinite only by way of the Infinite; we know God only by encountering God. Otherwise, we could not know that we are finite.

Here again, Jewish and Christian theologians share common sources in the biblical narrative of God's intimate relation to the people Israel. The Hebrew term for this knowledge is *yedi'ah*, a word that also carries sexual connotations and that in the biblical record refers to the intimacy of human intercourse with God, who says, "I fell in love with Israel when he was still a child" (Hos. 11:1). In the New Testament, the intimacy is extended to God's relation to the one Jew, Jesus: "His beloved Son" (Col. 1:13).

Knowledge by the Infinite: As finite creatures, we cannot be agents who *actively* "know" the Infinite, since our acts are finite. We therefore cannot construct a conception of the Infinite, but we can *discover* ourselves as those who may belong to an infinite. To represent this quality of belonging, theologians often use passive verbs to portray our relation to the Infinite: we "are known by" God, or we "are made" in God's image.

One meaning of the English word "suffer" is "to be brought passively into an experience or relation"; in *this* sense, "suffering" is the condition of the finite creature's knowledge of God. There are many strong images in the Bible of Israel's suffering in the more obvious, physical sense and of God coming to their aid. "I . . . have heeded their outcry. . . . I have come down to rescue them" (Ex 3:7–8). God's presence here is an "outstretched arm" that comes directly to Israel—"I even I alone, and not a fiery angel."[20] Even these accounts of suffering and rescue, however, may also be interpreted on a second level as an illustration of Israel's "being brought into" rather than initiating relation with God.

In Christian tradition, it is Jesus who suffers on behalf of all humanity. For Robert Jenson, this event does not supplant Israel but represents the Israel that dies and is resurrected in Egypt.[21] In other words, in both Israel's suffering and Jesus' suffering, humanity is known by God.

The Infinite as a subject who knows: Describing the finite creature as "being known by" the Infinite is to personify the Infinite. This is a troubling case of anthropomorphism, but the alternative appears to be worse. To portray the Infinite as being passively known by the finite creature would be to claim that *we* could subject "the Infinite" to our finite rules of knowledge. Secular rationalists appear to make presumptuous claims of this kind.

For both Jewish and Christian sources, God's act of knowing us is disclosed, in part, in God's speech to Israel. "God spoke to Moses, saying . . ." When Israel is portrayed as suffering, God's speech brings means of redemption, primarily through instructions. "Torah" is the primary term used to portray God's word to Israel as instruction.

The rabbinic sages write that when God gives instructions to bring justice to earth, He displays *midat ha-din*, His attribute of justice, of which one name is *elohim*. When God gives instructions to redeem Israel, He displays *midat ha-rachamim*, His attribute of mercy, of which one name is *YHVH*. As God of mercy, God is often addressed as *av ha-rachamim* (Merciful Father). In Jewish tradition, God's speech brings God's word *(dibur)* into the world, and through this word God creates the things of the world *(devarim)* and teaches Israel and the nations to obey Him and imitate His actions.

For some Christian Trinitarian theologians, God tends to be named "God the Father" when He is addressed as the author of his spoken word. In classical terms, "Father" is one of the "persons" of God; in Jenson's more helpful phrase, it is one of God's "identities." To be Father is, however, to have one's identity in relation to another, whom Trinitarian theologians call the "Son" and consider a second identity of God: "the Father sees Himself and his works in the Son."[22] Jenson notes that in the early church (before the Antiochenes), "'Christ is the word of God' meant that the Father speaks and Christ is the speech."[23] The Jewish concept of God's being author of the divine speech is therefore analogous in Trinitarian theology to the Father's begetting his divine Son.[24]

The two brief discussions of suffering earlier in this essay provide another means of understanding the Trinity. Trinitarian theologians identify God the Son also with the Suffering Servant of Isaiah: "This is My servant, whom I uphold; My chosen one. . . . He was despised, we held him of no account. Yet it was our sickness that he was bearing, our suffering that he endured. . . . He was wounded because of our sins, . . . and by his bruises we were healed" (Is. 42:1, 53: 3–5). For Jenson, this Servant refers both to the people Israel *and* to the one Jew, Jesus. "The only Logos or Son we . . . may reckon with is the Suffering Servant. . . . The Logos that God speaks to command heaven and earth into being is no other Word than the Word of the cross, the Word the Father speaks by the mission, death and resurrection of Israel [in Egypt, and in each destruction] and this Israelite [Jesus]."[25] This Christian notion is perplexing. But Jews can find a bridge to discussion in the biblical analogy of Israel's own suffering for humanity and in the theological reflection that Israel knows God the Infinite only by "suffering" (that is, receiving) God's presence. In Jewish terms, the Christian claim that Jesus is the Suffering Servant means that Christians believe, on one level, that the end of days has come and that the Messiah who takes on Israel's burden is Jesus. On a second level, this Christian claim means they believe that the Messiah not only receives but also fully embodies

God's Torah for redeeming all human suffering. On a third level, this Christian claim means they believe that full embodiment of God's word is itself an identity of God.

Perhaps the Infinite "suffers" finitude in some way: To speak of the Infinite "acting" in relation to us would, ironically, also imply *its* "suffering"—in the sense of "tolerating"—such a relationship. Some rationalist Jewish philosophers, in medieval and modern times, have for this reason refused to write even of God's acting. To "give us a Torah" or "punish us" means to suffer relationship with us. For these rationalists, "Infinite is infinite," "finite is finite," and the two definitions admit of no admixture. Thus, these rationalists also conclude that the Bible is strictly metaphorical; there is no sense in which God can give to or take from us. We may respond that if there is no relation at all between Infinite and finite, then these rationalists have no basis for speaking about the Infinite *or* about the finite that is limited by the Infinite! On the other hand, we who speak of the difference between our finitude and God's Infinity must, if we reason consistently, also talk about our "suffering" (sharing in) a relation to God and God's suffering a relation to us, however mysterious this notion may remain to us.

Not surprisingly, the study of Infinity, and of the possibility that the Infinite suffers a relationship with the finite, leads eventually to the notion of mystery. In Christian theology, reflection on mystery leads, among other things, to reflections on the Trinitarian doctrine of the Holy Spirit. Jenson cites the characteristic Gospel source: "The *pneuma* [Greek: spirit] blows where it will, and you hear the sounds of it, but you do not know where it comes from or where it goes. So it is with everyone who is born of the spirit." The Spirit, says Jenson, is the identity of "God's freedom, God's openness to the future."[26] According to the early sages of the eastern church, "the whole divine life begins with the Father and is actual through the Son and is perfected with the Holy Spirit." This statement implies, for Jenson, that "the Spirit receives his existence from the Father, but lives eternally with and in the Son."[27] How will Jewish thinkers possibly make sense of such a claim?

In rabbinic literature, the terms *ruach ha-kodesh* (holy spirit) and *shechina* (divine Presence) are employed at times in overlapping ways: as, for example, in the phrases "the holy spirit rests on them; if they are not prophets, they are sons of prophets";[28] and "Hillel . . . had eighty disciples, thirty of whom were worthy of having the divine Presence rest on them."[29] In these cases, the terms refer to that which brings prophecy or, when applied to rabbinic sages, to what we might call touches of divine wisdom or mystical experience. There is some bridge here to understanding the Trinitarian usage, since the Holy Spirit also concerns the direct touch of God. But a bridge to fuller discussion of this Trinitarian notion needs something less overt: a study of how the community of Israel transmits and reinterprets the Oral Torah:

> [R. Yose said,] "Had the Torah not been revealed to Moses, it would have been revealed to Ezra." [B Sanh. 21b] . . . The Torah was revealed to Moses, but received, hundreds of years later, under Ezra. Yet the two prophetic figures are not entirely analogous. Whereas Moses must be seen as a passive conduit, the recipient of a perfect, divine Torah, Ezra must be seen as a prophet whose task was to rebuild that Torah . . . [after] centuries of neglect.[30]

These words introduce the interpretation of David Halivni, for whom Ezra's work is a prototype for all sages of the Oral Torah. The Torah is not fully disclosed to Israel all at once, but only through the entire history of Israel's reception and retransmission of the divine word. The infinite word suffers being delivered to a finite people, among whom its meaning and identity is fully disclosed only at the end of its infinite history with them: "when God will be one and His name will be one." We have not referred here to the Spirit or to the divine Presence. Nevertheless, by comparing Halivni's and Jenson's accounts, the reader may observe some parallels and some significant differences between Jewish and Christian theologies of how God's word and purpose moves through history.

Concluding with a Caution

In modern times, we may be accustomed to associating "secularism" with a kind of tolerance: secularists are humble about their ability to know more than we can know, so they are tolerant of whatever their neighbor wants to believe, as long as the belief isn't imposed on others. This essay is guided by another hypothesis: that a greater sign of humility is to accept ("suffer") the wisdoms one has inherited from age-old traditions, except where those traditions have proved themselves wrong or unjust or oppressive. If "secularism" refers to the wholesale dismissal of age-old Jewish and Christian traditions about humanity's relation to God, then we should not identify secularism with a tolerant or humble position. What if, however, there are individuals who call themselves "secular" because they are not prepared to identify themselves, incautiously, with traditions that they believe are now practiced dogmatically and oppressively? "Secularism" of this kind—what I have been calling "skepticism" or "rationalism"—should be welcomed *into* Jewish and Christian communities as representative of the Bible's own prophetic voice. Judaism and Christianity are both called to perennial self-critique. One challenge for Jews and Christians today is to identify forces that muffle such self-criticism both inside and outside the religious communities.

The Christian theologian Robert Jenson and the Jewish philosopher Emmanuel Levinas offer overlapping criticisms of one of these forces: the tendency toward "totalistic thinking" that affects secularists as well as religious Christians and Jews. This is thinking that claims to identify the one set of clear principles upon which all human life should be based. A secular example is the adoption of some one "ism" (such as communism) as an exclusive program for social organization. Jewish examples include efforts to identify one aspect of Judaism as defining the purpose of all the others (such as "the halachah," or "prophetic ethics," or Zionism). The Christian example most pertinent to this book is supersessionism.

Jenson argues that a major source of this totalistic tendency is an admixture of biblical religion with the Greek philosophic concept of "timeless being"—the concept that for something to exist truly, it must be immune to change and to relationship with whatever changes. The God portrayed in the biblical narratives appears to wield absolute authority over all creation, to declare His intentions to humanity, but also to enter into close relations with His creatures, as well as to change His opinions about them. When this God is assimilated to the Greek philosophic concept of deity, what often results is the portrayal of an absolute deity whose intentions are unchangeable but knowable by at least a select portion of humanity. This portion of humanity may be elected to comprehend the entire world and also to rule over it. For Levinas, worship of "timeless being" in this way is a source of modern totalitarianism, secular as well as religious.

The biblical God is not to be confused, however, with the deity conceived out of philosophic reflections on the biblical narratives. Although Jewish thinkers have also been tempted by this error, the profound influence of Greco-Roman philosophic culture on European Christianity has rendered this a more typically Christian temptation.

The temptation is strongest among Christian thinkers whose reasoning is farthest removed from the plain sense of the biblical sources. Among them are theologians who interpret the Trinity as an account only of the eternal, unchanging self-relation of God as Father, Son, and Holy Spirit, unmoved by the temporal life of His people. Jenson is not such a theologian. Jewish thinkers who share Levinas's concerns may therefore find an ally in Jenson and his colleagues.[31]

Of course, by stressing the biblical sources, I do not mean to suggest that there is no place for philosophy in Judaism or Christianity: Moses and his fellow prophets questioned, reasoned, and wondered like philosophers. But their philosophy began with the scriptural word and the questions it raised. Some of these questions concerned *being*, but not in the abstract; rather they were questions about the being *of God's word* and its relation to the world, to their lives, and to suffering. In the Exodus account, God said to Moses "I will be what I will be" and "I will be with you in your suffering." This third epoch of Jewish theology may be a time for Jewish thinkers to remember the God who is with us in our suffering—"for I am with you, declares YHVH, in your suffering" (Jer. 1:19)—and a time to lend support to others who remember Him, too.

A Jewish View of the Christian God: Some Cautionary and Hopeful Remarks

DAVID ELLENSON

Jewish teachings have long viewed the Christian doctrine of Incarnation and the concomitant Christian affirmation of a triune God as lying beyond the boundaries of acceptable Jewish faith. The objects of Jewish polemic for generations, these notions, as Peter Ochs has indicated, have proven difficult for Jews to appreciate and grasp, much less affirm. This essay will first explore the classical Jewish theological grounds for the negative depiction of these Christian notions, and it will then indicate what resources Judaism possesses for a reassessment of this position. The essay will conclude by reflecting briefly on how contemporary Jews standing on the threshold of a new Christian millennium might evaluate Christian approaches to faith so as to renew and redirect efforts at Jewish–Christian conversation in our day.

Classical Sources and Medieval Polemics

According to classical Jewish tradition, God established an eternal Covenant with the people Israel through their father Abraham in Genesis 15. However, Judaism also teaches that God stands not only in particularistic relationship with the Jewish people, but also in a universal relationship with all humanity. The rabbis of the Talmud posit this relationship in Sanhedrin 56a, on the basis of the Noah story in Genesis 9. This relationship, known in Jewish tradition as the Noahide Covenant, caused the rabbis to assert that God issued seven commandments through Noah to all humankind. These commandments were later viewed as constituting the minimal moral demands that God made, and makes, upon all non-Jews. One commandment was positive—to establish courts of justice for society; the other six were negative and included prohibitions against eating flesh from a living animal, adultery, murder, robbery, blasphemy, and idolatry.

Precisely because these commandments were viewed as being enjoined by God upon all Gentiles, the Talmud ruled that no Jew could ever cause a non-Jew to commit sins of blasphemy or idolatry. It therefore prohibited the Jew from engaging in any transaction with a Gentile that might serve as the occasion for that Gentile to swear an oath to a deity that would be regarded, according to the standards established in the Noahide commandments, as a "false god." As the Talmud states in Sanhedrin 63b:

> *Mishnah*—He who vows or swears by its name violates a negative precept. *Gemara*—Whence do we know this? It has been taught, "And make no mention of other gods" (Exodus 23:13). This means, one must not say to his neighbor, "Wait for me at the side of this idol."
>
> "Neither let it be heard out of your mouth" (Exodus 23:13). One should not vow or swear by its name, nor cause others (heathens) to swear by the name. . . .

"Nor cause others (heathens) to swear by its name." This supports the dictum of Samuel's father. For the father of Samuel said, "One may not enter into a business partnership with a heathen, lest the latter be obliged to take an oath [in connection with a business dispute], and he swear by his idol. For the Torah has said, "Neither let it be heard out of your mouth."

In sum, if the Jew were responsible for creating a situation in which the non-Jew would swear by his "false god," then the Jew would be deemed culpable, for the Jew would be viewed as the proximate cause for the transgression of the Noahide prohibition that would transpire. The Jew would be guilty of having violated the biblical injunction, "You shall not place a stumbling block before the blind" (Lev. 19:14).

The relevance of these dicta for our discussion is that they led rabbinic authorities to consider the nature of Christian faith in order to determine whether Christian belief in God violated the Noahide stricture against idolatry, or whether it constituted an acceptable form of monotheism for Gentiles. Of course, Christians insisted that their doctrines regarding God adhered to monotheistic standards, and, according to the Talmud, they even interpreted Scripture to support their claim. For example, the Jerusalem Talmud, Berachot 9:1, reports that Christians claimed that the three Hebrew names for God, *El*, *Elohim*, and *YHVH*, demonstrated that the Hebrew Bible reflected a triune conception of the Godhead. Rabbi Simlai rebutted this notion, asserting that these terms all referred to the one God, and that the employment of three names to signal the one God was analogous to how persons might employ the terms "King, Emperor, Augustus" to refer to the single ruler of Rome. Other talmudic sages were not content with simple rebuttal, and they explicitly condemned early Christian expressions concerning the doctrines of Trinity and the incarnate man-God Jesus as untrue and in opposition to genuine monotheism.

One oft-cited midrash on Exodus 20:2, "I am the Lord your God," illustrates this position:

Another explanation of "I am the Lord your God." R. Abbahu illustrated thus—A human king may rule, but he has a father and brother, but God said, "I am not thus." I am the first, for I have no father, and I am the last, for I have no other, and besides Me there is no God, for I have no son (Ex. R. 29:5).

In another passage, the Jerusalem Talmud reports on a discussion that Rabbi Abbahu held with a Christian sectarian. In commenting upon Numbers 23:19—"God is not a human being that he should lie, nor the son of a human being that He should repent of a decision. Has he said and not acted, or spoken and not accomplished it?"—this fourth-century Palestinian sage said, "If a person says to you, 'I am God,' he lies. 'I am the son of Man,' he shall regret it in the end. 'I shall rise up to Heaven.' That one [Jesus] said it and did not accomplish it" (TJ Ta'an. 2:1).

By the Middle Ages, these negative attitudes toward Christianity and its visions of God had hardened in many Jewish precincts. The view of a Trinitarian Godhead and the notion of an incarnate deity were the foci of attacks by many Jewish polemicists. In Jewish philosophical circles, the critique was particularly pointed. In his "Preface" to his fourteenth-century polemic *The Refutation of the Christian Principles*, Hasdai Crescas summarized succinctly what he considered the points of similarity and distinction between Jewish and Christian beliefs about the nature of God. Crescas wrote:

> Concerning the third principle: trinity. There are seven common premises [between Jewish and Christian doctrine]: (1) God's existence is necessary, that is, His existence comes from Himself, not from anything else; (2) the divine quiddity has all perfections eternally; (3) His simplicity is absolutely, infinitely simple; (4) He has in Him eternal life, power, wisdom, will, and other eternal perfections; (5) there is no internal inconsistency in Him; (6) He is not subject to any composition at all; (7) there is nothing in God, may He be blessed, which is not divine. There is disagreement concerning three premises: (1) the Christian says God, may He be blessed, has three separate attributes, which he calls Persons, and the Jew denies this; (2) the Christian believes that God, may He be blessed, has an attribute called Son, generated from the Father, and the Jew denies this; (3) the Christian believes that God, may He be blessed, has an attribute which proceeded from the Father and the Son called Spirit, and the Jew denies this.

> Concerning the fourth principle: incarnation. The Christian believes that the Son took on flesh in the womb of the virgin. This incarnation was indivisible and inseparable in the same unity and even greater than the conjunction of the human soul to man, such that even after he was crucified and died, the divinity remained conjoined to and united with

the flesh and soul, namely with each one separately. The Jew denies all of this.[1]

No less a figure than Moses Maimonides considered these doctrinal differences to be of such import that he consigned Christians to the talmudic category of *ovdei kochavim u-mazalot* (worshippers of idols) in both his *Commentary on the Mishnah* (1163; *Avodah Zarah* 1:3) and the *Mishneh Torah* (1180; *Hilchot Avodat Kochavim* 9:4). These Maimonidean legal sources not only reflect the doctrinal emphases that have classically distinguished Jewish from Christian faith but also indicate that these differences—as the Talmud in Sanhedrin 63b had suggested—possess normative implications that would circumscribe Jewish–Christian interactions.

However, other voices in Jewish tradition took a different stance on these matters. They would not consign Christianity to the category of "idolatry," nor, by extension, would they accept a definition of Christians as "idol-worshippers." It is to a consideration of these other views that we now turn.

New Directions

A tendency toward Jewish religious tolerance—one might even say appreciation—of Christianity as a form of monotheism began to appear among the Jews of Christian Europe in the twelfth century. In a comment upon Sanhedrin 63b, Rabbi Isaac, a medieval authority, spoke of Christians and Christianity in the following terms:

> Although they [Christians] mention the name of Heaven, meaning thereby Jesus of Nazareth, they do not at all events mention a strange deity, and moreover, they mean thereby the Maker of Heaven and Earth too; and despite the fact that they associate the name of Heaven with an alien deity, we do not find that it is forbidden to cause Gentiles to make such an association, . . . *since such an association (shituf) is not forbidden to the sons of Noah.*[2]

In taking this stance, Rabbi Isaac offered a distinction that was unknown in talmudic Judaism—that although Trinitarianism constituted idolatry for Jews, it did not for Christians. One should not dismiss the value this distinction held for a novel Jewish approach to Christian belief. Indeed, the historian Jacob Katz has characterized its significance as follows: "The assertion that the Gentiles are not bound to uphold the strict unity of the Godhead opens up the possibility of condoning Christian adherence to the doctrine of the Trinity so far as the Gentiles, though not the Jews, are concerned."[3]

Katz notes further that this view was taken up and expanded upon by Rabbi Menachem Ha-Me'iri of Provence, who, writing in the early 1300s, stated that Christians "recognize the Godhead" and "believe in God's existence, His unity and power, although they misconceive some points according to our belief." In fact, Ha-Me'iri explicitly refused to place contemporaneous Christians in the talmudic category of "idol-worshippers," declaring, "Now idolatry has disappeared from most places."[4] Katz, commenting upon these writings of Ha-Me'iri, has noted "that the exclusion of Christians . . . from the category of the idolatrous—an exclusion that had been suggested purely casuistically by earlier halakhists—*was to be acknowledged as a firm and comprehensive principle.*"[5]

The trajectory that marked these rulings came to dominate among later generations of Jewish legal writers. The eighteenth-century rabbi Yehuda Ashkenazi, writing on the *Shulchan Aruch* (*Yoreh Deah*, 151:2), in his authoritative *Be'er Heitev*, echoed both Rabbi Isaac and Ha-Me'iri and granted their position normative Jewish legal status. His commentary there on Christians and their faith states, "In our era, . . . when the gentiles in whose midst we dwell . . . [speak of God], their intention is directed towards the One Who made Heaven and Earth, albeit that they associate another personality with God. However, this does not constitute a violation of Leviticus 19:14, 'You shall not place a stumbling block before the blind,' for non-Jews are not warned against such association (*shituf*)."

At the same time, the central European rabbi Jacob Emden (1697–1776) carried this posture to new heights. In a commentary upon *Mishna Avot* 4:11—"Every assembly that is for the sake of Heaven will in the end be established"—he stated, speaking of both Islam and Christianity, "Their assembly is also for the sake of Heaven, to make Godliness known among the nations, to speak of Him in distant places."[6] Elsewhere, he declared that Jesus, "the Nazarene, brought about a double kindness in the world. On the one hand, he strengthened the Torah of Moses majestically. . . . On the other hand, he did much good for the gentiles . . . by doing away with idolatry and removing the images from their midst. He obligated them with the Seven Commandments so that they should not be as the beasts of the field."[7]

These postures permitted Rabbi Marcus Horovitz (1844–1910) of Frankfurt to answer affirmatively when asked by a rabbinical colleague whether it was permissible for a Jew to contribute funds to the building of a Christian church. Rabbi Horovitz, relying on the sources cited here, stated that Christians were not "idolaters." They, like Jews, worshipped "the Maker of Heaven and Earth." *Shituf* was permitted for non-Jews. No less an authority than Rabbi Moses Isserles, whose glosses on the *Shulchan Aruch* were incorporated into its text, had so ruled.[8] Since normative Jewish law held that Christianity was a form of monotheism, Horovitz stated that it was a commandment *(mitzvah)* for a Jew to donate charity money to a church. He concluded his responsum by thanking God for allowing Christians, through their teachings, "to be among the pious and great men of the nations of the world."[9]

In these later writings, Jewish faith in God remains superior to Christian conceptions of the deity. However, the tone here clearly departs from that of earlier rabbinic writings on this topic. Furthermore, the substance is distinct as well. These authorities reflect a genuine appreciation for Christianity as monotheism, and they clearly recognize that Christian faith in God directs Christians, no less than Jews, to become involved in the ethical tasks incumbent upon all persons of goodwill in this world.

Concluding Thoughts

In the statement of principles accompanying this book, the editors assert, "Jews and Christians worship the same God," and contend, "As Jewish theologians, we rejoice that through Christianity hundreds of millions of people have entered into relationship with the God of Israel." Furthermore, the editors affirm that "Jews and Christians share a common morality. Jews and Christians accept the moral principles of Torah. Central to the moral principles of Torah are the unalienable sanctity and dignity of every human being." These principles alone establish much common ground for dialogue and action between Jews and Christians. Nothing in Jewish tradition as contained in the dominant legal tradition counters these assertions.

At the same time, doctrinal differences must be acknowledged. Jewish views of God diverge, in several significant ways, from Christian conceptions, and, as the editors' principles state, "Christian worship is not a viable religious choice for Jews." Indeed, there is no reason it should be. Again in the words of the statement, "Neither Jew nor Christian should be pressed into affirming the teaching of the other community." Differences on certain points may be "irreconcilable." Yet Jews should not exaggerate these differences and should search, as rabbis ranging from Ha-Me'iri to Horovitz did, to affirm elements of commonality that mark these two faith traditions.

Finally, we should remember that Jewish and Christian human beings, men and women marked by finitude and foibles, have put forth these diverse conceptions of God. As a result, the visions contained in them are by definition limited. In Jewish tradition, these limitations were frankly acknowledged by the twelfth-century German kabbalist and pietist Judah the Pious. Rabbi Judah composed a hymn, *Shir Ha-kavod* (the song of glory), that is still sung weekly in many Jewish services. One line is particularly relevant to this concluding discussion. In speaking of the ineffability of God, Rabbi Judah writes, "I tell of Your glory, though I have not seen You. I imagine You, and I call You by name, though I know You not."

When I consider these words, I am reminded how difficult it is to describe God. Each human effort to know God is condemned to incompleteness, for the Infinite Reality that is God must always lie beyond our finite attempts at description and understanding. Whatever metaphors humans construct to capture and define God are at best fragile and tentative gropings. No image or thought created or mediated through human agency could ever fully contain God, Whose fullness must always be beyond all words and rituals. Mystery and infinity lie at the heart of religious faith.

For this reason alone, religious dialogue is always crucial, as elements of truth concerning God may emerge in conversations and exchanges that would otherwise be ignored or overlooked in a particular religious tradition. There are substantial differences between Jews and Christians as they seek to comprehend the divine. The doctrines of Trinity and Incarnation remain non-Jewish understandings of the Godhead. Nevertheless, Christians clearly know a great deal about the God of Israel, and this knowledge directs them, no less than Jews, to God's service. At the threshold of a new millennium, there is a great deal to celebrate in this recognition, as Jew and Christian together seek peacefully to aid God in the ultimate messianic task of repairing the world.

God as Trinitarian:
A Christian Response to Peter Ochs

DAVID TRACY

Professor Peter Ochs's exceptionally clear, finely tuned, and persuasive essay makes it possible for this Christian theological respondent to say, by way of response, Amen. His reflections on modernity and Judaism, together with his interpretation of Christian theology, at once accurate and generous, make possible the longed-for dialogue between Christian and Jewish thinkers. The Christian God, as many Christian scholars have argued, is none other than YHVH named anew by the Christian tradition as Trinity. Our commonality is clear here: the one and only God is YHVH of the Hebrew revelation. Our difference is also, as Professor Ochs states, clear: Christians, inspired by the revelation of Jesus as the Christ, also (*not* instead) name our God as Father, Son, and Spirit.

Across many forms of Christian thought, the great effort is to eliminate supersessionist (and triumphalist) interpretations of Christianity in relationship to Judaism. Once Christians drop talk of a "new" (i.e., traditionally, often a supersessionist) covenant and hold, with Judaism, to YHVH alone, the question is the difference of the Trinitarian naming of God. That is the question Professor Ochs emphasizes, as shall I in my response.

Monotheism and Its Different Meanings

The first problem is the meaning of the word "monotheism." Although its basic meaning is clear (monos theos: the one-God), that meaning changes into a surprising multiplicity as the horizon for understanding the word shifts. Wittgenstein's insistence that meaning is not an abstract property of words but is discovered by noting the *use* of a word in a context is nowhere more true than in this case. Ever-shifting contexts change the meaning of monotheism for Jews, Christians, Muslims, and their interpreters.

At least three contexts are worth noting here. First, "monotheism" is a modern philosophical word meaning an abstract property (oneness) that belongs to God alone. More exactly, monotheism is an Enlightenment invention (Henry More, 1614–1687; David Hume, 1711–1776) that bears all the marks of Enlightenment rationalism. Monotheism, in this not so secretly evolutionary view, stands in contrast to "polytheism"; by Enlightenment standards, monotheism is a more rational understanding of the logic of the divine, since it implies a unity of divine power instead of a dispersal of that power into many gods and goddesses. Like the other famous "isms" of the Enlightenment (deism, pantheism, theism, panentheism), modern philosophical monotheism is, above all, "rational" and "ethical" (Hermann Cohen, 1842–1919). The relationship of this Enlightenment notion of monotheism to the historical religions (especially, but not solely, Judaism, Christianity, and Islam) is often obscured by the Enlightenment prejudice against "positive" (i.e., historical) religions in contrast to "natural religion." Unfortunately, most philosophical and many theological uses of the word "monotheism" still bear this dehistoricized and decontextualized Enlightenment meaning.

A second context for understanding the word "monotheism" is the history of religions. Here "monotheism" is a category employed to describe the "family resemblances" among different religious phenomena: the "high gods" of some primal traditions; the philosophical reflections on the logic of unicity among Greek thinkers from Xenophanes to Aristotle; a possible name for some Indian thinkers (especially Ramanujan); a name for the God of such religions as Sikhism and Zoroastrianism; the revisionary monotheism of the reforming pharaoh Akhenaton; above all, of course, the three classical "religions of the book," or, in history of religions terms, the historical, ethical, and prophetic monotheism of Judaism, Christianity, and Islam. Clearly such "history of religions" reflections on monotheism have influenced modern scholarship on the history of ancient Israel and on the history of early Islam and Christianity. Many scholarly studies show the final emergence of radical monotheism in the "YHVH alone" prophets (especially Amos, Elijah, and Hosea). This movement culminated in the prophet of the Babylonian exile (Deutero-Isaiah). There YHVH is clearly not only the God of Israel but also both creator of the whole world and the one and only God who determines not only Israel's history but all history: recall Deutero-Isaiah's reading of the Persian king Cyrus as the "Messiah" appointed by YHVH. This understanding of YHVH will influence the theological—that is, radical monotheistic—reading of Israel's history. After Deutero-Isaiah, the central religious affirmation of Judaism, Christianity, and Islam will be the classic *shema Yisrael* of Deuteronomy 6:4–5: "Hear, O Israel: The Lord our God is one Lord; and you shall love the Lord your God with all your heart, and with all your soul, and with all your might!"

The route to this radical monotheism, however, was a long and complex one whose many twists and turns are still debated among scholars. Indeed, there are few more fascinating debates in the history of religions than the conflict of interpretations among scholars of ancient Israel on the most likely history of the emergence of radical monotheism from polytheism, henotheism, monarchic monotheism, and monolatry. In strictly historical terms, radical monotheism is a relatively late arrival in the history of ancient Israel. But the principal theological question of today for Jews, Christians, and Muslims does not concern the theological implications of the various names and forms of the divine in the complex history of ancient Israel. Rather, the contemporary theological question concerns the different ways of experiencing, naming, and understanding the divine reality that have developed since the emergence of radical monotheism.

Hence, the third, and for present purposes principal, context for understanding the word "monotheism" is the strictly theological context of monotheistic Judaism, Christianity, and Islam. For the purpose of clarity, this context bears the following characteristics:

1. God is one: an individual distinct from all the rest of reality.
2. God is the origin, sustainer, and end of all reality.
3. God, therefore, is the One with the person-like characteristics of individuality, intelligence, and love.
4. God, and God alone, is related to all reality. Indeed God is Creator of all reality both natural and historical.
5. In sum, God, and God alone as the Wholly Other One, is both transcendent to all reality and totally immanent in all reality.
6. God discloses Godself in chosen prophets, historical events, and Scripture.

Christian Realism: Narrative, Doctrine, and Liturgy

To understand the many faces of the divine in Christianity is to understand who God is in and through the revelatory event that is, for the Christian, the decisive mediation, as self-revelation, of God: the person of Jesus Christ. A Christian understanding of God becomes the question of God's identity: Who is God? For the Christian, God is the One who revealed Godself in the history of Israel and in the ministry and message, the cross and resurrection of Jesus Christ. A Christian theological understanding of God cannot ultimately be divorced from this revelation of God in ancient Israel and in Jesus Christ. The full Christian doctrine of God discloses God as named in Hebrew Scripture and as specified by the Trinitarian names for the divine reality that must inform every symbol and doctrine. A theological insistence on the interconnection of the central mysteries of Christianity is important for all aspects of the faith, but this insistence is especially crucial when the question concerns God's identity. Christian theology must always be radically theocentric (God-centered) so that no single symbol or doctrine in the whole system of doctrines can be adequately understood without explicitly relating that symbol to the reality of God as disclosed in ancient Israel and in Jesus Christ. In other words, Christian theologians should maintain a "Christian realism"—the belief that Christianity provides a means of knowing God in everyday life (or, in Professor Ochs's terms, of knowing God in everyday "practice" via a "received tradition").

Christianity provides realistic knowledge of God in three principal ways: through its Gospel narratives, its doctrines, and its liturgy. These three principal institutions of Christian realism require that Christians maintain a Trinitarian understanding of God: whether that is disclosed in everyday terms or through the development of more conceptual namings of the Trinitarian God.

Hans Frei nicely describes the passion narratives of Jesus as the Christ as "history-like" and "realistic." Thus, we need not enter into the debates of those who argue that these Gospel narratives are like journalistic histories, or metaphoric stories, or supernatural myths. The bottom line is that these narratives function in the Christian community the same way histories function, delivering real knowledge of their subject. The Gospels disclose the most basic Christian understanding, not only of the real identity of Jesus Christ but also, through that identity, of the real identity of God who acts for Christians with the "face" of YHVH in and through the actions and suffering of Jesus of Nazareth.

Any realistic narrative portrays some hero's identity through the way that unique (or unsubstitutable) character interacts with some unique events, producing what we call the "plot" of the narrative. The passion narratives portray the identity of Jesus as the Christ through the events of the betrayal, the cross, the resurrection, and the promised second coming. Christian understanding of the one God is therefore grounded in knowledge of God as YHVH, disclosed through the concrete history of ancient Israel, and in knowledge of God as Father-Son-Spirit, disclosed through the passion narrative. These realist histories—rather than any general philosophical theory of monotheism—represent the theological foundation of all properly Christian Trinitarian understandings of God. This is what contemporary Lutheran and Reformed Trinitarian theologies (Karl Barth, Jürgen Moltmann, Eberhard Jüngel, Hans Frei, George Lindbeck, and, as Ochs explains so well, Robert Jenson and Stanley Hauerwas) see so clearly in their close attention to the details of the realistic biblical narratives (not, it is important to recall, in the historically reconstructed narratives) and in the everyday life of ecclesial communities.

The central passion narrative, moreover, should not remain isolated from the rest of Scripture, especially the Hebrew Bible (for Christians, the First [not old] Testament), or from the later creeds. Rather, the Christian passion narrative, as foundation and focus of all distinctly Christian understandings of God, should open up to the already declared name of YHVH and to the larger Gospel narratives on the message and ministry of Jesus, the theologies of Paul and John, the Pastorals, the Book of Revelation, and all the rest of the Christian Testament and Hebrew Scripture. For the Christian, the many faces of God are found, therefore, not only in the passion narratives of Jesus the Christ but also in the pre-passion actions of YHVH in ancient Israel and in the ministry and message of Jesus of Nazareth as they are rendered in importantly different ways in the four Gospels.

The typical speech of Jesus, for example, becomes part of the way through which Christians understand God: the parabolic discourse on the Reign of God discloses God's face as an excess of both power and love (e.g., the Prodigal Son); the typical word of Jesus for God, *Abba*, becomes crucial for any Christian understanding of the Power ("Lord") and Mercy (Father) of the mysterious face of God disclosed for Christians through Jesus; the centrality of the cross in the apocalyptic tale told by Mark and the dialectical language of Paul also open later Christians to the *tremendum et fascinans* face of God disclosed in the hidden-revealed Trinitarian God of Luther, Calvin, and Pascal; the intrinsic link of Jesus' actions to the poor, the oppressed, and the marginal, especially in Luke and Mark, open many contemporary Christian thinkers (political, liberation, and feminist-womanist-mujerista theologians) to discover the face of God anew above all in the faces of the victims of history and all those involved in the prophetic struggle against all oppression.

At the same time, the Christian understanding of God should open to the complex and profound disclosures of God's identity in the history of Israel as that identity is rendered in the many genres and forms (narrative, law, praise, lamentation, wisdom) of the First Testament. For the Christian, God is above all the One who not only disclosed the authentic face of God in raising Jesus of Nazareth from the dead but also in the Exodus of ancient Israel. God, for the Christian, is the One who revealed who God is in and through the texts of Hebrew Scripture. The most profound Christian metaphor for the true face of God remains the metaphor of 1 John: God is love (4:16). To understand that metaphor is, in part, to understand, on inner-Christian terms, what has been revealed by God of God's very identity as agent and as the very face of love in the history of ancient Israel.

For the Christian faithful to the self-disclosure of God in the Hebrew Bible and in Jesus Christ, the answer to the question "Who is God?" is: God is love, and Christians are those agents commanded and empowered by God to love and struggle, with Jews and Muslims, for love and justice. However, if this classic Johannine metaphor is not grounded in, and thereby interpreted by means of, the harsh and demanding reality of the entire Hebrew Bible (e.g., Job and Lamentations) and the whole of the message and ministry, cross and resurrection of this unsubstitutable Jesus—who, as the Christ, discloses God's face turned to us as love—then Christians may be tempted to sentimentalize the metaphor by reversing it into "Love is God." But this great reversal, on inner-Christian terms, is hermeneutically impossible. "God is love": the Christian experiences this identity of God in and through the history of God's actions and self-disclosures as merciful YHVH in ancient Israel and as Jesus Christ, the parable and face of God.

To affirm that God is love (that most relational of all categories) is also to affirm that the radically monotheistic God that Christians trust, worship, and have loyalty to is the radically relational (and, therefore, personal) origin, sustainer, and end of all reality. To affirm that God is love, moreover, grounds a theological understanding of the so-called economic Trinity (i.e., God experienced as Father, Son, and Spirit in the ordinary and liturgical lives of Christians as individuals and as a community) in the primary Christian confession of Jesus Christ. It also suggests that the so-called immanent Trinity (i.e., God is Godself as radically relational Father-Son-Spirit) can be partly, analogously but really, understood in and through the economic Trinity.

Christian monotheism is a Trinitarian monotheism, as the realistic Christian narratives, doctrines, and liturgy all witness exoterically, for the Trinitarian understanding of God can never be separated from YHVH as the *Christian* theological understanding of the radical, relational, loving God who revealed Godself in and through the history of ancient Israel and in and through the incarnation, the ministry (healing, preaching, actions), the cross, and the resurrection of Jesus of Nazareth. The Trinitarian understanding of God is also expressed in the promise and thrust of a second messianic coming and in the disclosure of this Jesus as the Christ through the power and activity of the Spirit as proclaimed for Christians in Word and celebrated in sacrament, especially the Trinitarian sacraments of baptism and Eucharist (to the Father through the Son in the Spirit). It is impossible for Christians to separate Trinitarian theology, Christology, and YHVH. In that sense, the Christian understanding of the "existence" and "nature" of the radically monotheistic God must be grounded in the "identity" of the God disclosed in the history and effects of ancient Israel (YHVH) and in Jesus Christ.

In Defense of the Speculative
Esoteric Form of Trinitarian Theology

Although grounded in the three classic forms of Christian realism— narrative, doctrine, liturgy—Christian reflection on the Trinitarian reality of God is also open to speculation. Speculative Trinitarian thought tends to begin with discussion of "the economic Trinity": the Trinity as disclosed in the realistic histories of Israel, Jesus Christ, and the church and as articulated in the realistic forms of church life, liturgy, Gospel narratives, hymns, and creeds. This thought then tends to move into more conceptual and abstract forms of reflection on the "immanent Trinity," that is, speculative reflection on God as God is in Godself. Both Karl Rahner and Karl Barth insisted on the priority of the economic Trinity as experienced by Christians over any esoteric speculation on the immanent Trinity. This priority can be understood, however, as the chronological and ontological priority of realistic narrative, doctrine, and liturgy, which in turn ground any speculation on the immanent Trinity.

I continue to believe, for example, that the brilliant use of the analogies of intelligence and love by the western Trinitarian theologies of Augustine and Aquinas are splendid, plausible, and modest analogically speculative forms for reflection on the immanent Trinity without any loss of a grounding in the realistic forms (here, especially, doctrine, confession, and liturgy) of articulating the economic Trinity. Even in less modest and more daring Trinitarian speculative theologies, that realistic grounding can reappear in the heart of speculation itself, as is especially apparent in the relationship between radical negative theology or apophaticism and Trinitarian theology.

Speculations about the immanent Trinity do not remove in any way either the Christian–Jewish foundational belief in YHVH as the one and only God, or the difference of the Christian belief in the economic Trinity as a radically relational Christian second naming of God as Father-Son-Spirit (which should never be either separated from or substituted for the name YHVH). Professor Peter Ochs's brilliant reflections on the principal commonalities and differences in Jewish and Christian namings of God help clarify what it means to name God YHVH, the God who rescued Israel from Egypt and who, for Christians, raised Jesus the Jew from the dead and promised his return for judgment on Christians, including, of course, their real historical role in the horror of anti-Semitism.

5

SCRIPTURE

Searching the Scriptures:
Jews, Christians, and the Book

MICHAEL A. SIGNER

The Centrality of *Derash* or "Seeking"

In their weekly Sabbath services, Jewish congregations hold a procession with the scroll of the *Sefer Torah*. Members of the congregation surge forward into the aisles of the synagogue to touch it. The scroll is carried to a lectern in the midst of the congregation where members of the community are given the "honor" of reciting blessings and reading from the scroll itself. In many synagogues, the rabbi or a member of the community offers a *Devar Torah*, a "word of Torah" that applies the weekly portion to the lives of those who have assembled to pray. This outpouring of attention and affection is a concrete demonstration of the centrality of Torah in Jewish life.

Although many Jews are not aware of it, there is a similar demonstration of honor and affection for Scripture in Christian worship. In Catholic and Orthodox churches, there is often a procession where the book of the Gospel is carried forward and placed on the altar. When the Scripture is read, the congregation rises. After the weekly reading, the worshippers anticipate a homily or sermon where the priest or pastor will provide nurture from Scripture to enrich the lives of those who have gathered.

The similarity of these rituals demonstrates a significant point of contact between Jews and Christians. Scripture, the written word, is a foundation for their communities. However, there are many Jews and Christians who would argue that the canon of Scripture—those books that have religious authority—is constructed very differently. Jews read and revere the TaNaCH (Torah, Nevi'im, and Ketuvim). When Christians refer to the Bible, they mean the Old and New Testaments. Some Christian communities also hold a collection of books called Apocrypha as part of their canon. When Jews open a Gideon Bible in their hotel rooms, they might ask themselves, "Do we read the same book?" The comfortable response would be "no." However, a more careful evaluation of the place of the Book in both religious communities might reveal deeper insights and lead to more productive discussions between them. Jews and Christians may have serious disagreements about what is included in the books they call "holy." They may not find consensus in the translation of their ancient texts. However, when we examine the discussions and disputations about the content of Scripture, we will see that continuing efforts to understand how to build ethical communities are at the heart of Jewish and Christian strivings to bring sanctity and meaning to the world that surrounds us.

We might begin with a simple observation. Both Jews and Christians seek out meaning of God's word for their lives in Scripture. The word for "seeking" in Hebrew is *darash*. To seek meaning in Scripture is not a casual or cursory reading. We approach its words as both familiar and strange. They are familiar to us because we have heard their stories since our childhood. Yet with more careful listening or reading, we can open ourselves to how "strange" some of the practices and stories are to our modern sensitivities. The strange or foreign aspect of these ancient texts is more than exotic or alluring. We want to create a bridge between the ancient texts and ourselves. In our search for religious meaning, we want to bring our lives to the text and the text into our lives.

This search for meaning is not new to our generation. It reaches back to the origins of Judaism and Christianity. The revered teaching of the ancient rabbis lives on in the study groups found in our synagogues and in the sermons or *derashot* that we hear. The earliest teachers in the Christian community delivered discourses on Scripture.

Through many generations, Christians have pondered the writings of their theologians, priests, and pastors. The excitement generated by the television series "Genesis" indicates that many people in America—even those who feel estranged from their religious roots—have a new desire to engage both the scriptural text and the ancestral traditions that have shaped its meaning. If we explore how Jews and Christians have searched the Scriptures, we will learn that their disputations and discussions have enriched both communities.

An ancient rabbinic text opens our eyes to the centrality of Scripture in the search for knowledge: "Turn it, and turn it again, for everything is contained in it" (M. *Avot* 5:26). This teaching of the rabbinic sage Ben Bag Bag asserts that the life of examining Scripture from every angle will produce wisdom. His prescription for "turning" indicates that *derash* or seeking knowledge is an active process. Writing nearly one thousand years later, the Christian scholar Hugh of St. Victor held a similar attitude toward the Bible. He composed a manual of scriptural interpretation for his students. He urged them to study the liberal and practical arts to prepare themselves for the study of Scripture. He exhorted his students, "Learn all things. Afterwards you find that nothing is superfluous" (*Didascalicon*, Book 6, 6). Both scholars reflect a similar attitude about the capacity of the Bible to inform their respective communities: The answer to every question may be discovered within the Bible when a reliable authority interprets it. The history of scriptural interpretation provides a significant point of entry for understanding the nature of the relationship between Judaism and Christianity during the past two millennia.

Searching: A Common Foundation

The centrality of the search for meaning in Scripture began at least as early as the return from Babylonian exile. The people who worshipped the God of Israel invested the text of the Bible with the power to provide the presence of God in their midst even when they could no longer literally "hear" his voice. Nehemiah 9 provides the image of a community assembled around its teachers on the New Year's festival. In that assembly, Ezra the scribe read the text, and the Levites provided an interpretation and translation for the people. This community described even non-Israelite monarchs as acknowledging the authority of Scripture. King Cyrus of Persia attributed his release of the Israelite exiles as the fulfillment of "the word of the Lord spoken through Jeremiah" (2 Chron. 36:22). Other communities of Jews would search these texts for direction in the proper conduct of the Temple cult and its festival calendar. The books of Enoch and Jubilees indicate efforts to reinterpret the Bible and to retell biblical stories to provide the foundations for their practice. The communities that composed the Dead Sea Scrolls wrote law books, liturgies, and eschatological interpretations of biblical prophecies. The Scrolls provide valuable information about the vehement disagreements over the meaning of Scripture among Jewish communities who lived in Palestine. The armies of Alexander the Great and his successors (fourth to second century B.C.E.) provided a new challenge to those who worshipped the God of Israel. When faced with persecution and the desecration of the Temple by Antiochus Epiphanes (r. 175–164), Jews turned to earlier prophecies and elaborated them. The biblical book of Daniel provides an example of this new style of biblical interpretation, called "apocalyptic." In writing apocalyptic works, the authors sought to discover when deliverance from persecution would come and who would liberate the people.

The cultural conflict between Judaism and Hellenism within the communities in the land of Israel inspired cultural developments in the Diaspora communities, most notably in Alexandria. In that city, the Jewish community developed its own interpretations of the Hebrew Bible in Greek translation. From the *Letter of Aristeas to Philocrates* we learn that these people understood this translation to have been guided by the prophetic spirit of God. Even the writings of the Greek philosophers were not beyond the boundaries of the Bible. Philo (20 B.C.E.–50 C.E.) utilized the contemporary tools of Greek literary practice—the allegorical method—to demonstrate that the Hebrew Bible contained all of the great truths in Greek philosophy and that Plato sat at the feet of Moses to learn wisdom.

Roots and Branches:
The Development of Jewish and
Christian Communities of Interpretation

The renaissance of biblical study among the Jewish communities from the fourth century B.C.E. until the first century C.E. reveals a creative spirit that would not diminish. In the wake of the destruction of the Jerusalem Temple in 70 C.E. and of the failed attempt by Bar Kochba to reestablish Jewish sovereignty in 135 C.E., two dominant communities emerged, and both of them sought guidance from the Hebrew Bible. By the middle of the second century C.E., we can speak of communities of rabbinic Jews and of Christians who lived in the land of Israel and in the Mediterranean region. Scholars are still engaged in explaining the "parting of the ways" between Jews and Christians. They agree that the interpretation of Scripture was at the heart of the separation.

Rabbinic Jews followed the teachings of their Pharisaic predecessors, who propounded the idea of Oral Torah *(Torah shebe'al peh)* as the primary framework for expanding the written words of Scripture *(Torah she-bichtav)*. They considered their oral traditions to be part of the continuous revelation that God had given Moses at Sinai (M. *Avot* 1:1).

By the third century, the foundational document of the Oral Torah, the Mishnah, appeared in written form and provided a compendium of rabbinic oral traditions. Although the Mishnah is not guided by the order of the biblical books, it presumes the TaNaCH as its foundation. The Mishnah, in turn, was the foundation of the Talmud, a complex literary document that presents both Halachah and Aggadah—extended discussions on how the rabbis expanded the laws in the Pentateuch and its moral teachings. Additionally, in collections of Midrash, the rabbis followed the order of the biblical text and expounded Scripture. Throughout their centers in the Byzantine and Persian Empires, the rabbis continued to master the Written Torah and make it the central authority for Jewish thought and practice.

From the documents of nascent Christianity, we can discern that the early followers of Jesus of Nazareth built their foundations on the Hebrew Scriptures. The documents of the New Testament present an extended meditation on the meaning of the Hebrew Bible that is analogous to the process used by the rabbis in Talmud and Midrash. For example, the infancy narratives in the Gospels of Matthew and Luke were composed in the same style as the genealogies in Genesis and Chronicles. Matthew's narration of the events in the life of Jesus often concludes with the formula, "All this happened in order to fulfill what the Lord declared through the prophet" (Mt. 1:22–25; 2:5–6).

Matthew often depicts Jesus as a teacher of Torah who claims that he did not come to abolish the Law and the Prophets but to complete or fulfill them (Mt. 5:17–19). Jesus expands the meaning of the commandments in the Decalogue and speaks with his own authority (Mt. 5:21–48). Luke depicts Jesus as a teacher of Scripture who attends the synagogue and reads from the scroll of Isaiah 61:1–2 (Lk. 4:16–21). The authority of Jesus is frequently asserted in disputations with teachers from the Pharisaic schools (Mt. 23). However, it should be noted that when Jesus is asked to name the most important commandments, he responds with direct quotations from the Torah: "Love the Lord your God with all your heart, with all your soul, with all your strength, and with all your mind (Deut. 6:5) and "Love your neighbor as yourself" (Lev. 19:18). Despite all his arguments with other Jewish teachers, the Hebrew Bible is at the center of his teaching about how humanity should relate to God and to all of God's creatures.

The most important early discussions of the *meaning* of Jesus as the risen Christ are in the letters of Paul. These letters provide evidence that Paul addressed his audiences by utilizing Hellenistic forms of persuasion. However, he frequently calls upon the Hebrew Bible—albeit in Greek translation—as an authority for his arguments. At the center of Paul's interpretations is the experience of the resurrected Jesus as Christ. For Paul, this fact makes Jesus a stumbling block to Jews and pagans (1 Cor. 1:23). Without the prism of Christ, reading the Hebrew Bible is like looking through a veil (2 Cor. 3:6–18). Yet, an understanding of the narratives in the Hebrew Bible provides the appropriate foundation for participating in the life of the community of the new covenant: "You understand, my brothers, that our ancestors were all under the pillar of cloud, and all of them passed through the Red Sea; and so they all received baptism into the fellowship of Moses in cloud and sea (1 Cor. 10:1–5).

For Paul, these events are "symbols" that were "recorded for our benefit as a warning" (1 Cor. 10:11). Paul called Christians to read the Old Testament through the new spirit offered in Jesus Christ. This "spiritual reading" of earlier events would provide guidance for pagans who had become Christians. They would not be tempted into following the practices of those who lived according to the letter of the commandments. In chapter 3 of his letter to the Galatians, Paul rereads Genesis 15:6 as an indication that the covenant relationship between God and Abraham was firmly established before the commandment of circumcision in Genesis 17. Paul concludes his argument against the necessity of circumcision by indicating that the Old Covenant had a time-restricted value. It was a "protector" or "pedagogue" until Jesus came (Gal. 3:24). Nonetheless, in chapters 9–12 of his letter to the Romans, the Law or Old Testament occupies a significant place in Paul's description of the salvation of humanity.

The Epistle to the Hebrews defines the reading of the Old and New Testaments as one book as fundamental to Christianity. Drawing upon Paul's narrative of salvation through Christ, Hebrews provides Christians with a "guide" for reading the Old Testament. The message of God "in former times" was spoken by the prophets in "fragmentary and varied ways." With the advent of Jesus, everything is now clear and filled with light (Heb. 1:1–4). Borrowing from the image of Jesus as the divine word in the Gospel of John, the author of Hebrews offers a Christological reading of passages in the Hebrew Bible (Heb. 1:5–2). The remaining chapters of the letter describe the "fulfillment" of the tasks of Moses and Aaron by the high priesthood of Jesus (Heb.4–7), and the sacrifices of the Day of Atonement as subsumed in the death of Jesus on the cross (Heb. 8–10). The letter concludes its biblical "searching" with a retelling of the story of biblical Israel through the power of faith (Heb. 11).

I have attempted to present a strong argument for the conjunction of New and Old Testament. It is fair to claim that the conceptual vocabulary and the narrative framework of the New Testament are almost impossible to understand apart from their roots in the Hebrew Bible. The New Testament presents a paradox with respect to the fundamental importance of the Hebrew Bible. It suggests that the life and teaching of Jesus and the activity of his disciples offer a "new way" to salvation for humankind. At the same time, it is impossible to understand the most important concepts of the New Testament—such as "sin," "redemption," or "salvation"—apart from the Hebrew Bible.

In their search to distinguish their teachings from the Jewish communities, early Christian writings such as the Epistle of Barnabas (ca. 130–135) and the Didache (ca. 80–100) emphasize those elements in the New Testament that describe the superiority of the way of Jesus. These documents speak about Christianity as the way of light and Judaism as the way of darkness. They indicate that narratives in the Hebrew Bible already demonstrate the diminished status of the Jewish people. For example, when Moses shatters the tablets of the Ten Commandments, God replaces the first tablets with a "law of punishment." This "law of punishment" is replaced only with the coming of Jesus (Barn. 14:1). By contrast, some of the actions by Moses in the Torah are explained as foreshadowings of Jesus. For example, Barnabas interprets the posture of Moses with his arms outstretched and supported by Aaron and Joshua during the battle against the

Amalekites (Ex. 27:8–13) as anticipating Jesus on the cross (Barn. 12:2–3). In the homily of Melito of Sardis (d. ca. 190), the Exodus narratives demonstrate the election of the church and the rejection of the Jews who did not recognize Jesus as the Messiah.

Many modern scholars have demonstrated that these early texts have contributed to the "teachings of contempt," the cumulative body of Christian teachings developed over the centuries that call for the rejection of Judaism and declare Christianity the "True Israel." If we read Melito or Barnabas in their historical context, they reveal the dilemmas of the first generation of Christian teachers. Many pagans were attracted to Christianity because it offered the promise of salvation to those who possessed a "gnosis," the Greek word for "secret knowledge." For these Christians, Jesus Christ and his teachings were the "way of the spirit" and permitted them to reject the material world. One of their teachers, Marcion (d. ca. 160), taught that only the spiritual life of the risen Jesus Christ was religiously significant. He argued that the Old Testament and even the books of the New Testament like the Gospels that described the earthly life of Jesus and his disciples were unnecessary for Christian believers.

The effort by Marcion and other Gnostics to eliminate the Old Testament evoked an internal Christian argument. Opponents of the Gnostic argument to "spiritualize" Christianity insisted on the importance of the Old Testament as the "preparation" for the truth of Jesus Christ. These theologians were trained in the philosophical schools of late antiquity. Their approach to Christian Scripture was grounded in their rhetorical training, which they received through guidebooks or manuals to Greco-Roman literature. They set themselves the project of constructing an approach to the study of Scripture that would distinguish Christian belief and practice from both internal opponents (the Gnostics) and rabbinic Judaism. Two of these teachers, Clement of Alexandria (ca. 150–215) and Irenaeus of Lyons (ca. 130–200), composed lengthy works to combat heresy. They emphasized the continuity of Christian teaching with the Hebrew Bible by combining the allegorical method developed by Philo of Alexandria and the typological method of foreshadowing that they learned in their meditations on the New Testament. Both allegory and typology led to interpretations of the Hebrew Bible as a text that pointed to something beyond its own immediate contents. Philo's allegory demonstrated that the Hebrew Bible was clearly compatible with Greek philosophy. Paul had used typology to demonstrate that the Hebrew Bible provided the "type" that would be fulfilled in the "antitype" of the New Testament. As a method of Christian interpretation, typology insured that the Hebrew Bible revealed Christian truth, from the creation of the world until the second coming of Jesus Christ. Christian teachers in the eastern churches such as Antioch also developed methods of revealing the continuities between the two testaments. These Syriac-speaking Christian eschewed the allegorical method and focused their teaching on demonstrating that the connection between the two testaments was based on similar patterns of language and story rather than on typology.

By the third century, Origen (ca. 185–253/4)—a teacher in Alexandria and then in Caesaria—wrote *Peri Archon* (On first principles), a systematic guide to the interpretation of Scripture. Modeled on the rhetorical manuals of the day, this text attempted to guide students to read the Hebrew Bible as Christians. Origen also wanted Christians to have an accurate text of the Bible as the basis for developing their theology. This concern led him to compose the *Hexapla*, which presented the Hebrew, Greek, and Aramaic versions of the biblical text in parallel columns. Drawing upon methods also used by Philo, Origen made it possible for Christians to learn how the narratives and laws of the Hebrew Bible could be read as shadows that illumined and enriched Christian life. In his book *Contra Celsum*, Origen defended Christian theology, particularly biblical interpretation, against the arguments of the pagan philosophers.

In addition to his response to the pagans, Origen encountered the rabbis in Caesaria and disputed with them about the proper interpretation of the Hebrew Bible. His sermons and biblical commentaries reflect his efforts to respond to the rabbinic claims about the true meaning of the text. Two centuries later, Origen's example would inspire Jerome to move from Italy to Bethlehem, where he would study Hebrew, argue with the rabbis, and translate the Old Testament into Latin. From the examples of Origen and Jerome we gain some new perspectives on Christian efforts to interpret the Hebrew Bible. They had to answer the questions raised by pagan philosophers who claimed that there was nothing unique about Jesus Christ and the Christian faith. In addition, they had to contend with dissenters within the church who asserted that the Hebrew Bible was not essential to Christian belief. Origen and Jerome developed their responses to pagans and Gnostics based on their study with the rabbis. To be sure, they argued with the rabbis. But their exchanges with the rabbis sharpened their own Christian perspective.

How did the rabbis and Jewish communities respond to the early Christians? It is difficult to establish a precise chronology of their reactions. We know that the early rabbis accepted the authenticity of the Greek translation of Scriptures, even though they themselves used the Aramaic translation or *Targum*. A deeper look into rabbinic culture reveals that they did develop a structure for interpretation that had parallels with those used by Christians. Both rabbis and early Christian teachers were confronted by the problems of deriving meaning from the Bible and instructing their respective communities. They both understood the Scriptures to be the revealed word of God. The power of divine revelation implied that the words of Scripture pointed beyond themselves and could speak to all eras, from creation until the end of the world when those who had been faithful to God's covenant would be rewarded or punished. This common task of promoting the "word of God" called upon both communities to create frameworks for biblical interpretation that would validate the text of Scripture as the bearer of divine revelation.

For the rabbis, the biblical text could support many interpretations. When Jeremiah said, "Behold, My word is like fire says the Lord; and like a hammer that shatters rock" (Jer. 23:29), the rabbis understood his words in the following way: "Just as a hammer shatters rock into numerous splinters, so may a single biblical verse yield a multiplicity of meanings" (B Sanh. 34a). However, not all interpretations were correct. When they engaged in developing Halachah on the basis of the biblical verse, the rabbis insisted that "no Scriptural verse can transgress its *peshat* or plain meaning" (B. Shab. 63a; B. Yeb. 11b, 24a). Nevertheless, the rabbis continued to debate the elasticity of scriptural language. Rabbi Akiba argued that every particle of speech and even the special signs on the top of letters were an occasion to probe the biblical text and expand its meanings. His colleague Rabbi Ishmael rejected such a supernatural approach to language. Rather, Rabbi Ishmael held that "the Torah speaks in human language." For Ishmael, all expansions of a biblical passage could be derived only from the rules of grammar and from the rational method of deduction.

In their efforts to search out the meaning of Scripture, the ancient rabbis were conscious of the need to distinguish between *peshat* as "plain meaning" and *derash* as derived meaning. For the rabbis, both *peshat* and *derash* are intrinsic to the Bible itself and are not meanings that they "read in." Yet, the idea of *derash* carries with it a more profound sense of active reasoning than does *peshat*, as the rabbis work to arrive at the meaning of the text. David Weiss Halivni points out, however, that we should not confuse the rabbis' understanding of *peshat* with our modern ideas of lexicography or historical meaning. The discussion of how *peshat* and *derash* develop through the history of Judaism is complex and stands as an example of the vitality of Jewish intellectual life.[1] From antiquity through the modern era, Jewish scholars continued their debate about the relationship between those interpretations based on scriptural language and those based on inductive or deductive reasoning.

We find a similar intellectual vigor present in Christian communities and their efforts to understand the Bible. Christians have framed their discussions about the Hebrew Bible in terms of the "letter" and the "spirit." These two terms derive from the writings of Paul, who distinguished between the "letter that kills" and "the spirit that gives life" (2 Cor. 3:6–7). Early Christians read the Old Covenant through the lens of Christ—the New Covenant. There was always the danger that some Christian readings would demean the literal sense of the biblical text. However, Origen put "letter" and "spirit" into proper perspective. He described Scripture as possessing both a body and a spirit. Both elements were necessary for the healthy body of the church.

The teachers of the church insisted that the "New Covenant lies hidden in the Old; and the Old Covenant becomes clear in the New Covenant." Two of these teachers, Augustine (354–430) and Gregory the Great (590–604), created the basic framework for scriptural interpretation in the western church. Gregory compared Scripture to a house; he asserted that the letter was like the foundation. Only with a solid foundation of understanding the literal meaning could a Christian build proper spiritual interpretations. The "spiritual" meaning was later divided into three categories or "senses": The allegorical sense taught Christians what they should believe; the tropological or moral sense guided them to proper behavior; and the mystical sense provided hints at the inner life of God.

Christian theologians argued about the proper method for discriminating between the four senses of Scripture. Ideally, the spiritual meaning should always be based on the letter. In reality, the exigencies of instructing the Christian community in beliefs and behaviors often led to minimal descriptions of the letter in order to pass to "higher levels of meaning." However, throughout the history of Christian interpretation there have been strong advocates of the literal sense— and of the notion that some knowledge of Hebrew is necessary for a

Christian understanding of the Old Testament. We can observe these internal Christian discussions in late antiquity when Augustine and Jerome agreed on the importance of Hebrew language.

Jerome, who actually studied Hebrew with Jewish instructors in Bethlehem, bequeathed to the church a Latin translation of the Old Testament, the Vulgate, that was based on a study of the Hebrew. In twelfth-century Paris, Christian scholars at the Abbey of St. Victor consulted with contemporary Jews and included Jewish explanations (in Latin translation) in their own commentaries. At the University of Paris in the thirteenth and fourteenth centuries, Thomas Aquinas (1225–1274), a Dominican, and Nicholas of Lyra (1270–1349), a Franciscan, turned to Maimonides (1135–1204) and Rashi (1040–1105) for novel approaches to the interpretation of the Bible. During the period of the Renaissance and Reformation, Christians turned to the study of Hebrew and rabbinic traditions as the basis of their inquiries into Scripture and arrived at new views of the relationship between Scripture and the accumulated teaching of their tradition.

At the dawn of modernity, Richard Simon (1638–1712) and Baruch Spinoza (1632–1677) provided the weapons for the separation of letter and spirit. For both Spinoza and Simon, the primary value of biblical study was historical. The Bible could best be understood as part of the ancient world. The reduction of biblical studies to ancient history and textual criticism challenged all previous generations of Christian exegesis, and its echoes resonate in many contemporary Protestant denominations.

Beyond the discussion about letter and spirit, we might observe that the divisions among Christians originate in questions over how Scripture is best interpreted. Three elements constitute these internal Christian discussions: Scripture, tradition, and theology. First, Catholics and Protestants do not agree on what constitutes the canon—the authoritative books of Scripture. Although they both hold the Old and New Testaments as authorities, Catholics consider Maccabees, Ben Sirach, and other books to be part of Scripture. Protestants call them "Apocrypha." Next, with respect to tradition, Orthodox Christians believe that the writings of the church fathers and the decisions of the councils compose the framework for interpretation. For Catholics the tradition is carried on through the teaching office of the church (the *Magisterium*), in dialogue with theologians. Mainline Protestant traditions carry out their interpretation of Scripture in light of their church confessions. However, many Protestants deny the authority of any traditional interpretation. They rely upon the careful reading of Scripture as *ipsissima verba*, the very word of God. Only prayer and the Bible are constitutive of the life of faith.

Theology, the third element in Christian biblical interpretation, is the use of reason, particularly philosophical method, to arrive at normative belief and behavior for the Christian community. Differing attitudes toward tradition are reflected in different understandings of the relationship between Scripture and theology. Catholic theology begins with Scripture but utilizes the church fathers, church councils, and papal documents. Orthodox theology utilizes the authority of the church fathers. Protestant theology places most of its emphasis on Scripture itself.

Discussions and apologetics about Scripture that are internal to Christianity have often been as acrimonious as the rhetorical assaults on Jewish misunderstandings. These internal arguments have often marginalized and obscured what I would call the "hidden dialogue" between Christians and Jews throughout their generations. This hidden dialogue takes place at the deepest level of Jewish and Christian hopes to live as God's creatures and care for the world. Both Jews and Christians read the Bible and seek its meaning in order to live in the presence of God. By revealing this continuing search for the significance of the Bible in daily life, we can discover profound points of agreement between Jews and Christians: In both traditions, Scripture is central to worship and calendar, to preaching and private devotion or study. When the study of Scripture is viewed in this binocular fashion—through the eyes of both traditions—we can observe both the similarities and differences between Jews and Christians. We can sort out the animosity and the need to displace one another's efforts and move toward respecting our differing perspectives.

We can conclude, then, that the debates about how to interpret the Bible will continue within each community and between Jews and Christians. With the new approaches to Judaism that have awakened among Christians since the Shoah, there is now the possibility for both religious communities to study the ways our ancestors searched for meaning in Scripture. Their "searching" can become the foundation of an active discussion between Jews and Christians. We need not disdain our ancestors' lack of historical knowledge about the ancient Near East. Rather, we can appreciate their efforts to discover the profound truths that enriched their lives.

If we look at the tensions that surrounded discussions about the framework of premodern scriptural interpretation, we may discover that "letter" and "spirit," or the four "senses" of Scripture, provide a new lens that links our respective communities to the richness of our ancestral traditions. In this common study of Scripture there are, I would argue, two "senses" that might allow Christians and Jews to fully share their findings with one another and reach a broad range of consensus or even agreement. First, we can explore the literal sense of Scripture. Our studies would focus on the historical meaning of the biblical passage in its biblical context. This study has been the exclusive province of academic biblical studies for at least a century. During the past fifty years, however, there has been a collaboration between Christians and Jews that has opened up the complex historical background of the era that produced both the Old and New Testaments. The rich and diverse voices of Second Temple Judaism resonate with the polyphony of our own era. Second, as Christians and Jews we can read the Scriptures for the moral sense that presents models of ethical behavior.

Explorations of the two other "senses" of Scripture—the allegorical and the mystical—will not yield a similar consensus or agreement, but, nonetheless, they can provide an important link between the Jewish and Christian communities. For Christians, the allegorical sense presents the Hebrew Bible through the mirror of the New Testament, whereas for Jews, the *derash* of the Hebrew Bible always seeks correlation with the tradition of Oral Torah. If Jews can learn how Christians unite the Old Testament with the New via allegory, they can understand what binds the Christian community to biblical Israel and its progeny—the Jewish people. The fact that Christians can share their allegory without oppressive proselytizing is most important here. Rather, Christians must speak openly about how the Hebrew Bible has an impact on their lives. That will help Jews gain understanding of Christianity as a profound exploration—or *derash*—of the way God operates among humanity. Once we pass over the threshold of the core tradition of allegory or *derash*, the mystical tradition differs because the intimate symbolism of each tradition excludes the possibility of the other. However, it is precisely the inability to grasp the whole of Scripture's meaning that can create a spirit of collaboration between our two communities, and so even here there is promise. No single tradition can or ought to dominate the other. The ability to share our readings of "spirit" or *derash* may be the model for a future reconciliation that recognizes both our profound differences and the imperative to become partners in understanding the divine word to be a blessing to the entire world.

The Writings and Reception of
Philo of Alexandria

HINDY NAJMAN

As early as the inauguration of the Second Temple community under Ezra the scribe, authoritative Scripture played a central role in constituting Jewish life. Instead of appealing to a king or a prophet, the people consulted scribes whose authority rested on their access to the sacred Scripture that represented Israel's past and present covenantal relationship with God. Because much of Scripture had been written for earlier generations, scribes needed not only to read but also to interpret Scripture, to render it relevant and applicable under new conditions. As differences of interpretation emerged, various groups claimed that their interpretations captured the true meanings of the ancient laws and narratives. Sometimes they asserted that like Scripture itself, their interpretations were divinely inspired. Interpretive disagreements sometimes grew into sectarian divisions, and, ultimately, some groups could no longer recognize other groups as members of the same religious community. This dynamic contributed to the eventual parting of ways between rabbinic Judaism and Christianity, both of which emerged out of the interpretive practices of various Jewish groups in the late Second Temple period. Despite their differences, the reading and interpretation of Scripture remained central to both rabbinic Judaism and Christianity. Indeed both Judaism and Christianity inherited a wealth of shared interpretations of their sacred Scripture, although each tradition developed these interpretations in distinct and sometimes opposing ways. The study of Philo of Alexandria (ca. 20 B.C.E.–50 C.E.) makes a singular and unusual contribution to our understanding of the parallel and overlapping histories of Jewish and Christian scriptural interpretation. Philo, who lived before Judaism and Christianity separated into two distinct religions, left behind a rich legacy of exegetical writings—including philosophical essays, allegorical interpretations, explications of biblical laws, questions and answers on Genesis and Exodus—and apologetic writings. His variegated writings provide a window through which we can examine intellectual developments in Second Temple Judaism, prior to the split between Judaism and Christianity. Apparently lost to later Jewish exegetes and philosophers, Philo was appropriated so completely by some Christians that he was regarded as a Christian. Only centuries later, during the Reformation, was it recalled that Philo Christianus had in fact been Philo Judaeus. This recognition generated renewed interest by Jewish scholars and repudiation by some Christian scholars. To this day, some scholars describe Philo as a proto-Christian, whereas others interpret his writings as those of a proto-rabbinic Jew. The work of Philo and the story of the reception of his writings illuminate the intimate entanglement of Judaism and Christianity, as well as the difficulty and hope of conversation between them.

The Writings of Philo of Alexandria

Throughout his writings, Philo links the Hellenistic philosophical traditions of his day and the Jewish interpretive traditions he inherited.[1] He weaves Greek philosophical concepts even into his explicitly Jewish traditional interpretations, a synthesis of Judaism and Greek philosophy absent from classical rabbinic traditions. The challenge that Philo faced was that Greek philosophy encouraged a valuation only of ways of life relevant to all humans, whereas Mosaic Law seemed of particular relevance only to Jews and was therefore suspected of misanthropy.

Philo met this challenge by claiming that Mosaic Law had a unique relationship to what Hellenistic philosophers called natural law. This relationship distinguished Mosaic Law and its traditions from the laws of all other nations. The idea of nature as a divinely created cosmic order providing normative guidance for human action was absent from early Greek thought but must have emerged shortly before the time of Philo. However, Philo faced formidable obstacles in his employment of this strategy. To put the problem in its general form: the law of nature was surely of universal significance for all peoples, but the Law of Moses appeared to be concerned, for the most part, with the obligations of a particular people arising from its particular history and relationship with God. How could biblical traditions display the universality of natural law without losing their connection to the particular observances of the Jews?

Philo's interpretations of biblical personalities and laws were intended to address this problem. Philo portrayed Moses as the paradigmatic leader, the unique combination, in one person, of all Greek ideals of humanity—a "divine human." As such a figure, Moses had the authority and wisdom to compose an eternally binding law that was more excellent than the laws of the great Athenian legislators, Solon and Lycurgus.

Philo's biography of Moses reflects the Hellenistic tendency to display the divine status of philosophical and political heroes. Philo not only defended the philosophical significance of Moses but also concerned himself with Israel's pre-Mosaic ancestors, most notably, Abraham. Philo ensured that Abraham's acts of faith and obedience were explained in terms that granted Abraham universal significance.

Abraham was the first to know God, yet he lived prior to the giving of the Torah. Philo explained this knowledge as a mark of Abraham's ability to grasp the unwritten law of nature by means of his own reason. This was a remarkable achievement, which set Abraham apart from those who were fortunate enough to live after the time of Moses and needed only to obey the written law (*On Abraham*, 16). Abraham's achievement did not, however, imply that the unwritten law was greater than the written law. Rather, the written Mosaic Law embodied the unwritten law of nature and was therefore "stamped, as it were, with the seals of nature itself" (*Life of Moses*, 2:14). For Philo, the Mosaic Law was the most perfect, particular, written copy of natural law; natural law was thus embodied in the laws of the Pentateuch as well as in the subsequent laws and traditions of the Jews.

Philo maintained that even the most particular laws had a universal significance that could be brought out by allegorical interpretation. For Philo, allegory draws equivalences between scriptural terms and a set of terms that are never explicitly mentioned in Scripture, terms most often rooted in the Hellenistic philosophical teachings of his day. For example, Philo established equivalences between the three patriarchs and the three dispositions of the soul: "The first, who is named Abraham, is a symbol of that virtue which is derived from instruction; the intermediate Isaac is an emblem of natural virtue; the third, Jacob, of that virtue which is devoted to and derived from practice" (*On Abraham*, 52).

Philo's universalizing reinterpretations of Scripture did not mean that the law revealed in the Torah was to govern all peoples or that Jews who understood the law's meaning were thereby exempt from obeying it. For example, Philo explained circumcision as a law that improves the virtue of men and controls their passions (*Special Laws*, 1:2–11). However, Philo never suggested that Gentiles should adopt this particular way of controlling their passions, nor did he ever suggest that Jews who could control their passions in some other way were exempt from fulfilling this commandment. Philo was critical of Jews who thought that the allegorical interpretation of Scripture superseded the authority of the Law.

In general, the authority of an interpretive tradition did not rest, for Philo, as it did for the rabbis, on God's transmission of those traditions to the interpreter by way of Moses and a chain of tradents. It rested rather on the tradition's ability to show the unparalleled authority of Mosaic Torah and to display the universal significance of Mosaic Torah by demonstrating the congruence of Mosaic Torah with the law of nature. Consequently, Philo did not always claim that his allegorical interpretations were inherited from the elders or the fathers. He sometimes took the liberty of interpreting Mosaic Law on his own by using his "love of knowledge to peer into each of them [sacred messages] and unfold and reveal what is not known to the multitude" (*Special Laws*, 3:6). Overall, Philo's concern was to authorize the Law of Moses in the universal terms appropriate to his Hellenistic context, *without compromising the particularity of the law* and its place in particular Jewish society.[2]

Philo's Christian Reception

Tragically, the Jewish community in Alexandria did not survive long after Philo's death. Philo traveled to Rome to protest the anti-Jewish riots in 38–41 C.E. But that was not to be the final pogrom against the Jewish community in Alexandria. The final decimation of the Jewish community occurred in 117, under the direction of the Roman emperor Trajan. Not Jews, but Christian church fathers such as Clement of Alexandria (ca. 150–220) and Origen (184–253) were thus the direct inheritors of the legacy of Philo and Hellenistic Judaism. Philo offered these recent converts to Christianity a way of incorporating their philosophical training into their appreciation of Scripture. These interpreters made great use of Philo and were ultimately responsible for the preservation of Philo's writings.

A little over a century after Philo's death, Clement was living in Alexandria as a Christian, studying in what is known as the Catechetical School. Clement made only four explicit references to Philo in his *Stromateis* (Miscellanies), but he made implicit use of Philo's biblical interpretations throughout his writings, appropriating many of Philo's ideas and recasting them to address the problems of Alexandrian Christians. Was a well-educated Gentile convert to Christianity supposed to renounce his Hellenistic education and universalistic background in order to adopt the particular tradition of the Jews as interpreted by Christianity? Since Philo had interpreted the Jewish Torah as a universally significant philosophy, Clement was able to interpret the philosophical tradition as a sort of Gentile Torah. Philosophy had prepared the Gentiles for Christianity, just as Torah had prepared the Jews. Thus Clement wrote:

> God is responsible for all good things: of some, like the blessings of the Old and New Covenants, directly: of others, like the riches of philosophy, indirectly. Perhaps philosophy too was a direct gift of God to the Greeks before the Lord extended his appeal to the Greeks. For philosophy was to the Greek world what the Law was to the Hebrews, a tutor escorting them to Christ. So philosophy is a preparatory process; it opens the road for the person whom Christ brings to his final goal. (*Stromateis*, bk. 1:3)

Hence Gentile and Jew were equally prepared for Christianity, and both philosophy and Scripture could be properly read through Christian eyes alone. This new synthesis of particularity and universality would hardly have been possible without Philo's prior synthesis. In the same section of the *Stromateis*, Clement cited Philo's allegorical interpretation of Abraham's relationship with his wife's Egyptian maid as proof that Scripture supported his idea: lady wisdom (Sarah) permitted faith (Abraham) to have a fruitful encounter with secular philosophy (Hagar), because such an encounter was preparation for a productive relationship with wisdom herself. Philo could not have accepted the Christian idea that the particularities of Jewish law and life were no longer necessary, but he had helped lay the groundwork for Christianity's universalistic interpretation of Scripture, nonetheless.

Many church fathers who incorporated Philo's interpretations into their writings acknowledged his Jewishness, often considering it a limitation to Philo's own success as an interpreter. But at moments in the history of Christian interpretation, Philo was remembered as a Christian. Various legends about his alleged conversion can be found in the literature of the church fathers. Perhaps one should understand these fabrications in light of the ongoing Christian struggle with the survival of recalcitrant Judaism. It was no simple matter to appropriate Philo's interpretations without recasting Philo himself as a Christian.

Although the extent of Philo's impact on early Christianity can be debated, it is certain that his writings were read by Christians through the fourth century, and that for centuries after this his methods and ideas remained an integral part of Christian biblical interpretation, even if his texts were not as widely read.

Philo's Jewish Legacy

In stark contrast to the Christian response, Philo is never explicitly cited or even mentioned in any of the rabbinic writings. What are we to make of this silence? Does this suggest that Philo should really be understood as a proto-Christian? Why was Philo's rich corpus of interpretation forgotten?

Philo's allegiance to Second Temple Judaism is omnipresent in his writings. His repeated deference to inherited interpretations of the fathers and his idealization of the Mosaic Law as the most perfect universal law attest to his unswerving commitment to Jewish law and to the perpetuation of Jewish tradition. Philo undertook to render the authority of Mosaic Torah and its interpretations intelligible to Hellenistic Jews such as himself, while simultaneously responding to the uncomprehending hostility of some non-Jews. However, the universal appeal of Philo's interpretations resonated well with later developments in Pauline Christianity; at the same time, rabbinic theology consciously relinquished many concepts that had been part of Second Temple Judaism in order to ensure the survival of Judaism. The rabbis sought to accomplish their task by distinguishing the distinctiveness of the biblical message from the unalloyed universalism that was promoted by Christianity. This perceived need for separation and distinction may have contributed to the rabbis' neglect of Philo. However, it is worth noting the extensive corpus of shared interpretive traditions that one can find in Philo and later rabbinic texts. Although I do not think these shared traditions testify to rabbinic dependency on Philo, they demonstrate that a great many biblical interpretations available to Philo in Alexandria continued to circulate among rabbinic interpreters.

Philo's contribution to the history of Jewish philosophy is an even more complicated matter. There is no evidence that Geonic and later medieval Jewish philosophical traditions drew directly on the work of Philo. Nevertheless, many of the philosophical issues raised by Philo were revisited centuries later in the work of figures such as Sa'adiyah Gaon (882–942) and Moses Maimonides (1135–1204), both of whom may have been influenced by traditions that ultimately led back to Philo.

The controversies about philosophical Judaism in the centuries following Maimonides' publication of the *Guide to the Perplexed* may help us understand why Philo's writings were apparently not preserved in ancient rabbinic academies. The Maimonidean controversy concerned, in part, the compatibility of universalizing allegorical interpretation with the particular demands of the Law. Maimonides' allegorical approach, perhaps indirectly inherited from Philo, was developed by interpreters like Rabbi Ya'akov Anatoli (thirteenth century), whose *Malmad Hatalmidim* (Goad of the Students) was studied every week in some synagogues. However, halachists such as Rabbi Shlomo ben Adret (1235–1310) warned that allegorical interpretation was weakening faith and observance, and he placed some of its practitioners under the ban. For example, he banned those who interpreted the personalities of Abraham and Sarah as representations of universally significant Greek philosophical concepts. But this was exactly the exegetical approach pioneered by Philo. The kind of philosophical interpretation embodied in the works of Philo and Maimonides never vanished from Judaism, yet its complex relation to Jewish particularity made it a minority interest, under occasional clouds of suspicion.

Finally, during the period of the Reformation a striking change occurred. Just when some Protestants rejected Philo of Alexandria as Philo Judaeus, Jewish scholars, notably Azariah dei Rossi (1511–1578), rediscovered him. Philo's storehouse of Jewish interpretation was reopened to Jewish scholars. More than three centuries after this rediscovery, Harry Austryn Wolfson (1887–1974), pioneer of Jewish studies in America, developed an interpretation of the intellectual history of the West in which Philo was the seminal figure, the founder of a philosophical tradition without which the classical philosophical works of Judaism, Christianity, and Islam would have been impossible.

Conclusion

Philo's work was motivated by a question that later divided Judaism and Christianity: can the religious experiences and traditions of ancient Israel have universal significance and yet retain their linkage to the particular practices of the Jewish people? Philo's writings can encourage Christians to appreciate the particularity of halachah and interpretation emphasized by Jews, while encouraging Jews to appreciate the universality of the divine encounter with the human emphasized by Christians. To study Philo and the complex story of his reception by Jews and Christians is at the same time to reflect on the relationship between two intimately separate traditions.[3]

Postmodern Hermeneutics and Jewish–Christian Dialogue: A Case Study

GEORGE LINDBECK

Christians and Jews continue to differ over scriptural interpretation but not, fortunately, with the aggressive and defensive bitterness they once deployed. Michael Signer's account of the two traditions is as acceptable to Christians as I assume it is to Jews. There is to my knowledge no better brief sketch of the last two thousand odd years of biblical hermeneutics, and I shall adopt it as the historical springboard for the musings that follow.

The Question

Signer concludes that Jews and Christians can agree on two areas of interpretation. First, in reference to the letter of the text, Jews and Christians can agree on "the historical meaning of the biblical passage in its biblical context." Second, in regard to the spirit of the text, their accord can extend to "the moral [or tropological] sense that presents models of ethical behavior." Regarding the two other spiritual senses, however—the allegorical (now more often called the typological) and the mystical (cf. devotional)—Signer concludes the Jews and Christians will not arrive at agreement; indeed, in the case of the mystical (or devotional) sense in particular, the "intimate symbolism of each tradition excludes the possibility of the other . . . [and thus] precludes agreement."

These are historically sound Enlightenment generalizations, and they provide a way of summarizing the strengths and weaknesses of modern methods of deflating interpretive conflicts. On the positive side, these modern methods enable us to agree on the literal sense of the text to the extent that this is possible. These methods, like premodern methods, also allow some agreement on the moral sense. On the negative side, however, they say nothing about the allegorical and mystical meanings through which scriptural realities become present to the faithful here and now. Allegorical and mystical meanings are nonexistent for the disenchanted modern world; so also, therefore, are religiously significant Jewish and Christian disagreements. Modernity, one might say, creates a religious desert and calls it religious peace.

Historical-critical methods are not in themselves the problem. These methods as increasingly practiced since the days of Richard Simon and Baruch Spinoza have played an indispensable role in freeing Christian and Jewish biblical studies from premodern prejudices and polemics (although these have often been supplanted by modern ones). Without these newer studies, the intense Jewishness of Jesus and Paul, for example, would be as invisible to Christians in our day as it was in patristic times, and the official mea culpa of the churches for Christian anti-Semitism, inadequate though they are in some respects, would be unthinkable. Critical history is one modern achievement that cannot be jettisoned in any postmodern era worth entering.

But can critical history survive if modern certainties crumble and are replaced by postmodern doubts? I do not want to tackle this question, but I want to emphasize that criticism is most effective when it appeals not to universal norms but to specific, concrete, and local standards of the particular communities for which and in which the work is being done. This basic understanding, which is fundamental to what is called "Anglo-American postmodernism," frees Jews and Christians to retrieve precritical interpretive strategies without rejecting critical ones. Once it is stripped of the modernist pretension to universal truth and objectivity, historical criticism can correct each community's understanding of the plain sense of the Bible without dictating it. Each community should make its own selection from among all available historical-critical, commonsensical, and spiritual readings. Premodern distortions led modern readers to reject all the old communal readings—a religiously suicidal instance of throwing the baby out with the dirty bath water. Can the baby be rescued? Is it possible in contemporary circumstances for critically retrieved classical biblical hermeneutics to retain enough of their ancient power to sustain and enliven communities of faith? Only the future can tell, but there are reasons for hope.

To illustrate what I am saying, I will concentrate on one premodern reading that I would retrieve in a corrected form: the church's understanding of itself as Israel. Can we bring back a nonsupersessionist understanding of the church as Israel? To a large extent, Christian discourse employs Jewish terminology and concepts. And the way Christians understand Judaism has influenced every aspect of what they read or do not read in the Bible. Judaism has had no comparable impact on Christianity. As Paul puts it in Romans 11, Israel is the tree, and the Gentile church is an engrafted branch. Changes in the way Christians conceive Judaism necessarily influence their understanding of the Bible and of their religious identity, whereas Jews can reconceive Christianity without in the least altering what they think theologically of themselves or their Scriptures. Perhaps this asymmetry will become less pronounced in the postmodern future that this essay speculatively probes, but that is a question for Jews to explore. The task for Christians is to ask whether and how the correction of a long-eclipsed understanding of the church can and should lead to its retrieval and to a correspondingly rectified postmodern hermeneutic.

Hermeneutical Consequences

It was inevitable that early Christians thought of themselves as Israel. After all, it was generations after Christ before the church formed a New Testament canon; until then, its authoritative text was the one it shared with the synagogue. Christians and Jews both lived imaginatively within the textually projected and all-embracing cosmic drama of which God was both creator and chief protagonist and in which Israel played the second lead. That drama was interpreted by Christians through the orally transmitted memories of Jesus and his teachings, and through the rituals, especially baptism and Eucharist, that celebrated his life, death, and resurrection; but it was the pre-Christian Scriptures that supplied the basic plot and content of this drama.

Christians would have had no distinctive identity without the Old Testament. It was the need to articulate who and what Jesus was and who they were as his followers that led even Gentile Christians to claim to be Israel, rightful interpreters of what for them was the only written Word of God.

An example of the use of the Old Testament may help. The New Testament tells Christians to baptize but says little about why baptism, and not some other ritual, serves as their initiation into the faith. Patristic writers, building on hints in the New Testament, undertake to fill the gap by utilizing Old Testament materials. Thus to be baptized is, among other things, to pass through the Red Sea waters that are perpetually present in the baptismal font and to participate in the dying and rising of Christ, the Passover lamb, whose blood shielded the children of Israelites from death in Egypt just as it now shields Christians. Later, Aquinas said that circumcision communicates the same grace as baptism; both rituals are prefigurations that God uses to create the same reality. Thus what happened to Israel in Abraham's call and circumcision and in the Exodus from Egypt happens to the church, and what happens to the church in Christ happened to Israel. The Old Testament's contribution to the church's understanding of baptism is fundamental; without it, for instance, it is hard to see how the baptism of infants could have become universal: there are no explicit New Testament precedents.

Conversely, when Christians after the sixteenth century increasingly replaced the Old with the New Testament as the main source for understanding church and sacraments, the proportion of those who practiced infant baptism declined, and those who denied the validity of infant baptism increased. Adult baptism now accounts for perhaps half of all baptisms among present-day Protestants, and it is making great inroads, especially through Pentecostalism, in historically Roman Catholic and Eastern Orthodox populations. Furthermore, neither those who practice infant baptism nor those who baptize only adults think of the church as Israel. Modernity has changed the way people think of the church, and as a result infant baptism has become a familial or social affair instead of a public, community-creating event.

Losing the image of the church as Israel destroys the self-image of the church as a community chosen by God. However, retrieving this image cannot, by itself, restore the church's sense of community. The prevailing ethos of American culture is individualistic, and churches have thus become voluntary societies of like-minded individuals. Such "communities" are too weak to support the adoption of the biblical image of the church as Israel. Nonetheless, the loss of this image has had enormous consequences, ranging from failures to act to utter disasters. Bringing back the image of the church as Israel may repair these failures and block future disasters.

Among the failures is the fact that the renewal of the Old Testament's prophetic concern for justice in the movement known as the Social Gospel neglected the church itself. In this movement, churches viewed themselves as instrumental to the struggle for reform in the wider society and paid little attention to their own communal welfare. This weakened the liberal mainline denominations, which were the leaders in the struggle for social reform. Their activist members focused on what they could do for society and tended to treat the church as a disposable means to a higher end.

A more poignant failure is the ecclesial weakness of African American Christians who, starting in the days of antebellum slavery, lived imaginatively in a world shaped by biblical stories drawn largely from the Old Testament. They came to experience themselves as Israel in Egypt and in the Exodus and outside the walls of Jericho; this experience continues to inform their sense of community but not their theological understanding of their church life. African American Christians have capitulated to the individualistic religiosity of most Americans and see nothing wrong with choosing membership in the church that best suits their felt needs.

In addition to preventing such failures and reclaiming the corporate character of baptism, what other consequences follow when the church appropriates the identity of Israel without expropriating it? First and most fundamentally, the church is delivered from the triumphalism that follows from its expropriation. When the church "expropriates the identity of Israel" it replaces the Jews as Israel; when the church "appropriates the identity of Israel," it claims to be Israel without replacing the Jews. Christians who expropriate the identity of Israel assume that to remain in covenant with God, Israel must be without fundamental error. They conclude that because Israel was errant, it was not worthy of being God's covenant partner. God consequently transferred all of God's promises to the church. In the expropriator's view, therefore, it was Israel's sin that made God revoke the covenant. But if the church is to endure until the end of ages, as the New Testament promises, it must be incapable of comparable unfaithfulness; it must be truthful and holy in a way that Israel was not. The error in this view is the conviction, essential to supersessionism, that God's patience is exhaustible and his covenant conditional. The Bible itself corrects the error of expropriation, for it informs us that God keeps his promises no matter how errant his people. For good reason, then, Paul argued that God's covenant with the Jews is unconditional, as Christians are now increasingly willing to grant. But if we apply Paul's argument to the church, then the covenant between God and the church as Israel is also unconditional, and the logic of supersessionism—and of a wide range of other triumphalisms to which Christendom has been vulnerable—falters.

A second hermeneutical consequence of Christians appropriating Israel's Scriptures without expropriating them is the notion that God speaks, so to speak, bivocally through the same text: the Old Testament for Christians and the Tanach for Jews. As a matter of principle, historical-critical scholarship ignores the possibility that the Bible has multiple meanings. This scholarship focuses narrowly on what the Bible meant for its original author and audience. But, within a given communal tradition, the concept of multiple meanings is both traditional and commonsensical. Trading on the familiar idea that the literal sense is what the author intends, Aquinas points out that God in his omniscience might very well intend a given passage to mean different things in different times and places, and if so, it has multiple literal meanings. Common sense can arrive at a similar conclusion without appealing to omniscience. When a mother says to her assembled family, "You know I love each one of you," she does not communicate a general truth but a number of incompatible meanings calling for distinct physical, verbal, and emotional responses. The husband does not hear the words as do the children, nor the five-year-old as does the twenty-year-old, and yet each may rightly understand what the mother and wife intend. This elementary point makes easier the notion of communal bivocality, as I have called it: God may intend Jews and Christians to hear very different messages through one and the same text.

What, however, if God's Words to Jews and Christians are not only different but also contradictory? The conviction that God speaks bivocally through one and same sacred text—interpreted by the Oral Torah and New Testament, respectively—does not resolve all problems. Perhaps the most acute conflict at present is between the apparently exceptionless New Testament command "to make disciples of all the nations" (Mt. 28:19) and the Jewish conviction that missions to the Jews are inescapably supersessionist: they imply in practice, whatever the theological theory, that the covenant with Israel has been revoked and that the endurance of Torah-observant Judaism until the end of history as a witness and blessing to all nations is not willed by God. Confronted by this conflict, increasing numbers of Christians agree that two millennia of survival sustained by the Oral Torah in the midst of hostile Christendom enables Jews to hear God's Word and will about Israel's survival better than Christians can, unless they are willing to listen together with Jews. Even some missionary-minded Christians ask whether the Great Commission, as they call it, is utterly exceptionless as far as the Jews are concerned. Perhaps God's normal call to them in our day is first and above all to be good Jews for the sake of their people's flourishing; if so, then the church must take care, as did Gamaliel in the New Testament, not to contradict God's will (cf. Acts 5:33–39).

Finally, the appropriation of Israelhood without expropriation would enlarge the deep though incomplete spiritual sharing of specifically mystical or devotional readings of the Bible that shape personal spirituality. For Michael Signer, these are the least sharable of all the scriptural senses. Perhaps this is truer for Jews than for Christians. There is scarcely anything in the Jewish liturgy that Christians cannot sing and pray in the confidence that Jesus and Paul could have done the same. Indeed, Protestants not infrequently say that they are more at home in synagogue services than in Roman Catholic services, where they find themselves spiritually alienated by the scriptural interpretations embedded in prayers to Mary and in the veneration of the saints. It would be strange if Trinitarian and Christ-centered devotions were not at least equally disconcerting to Jews; but familiarity and friendship can overcome antipathies even when disagreements remain, as many Christian readers of Abraham Heschel (and of scholars such as Moshe Greenberg) can testify.

Hermeneutical rapprochement has its dangers because Scripture is central to both Judaism and Christianity. The erosion of distinctly Jewish and Christian interpretations cannot help but weaken each community's identity and power, resulting in a tastelessly lukewarm Judeo-Christian tradition good for nothing except to be spewed out, as the Book of Revelation says of the church at Laodicea. It was something like this weakening of identity that John Chrysostom feared when he preached his anti-Jewish diatribes in fourth-century Antioch:

his Gentile flock found Judaism so much like Christianity that they cheerfully thronged the synagogues on festive occasions. Nowadays it is Jews who fight assimilation, and rightly so. The imperative of survival is a corollary of the unbroken covenant, and it is an imperative that rests also on Christians.

6

COMMANDMENT

Mitsvah

DAVID NOVAK

Legalism and Antinomianism

For too long, many Jews and Christians have assumed an essential impasse between Judaism and Christianity over what Jews call *mitsvah* (commandment) and Christians call "the law" (Greek: *ho nomos*).[1] Many Christians have assumed that in Judaism the successful keeping of the commandments of the Torah automatically leads to salvation, to full reconciliation with God in the world to come. Some Christians refer to this view as "Jewish legalism" and criticize it as "works righteousness," the idea that human beings themselves, by successfully keeping all of God's law, can effect their own salvation. This charge of legalism seems to divinize human achievement and comes very close to the claim that Judaism is idolatrous, making "their fear of Me like a human commandment learned by rote" (Is. 29:13). To this charge, many Jews have responded with the countercharge that Christians have rejected the law of God in favor of a human creation, the church; Jews have even concluded that Christian law and worship are idolatrous.[2]

Charges of "idolatry," even if only by connotation, prevent any empathetic appreciation of another religious tradition; they kill the dialogue before it begins. When Christians stop seeing Judaism as legalism, they will be in a much better position to realize the importance of law in Christianity. And when Jews stop seeing Christianity as antinomian, as against the law, they will be in a much better position to realize the importance of grace in Judaism. Indeed, such understanding of each side by the other might lead each tradition not only to a better understanding of the other but to a better understanding of itself. Jewish–Christian dialogue is more than just externally directed apologetics.

When Christians drop the charge of legalism, they can see that the Jewish devotion to the commandments of the Torah, including our ongoing tradition of interpretation and application, is not a replacement of the work of God by the works of humans.[3] The very need for forgiveness of and atonement for sins shows that by keeping the commandments we participate in a larger cosmic reality, which human effort alone neither has initiated nor will complete. We are grateful to God for allowing the people of Israel, by keeping the *mitsvot*, to become his junior partners in the full work of creation. "I am the first and I am the last, and there is no God other than Me" (Is. 44:6).[4]

Of course, Christians are still justified in questioning whether this Jewish keeping of the *mitsvot* is adequate as the highest and most complete worship of the Lord God of Israel. Christians make a rival claim about the best worship of the God who stated about Himself, "I am the Lord your God, who took you out of the land of Egypt, out of the house of bondage" (Ex. 20:2).[5] Their claim centers not on keeping the commandments of the Torah but on imitating the life, death, and resurrection of Jesus of Nazareth. But even when making their rival claim, Christians should recognize that Jewish piety in keeping the *mitsvot* as ordered by the legal system called *halachah* can be, for Christians, a lesser but legitimate mode of piety. When Christians overcome the false charge of Jewish legalism, they can begin to move away from antinomian temptations. Christian questioning of the sufficiency of "the law" is not a rejection of law per se; instead, it is only the question of what the true content of the law of God is. And since the content of the law can be known and practiced only in the context of a real historical community, keeping the law is a matter of choosing within which community, Jewish or Christian, one is to hear the commandments of the Lord God of Israel.

The great divide between Judaism and Christianity does not revolve around whether law is or is not part of the relationship with God. Instead, it is better to say that the need for law, which is the keeping of the commandments of the Lord God of Israel, is what is common to both Judaism and Christianity. How could the Lord God of Israel, the creator of heaven and earth, whom both Jews and Christians worship, not command us? Is not every act in relation to this God a response to one kind of commandment or another? Is not our relationship with this God a covenant? And is not a covenant a political reality? And could there be any polity not governed by law? So, *the* divide between us is not over law per se. The divide is over *what* those immutable commandments are, and this *what* depends on *when* and *where* one hears them and *how* one is to do them.

Antinomianism is as much a distortion of Christianity as legalism is a distortion of Judaism. Christians can no more be antinomian than Jews can be legalistic with theological cogency. At the key point of human action, both of these extremes replace the divine with the human. Legalism errs by placing the kingdom of God in human hands; antinomianism, accompanied as it is by radical individualism, errs by denying the kingdom altogether. The rabbis saw antinomianism at the heart of the rejection of God's authority. The antinomian individual lives in a morally absurd universe, acting as if "there were no law *(din)* and no judge *(dayan)*."[6] He or she is the immoral "fool *(naval)* who says in his [or her] heart there is no judging God *(elohim)*" (Ps. 53:2). The task for Jews who wish to appreciate Christianity authentically is to understand how Christian lawfulness is consistent with, but not subordinate to, Jewish lawfulness.

Noahide Law

From rabbinic times on, Jews have developed a rubric for dealing with the issue of Gentile lawfulness. That rubric is the concept of the "seven commandments of the children of Noah": (1) the mandate for a society to set up courts of justice; (2) the prohibition of blasphemy; (3) the prohibition of idolatry; (4) the prohibition of killing innocent human life; (5) the prohibition of the sexual practices of incest, adultery, homosexuality, and bestiality; (6) the prohibition of robbery; (7) the prohibition of tearing a limb from a living animal for food. These commandments are addressed to the "Noahides" *(benei Noah)*—that is, all humankind, who after the flood are the descendants of Noah—

and they are discussed in many places in rabbinic and post-rabbinic writings.[7] In one way or another, all of these commandments are based on Scripture, and it is important to note that according to tradition, the three most central commandments are the prohibitions against idolatry, killing innocent human life, and sexual immorality.[8] These three prohibitions admit of no exceptions, and a Jew is to die as a martyr rather than transgress them; they are the sine qua non of Judaism and, as far as Judaism is concerned, of Gentile existence as well.[9] These three laws can never be violated, even to save one's own life, and they are the most fundamental of all commonalities between Judaism and any Gentile tradition on earth.

Since Christians base their morality on the Scripture they call the "Old Testament," and since the Noahide laws are found in this Scripture, Christians are the most likely candidates for the category of "Noahides." In fact, when Maimonides designates those Gentiles whom he considers worthy to join "all Israel" in the world to come, he specifies that they are those who "accept and practice them [the Noahide laws] because God commanded them in the Torah and let us know through Moses our master that the children of Noah were commanded concerning them beforehand."[10] It could very well be that only Christians fit this description. They have the only non-Jewish tradition that sees its morality as fundamentally biblical in origin. Maimonides (and others) also regard these laws as rationally discernible; however, even though other Gentiles can thus live a moral life that is consistent with what Jews regard to be minimal non-Jewish morality, one could very well say that Christians are the only Gentiles who are part of the transcendent trajectory Jews see as the ultimate end of all human striving, striving that begins with devotion to justice in this world.

Some Jewish and Christian advocates of a richer Jewish–Christian relationship are wary of the concept of the Noahide. They see the concept and its accompanying commandments as much too minimal in scope and depth to account for the richness of the commonalities and parallels between Judaism and Christianity.[11] However, these concerns miss the point of this rabbinic innovation. The rabbis regarded the Noahide laws as the necessary but not sufficient condition for any human community to be considered as living according to divine law. Granted, Noahide law is too "thin" to constitute the "thickness" of a historical tradition like Judaism or Christianity. No human community could live by Noahide law alone; on the other hand, no human community is worthy of the loyalty of humans created in the image of God who does not affirm it.

The best way to see this point is to look at how the rabbis dealt with Gentile idolatry. The rabbis defined a Noahide *(ben Noah)* as a Gentile who has discovered that the prohibition against idolatry is universal in scope and that, therefore, Gentiles as well as Jews, at least in principle, are obligated to uphold it. It is quite clear that the rabbis' main concern was whether any Gentile they confronted was or was not an idolater. In fact, in later versions of rabbinic texts, Gentiles who are penalized in one way or another according to Jewish law are generically termed "idolaters" *(ovdei avodah zarah)*.[12] It seems that the rabbis thought that once idolatry had been rejected by Gentiles, acceptance of the other moral laws would follow inevitably. Conversely, it also seems that when the rabbis saw Gentile respect for the other Noahide laws, especially the respect for human life involved in the prohibition of bloodshed, they had a tendency to regard any cultural vestiges of idolatry in such societies quite leniently. This leniency indicates the close relation Jews have always seen between theology and ethics. Theology entails ethics, since ethics presupposes theology in any monotheistic system based in revelation (namely, Judaism, Christianity, and Islam).

To link ethics so closely to theology and theology to revelation might seem to undermine the universal character of the Noahide law. It can apply only to those who have received the revelation. In fact, however, the Noahide law is natural law and is thus available to everyone. The Noahide law applies to all humankind, to all those deemed to partake of human nature, who are the descendants of the first man and the first woman.[13] Those who think Noahide law is natural law, not only because of its universal scope but because of its universal accessibility to human reason, hold that it can be known when human beings truly ponder what it means to be human and what makes a society worthy of the loyalty of the human beings who compose it. In this Jewish point of view, with which I identify, the revelation of basic moral law in Scripture is a confirmation and deepening of natural law. Nevertheless, neither natural law as God's general revelation to all humankind through reason, nor scriptural law as God's special revelation to Israel through history, are products of human reason. The humanly inhabited world is the most general political context of Noahide law, a context that includes some basic recognition of God as sovereign. Only a sovereign can make law that is to be obeyed by his subjects.

The idea that all law is divine law in essence, with human law as its interpretation and application, seems to involve a notion of divine kingship, however remote that king is before covenantal revelation occurs.

Jews can very well see in Christians those human beings outside the people of Israel who have understood the truths of the Noahide commandments best. I think a natural law perspective best explains the normative commonalities between Judaism and Christianity, but one can still recognize these commonalities even if one assumes that moral law must be originally located in special revelation and a tradition that passes on its content.[14] A community that sees the authority of the Lord God, maker of heaven and earth, as supreme, which is a community having a cosmic intention, is a community with which Jews share a common understanding of the essence of law.[15] And when recognition of God's supremacy includes respect for the historical claims of the Jewish people and for the cosmic significance of these claims, then there is additional commonality. For Christians, for whom the Lord God, maker of heaven and earth, is manifest as the Lord God of Israel, the historical claims of the Jewish people are more readily acceptable than they are for anyone else.

The Partial Torah and the Impossibility of a Jewish–Christian Polity

Both Jews and Christians can agree that Christianity has appropriated only part of the law of the Torah for itself, the part that includes the moral law of the Torah in general, including basic obligations of love and respect first to God and then to fellow humans.[16] The part of the Torah not appropriated by Christianity has consisted of those commandments that are addressed to the people of Israel in their very separateness, such as the purity laws pertaining to diet, dress, and marital relations. It also includes those practices like Passover that celebrate pre-messianic events in the life of the people of Israel. The church has replaced these commandments with the sacraments that celebrate the life, death, and resurrection of Jesus.[17] Here the church seems to have based itself on an ancient Jewish belief that when the Messiah comes, the more ethnically specific parts of the Torah will have already fulfilled their function and thus be overcome, that is, no longer binding on Israel of the new (better, renewed) covenant *(brit chadashah)*.[18] Perhaps because of its use by Christianity in its separation from Judaism,

Jews suppressed the notion that the "ritual" commandments will be abrogated in the messianic age.[19] In fact, Maimonides states that the prime function of the Messiah, when he comes, will be to reestablish the full hegemony of all the laws of the Torah, even though Gentiles need not accept any of these laws but the Noahide commandments.[20]

Even the appropriation of part of the law of the Torah has not been without debate in the history of Christianity. Very early in Christian history, the monk Marcion advocated a total break with the Jewish legacy of the church and thus with Jewish law. The fact that Marcionism was declared the very first heresy by the early church itself indicates that despite its ultimate differences with Judaism, the church did not want to break away from its Jewish origins and its partial connection to Jewish law, at least in its scriptural core, the Ten Commandments.[21] Thus whenever Christians have had to consider what a Christian polity would actually be like, they have had to return to the law of the Old Testament, and Christian scholars have frequently sought out Jewish interpretations of scriptural law for their own enlightenment. Even today, when most Jews and Christians have accepted the necessity of a secular polity, Jews and Christians, because of that part of the Torah they share, have discovered important commonalities in their attempts to influence moral and political issues.

The key Jewish problem with Christian acceptance of the law has been that it seems partial and selective. In fact, one of the reasons the reading of the Ten Commandments is no longer a feature of the daily Jewish liturgy (although they are still read within the full cycle of scriptural readings in the synagogue) has to do with the "charges of the sectarians" *(minim)*. These charges are that "only the Ten Commandments were given at Sinai."[22] Even though the meaning of "sectarians" is often unclear, it seems that in this talmudic discussion the rabbis had the Jewish Christians in mind. The rabbis offer this diminution of the full range of the binding norms of the Torah as the prime reason for their rejection of the Christianity of these Jewish Christians as an acceptable form of Judaism itself. For Christians, of course, their treatment of the Torah is not a diminution of God's law inasmuch as it is an indication that the Old Law was only a temporal preparation for the full law of God revealed in the New Law of the New Covenant. At this point, anyway, there seems to be an unbridgeable gap between what Jews see as partialness and what Christians see as fulfillment.

Nevertheless, the possibility of getting beyond this impasse depends on the essential status of the Christian community, the church itself, in

Jewish eyes. When the church (Greek: *ekklesia*) was a predominantly Jewish community made up of persons whom the rabbis had to consider bona fide Jews plus some questionable converts, the rabbis had to deem the Christian attitude toward the Torah an unacceptable deviation from Judaism by a group of Jewish sectarians. However, when the church soon became an essentially Gentile community, such was not the case. There is a fundamental difference between a group of Jews lessening the number of the commandments of the Torah they consider binding on themselves and a group of Gentiles adopting some of the commandments of the Torah as binding on themselves, especially those commandments of the Torah the Jewish tradition considers binding on both Jews and Gentiles universally, here and now.[23]

Jews began to deliberate about Christian lawfulness in the Middle Ages, by which time the church was an undeniably Gentile community both by her own criteria and by the criteria of Judaism. From the Jewish perspective, Gentiles moving *away* from zero lawfulness, upward, are quite different from Jews moving *toward* zero lawfulness, downward. The former group is to be encouraged; the latter group is to be discouraged. That is why the rabbis criticized the Jewish Christians but later assigned Gentile Christians a valid status. Jews who practice Christianity are apostates *(meshumadim)*, but not so for Gentiles. To employ a metaphor, the difference between Jewish Christians and Gentile Christians is like the difference between seeing a glass as half empty or half full. It depends on who is drinking from the glass. Is it someone who once had more and has now taken less, or is it someone who had less and has now taken more?[24]

Despite certain legal commonalities between Judaism and Christianity, Jews and Christians cannot establish a joint Jewish–Christian community as any kind of political order. Such a political order would inevitably entail the unacceptable subordination of one community to the other. Jews and Christians cannot both compose the people *Israel* in a cogent way. That is why I think the legal commonalities between Judaism and Christianity are best negotiated and developed in secular political space, where both Jews and Christians are struggling to survive in similar ways for similar reasons and where neither community can seize political power for itself. In a secular polity, Jews and Christians can display their legal commonalities in the form of moral guidance in a realm where they and everybody else are equal. To see the problem with establishing a joint Jewish-Christian community, we can look to ancient Israel.

From a Jewish perspective, the only way Christians could live in a Jewish polity, governed by Jewish law, would be in sort of resident alien status, a status held by one whom Scripture calls "the sojourner in the city" (Ex. 20:10) and whom the rabbis called the *ger toshav*. In ancient Israel, these tolerated Gentiles lived under Jewish rule with definite rights and responsibilities; they were both subjects and objects of a definite segment of Jewish law, that is, there were laws these Gentiles had to keep when living with the Jews and there were laws that Jews had to keep when living with them. However, there was no doubt at any time that these Gentiles were a subordinate group of second-class citizens. Jews themselves could well recognize the meaning of such a compromised status since they often had to make the same type of arrangements with the Gentile societies that tolerated them. But such arrangements are the result of political necessity rather than any sort of desideratum. Neither Jews nor Christians can cogently desire to be "sojourners" in each other's house, even if that is the best the other community can do for them in good faith.

This is the problem with Paul's famous metaphor of the church as "the branch grafted onto the tree" (Rom. 11:17–24). The metaphor would be apt if Christians (Gentile Christians, that is) simply regarded themselves as a group subordinate to the Jews because of their adoption of some of Jewish law, indeed, that segment of Jewish law that also pertains to the Gentiles. But the fact is that Christians have regarded themselves as a community that has superseded the Jews.[25] And even if that supersessionism (consistent with Paul's refusal to give up on the Jews in his view of Israel) does not reject the Jews from being forever *part of* Israel, it still has to assert two things: one, the Jews are no longer solely identical with Israel; two, the church has the more authentic definition of Israel. To bring Paul's ancient agricultural metaphor up to date with a modern urban one: even if the suburbs of the new settlers do not displace the old inner city altogether, they certainly displace its normative centrality in the urban scheme of things.[26] Needless to say, no Jew who is loyal to Judaism could possibly accept such a subordinate role for Judaism with any Jewish authenticity. That is why there are hardly any Jews who would look forward to a return of "Christendom" in any form whatsoever.[27] And, of course, Christians would have as hard a time with the political privileging of Judaism as Jews have had with the political privileging of Christianity.

Jewish and Christian Law

It is better to see the normative commonalities between Judaism and Christianity as a matter of significant overlappings between two separate communities than as mere denominational differences within one overarching community, like party differences within one democratic polity. *This view preserves the truth that the difference of Judaism from Christianity and Christianity from Judaism is still greater than any commonalities the two communities now share.* To see greater commonality than difference would surely supply the rationale for the assimilation of the weaker party by the stronger, a kind of theological "survival of the fittest." The fact that Christianity succeeds Judaism historically and that it has been much more politically successful than Judaism would give Christianity a decided edge in any sort of communal identity. Christianity can absorb Judaism (and has attempted to do so repeatedly) in a way that Judaism cannot absorb Christianity.

The logic of overlapping, on the other hand, provides a more even playing field for the new encounter between Judaism and Christianity.[28] There need not be prior agreement on first principles or agreement on final conclusions. The recognition of commonalities can lead to the subsequent enunciation of principles, although final agreement on first principles is beyond the grasp of human intelligence here and now. As for final conclusions, they are still only tentative insofar as they are still hidden behind an eschatological horizon. Only when we know the end will we thereby know the beginning. Law and commandments are especially well suited to be the subject of this new relationship between Jews and Christians because they lie in between the foundations that are their source and the goal that is their final intention: the kingdom of God. The process of recognizing and developing these partial commonalities takes two forms.

First, the recognition of normative commonalities is located in the broad area of ethics: the proper structure of human relationships. Here the common reliance on the Hebrew Bible—the *Tanach* or the Old Testament—is most evident. It is not a matter of adjudicating cases of moral difficulty according to biblical law as much as it is a matter of discovering the underlying principles of scriptural judgments concerning human personhood and human community. We can begin to undertake this discovery by returning to the three most basic Noahide laws (or, better, normative categories): the prohibitions of idolatry, bloodshed, and sexual immorality.

Jews and Christians need to be especially sensitive to the manifestations of idolatry in our time. Although a universal ethics cannot prove the existence of God, much less constitute what the human relationship with God is to consist of, it must still argue against those modern ideologies of absolutized individuals or absolutized collectives that by definition, be it by their explicit or implicit atheism, make no room for any relationship with the Lord God, creator of heaven and earth.[29] It is no accident that the most prominent of these ideologies, communism and fascism, have directed their particular attacks on Judaism or Christianity or both. It is also no accident that doctrinaire liberal secularism, although it has not been the basis of the sort of atrocities committed by communism and fascism, has been almost as hostile to Judaism and Christianity, at least in principle. It is the ethical task of Jews and Christians together to secure religious liberty as the most basic of all rights in a secular society and to proclaim that the denial or belittling of the human quest for God entails an assault on human dignity and destiny.

Regarding bloodshed, Jews and Christians need to work together for the broadest possible definition of human personhood in order to include everyone genetically human within the prohibition of homicide. As long as there is some agreement about the uniqueness of human personhood, it is hard to argue for homicide per se; thus those who have in fact advocated homicide have had to preclude certain segments of humankind from the category of human personhood. They have argued for what they consider the killing of less than human life. But for Judaism and Christianity, anyone descended of human parents, who is thereby descended from the original human couple, is made in the image of God and, hence, the object of special protection and care. Anything less than this definition of humanness/humankind is based on only some features of the human condition, arbitrarily selected by those humans having power over other humans. Ultimately, the criterion of selection turns out to be racism of one form or another. Jews and Christians must become the advocates and protectors of all those who could easily be precluded from human personhood when its essence is taken to be something less than the image of God.[30]

Regarding sexual immorality, Judaism and Christianity must teach that certain acts are universally prohibited (incest, adultery, homosexuality, and bestiality)—all for the sake of the traditional family as the core of authentic human community and the arena for acceptable sexuality. Jews and Christians need to be advocates of family life in the face of an unprecedented assault on sexual morality, one that sees sexuality as a private preference between consenting adults or as a matter of irresistible physical desire. Both of these views render sexuality per se amoral: the former by denying it universality; the latter by denying it freedom of choice.[31] Traditional Christian moral teaching on sexuality has remained faithful to its Jewish roots and has insisted that sexuality is legitimate only within the confines of the marital covenant.[32]

The recognition of these ethical overlaps provides a starting point for a new relationship between Jews and Christians. There is, however, a second way that Jews and Christians can begin to recognize and develop their partial commonalities. In this case, the task involves seeing analogies rather than making simple identifications. These analogies are mostly in the area of cult and ritual, in what the Jewish tradition calls the area "between humans and God." Here the commonalities involve those acts that have God as their direct object, like prayer and worship.[33] In this arena, Jews and Christians cannot develop a common life without one side capitulating to the other or without sliding into syncretism. Nevertheless, we Jews and Christians can still learn something from each other's "religious" beliefs and practices, something that goes far beyond the discovery of "interesting" similarities and differences between Judaism and Christianity. Such superficial similarities can be found between any two religions or philosophies. Jews and Christians, on the other hand, can learn much from each other, even up to the point of empathy, because our religious ways of life are both developments of God's covenant with Israel. Throughout our historical interaction, Christians have learned significant things from Jewish piety and Jews have learned significant things from Christian piety. That is because we have been commanded by the same God. Thus it is the centrality of the *mitsvah* to us both that offers the greatest content and the greatest hope for our relationship in this world and the next.

Another Jewish View of Ethics, Christian and Jewish

ELLIOT N. DORFF

Professor Novak and I share a commitment to the Jewish tradition and to Jewish–Christian dialogue, not only in conviction but through many and diverse activities in our lives. We understand the Jewish tradition somewhat differently, though, and that leads us to some differences in how we understand both Jewish ethics and also Christian ethics from a Jewish point of view.

Belief and Practice

Let me begin with a point that we share. Professor Novak is certainly right when he calls on Christians to stop looking at Judaism as legalistic (hypernomianism) and at Christianity as lacking in law altogether (antinomianism). Or, put another way, it is a mistake to assume that Jews are concerned with practice and not belief, whereas Christians are concerned with belief but not practice. Both Judaism and Christianity, in all their forms, affirm various beliefs and practices, and to focus abstractly on "the Law" and ignore Jewish beliefs or Christian practices is to distort the reality of those two faiths in the past and present.

However, the relative emphasis placed on belief and practice within the two religions is different: Judaism goes to great lengths to define proper behavior in both ritual and moral aspects of life and lets the beliefs emerge from the practice, whereas Christianity takes pains to define proper beliefs and lets the practice that is appropriate to one who holds such beliefs remain largely undefined.

Judaism does affirm a set of beliefs; but Judaism has not insisted that practicing Jews affirm a particular formulation of those beliefs. Instead, within certain wide bounds, the tradition assumes that each individual will respond to Judaism's intricate weave of actions, stories, study, and community in his or her own unique way. The Torah, by the tradition's count, includes 613 commandments, and, with the possible exception of the first of the Ten Commandments, not a single one demands that we *believe* or *deny* something; they all instead require that we *do* something or *refrain from doing* something. Moreover, although some medieval Jewish thinkers, largely under Christian influence, proposed a variety of articulations of fundamental Jewish beliefs, none of those formulations attained the status of becoming an authoritative definition of who is, and who is not, a Jew; instead, Jews, in a mode typical of us, pounced on each of the proposals with criticism, questions, and proposed changes. In contrast, Christianity has taken its creeds very seriously, sometimes to the point of heresy trials and even wars.

When we turn from Jewish belief to Christian practice, we see that the New Testament is clear that faith must bear fruits in action if the faith is to be considered powerful and real: "What good is it to profess faith without practicing it? Such faith has no power to save one, has it? If a brother or sister has nothing to wear and no food for the day and you say to them, 'Good-bye and good luck! Keep warm and well fed,' but do not meet their bodily needs, what good is that? Faith is like that: if good works do not go with it, it is quite dead" (Jam. 2:14–17). Moreover, many Christian denominations have enunciated at least a few specific practices that Christian belief, as they see it, requires. Thus Catholics, in living out their faith, are supposed to eschew artificial means of birth control and abortion; Southern Baptists are prohibited from drinking alcohol, and Mormons add caffeine to that ban; Quakers are supposed to refrain from war at all costs; and, positively, all forms of Christianity urge followers to model their lives after Jesus, including his love, kindness, and charity. On a social level, this imitation of Jesus has led many denominations to establish hospitals and social service agencies. With all that, though, an old Christian doctrine dating from the New Testament maintains that salvation is by faith and *not* by works.[1]

In contrast to this traditional Christian doctrine, biblical and rabbinic passages routinely demand that Jews obey God's commandments, and God, according to those texts, rewards us for adhering to those commandments and punishes us for violating them.[2] There are some beliefs, of course, very near the surface of these commandments. Most especially, we are to shun idolatry, for Israel is to worship only the one, "jealous" God rather than go whoring after false gods. The Jews of antiquity were also to hold the Torah up as the binding, authoritative revelation of God and to deny the legitimacy of any prophets after the closing of the canon of the Hebrew Bible; of course, this denial undermined the prophetic status of Jesus and Mohammed.[3] But Jews are not held to any specific formulation of the belief in God, revelation, or the world to come and, in fact, have historically embraced many versions of those beliefs.

On the other hand, the demands of Jewish practice are spelled out in detail, and even though communities might vary somewhat in how they carry out those demands, ultimately the Bible and Talmud make clear that God's judgment of us focuses primarily on what we do. Thus the prophets castigated the Israelites, who were to be God's model people, for aggravating rather than alleviating the plight of the poor, widows, and orphans and for living their lives unjustly—as well as for engaging in the practices of idolatry.[4] In justly famous passages, Micah and the psalmist summarize what God really wants of us—actions that bespeak our faith in God:

He has told you, O man, what is good, and what the Lord requires of you: Only to do justice, and to love mercy, and to walk modestly with your God.

Who is the man who is eager for life, and who desires years of good fortune? Guard your tongue from evil, your lips from deceitful speech. Shun evil and do good, seek peace and pursue it.[5]

Similarly, although the rabbis maintain that only those who believe that the Torah promises resurrection will enjoy that reward, they depict God as asking those who have died about their actions, first, and then about their beliefs and hopes: "Did you transact your business honestly? Did you fix times for the study of Torah? Did you fulfill your duty with respect to establishing a family? Did you hope for the salvation [of the Messiah]? Did you search for wisdom? Did you try to deduce one thing from another [in study]?"[6]

It is thus not surprising that although the curriculum in Jewish schools of all denominations includes some discussion of Jewish beliefs, its central focus is on the knowledge, skills, and values that Jews need to live their lives as Jews. And a Jewish child becomes an adult in a ceremony of Bar Mitsvah or Bat Mitsvah (a "son of the commandment" or a "daughter of the commandment") at the age when they become legally obligated to obey all the *commandments* of the tradition and are thus responsible for their *acts*. In contrast, the standard religious education that Christians give their children includes considerable discussion of the beliefs of the church (the "catechism," in some denominations), and children are ultimately confirmed in their faith by demonstrating their knowledge and acceptance of those beliefs and their commitment to them.

The Ethical Method of Conservative Judaism

This discussion of Judaism's stress on practice has so far left open the question of how we are to define what acts are required of us. Here the modern movements in Judaism—the Reform, Orthodox, and Conservative—take very different tacks. For the Reform movement, each individual must learn the tradition as much as possible and then decide autonomously which acts he or she sees as obligatory. For the Orthodox, the law as it has come down to us governs absolutely, for it is the divine revelation given at Mount Sinai. Even the Orthodox, though, are not fundamentalists in the Protestant sense of that term, for they also believe that the Torah must be interpreted through the prism of the rabbis' interpretations and applications through the ages. The Conservative movement, of which I am a part, agrees with the Orthodox tenet that we are bound by Jewish law, but it understands the entire Jewish tradition historically and applies Jewish law with that historical perspective in mind. In practice, this historical perspective means that in the Conservative movement, Jewish theology, law, and ethics intertwine much more tightly than they do in most Orthodox interpretations, for historically Jewish law, especially in its most creative periods, manifested an openness to outside cultures, an engagement with their ideas and practices, and an adaptation of some of them. Conservative Jews' historical rootedness, then, makes them, as a whole, much more open to considering contributions from other cultures in judging how Judaism should be understood and lived in our time. Reform thinkers take a historical approach to understanding the Jewish tradition, too, but the Conservative movement insists that it must be the contemporary community, rather than each individual, that determines what God wants of us in our day if Judaism is to retain its coherence, normativeness, and its very identity.

Jewish ethics within the Conservative framework deliberately continues the same methodology that was used by the rabbis and their successors over the generations. When Jews had a question about what Judaism demanded of them in a given situation—or, in the absence of a demand, what Judaism advised or encouraged them to do—they would ask their local rabbi. His (until 1973, all rabbis were men) answer was authoritative because his knowledge of the content of the tradition and of the methods by which it should be applied to modern circumstances had been certified by his ordination; also, the community had appointed him as their official interpreter of the tradition. In most cases, the rabbi would answer the question orally, sometimes taking some time to look something up and to think about it. In situations where he did not know how to respond, he would consult with another rabbi respected for his knowledge of that aspect of Jewish law and tradition. Ultimately, though, it was the local rabbi's use of the expert's answer that gave it authority for the questioner, and so most moral questions (as well as most ritual ones) were decided through the *mara d'atra*, the rabbi of the local community.

Some Jewish communities were sufficiently well organized to have a central body to make decisions for the region.[7] In all places and times, the law as lived, though, was not only a matter of what the rabbis said, either individually or collectively, but also a product of the interaction between rabbinic rulings and the practices and customs of the people—just as it is in any living legal system.

In line with these historical precedents, Conservative Jews with moral questions first address them to their local rabbi. Since virtually all Jews nowadays live in societies where freedom of religion is guaranteed, the rabbi's decision will not be enforced by the police power of the community or the state, as it was in pre-Enlightenment times. Rather, the rabbi must convince the questioner of the Jewish authenticity and wisdom of his or her decision, pointing out the historical precedents on which it is based, the reasons it should make sense to us today, and the ways in which it might be carried out in modern circumstances that often differ markedly from those of the past. The rabbi might consult with another rabbi with expertise in this particular area of law, and such consultations these days happen as much by telephone and e-mail as they do by formal letter. When the rabbi thinks that the entire Conservative community should consider the question, usually because there is not a clear precedent in traditional Jewish law or because the precedent on the books poses some moral or logistical problems in our time, he or she sends it to the Conservative movement's Committee on Jewish Law and Standards—a body of twenty-five rabbis and five, nonvoting lay representatives—for a decision.

This method of making moral decisions is, of course, very different from the methods of other communities. As Americans, we are used to deciding questions—including moral questions about such things as abortion and the treatment of the poor—through our legislatures and courts, ultimately, in other words, through majority vote. Catholics see their priest, bishop, and, finally, the pope as the arbiter of moral norms and values. Protestants bid individuals to consult their individual conscience. (Of course, there is some room for individual conscience in Catholic moral theology, and Protestant denominations have taken specific stances as a group on some issues.)

Why do Jews follow the method I have described to make their moral decisions? In part, they do so because theologically the Jewish tradition understands the rabbi's decision as nothing short of the Word of God. Although the Torah records some instances in which Moses gained new instructions from God through speaking with God directly,[8] it struggles with the question of how to distinguish a true prophet from a false one.[9] It also proclaims that when someone has a question, he or she should go to "the judge in charge at that time," and "you shall act in accordance with the instructions given you and the ruling handed down to you; you must not deviate from the verdict that they announce to you either to the right or the left."[10] Following this biblical direction, the rabbis declared that God no longer speaks to us through prophets but rather through ongoing interpretations of the one accepted revelation, the Torah, including the Written Torah and the continuing tradition of interpretations, precedents, and customs (the Oral Torah).[11] So Jews use a legal methodology to address moral questions because that is how we are to discern the will of God in the postbiblical period.

Beyond the task of discerning God's will, there are some important practical advantages in using the law to respond to moral questions.[12] First, the law is a *public* vehicle for both the discussion and determination of moral policy and thus provides a much stronger base than either individual conscience or the decrees of an authority figure for discerning the good. The decisions of conscience or the decrees of an authority figure may be wise and benevolent, but also arbitrary and unsound; in contrast, a legal decision gains its authority from the fact that it is a *reasoned* argument based on accepted *precedent*, and, as such, it is open to argument, challenge, and public debate. Deciding moral matters in legal form also enables a community to adapt its norms to the changing circumstances of everyday life, and yet because legal decisions rely on precedent, these adaptations are protected from simply expressing the current whim of the majority. Law-based morality can accommodate new circumstances and yet also has continuity and staying power. It thus provides a good balance between change and tradition.

Using law to decide moral issues, for all its virtues, is, like all methods, incomplete. As a result, the rabbis demand that we go "beyond the letter of the law" *(lifnim mi-shurat ha-din)* in modeling ourselves after God and in trying to be a holy people. Jewish law is stringent and specific in its demands, but we must aspire to even greater moral heights. To foster these aspirations, Jewish law must be interpreted in the context of, and supplemented by, Jewish moral maxims, stories, and theological beliefs, and it must learn also from other religions and secular philosophies. Conservative rabbis tend to see and invoke that broader context of Jewish moral decisionmaking more often than Orthodox rabbis do. In contrast to Reform writers, who see the law, at most, as a possible guide for an individual's autonomous choice, Conservative writers begin their moral discussions with a consideration of the requirements of Jewish law and base themselves primarily upon it.

Jewish and Christian Commonality

So far, I have sketched some of the differences between Jewish and Christian conceptions of belief and practice as well as the way in which Conservative Jews approach moral questions. I have offered this sketch as a way of joining Professor Novak in his call for an end to the oversimplifications that have characterized Christian understandings of Judaism as hypernomian and Jewish understandings of Christianity as antinomian. In closing, let me return to Professor Novak's essay, specifically to his depiction of the congruence of the Jewish and Christian moral visions, a depiction that is, I think, much too rosy.

Professor Novak maintains that the prohibitions against idolatry, killing innocent human life, and sexual immorality, the three commands that Jews are not supposed to violate even at the cost of their lives, constitute "the most fundamental of all commonalities between Judaism and any Gentile tradition on earth." That, though, is his Jewish interpretation of other faiths. Even if other faiths prohibit those things, they may not interpret them the same way or give them the same degree of emphasis as Judaism does. For that matter, within and among Christian and Jewish denominations themselves, past and contemporary debates abound as to the scope of those prohibitions; so, for example, in our own time, homosexual sex has been hotly debated within many Christian and Jewish groups. Thus, contrary to Professor Novak's claim, these prohibitions cannot constitute a strong and clear basis for interfaith—or even intrafaith—commonality.

More broadly, I doubt that Christians would assert that they "base their morality on the Scripture they call the 'Old Testament,'" as Professor Novak maintains, or that "whenever Christians have had to consider what a Christian polity would actually be like, they have had to return to the law of the Old Testament." Most textbooks on Christian ethics concentrate instead on the person and sayings of Jesus and, secondarily, on official statements and discussions within a particular Christian denomination. The classic view of Christian polity comes from the first Christian community described in the Book of Acts rather than from the Hebrew Bible, and then from later Christian political writers like Augustine and Thomas Aquinas.

It appears that Professor Novak has perhaps tried too hard to find common ground between Jews and Christians. One important guideline for interfaith relations, though, is that we must avoid reading our own faith into someone else's; we must instead understand the other person's faith in its own terms, with its own methods, texts, and emphases. Only then can we accurately look for similarities, differences, and common projects. As I said at the start, Professor Novak and I share a commitment to the Jewish tradition and to Jewish–Christian dialogue, but we differ when it comes to our assessment of what Jews and Christians share and, thus, of how we might begin to talk to each other.[13]

Christian Ethics in Jewish Terms: A Response to David Novak

STANLEY HAUERWAS

Beyond Christian Society

That Jews now think it important to understand Christians in Jewish terms may indicate that some extremely important changes have occurred or are occurring in Christianity itself. It is my impression that until very recently Jews have rightly regarded Christians primarily as a "problem." What Christians might mean when they say God is "Trinity" has not seemed important, given the challenge of Jewish survival in a world dominated by Christians. For Jews to engage in a Jewish theological assessment of Christian theological convictions may indicate that the world is no longer a Christian world.

Of course, many Christians, particularly in America, continue to think they live in a "Christian society" or, if society is becoming less Christian, that they should do all they can to stem the perverse tide of secularism. Though I have reason to regret developments such as abortion that may be the result of "secularization," I represent that part of the Christian tradition that has thought the attempt by Christians to rule through state agency (what has been called Constantinianism) to be a mistake. But representative theologians of "mainstream Protestant Christianity" regard my call for Christians to recover our status as "resident aliens" as a sectarian retreat from the Christian responsibility to "serve" the world.[1]

But why should Jews be interested in what seems to be an internal Christian debate? Moreover, what does such a debate have to do with understanding how Christians think about ethics? The short answer to the second question is "everything." And that answer, I hope to show, makes clear why Jews should care about how Christians understand the relation between church and world. For example, the concept of natural law in Christian theological ethics is not just a "given" but has a quite different content and function depending on how Christians understand their relationship to the societies in which they find themselves.

Christians and the Law

For Christians, our "ethics" cannot be abstracted from our conviction that Jesus Christ is God's messiah—very God and very man. Christologies that fail to acknowledge the full reality of Jesus' humanity—a humanity that is unavoidably Jewish—are often implied in natural law accounts of Christian ethics that separate what is required of Christians from the salvation into which we have been incorporated through the work of Jesus Christ. The church may have decisively rejected Marcion and his rejection of Judaism, but that decision may well have hidden from Christians the fact that we continued in our politics and ethics to live as if the law and the materiality of our faith that the law represents can be left behind.

Therefore, David Novak's recognition that Christians are not antinomian is an extremely welcome Jewish reading of Christian ethics. Christians do share with Jews the conviction that our relationship to God has been determined through God's gracious gift of the law. Karl Barth, for example, begins his reflection on ethics in the *Church Dogmatics* with the claim:

> As the doctrine of God's command, ethics interprets the Law as the form of the Gospel, i.e., as the sanctification which comes to man through the electing God. Because Jesus Christ is the holy God and sanctified man in One, it [the Law] has its basis in the knowledge of Jesus Christ. . . . Its function is to bear primary witness to the grace of God in so far as this is the saving engagement and commitment of man.[2]

Barth's Christological understanding of the law obviously names the difference between Jews and Christians, but it also makes clear that our differences about the law cannot be characterized by the familiar contrast: "Jews are a people of the law; Christians are a people of grace." During the Reformation, Protestant Christians often characterized Judaism as legalistic—not because they knew anything about Judaism but as part of their anti-Catholic polemic. In effect, Protestants were attempting to make Catholics the Jews of Christianity, and they did not mean that characterization to be a compliment. Yet as Novak makes clear, the very need for forgiveness and atonement for sins indicates that the keeping of the law for Jews is part of a larger covenantal reality that renders the charge of legalism a gross misrepresentation.

The conflicts among Christians make any attempt by Jews to assess Christianity particularly challenging because Jews must try to avoid being misled by the misrepresentations Christians make of one another's theology. For example, justification by grace through faith was Luther's way of criticizing medieval Catholicism; in time Luther's view of Catholics hardened into the notion that Jews are to the law as Christians are to grace. But it would have never occurred to Luther that justification made the Decalogue, for example, any less authoritative for Christians. After all, it is Luther who says in his *The Large Catechism* that "anyone who knows the Ten Commandments perfectly knows the entire Scripture."[3]

The New Testament obviously includes, particularly in the letters of Paul, an ongoing critique of the law. Paul says that those in Christ have "died to the law" so that they might "belong to him who has been raised from the dead," and so "bear fruit for God" (Rom. 7:4–6; Gal. 2:19). Now that Christ has come, those who still try to keep the law (by being circumcised or maintaining ritual purity) cut themselves off from Christ and lose his benefits (Galatians 5:2–6). Yet as Bruce Marshall maintains, these New Testament passages are not "against the law itself, but against treating the law and its observance as the way to salvation," a view that is not incompatible with the understanding of the law within Judaism. Marshall notes that Jews understand "their obedience to the commandments as acts of gratitude and thanksgiving to God for his electing love towards the Jewish people, and not as a means to salvation or to some other end."[4]

The purpose of the law for Christians, as Barth suggests, is our sanctification. The difference between Christians and Jews is not located in the law but in our different understandings of sanctification. Jesus has become for us the new law, making it possible for us to be his disciples. Discipleship is not a denial of the role of the law but rather, for Christians, names the way the law serves to make us manifestations of God's gracious election. What becomes crucial for us, therefore, is how the law helps us see the interconnection between our worship of the one true God, truth-telling, honoring parents, sharing goods, and rejoicing in our neighbor's good fortune.

This account of the role of the law in the Christian life may seem extremely odd from a Jewish perspective. After all, Christians think they can pick and choose which commands to follow by distinguishing the moral, ceremonial, and juridical law of the Old Testament. These very distinctions cannot help but suggest that Christians presume a freedom from the law that is incompatible with Judaism. And, indeed, Christians disagree with Jews about which laws are to be obeyed, as well as about how to obey the laws we have adopted as our own. However, it is crucial for Jews (and for Christians) to understand that Christians approach the law selectively not because we are against the law, but because we believe that God's election of us, the Gentiles, to participate in God's promise to Israel means the law has an inherent purpose to which we must be faithful.

For example, nothing distinguishes Christians and Jews more dramatically than our understanding of the family. Put simply, Christians are not bound by the law to have children. We must acknowledge that we are children by appropriately honoring our parents, but to honor our parents does not mean that we must make them grandparents. The stark fact of the matter is that Jesus was neither married nor had children. By itself, that fact does not explain why Christians do not have to be parents, but it does indicate our conviction that what God has done through the life of Jesus makes the existence of the church not only possible but necessary. What Jesus started did not continue because he had children but because his witness attracted strangers. Christians are not obligated to have children so that the tradition might continue; rather we believe that God through the cross and resurrection of Jesus and the sending of the Holy Spirit has made us a people who live through witness. In other words, the church grows through the conversion of strangers, who often turn out to be our biological children.

I do not want to leave the impression that Christians are antifamily or antichild. The point, rather, is that for Christians the single person does not have to justify her or his existence in the same way that married people do. Instead, those called to marriage—that is, those called to manifest to the world the Christian commitment to lifelong fidelity—bear the burden of proof, part of which is, indeed, a willingness to have children. Particularly in a liberal culture, Christians and Jews may appear to understand and practice the commandment to honor parents in similar ways, but our "similarity" may well hide quite different understandings of the end of the law. For example, contrary to Novak, family identity is not at the core of our identity as Christians.

Theology and Ethics

This example helps explain why I find Novak's account of natural law at once illuminating and problematic. Particularly after Kant, Christians have developed similar accounts of natural law.[5] My problem with such accounts is that they tend to occlude the fact that, as Novak puts it, "theology entails ethics, since ethics presupposes theology." Novak's claim that the Noahide law is universally accessible to human reason is in tension with his view of the inseparability of theology and ethics.

Though I am suspicious of appeals to universal human reason, my deeper concern about Novak's construal of the Noahide law as natural law is that his account may abstract the law from the law's purpose to form a holy people. Jews and Christians do not obey the law because it is the law, but because such obedience makes us people capable of faithfully worshiping the creator of heaven and earth. Therefore, as I tried to display in my discussion of our differing views of the family, if Jews and Christians disagree about the law, it is because we disagree about exactly what it means to be a holy people. I have no reason to object to Novak's use of the Noahide law as a means to understand the status of Christians. If Christians—from a Jewish perspective—obey the law of Noah, so much the better. But Jews should be careful not to make too much of Christian obedience. Indeed, I think Novak's suggestion that a natural law "ethic" should become the location for the recognition of commonalities between Jews and Christians, as well as a basis for how both traditions negotiate a secular society, is problematic. Such a strategy, I fear, tempts Jews and Christians alike to assume that our ethics can be separated from our most basic theological convictions and practices. Both Jews and Christians may obey the commandment to honor their parents, but a close look at the character this obedience has in each tradition will reveal as much about our differences as it will about our commonalities.

Novak identifies two kinds of commonality between Jews and Christians: those that are rooted in the universal character of the Noahide law, and those that exist only as analogies. He offers prayer and worship as an example of the latter and says that here "Jews and Christians cannot develop a common life without one side capitulating to the other or without sliding into syncretism." My own sense is that in the end all commonalities that matter exist only as analogies.

Christians do not have beliefs about God from which certain ethical practices follow; rather we believe that the right worship of God is our morality. Crucial for our understanding of the Decalogue is not just the authority of the individual commandments but why the so-called moral commandments are inseparable from the command to worship God on the Sabbath. Both Jews and Christians gather to worship God on the Sabbath. However, that we do not gather for worship on the same day of the week is an important aspect not only of our differing understandings of worship but also of our differing understandings of "ethics."

Toward Christian and Jewish Friendship

As I suggested at the beginning, Christians in the West are just beginning to learn to live the way Jews have had to live since Christians took over the world by making Caesar a member of the church. Put simply, we must learn from the Jews how to survive in a world that is not constituted by the recognition much less the worship of our God. In the process of acquiring the wisdom the Jews have hewn from their struggle to survive Christianity, Christians might also learn that our destiny is inseparable from the destiny of the Jews. I am convinced, however, that Christians cannot learn this lesson if, in an attempt to appear tolerant, we pretend that our ethics can be divorced from the conviction that God, through Jesus' life, death, and resurrection, has made us nothing less than heirs of Abraham. Accordingly, I think Jewish theological readings of Christianity must face the challenge that the existence of Christianity is not a mistake but is, rather, one of the ways God desires to make His covenant with Israel known to the nations.

That Christians must now struggle to understand Jewishness is not necessarily good news for Jews. I cannot offer an account of natural law that will ensure that we really share far more than we disagree on, or that will give us a common strategy to survive the challenges of an increasingly unfriendly social order. That we share much is no doubt due in part, as Novak argues, to our common humanity; but more important, we share God's election. Supported by that fact we should pray that God will make us capable of sustaining the slow and hard work of friendship through which we might discover that we are in fact commanded by the same God. For I believe that through the law, God intends nothing less than to make us His friends and, therefore, friends with one another.

7

ISRAEL

Judaism and Christianity: Covenants of Redemption

IRVING GREENBERG

God's Universal and Particular Covenants

The religion and the people of Israel came into being to mediate the conflict between bringing the *ideal* world (creation redeemed and history fulfilled) into existence and meaningful living in the *real* world (creation and history as they are now). According to Jewish tradition, God, out of love, self-limits—first to create and sustain existence, then to enable its ultimate perfection. Without yielding the conviction that people should live lives of full dignity, God allows history to go on in a flawed world and in societies full of degradation. Without giving up the desire that humans always act on the side of life and value, God respects human freedom and allows people to sin without destroying them. To reconcile the poles of the ideal and the real, God enters into covenant. The primordial self-limitation is expressed in establishing natural order/law and being bound by it. The regularity and dependability of the natural order gives humans the sense of trust to work and build the world and to feel responsible for their lives. Similarly, God does not continuously interfere with history; nor will the divine enter into human lives with constant miraculous intervention. Rather, God calls humanity into active partnership. Singly and collectively, human beings are commanded to use their God-like capacities to complete the world. In turn, God promises to be with humanity and to work with them all the way, neither to reject them nor to coerce them until all is realized.

All other living forms are genetically programmed to maximize creation of life and to live in the natural order. Humans alone have the fuller consciousness that enables them to understand and, then, to reject or to willingly join in the rhythms of creation. For humans to be summoned into covenant, then, is to be singled out in love; the call to do more and to get closer to God is the content of the experience of election.

Only divine self-control and a profound commitment to full human development can motivate God's promise to neither reject nor coerce human beings; only the recognition that coerced righteousness would violate human equality can evoke God's ongoing willingness to bear the pain of an unredeemed world. The covenant is grounded on an infinite divine respect for humanity; it is driven by a loving desire that human beings emerge out of the natural and historical process as fully independent, dignified creatures.

How can God move the world forward toward perfection and still allow humans to be free? God can do this by joining with humanity as it is (with mixed values, contradictory urges, and cross-purposes), where it is (in a world of shortages, limitations, and conflicting interests), in a partnership to work together for redemption. God joins with humanity in this way by establishing the Noahide covenant—a covenant with humanity that precedes the covenant with Israel. The goal is to fill the earth with life, life in the image of God (Gen. 9:1–2, 7).

The concept of partnership implies joint and parallel efforts and mutual obligations. This is one of the revolutionary insights of Israelite religion. The covenant mechanism is intended by its Initiator to give over a sense of stability and dignity to humans and to make them feel that God is deeply and equally involved with them. At the same time, the covenant teaches that humans should not view their power as absolute. Human authority comes into being within a framework of relationship and accountability to God; it is bound by the rules of the divine-human partnership, biblically called the Noahide covenant.

The Noahide covenant is permanent, but the Torah tells us that God chose Abraham, Sarah, and their children to be the bearers of an additional, particular covenant. Particular group covenants are needed because the emergence of a universal *brit* (covenant) brings with it a great risk implicit in the exercise of human power and freedom. Unified or centralized human power can inflict evil unchecked. Ironically, this danger is exacerbated by the very vision of perfecting the world. All these God-like capacities can be enlisted in the cause of totalitarianism, which, strengthened by good intentions and dreams of perfection, will stop at nothing to realize its goal. The glittering ideal of the perfect world can blind the eye to the cruelty being done in the name of advancing the cause. The music of redemption drowns out the anguished cries of the victims of progress and soothes the conflicts in the breast of killers for kindness. To prevent the possibility of utopian totalitarianism, one must break up the centralization of human culture, power, and institutions.

The particularization of the Noahide covenant and the sharing of the covenantal task between smaller (national) groups restores the human scale of the movement to perfect creation (*tikkun olam*: repairing the world). Small group covenants also open up the possibility of experimental, varied pathways toward perfection. Local successes can be spread around or imitated by other groups; failures or dangerous tendencies can be contained within the limits of the community or locale.

Of course there is a trade-off in adopting such a strategy of redemption. The use of human groups as agents of covenant may lead to the growth of parochial loyalties. The creation of an in-group/out-group mentality often leads to double-standard morality codes and to the reduction of the humanity of the outsider. Conflicts of interest frequently emerge between the group's needs and the cause of *tikkun olam*, the very cause for which the group has come into being. This danger of chauvinism can be offset only by engendering a moral universe in which particular human bonds of affection and morality are nurtured but are balanced by being set in an overarching culture of universal love and responsibility. This constant tension (and the inevitable recurring outbursts of tribalism or runaway universalism as one tendency or the other gains strength) will be a prominent aspect of Israel's covenantal history. On the other hand, the particular covenant opens the door to a more richly textured, more human religious experience. Each group can incorporate its own language, its own specific historical experiences and family memories, its own favorite symbols into the warp and woof of its religion.

Covenanting with smaller groupings of humanity also addresses the question of the pace of perfection. How can human beings be inspired with the vision of *tikkun olam* without being overwhelmed by constant pressure from divine revelation? How can humans be moved to change the status quo as quickly as possible? The answer that is most respectful of human dignity is: by calling into being an avant-garde to serve as pacesetter for humanity, a cadre of humans to undertake the task of working toward redemption at so high a level as to inspire others to greater efforts by their example. The vanguard is willing to work in a highly disciplined way and to be held accountable for this effort so as to become lead partners in humanity's covenant with God. The Bible works with one small group; the family of Abraham is elected to be the pacesetters for humanity. This family *brit* neither repeals nor replaces the universal covenant. After all, God's covenantal love, *hesed*, is steadfast; God's calling proves to be irrevocable.

In the development of the particular covenant out of the universal, the partnership with God is intensified. The human partner is further empowered, as evidenced by Abraham's intervention to plead for Sodom (Gen. 18), in contrast with Noah's passive acceptance of the divine decree to wipe out all life on Earth (Gen. 6:13–22).

The Abrahamic Covenant

The gift of election is given to Abraham and Sarah and their family and not to an individual. The goal of the mission is to advance the triumph of life. Only the family has the biological capability of creating life and also the bonds of love to nourish and raise it successfully. The family is the womb of humanness; its love confirms and deepens the individual's image of God. Affirming the family makes clear from day one that the natural affection and emotional links that bind the family are not to be thrust aside for the sake of the greater good, namely, the assignment to repair the world.

Covenant incorporates committed love, a love that is willing to be bound to the other. Entering the covenant represents the lover's promise to be steadfast in the face of obstacles and failure; the partner is binding herself to be there even when the emotion of love flags. The singling out is a proclamation of love and divine good purpose for the Abrahamic family and all of humanity (Gen. 12). Abraham's family is singled out to establish the human scale of redemption and to hasten its pace and, thereby, its arrival for all. Thus, when Abraham responded to his call, he changed from being a local notable to becoming a blessing for the other families of the earth. Moreover, the choosing of Abraham and Sarah is designed to pluralize the ways to salvation; by living in harmony with the divine order, their descendants are to release the channels of blessing already inherent in the creation. When the other peoples walk in Israel's footsteps, they, too, draw forth the divine abundance from the wells of blessing that lie beneath the surface of life. Thus Abraham is a source of blessing for all.

With election comes the promise that Abraham will receive the gift of the land, with the condition that only his descendants will inherit it. The future gift makes clear that having been asked to uproot in order to go ahead, Abraham's family will obtain a new place to settle. The divine faithfulness to this promise led to the great liberation in the Exodus that is the cornerstone of the Mosaic covenant. And the profound connection of land and calling confirms the dignity of embodiment and the significance of economic life and labor, now and forever.

The commanded sign of the covenant—circumcision—underscores the profound transformation of Abraham's condition as a result of his joining in this pact. The organ of generation is marked with a sign of dedication that, in turn, constantly evokes God's promise, the assurance of the expansion and victory of life in the world. Moreover, God's blessing is now intimately intertwined with God's human partner. Circumcision reminds both God and Abraham of their sacred undertaking and ultimately sets the children of Abraham inescapably apart in the eyes of their neighbors. Finally, circumcision makes it clear that Israel is of the flesh as well as of the spirit; this again underscores the affirmation of embodiment. The Israelite body sends the message that God-is-in-our-midst, incarnate.

Abraham and, later, the children of Israel are teachers to humanity everywhere; to many, they are the first to bring the message of the presence of God and the call to walk the way of the Lord through life. So closely is God's name associated with the people Israel that even if some circumcised Israelites do not want to testify, their existence is an involuntary witness.

The link between circumcision and covenant was directly challenged by the Apostle Paul and by Christian hermeneutics during and after the break between the two religions. In Paul's argument, the true Jew is one who is such inwardly, and the true circumcision is of the heart (Rom. 2:29). In defending Judaism, some Jews intensified the stress on the biology, the carnality, the law that Paul and other Christian theologians disputed. A rereading of Abraham's life, especially of the chapters on cutting the covenant (Gen. 15, 17), refutes the easy contrasts that developed out of these early, polemical disputes: Abraham as the icon of pure faith versus Abraham the one who is given specific commandments and who undergoes circumcision in response; Abraham the universalist father of many nations versus Abraham the particularist father of a family that stands alone. Such partisan readings are simplistic; the chosen's function is richly complex. Abraham's call includes acting as all of the above. The covenantal instructions extend across a continuum of meaning.

The Covenant of Sinai

At Sinai, the Abrahamic covenant was renewed, deepened, and extended to a whole people. Abraham's *brit* had all the great strengths of a family covenant; it also had all the limitations of a family covenant. Blood ties make the exercise of mutual responsibility elemental. The frame is too biological, running the risk of excluding others not born into the system.

A nation incorporates people beyond the immediate family. At Sinai, the people of Israel, including absorbed mixed multitudes, were elected to be God's people. The nation's experience of being chosen was spelled out in the later synagogal liturgy, which includes references to being singled out, being loved and desired by God, being exalted. In grateful response, the Israelites accepted the partnership offered at Sinai. The covenant that came with chosenness included making the nation holy/special through additional commandments that made the people Israel an avant-garde in God's service. The Sinaitic covenant was powerfully influenced by the Exodus. Liberation was the act that singled out the people Israel. The Exodus challenges the reigning status quo and points to a future perfection even as it affirms the meaningfulness of history. Thus the Exodus generates the dialectical tension between the real and the ideal; and the events at Sinai again make the point that a covenant is required to close the gap and to guide living along the way to redemption.

By focusing on the Exodus, the Sinaitic covenant deepens Israel's commitment to the perfection of time (history) and not just space (creation) or spirit (humans). God's mighty acts of redemption *are* in history and not in some mythic realm. Of course, Israel's religion is not simply the product of the victory of the Exodus: the people of Israel will continue to testify in exile and after defeat.

The mission to testify places an enormous weight on the shoulders of the chosen people. Every day they must witness to infinite value in a world where values are degraded. In their behaviors, they must act responsibly when others "unburdened" by covenant may take advantage. When external events bring crushing forces to bear on them, they must find the internal fortitude to persist in hope and testimony. Given the incredible faithfulness and persistence in the face of suffering that the covenantal people have shown, one is almost convinced that God knew exactly what God was getting in selecting this family. In any event, at every step, covenantal actions summon up distinctive blessing for the covenant people; simultaneously, these blessings operate in exemplary fashion and extend to all humanity.

Israel and Its Blessings

God's promise to establish Israel in dignity in its own land is an example of the blessing bestowed upon the covenant people and of the extension of this blessing to the world. The promise implies that the soul of Abraham's children is bound to this land in a special way and that the land is uniquely responsive to them. At the same time, the right to live somewhere is the anchor of self-worth. The covenant model suggests that all peoples should have a homeland where their right to exist is self-evident and unquestioned. Unfortunately, most people tend to slip into the corruptions of being landed—becoming tribal, exploiting or excluding the outsider, worshiping the gods of this space, however morally outrageous their demands may be. Moreover, people do not necessarily feel an obligation to turn their land into the locus of a moral, humane society. In the act of election, God asks the beloved to step up and lead the way for humanity by making the promised land a microcosm of perfection, a land in which economic equality, righteousness, justice, and equal treatment before the law will be the lot and right of everyone, citizen and stranger alike.

When the people of Israel did not step up and lead the world in this way, they were degraded or exiled, God's Name was profaned, and the covenantal message was damaged. The other nations misread the sight of Israel in exile as proof that there is no profit in living covenantally.

The nations misunderstood the situation in two ways. First, they failed to discern that the expulsion occurred because Israel had not lived up to the convenantal standard that is demanded of God's people; second, they failed to grasp that since Israel is planted in God, exile cannot make it lose its soul or its way; it can move from one land to another and maintain its values and its being because it is grounded in God. It is also the case that when living in its homeland, this very groundedness in God should prevent Israel from absolutizing land possession and should remind Jews of their part in *tikkun olam*, of their role as a blessing to the nations.

To be a blessing to the world, Israel must play three roles. It must be a teacher, a model, and a coworker. As a *teacher*, each living generation must pass on its values to others, starting with its own children. Because the goal of perfection cannot be achieved in one generation, the covenant is, of necessity, a treaty among all the generations, as well as between them and God. If one generation would reject or fail to pass on the covenant to the next one, then the efforts and sacrifices of all past (and future) generations are wasted as well. The encounter with God and the experience of cosmic care gives Israel insight and girds it with strength to teach covenantal values. As teacher of humanity, Israel becomes God's witness (Is. 43:10, 12). In a flawed world, however, the faithful can only testify to their experience of the divine presence and of being saved, and this testimony may well fail: if the messenger suppresses his testimony, or if her behavior contradicts the message, or if the facts of life and the condition of other people are dissonant with the affirmation, then the witness will bear no fruit.

As a *model* for humanity, Israel must be a community within which covenantal values are maximally lived, at least to the extent realizable now in an imperfect world. By so doing, Israel can create a liberated zone—a land within which equality is respected. In serving as a model, Israel becomes "a light of nations" (Is. 42:6). The term "model" must not be idealized. This model people are only human, with all the attendant limitations. At times, Israel looks out only for itself and fails to teach; at times, its behavior contradicts its witness. At such times, Israel is a model of what not to do. When Israel does rise to heights of faithfulness, courage, and responsibility, it is worthy of emulation.

Finally Israel must be a *coworker* for redemption. One people cannot lift up the whole globe by itself; Israel must work with others. At times, some people have been tempted to dream of an apocalyptic ending that will burn away all the wicked (all the others?) and leave Israel alone, victoriously vindicated. This event would certainly be a morally unsatisfactory outcome of the divine election of Abraham. Throughout the Bible and thereafter, there are echoes of valid revelations to other peoples and traces of mighty redemptive acts bestowed on other nations (Gen. 14, 18ff; Num. 22–24; Is. 20, 21, 23; Jer. 1:4–10). Suffice it to say that at the end of days when the whole world is redeemed, other nations will have contributed their portion and will share in it fully (Is. 2:1–4; Mic. 4:1–5; Is. 57:6–7).

All the world is holy, suffused with divine presence. However, the transcendent is veiled by the evil and failure in the world. Someday perfection (life, peace, harmony with God and creation) will be manifest. In the interim, Israel is the holy place/nation/time where God's presence is more visible, and consequently, life is (more) triumphant there than elsewhere. In accepting the covenant, Israel agrees to become just such a nation of priests (teachers, role models) who offer an intense model to challenge the nations. If Israel lives up to its full commitment, it becomes the signpost to which all eyes turn to be inspired to work for the final perfection.

The New Covenant of Christianity

Each stage of the covenant has its own time. Rabbinic tradition counts the ten generations from Noah to Abraham as a measure of divine patience in the face of disappointment, that is, sin and the power of the status quo go on after the flood as before. In the increasing divine search for partners in *tikkun olam*, God chooses Abraham to initiate another experiment and to move the world toward perfection.

One can speculate on the timing of events in the first century. It was always God's plan to bring the vision of redemption and the covenantal way to more of humanity. After thousands of years, the Jewish people, as they would evidence in the aftermath of the destruction of the Second Temple, had sufficiently internalized the covenant to be able to take on new levels of responsibility. Challenged and enriched by Hellenism, they were capable of shifting to a more hidden holiness without losing their connection to the transcendent God.

At the same time, in the Hellenistic world, there was a high receptivity to the spiritual/ethical messages of the covenant, especially if they could be articulated in Hellenistic terms, to and for Gentiles. To reverse a classic image, then, it was God's purpose that a shoot of the stalk of Abraham be grafted onto the root of the Gentiles. Thus non-

Jews could be made aware that they were rooted in God also, and they could then bear redemptive fruit on their tree of life. Bringing considerably more people into covenantal relationships with God would be an important fulfillment (albeit not a complete one) of the promise that Abraham's people would be a blessing for the families of the earth.

The group that would bring the message of redemption to the rest of the nations had to grow out of the family and covenanted community of Israel. But the community was not intended to be a replacement for Abraham's family; nor were its achievements the proof of a divine repudiation of Sarah's covenant. The new avant-garde was to be an offshoot, a group to reach out to new masses of people in their language and images. To be heard and followed, this group had to swim in the sea of the Gentile people and their culture. This religion dared not be too Jewish (culturally or literally). Therefore, although the new articulation of the faith grew in the bosom of Judaism and was profoundly marked by Jewish interpretation of its symbols and history, it could and did take on the coloration of the people that it reached. Once one grasps that the emergence of this group was the expression of divine pluralism, God seeking to expand the number of covenantal channels to humanity without closing any of them, then the next step follows logically. The new development would have to become an independent religion or it would erode Jewish distinctiveness and undermine the capacity of the Jewish people to carry on a distinctively Jewish witness.

Christianity had to start within Judaism, but it had to grow into its own autonomous existence to preserve the particularity of the original covenantal ways while enabling deeper exploration of the polarities that characterize the covenantal dialectic. The signal that triggered the new growth was to be discernible to the minimum number it would take to start a new religion. It would not be heard by the bulk of Jewry, not because of spiritual deafness or arrogant hardheartedness, but because the signal was not intended for them. The Jewish majority was shortly to be called to its renewed covenant, its rabbinic flowering.

What was that initial signal? Was it a special teacher who gave new vitality and freshness to his followers' religious lives, communicating a sense of special closeness of the presence of God? Was it a revolutionary advocate for the poor and outcasts and/or against the Romans, proclaiming the kingdom of God, preaching a political, economic, and spiritual transformation out of which the first would be last and the last would be first? Was it some miracle maker whose truest miracle was to channel God's love and, hence, the sense of election to those who followed him? Or was the signal the miraculous, blazing glory proclaimed by some fundamentalists or everyday faithful Christians who read the Gospels quite literally today? By contemporary standards of proof, likely we shall never know the answer. In any event, the period of that initial signal was overtaken by the crisis of Jesus' crucifixion.

Was this shocking, God-mocking, torturous death the end of miracles? The proof that the brutal status quo would always win? The cruel refutation of the teaching of love? The ultimate phenomenology of Godforsakenness? The faithful few, thinking like Jews, concluded that death and destruction do not get the final word. On the contrary, defeat tests faith and opens the door to new and deeper understanding. Then they received another, activating signal: an empty tomb. The fact that Jesus did not even attain the minimal dignity of a final resting place—an undisturbed grave—should have been the final nail in the crucifixion of their faith. Instead, they increased hope and trust in God. Soon they experienced the same (or greater) presence in their midst as before. Once faith supplied the key of understanding, the empty tomb yielded the message of the resurrection. Whether they received this message within three days, as the Gospel story indicates, or within three decades, as the most probable scholarly account has it, is of secondary importance. Inspired, they redoubled their telling of their redemption story. Inspired, they interpreted every inherited symbol and tradition as foreshadowing their redeemer. Among Jews who were hearing other divine messages loud and clear, their preaching made little headway; among Gentiles, as was intended, it spread and spread.

The original people of God soon encountered their own crisis—the destruction of the Holy Temple in Jerusalem and the exile that soon followed. Was this catastrophe the end of the covenant? In light of Jewish religious/national fervor and their revolt against Rome out of loyalty to God, why did God not vanquish the Romans even as God had overwhelmed the Egyptians?

Instead of despairing, most Jews increased their hope and trust in God. The rabbis emerged to teach of God's self-limitation, of God's "hiddenness," which was designed to call the people of Israel to participate more fully in the covenant. In the Temple, the manifest God showed overwhelming power, speaking through prophet and breast-plate, and holiness was "concentrated" in Jerusalem. Now, God was calling on Israel to discern the divine that was hidden but present everywhere. To see God everywhere is a special skill; learning and law thus became the keys to religious understanding. The Jewish people, in biblical times an ignorant peasantry awed by sacramental, revela-tory experiences in the Temple (or elsewhere!) were now trained by the rabbis to study and speak through prayer to a God who no longer revealed Godself directly/visibly to Israel. The sacramental religion of the Bible was transformed into the internalized, more participatory faith of the rabbinic period. Even as Christians responded to their great religious experiences by proclaiming a New Covenant, Jews re-sponded to their extraordinary flowering by affirming a *renewal* of the covenant.

In the aftermath of the destruction came the tragedy in the parting of the ways (note: *in* the parting of the ways, not *of* the parting of the ways). As Christianity spread among Gentiles, they heard the message in a way that made Jesus more literally God-like. Jews looked away from the shared values, the shared sense of covenant, the shared mem-ories and focused on the Christian teaching that Jesus was God—which made Christian teaching more unacceptable, indeed inferior, in Jewish eyes. Soon gone from Judaism, or rather muted within it, were the themes of grace, love, and the pathos of divine suffering—covenantal all, but now deemed to be too Christian.

At the same time, as Christianity spread among Gentiles, it elabo-rated a theology that eliminated *halachah* (starting with the practices that separated Jews from non-Jews). Furthermore, to the constant Jewish critique that the world was manifestly unredeemed (therefore, Jesus could be no true redeemer), Christianity responded by spiritual-izing redemption (and dismissing Judaism as a "carnal" religion). The conjunction of anti-halachic thinking and the dismissal of biology (Christians are children of Abraham in the spirit) encouraged an oth-erworldly focus and reinforced a dualism that often pitted the soul against the body, the flesh against the spirit. Rootedness in the land also was spiritualized away; no land was sacred, and only the heavenly Jerusalem really mattered. Christianity preserved the covenantal di-alectic between the ideal and the real. However, in its main thrust it leaned to one side of this dialectic, a skewing that was reinforced by its projection of Judaism as the devil's advocate, rather than as God's bal-ancing voice.

Experiencing their own real sense of God's love as election, Christians assumed that the Jews must have lost theirs. Then Christians became convinced that their interpretation of the common symbols was the only one. As Christians saw it, the destruction of the Temple and the subsequent exile of the Jews was decisive proof of their interpretation of God's intentions. Precisely because of the Jewish origins of Jesus and shared patrimony with the Jews, the Christians were driven to insist that Judaism was superseded. The final confirmation of Christian supersessionism came with the success of Christianity in the Roman Empire. A triumph of the spirit—that is, bringing God, love, covenant, redemption, ethics to countless pagans—turned into a victory for a politically established religion and a license for triumphalism.

In their triumphalism, Christians overlooked the extent to which theirs was a one-sided and partial reading of the biblical tradition in the light of their redemptive experience; they ignored the possibility that God had supplied the Jews with a different interpretive key. Instead, Christians concluded that the Jews had to be spiritually deaf and dumb or willfully devilish to resist Christian understandings. From this conclusion it was not a big jump to medieval Christianity's demonizing and dehumanizing of the Jews and, from there, to the Holocaust. Thus a gospel of love—which often acted that way among Gentiles—turned into a privileged sanctuary for hatred of the original people of Israel, especially as election became self-centered and the experience of chosenness turned into a claim to hold a monopoly on God's love.

The narrowing of its messages that grew out of its unconditional rejection of Judaism penalized Christianity itself in no small measure. The focus on crucifixion strengthened ascetic tendencies and devalued the spiritual significance of pleasure. The model of self-abnegating sacrifice as the key relationship to God generated fideism, sometimes at the expense of reason; it also nurtured the self-image of a powerless human, dependent on a mediator, unable to help himself or play a fully dignified role in the covenant. Sometimes, such attitudes spread to other cultural disciplines.

For their part, the rabbis could only envision a covenantal pluralism inside Judaism. They understood the Christian claim that if Christianity was right, Judaism was wrong. Since Jews experienced ongoing religious vitality and the presence of Holy Spirit in their community, they concluded that Christianity was an illusion and that Jesus was a false Messiah. Precisely because of a shared Bible and because of the Jewish origins of Christianity, Jews were driven to insist that Christianity was idolatrous, that is, it advocated the worship of a man. Just as the Christian rejection of Judaism penalized and distorted Christianity, so, too, Judaism was no less skewed by Jewry's inability to admit the vitality of Christian religion and its contribution to meaning and ethics around the world. To reduce the impact of Christianity's triumph among Gentiles, Jewry dismissed the significance of this world and of politics and military power. Law and learning were stressed in counterpoint to the grace and love of the gospel, to the extent that tendencies to legalism or underrating the spirit were stimulated. Also, a certain narrowing of Jewish concern from all of humanity to the tribe of Israel took place.

Covenant After the Shoah

The Shoah was the *reductio ad* demonic *absurdum* of interethnic, interreligious hatred. The Nazi demonizing of the Jews drew upon the subculture of degradation and hostility that grew out of past Christian teachings of contempt. After the Shoah, the burden of this past teaching was insufferable to repentant Christians. The Shoah made clear the overriding need to end all circles of hatred that surrounded and isolated groups of others. The isolation not only made Jews vulnerable but also tempted bystanders into indifference and silence. Jews had to ask themselves if they would not be guilty of similar failures were the people and religions that they disrespected at risk. Responding to the Holocaust created an overwhelming moral need to restore the image of God to the other. This restoration required recovering the uniqueness of the other by throwing off the lenses of stereotype and of caricature. The Nazi absolute—a combination of centralized power and unlimited ideology—made the Holocaust possible. The commitment to "never again" demanded the breakup of all concentrated power and absolutisms—even cultural and religious ones. Pluralism—the setting of healthy limits on absolutes, valid or otherwise—emerged as a key corrective to the abusive tendencies built into all traditions of ultimate meaning. The more people of faith were committed to restore God and the image of God in a devastated post-Shoah world, the more they were driven to recognize God's intended pluralism.

Jews, too, must understand that theological contempt cannot be separated from human responsibility. As Hillel said, in summary of the whole Torah, "What is hateful to you, do not do to others." Jews must recognize the full implications of the truth that "God has many messengers." It is not enough to speak of the tradition that there is salvation for individuals outside of Judaism. This generality does not do justice to the full spiritual dignity of others who live their lives in religious communities, and not just as individuals.

In this spirit, one can make the following declaration about Christianity from a Jewish perspective. Both religions grow out of Abraham's covenant and out of the Exodus. The Exodus, as understood by the Hebrew prophets, is an event that points beyond itself to future, expanded redemptions. The messianic impulse is a fundamental expression of Judaism's ongoing vitality. In that sense, Christianity is not a mere deviation or misunderstanding; it is an organic outgrowth of Judaism itself. As I have argued above, Christianity is a divinely inspired attempt to bring the covenant of *tikkun olam* to a wider circle of Gentiles. God intended that Judaism and Christianity both work for the perfection of the world (the kingdom of God). Together, both religions do greater justice to the dialectical tensions of covenant than either religion can do alone.

Judaism's focus on family as the context for *brit* is constructive; pursued one-sidedly it can lead to tribalism and amoral familialism. The religion needs to be corrected by a faith that breaks out of the family model and explores the power of a universal, self-defined belief group. Rabbinic Judaism brings humans more powerfully into participation in the covenant; but it needs a counterpart religion to explore the element of grace and transcendence in a more central way. In this perspective, Jewish covenant peoplehood and Christian faith community are both validated. Both models are a necessary expression of the plenitude of divine love and of the comprehensiveness and range of human roles in the covenant. By the same token, it is not too late for Christians to enrich their own revelation by learning from rabbinic response and the development of halachah how humans become (in Joseph Soloveitchik's words) cocreators of Torah, the divine word. Nor is it too late for Jews to enrich their own way by focusing again on grace and the sacramental and universal motifs played out in Christianity.

There are many dialectical tensions built into the covenantal structure. There is grace: the divine role in the partnership and the extraordinary initiative of God's love. Yet, the counterpart is the centrality of humans and the fullest participation of the human in the process.

When they focus on grace, both individuals and communities find it difficult to explore the limits and potential of human participation in covenant. Similarly, if one concentrates on continuity in the covenant, it is difficult to plumb the depths of change and transformation in history. If, on the other hand, there is a community that is particularly quick to understand the role of transformation or change, it finds it difficult to adjust to the ongoing validity of tradition. Humans cannot keep the covenantal tensions in perfect balance. The key to upholding the totality of covenant and the fullest realization of the goal is that there be multiple communities working on many roads toward perfection, and that there be mutual, loving criticism to keep standards high. Perhaps this need for criticism and high standards is why the divine strategy utilized at least two covenantal communities. Even with Christianity and Judaism both in the world, neither religion has succeeded in bringing the final redemption to its fullest flowering.

From this perspective, Jesus is no false Messiah, that is, a would-be redeemer who teaches evil values. Rather, when Christianity, in his name, claims absolute authority and denigrates the right of Judaism or of Jews to exist, then it makes him into a false Messiah. Short of such claims, however, Jews should recognize Jesus as a failed Messiah. This recognition would allow Jews to affirm that for hundreds of millions of people, Christianity has been and continues to be a religion of love and consolation.

Does the recognition of Jesus as a failed Messiah demean classic Christian affirmations of Jesus' messiahship and the incarnation? Does it betray the classic Jewish insistence that the Messiah has not yet come, or does it breach Judaism's self-respecting boundary that excludes Christian claims?

I believe that none of these fears is warranted. The term "failed Messiah" allows for a variety of Christian and Jewish self-understandings. Some Christians will translate this term into their view of Jesus as a proleptic Messiah. Others will insist on their own traditional understanding of Jesus' messiahship but will see in the term a divinely willed, much needed spur to believers to confront the fact that the world is not yet perfect and that their task is unfinished. Still other Christians, those who insist on Jesus' Trinitarian status, will hear the phrase "failed Messiah" as a reminder that God's self-presentation is deeply humble, not triumphalist. God is identified with the weak and the defeated and with the power of persuasion by model rather than victory by intimidation.

Some Jews will understand the term "false Messiah" as a description of Jesus' actual role in Jewish history; others will understand it as an affirmation of the Jewish "no" to all claims to finality in this unredeemed world. Still others will understand the term as a tribute to Jesus' extraordinary accomplishments, since under the impact of his model, a major fraction of humanity has been brought closer to God and to redemption.

I have already suggested how one might respond to Christian claims that Jesus was the incarnation of God and that his resurrection in glory was decisive proof that Christianity is the only true religion. The resurrection signal was so ambiguous, so subject to alternate interpretations, that it was heard in diametrically opposed fashions—one way by the band elected to start the new faith, another way by the majority called to continue the classic covenantal mission. Only such a subtle signal would fully respect the free will and dignity of the disciples. Only a modest interpretation of the resurrection could prevent the hegemonic grandiosity of Christian claims and the spiritual arrogance that leads it to mistreat and abuse other religions.

From a Jewish perspective, one hopes that the growing Christian emphasis on Jesus as the path to the Father rather than on Jesus as God incarnate may yet win out as a more proper understanding. If it does not, then one may argue that Christianity is wrong on this understanding. But a single error, even on a major point, does not destroy the overall legitimacy of Christianity's covenantal way. Implicit in pluralism is the recognition that there are limits in my truth that leave room for others. Such limits may include the acknowledgment that erroneous doctrines do not necessarily delegitimize the faith that incorporates them.

If the Christian insistence that Jesus is literally God or part of God wins out, then many Jews will argue that closing the biblically portrayed gap between the human and the divine, between the real and the ideal, by incarnation is idolatrous or at least against the grain of the biblical way. But even if incarnation is contradictory to some biblical principles, the model itself is operating out of classic biblical modes—the need to achieve redemption, the desire to close the gap between the human and divine, the role of divine initiatives in redemption, and so on. Thus one can argue that incarnation is improbable and violates other given biblical principles, or that it is unnecessary in light of the continuing career of the Jewish people. But one can hardly rule out the option totally, particularly if it was intended for

Gentiles and not for Jews. Far be it from me as a committed Jew to dictate to God or to other faith communities what religious signals should be given or how they should be heard in those communities— unless they have evil consequences for others.

Both Judaism and Christianity share the totality of their dreams and the flawed finiteness of their methods; nonetheless, they differ so fundamentally that the traditional record is dominated by bitter conflict. However, from a pluralistic perspective—dare one say from the perspective of a divine strategy of redemption rather than from within the communities embedded in historical experience and needs?—both religions have more in common than they have been able to admit to themselves. Both Jews and Christians have a revolutionary dream of total transformation and yet remain willing to accept the finitude and limitations of humans and to proceed one step at a time. Both groups persist in preaching their messages despite the difficulties they have encountered along the way; they press ahead in the face of their historical suffering. And despite the terrible history of their relationship, each has witnessed to God and the human covenantal mission in its own way. For what often seems an eternity, both have hoped and waited, both have transmitted the message and worked for the final redemption. Both need each other's work (and that of others) to realize their deepest hopes.

All in all, the Christian experience of election is valid; they have experienced God's love that singles out the beloved and transforms and revivifies life. They must understand, however, that God's love is capable of singling out again and again; they are not the sole beneficiaries of chosenness.

There remains one question to be asked. When Christians carry on their covenanted mission, are they members of the house of Israel? Are they in a parallel covenant or part of a single covenant alongside Jewry? Personally, I believe that world religions such as Islam and noncovenantal faiths such a Buddhism and forms of Hinduism should be recognized as movements legitimately striving to fulfill the universal divine covenant with humanity. However, only Christians (although possibly also Muslims) may be deemed to be members of the people Israel, even as they practice differing religions than Jewry does. To articulate and defend this thesis would require another essay as long as this one. I adjure you, who love Jerusalem, by gazelles or by hinds of the field, let me not wake that love or rouse that enmity until [the time] please!

Israel, Judaism, and Christianity

DAVID FOX SANDMEL

"Hear, O Israel! The YHVH is our God, the YHVH alone."

Who Is Israel?

Traditionally, both Jews and Christians have considered themselves to be the heirs of biblical Israel, God's chosen people. Perhaps more than any other difference between Judaism and Christianity, this claim to be God's covenantal partner has defined the tragic history of relations between Jews and Christians. It is also the single aspect of Christian theology that has changed most radically since the Shoah, as a result of the process of Christian self-examination, of the dialogue between Jews and Christians, and of advances in critical scholarship concerning religion in the Greco-Roman world. After a brief look at the meaning of "Israel" for Jews, I will examine some classical and contemporary Christian understandings of what it means for Christians to be Israel.

Jews as Israel

For us Jews, the word "Israel" has three interrelated meanings. First, it refers to a *people* descended from the patriarchs and matriarchs. Second, this people Israel has a special *covenant* with God, first established with Abraham and subsequently renewed at Sinai. Third, according to our tradition, God has given us a specific *land*, the land of Israel. In English and in most other modern languages, we refer to ourselves as "Jews" (French, *Juifs*; German, *Juden*). The word "Jew," however, is not our original name. "Jew" occurs rarely in the Tanach or in the *siddur*.[1] Our oldest name is *Yisrael*, Israel; we call ourselves *'am Yisrael*, "the people of Israel," and *benei Yisrael*, "the children of Israel." In non-Orthodox prayer books, one of the first benedictions to be recited in the morning is "Praised are You our Eternal God, Sovereign of the Universe who has made me *Yisrael* (an Israelite)."[2] Similarly, in the Talmud we find, "A *Yisrael*, even though he (or she) sins is still a *Yisrael*."[3] The fact that most translators render *Yisrael* in both the morning benediction and the Talmudic dictum as "Jew" underscores the point. Indeed, the *Shema* doesn't make sense to some Jews until it is rephrased as "Hear, O *Jews!* The Lord is our God, the Lord alone." We, and others, may use the word "Jew," but our *name* is Israel.

As the children of Israel we are the descendants of our ancestors: Abraham and Sara; Isaac and Rebecca; and Jacob, Leah, and Rachel. Jacob was given the name Israel during his encounter with God described in Genesis 32. And Jacob had twelve sons who, in turn, became the twelve tribes of Israel. Thus Israel is a *people*, an extended family in which all Jews are related. But the family is open. Those who become "Jews by choice" are adopted into the Jewish people and become indistinguishable members of the family.[4]

"Israel" also refers to a particular event, since we are the people who entered into the *covenant* with God at Mount Sinai:

> *Israel* encamped there in front of the mountain, and Moses went up to God. YHVH called to him from the mountain, saying, "Thus shall you say to the house of Jacob and declare to the *children of Israel:* 'You have seen what I did to the Egyptians, how I bore you on eagles' wings and brought you to Me. Now then, if you will obey Me faithfully and keep My covenant, you shall be My treasured possession among all the peoples.'" (Ex. 19:2–5, emphasis added)

Finally, as Israel we have a deep emotional attachment to a particular *land* that we also call Israel. The phrase "land of Israel" is much older than the modern State of Israel; it is found in the Book of Samuel and is used regularly by Ezekiel. In the light of a history marked by persecution and genocide, the existence of an independent Jewish state, also called Israel, has made the connection to both the land and the state an integral part of what it means for contemporary Jews to be Israel.

Christians as Israel

The Christian understanding that the church has become God's covenantal partner—has become Israel—can be divided into three stages. The first stage was quite short, lasting only a generation or two after Jesus' execution, and can be found in the writings of Paul. During this stage, the earliest followers of Jesus, both Jewish and Gentile, saw themselves as part of, or at least in relationship to, the Jewish people and the Jewish tradition. The second stage began as Christianity started to develop an identity independent of Judaism, as early as the composition of the Gospels, and continued into the modern period. In this stage, Christianity came to view itself as the "new Israel." Christians are partners with God in a "new" covenant through Christ, and God's covenant with old Israel, with the Jews, is no longer in effect. As a result of their unfaithfulness to God, as recorded in the Tanach itself, and culminating in their rejection of Jesus Christ, the Jews are disqualified from continuing as God's covenantal partners. In its extreme and most dangerous forms, the church as "spiritual Israel" is diametrically opposed to the Jews as "carnal Israel"; the church is the "true Israel" and represents God and good; the Jews are the "false Israel" and represent Satan and evil. During the third stage, in the years since the Shoah, official church bodies and Christian theologians have been reconsidering what it means for both Christians and Jews to be Israel. I will now briefly examine each of these stages.

Paul's Conception of Israel

Christianity began as one of many groups within the complex religious world of Second Temple Judaism. As the movement that evolved from the followers of Jesus grew, it attracted relatively few Jews but was taken up by many Gentiles. By the middle of the second century C.E., Christianity and rabbinic Judaism were well on the way to becoming separate religions. One of the challenges for emerging Christianity was defining the relationship between an increasingly Gentile church and Christianity's Jewish roots. What did it mean to be a Gentile who believed that Jesus as the risen Christ was the Messiah promised *to Israel* by the *God of Israel*, especially when most Jews—Jesus' own people—did not accept Jesus? How could Gentiles share in God's promise to Israel and worship the God of Israel without being Israel?

Whereas the Gospels portray the tension between Judaism and emerging Christianity in the harsh rhetoric of religious polemic, it is the apostle Paul who first tries to provide a theological resolution for the question of the relationship of Christianity to the God of Israel.

This attempted resolution is found most succinctly in Romans 9–11. Paul begins by affirming God's covenants with the people Israel.[5] He then suggests that God's promise is not limited to the physical descendants of Abraham, that is, to the Jews. Rather, the essential aspect of God's covenant with the Jews is not the Jews per se but the fact that God made a choice and that God continues to have the power to choose whomever God wants. Paul states, citing Exodus 33:19, that it is God's choice, or God's grace, that ultimately determines whether mercy is bestowed upon a person or not. Likewise, and here Paul cites Hosea 2:23, God can choose other covenantal partners if that is God's will.

In this section of Romans, Paul also discusses the place of Jewish law in the new covenant. Paul believed that the law by itself was insufficient to ensure redemption or salvation. Faith in the risen Christ is essential: "If you confess with your lips that Jesus is Lord and believe in your heart that God raised him from the dead, you will be saved" (10:9). Thus for Paul, although God's choice of Israel is a historical fact and remains valid, God retains the freedom to choose whomever God wills; God's salvation is not restricted to Israel simply because God has a covenant with it. "There is no distinction between Jew and Greek; the same Lord is Lord of all and bestows his riches upon all who call upon him" (10:13).

As a Jew, Paul was greatly distressed that Israel had not heeded God's message of salvation brought through Jesus (10:14–21). Nonetheless, Paul steadfastly proclaims God's continued covenant with the people of Israel as well as his own allegiance to them. "I ask, then, has God rejected his people? By no means! I myself am an Israelite, a descendant of Abraham, a member of the tribe of Benjamin. God has not rejected his people whom he foreknew" (11:1–2). Indeed, Paul's mission to the Gentiles is, in part, an effort to bring Israel to faith in Christ by provoking their jealousy! (11:13)

At this point Paul invokes the famous metaphor of the olive tree from which some branches have been broken and onto which other branches have been grafted (11:16–24). The tree, both roots and branches, is Israel, the people with whom God made an everlasting covenant. The broken branches are those of Israel, the nation that has rejected the gospel of Jesus Christ. The grafted branches are those of the nations who have accepted the gospel. Gentiles who believe in Jesus become part of Israel—that is, God's covenantal partners—and are able to share in the salvation brought by the Savior who comes from

Israel. In Paul's view, it is Israel's rejection of Jesus that has made possible the election of the Gentiles, and the faith of the Gentiles is an essential part of God's plan for Israel. Paul has described a "new" or, more accurately, "true" Israel consisting of those who have faith in Jesus Christ. This true Israel is not made up of the descendants of Jacob/Israel (though they are not necessarily excluded from it); rather it is the community of both Jewish and Gentile believers, that is, the church.[6]

Paul understood the relationship between the old Israel (the descendants of Jacob) and the new Israel (the church) to be reciprocal; each needed the other in order to achieve final salvation. At the same time, Paul believed that God's promises to the old Israel were irrevocable and would be fulfilled, although admittedly, his understanding of that fulfillment—inasmuch as it required faith in Jesus as Christ—was not one that his contemporaries among the Jews would have accepted.

The Church as the True Israel

The first and second centuries were years of self-definition for both Judaism and Christianity. As Christianity grew and spread through the ancient world, it had to assert its own identity. As part of this process of self-definition and differentiation, each tradition drew distinct boundaries that excluded the other, and each claimed to be the exclusive heir of biblical Israel. The Christian understanding of the church as the "new" Israel came more and more to exclude the "old" Israel. This exclusion is found even in Gospel documents, which often portray the Jews rejecting Jesus and Jesus (and/or God), in turn, rejecting the Jews and turning to the Gentiles.[7] Whereas Paul saw a new Israel that included both "Jew and Greek," later Christianity saw (and some Christians today continue to see) the new Israel (Christianity) superseding the old Israel (Judaism). Justin Martyr (d. ca. 165), an important early church father, uses the term "true spiritual Israel" in referring to the church in his *Dialogue with Trypho*. Justin argues that since the God of Israel acted in Jesus Christ, it is in the church rather than in Israel that the God of Israel is now found.

An important difference between the position of Justin and the one articulated by Paul in Romans 9–11 is that Paul affirmed the irrevocable nature of God's promise to the people of Israel. Justin, and, thereafter, most of Christianity into the modern era, viewed God's relationship with "Abraham's physical descendants" as transient, at best.[8] The historical consequence of this theology was a growing antipathy to Jews and to Judaism in most of the Christian world.

Christianity Reconsiders Israel

We now come to the third stage in the development of Christian identity as Israel, in which the Shoah becomes a defining moment for Christianity. The long tradition of Christian anti-Semitism made the Shoah possible.[9] Many of the people who carried out Hitler's Final Solution considered themselves Christians. In confronting this stark reality, some post-Holocaust Christians have reexamined aspects of traditional Christian teaching, especially the concept of the church as the "true Israel," and have offered new definitions that differ from those of Paul and classical Christianity. Among the fundamental questions probed by theologians such as Paul van Buren, Rosemary Radford Reuther, George Lindbeck, and Franklin Littell are:

- What are Christians to make of the persistence of the Jewish people?
- Is the church the new Israel? If so, who are these people? If not, what happens to the doctrines of promise and fulfillment, law and grace?
- Is Jesus of the people Israel? For whom is he the Messiah?
- What of Israel's land and state?[10]

In addition, many official church bodies have issued public statements that reflect these concerns. In the documents of Vatican II, the Roman Catholic Church reassessed its teachings about Jews and Judaism; it has continued this reassessment in subsequent documents. Protestant churches have made similar pronouncements. For example, in 1987 the General Synod of the United Church of Christ adopted a resolution titled "The Relationship Between the United Church of Christ and the Jewish Community." It stated: "The United Church of Christ affirms its recognition that God's covenant with the Jewish people has not been rescinded or abrogated by God, but remains in full force, inasmuch as 'the gifts and the call of God are irrevocable' (Rom. 11:29)."[11]

The moral imperative to disavow triumphalist teachings that have led to atrocities in the past is the driving force behind the Christian theological reevaluation of Jews and Judaism. Hans Küng, a Roman Catholic theologian, examines the history of Jewish–Christian relations and states: "Only one thing is of any use now: a radical metanoia [reorientation], repentance and re-thinking; we must start on a new road, no longer leading away from the Jew, but toward them."[12] Küng concludes that the church's opposition to the Jews is tantamount to opposition to God. Furthermore, the church "must seek in every way to enter into sympathetic dialogue with the ancient people of God." Küng also argues that the church and Israel are two distinct peoples of God:

> Like Israel and following Israel the Church sees itself as the journeying people of God, constantly being delivered from bondage, constantly wandering through the wilderness of this age, constantly maintaining the tension between thankful commemoration and hopeful expectation and preparing itself for its entry into the promised land, the messianic kingdom, the goal that always lies in the future.[13]

The realities of history are also the starting point for Kendall Soulen's book *The God of Israel and Christian Theology*. In his critique of traditional Christian theology, Soulen argues that it has essentially omitted the history of Israel/Jews from its telling of its own story. In his reconstruction of what he calls "the standard canonical framework," there are four stages of history. First, God creates the world and humanity. Second, humanity, through the sin of Adam and Eve, disobeys and falls. Third, "lost humanity" is redeemed in Christ. Fourth, God brings the final redemption of the world at the "end of time." The church (that is, those who believe in Jesus as Christ) is Israel inasmuch as it has become the people of God through its fidelity to Jesus Christ, not because it is descended from a single ancestor. Its status as a people is not defined solely by the promises of Sinai, nor does it necessarily entail a connection to any particular land. Noticeably missing from this rehearsal of the Christian sacred story is any mention of what we Jews would consider the core of our history. In this view, the Jews and their story are irrelevant to the story of the new true Israel, Christianity.

Soulen notes, however, that "significant parts of the Christian church today reject supersessionism and affirm God's fidelity to the Jewish people. From there we ask: *what are the implications of this new development for the rest of Christian theology?*"[14] Soulen offers his own answer: "Christians should acknowledge that God's history with Israel and the nations is the permanent and enduring medium of God's work as the Consummator of human creation, and therefore it is also the permanent and enduring context of the gospel about Jesus."[15] Rather than viewing the history of Israel and the nations as preparation for the gospel, Soulen argues that this history "*surrounds* the gospel as its constant horizon, context, and goal."[16] Soulen suggests that Christianity cannot understand itself unless it posits an Israel whose covenant with God coexists with and informs the new covenant. Scott Bader-Saye, another Christian theologian who has considered the meaning of election for contemporary Christianity, refers to the church as "God's chosen people *with* Israel" (emphasis added).[17]

The concept of the church as the people of God along with the Jews, a concept that does not depend on denying Jews our identity and covenantal legitimacy, is a radical shift in Christian thinking. This step has required painful soul-searching and theological courage on the part of those Christians who have taken it. The Jewish community should view this shift positively; it signifies a real change in Christian understandings of Jews and Judaism and creates a profound basis for cooperation and exchange.

Above and beyond this basis of exchange, however, we ought to ask another question: does this new shift among Christians have theological implications for Jews? Does the recognition on the part of some Christians that we Jews continue to be Israel in covenant with God require that, in turn, we must acknowledge the legitimacy of the church's claim to identify with the name "Israel"? As I have tried to show in this brief essay, Jewish and Christian definitions of what it means to be Israel are quite different from one another. Jewish tradition already recognizes and affirms Gentiles who acknowledge the oneness of God. Jews can recognize Christians as people who believe in the God of Israel. From a Jewish perspective, however, that belief, in and of itself, does not make Christianity part of Israel, *as we understand Israel*, that is, a *people* that has a special *covenant* with God who has given us a specific *land*. Although Christians can acknowledge that Israel's covenant with God is eternal, fidelity to Jewish tradition precludes our recognition as Israel of those who do not meet our definitional criteria. This is but one of the enduring differences between Jews and Christians, and we both must not only accept but also affirm this difference if we are truly committed to supporting each other's integrity.

Changes in Christian theology regarding Jews and Judaism, how-ever, do challenge us to find new ways to relate to Christians and Christianity. Now that some in the Christian world affirm God's con-tinuing covenant with the Jews, we need to consider the theological implication of their claim to be in covenant with that same God.

Israel and the Church:
A Christian Response to
Irving Greenberg's Covenantal Pluralism

R. KENDALL SOULEN

A Brief Portrait of the Church

As a Christian, my task here is to state briefly how I understand the church and in doing so to respond to at least some of the points raised by Rabbi Greenberg.

In my view, the nature of the church can be clarified only by starting with what is generally agreed to be an odd claim (even by those who hold it to be true): the One God, the Creator and Consummator of all things, is the God of the Jews. If God is not God as he is portrayed in the Scriptures of the Jewish people—a God who makes promises to some for the benefit of all—then virtually nothing of what the church proclaims is worth bothering with. If, on the other hand, the Mystery-at-the-Heart-of-all-Things is the I AM who accosted Moses at the bush, then the gospel (the proclamation of which is the church's rai-son d'être) is at least possibly true. This is not to say that everything the church believes is already spelled out in what Christians tradition-ally call the Old Testament. But it is to say that only the God who made a beloved people Israel from Sarah's barren womb could have raised a beloved child Jesus from the dead.

According to Christian understanding, the church is what one might expect to come into existence once God's promise to Abraham—"in you all the families of the earth shall be blessed" (Gen. 12:3)—has been fulfilled. The Christian notion of a fulfilled promise is frequently misunderstood (not least by Christians), so let me define the term using the words of the Swiss theologian Karl Barth: "The promise is fulfilled does not mean: the promise comes to an end and is replaced by the actual thing promised. It means: the promise itself is now whole, complete, unambiguous, and hence already mighty."[1]

To put it another way, a fulfilled promise is still a promise, but one that has been "filled up" with the power of the promised future, so that the power spills over into the present. Christians believe that God's promise to Abraham—indeed, that *all* of God's promises—have been "filled up" in Jesus Christ. Oddly enough, this belief is tied directly to the fact that Jesus is, in Rabbi Greenberg's words, a failed Messiah, or, as Christians are more accustomed to saying, a crucified Messiah. A crucified Messiah is one on whom the forces of death and destruction have done their worst, so that—if he be raised—he is already their victor, and life's final victory over death has already begun to spill over into the present.

The church, then, can be compared to the commotion that happens after the ringing of a dinner bell but before everyone has settled down to dinner. Fittingly enough, life in the church begins with a good washing (baptism), and its central corporate act is a simple meal (Eucharist) that anticipates the end-time banquet of the new creation. Every act of Christian worship is accompanied by preaching, which echoes the good news of the first dinner bell. The commotion, beginning in Jerusalem, has gradually spread to the ends of the earth, so that now a sizable portion of the world is getting ready for I AM's supper in the name of Jesus.

This brief characterization of the church will have to suffice. The church is the company of those who believe that the promise of life's victory over death has been "filled up" in Jesus Christ, who seek to live according to the Spirit of that victory in the present time, and who look forward to the final triumph of life over death in the coming reign of Israel's God.

The Jewish–Christian Conundrum

The time has come to consider a major perplexity that confronts the view of the church that I have just presented: though Jews were the first to proclaim the gospel, it has been mostly Gentiles who have responded. In terms of our analogy, Jews rang the dinner bell, but Gentiles came to dinner. As for the bulk of Jewry and what eventually became normative Judaism, the response was simple: false alarm.

From his vantage point as a Jewish thinker, Rabbi Greenberg addresses this perplexity in a generous and profound manner by suggesting that the alarm was genuine but intended only for the Gentiles. He proposes a model of Judaism's relation to Christianity that I think might be called covenantal pluralism, according to which God's covenant with the Jews spins off other covenantal communities that are relatively independent of the Jewish people but nevertheless oriented toward a very Jewish hope—God's consummation and redemption of the world. From this point of view, the resurrection was the signal that initiated one such spin-off among the Gentiles. It was not an event intended for the Jewish people as a whole, nor one that "filled up" God's promises to Israel.[2]

Although I perceive elements of profound truth in Rabbi Greenberg's view, I do not believe that Christians can be completely satisfied with his answer. Christians, in my view, cannot easily yield on the idea that the resurrection of a crucified Messiah, if true at all, has significance for everyone. This claim may be puzzling and even offensive to many Jews. But it is tied up with the very notion of resurrection, which by its nature signals the dawn of new creation. It would make little sense, I think, for a Jew to say that God is Creator, but only of Jews. If God is Creator at all, God is Creator of Jews and Gentiles alike. Similarly, if Jesus inaugurates a new creation by his victory over death, then again he does so for all. True, neither Jesus' resurrection nor the dawn of new creation presents itself self-evidently to human experience. But the same thing is true of the affirmation that Israel is the chosen people of God, or, for that matter, that the universe is the good creation of God. Christians may be wrong that Jesus is raised from the dead, but, believing and trusting in this, it is all but impossible for them to relinquish the conviction that the gospel—the tidings of God's promises filled up in Christ—is good news for all.

But now we are back to our conundrum. If the gospel is for all, then why is it not also embraced by the Jews, who by all accounts know a thing or two about God and God's promises? There can be no denying that this circumstance has puzzled Christians from the earliest decades of the Christian movement. Paul, for one, grappled passionately with the issue at the climax of his most important letter (Rom. 9–11). What made the issue so difficult for Paul was his determination to maintain the truth of two seemingly irreconcilable convictions: the gospel was God's power of salvation for everyone, Jew and Gentile alike, *and* God's promises to Israel were irrevocable, including that part of Israel that did not believe in the gospel. Unfortunately, subsequent generations of Christians resolved the conundrum much more simply by just dropping the second of Paul's two great convictions. (Rabbi Greenberg for his part resolves the conundrum by dropping the first, but I have already explained why I believe Christians will have difficulty following him.) These Christians taught that God's covenant with the Jewish people was over, and that henceforth the church alone stood in its place. This teaching, often called supersessionism today, became the church's standard view on the matter, and it has prevailed among almost all branches of the Christian church until recent times.[3]

Jews, I need hardly say, have never found the teaching of supersessionism convincing. Many Christians (including myself) now concur with them on this point. If we find it difficult to yield on the gospel's universal implications, we find it equally impossible to continue to hold that God has annulled his covenant with the Jewish people on account of their posture toward the gospel. Christians have rediscovered the relevance of Paul's approach to the conundrum. In the climactic section of Romans, Paul warns his Gentile readers not to assume that God has withdrawn His faithfulness toward the Jewish people, even those who have not believed in Jesus. Although in a sense different from Rabbi Greenberg in his conclusion, Paul, too, is forced to conclude that the resurrection signal is not yet intended for most of Jewry. With a rare solemnity, Paul declares that Israel's "no" to the gospel is actually God's own doing, and that it serves the propagation of the gospel among the nations. Despite its "no," Israel remains God's beloved on account of the promises God gave to the patriarchs. "For the gifts and the calling of God are irrevocable" (Rom. 11:29), Paul concludes.

Had the church paid more attention to Paul's warning during the first centuries of its existence, it would never have adopted the simplistic theory that God has abrogated his covenant with the Jewish people and put a Gentile church in its place. In any case, during the past generation, Paul's warning has finally begun to register with many Christians. Citing the Pauline texts in question, many Christian communions have issued public declarations repudiating the idea that God has abrogated his covenant with the Jewish people on account of its "no" to the gospel about Jesus.[4]

"Carnal" Israel, "Spiritual" Church?

The picture that emerges from these considerations suggests that the church is related to the Jewish people in a way that incorporates elements of both independence and dependence, although these elements are configured somewhat differently than in Rabbi Greenberg's account. The church is independent of the Jewish people in the sense that it must represent the truth of the gospel by word and deed before all the nations, despite (or perhaps, thanks to!) the posture that most Jews take toward it. Yet the church is dependent on the Jewish people in the sense that the people Israel are not just one nation among the others, but the people who already and uniquely stand in covenant relationship to God, and who have already received the promise of life's victory over death, God's overflowing fidelity to which is the very content of the gospel itself. The gospel does not exclude the affirmation of God's fidelity to His promises to the Jews. The gospel requires it. Since these promises include at a minimum the survival and security of the Jews as an identifiable people (cf. Lk. 1:68–79), Christians should pray for and rejoice in everything that contributes to these ends in a manner consistent with the dignity and rights of the other families of the earth.

Rabbi Greenberg alludes to the destructive power of a second and more elaborate form of supersessionism that goes one step beyond the simple view that God has rejected the Jews on account of their refusal to believe the gospel. Since I agree with Rabbi Greenberg that this second view is at least as wrongheaded as the first, I want to address it directly.

At the heart of the second version of supersessionism is a dualistic (and therefore biblically suspect) contrast between what is carnal and transitory and what is spiritual and enduring. According to this view, God's covenant with Israel was carnal, since it was transmitted by carnal means (natural descent from the patriarchs) and since it focused on carnal goods (posterity, prosperity, and land). In contrast, the church is spiritual, since membership is conferred by faith and not by natural descent, and since it focuses on spiritual goods such as salvation from sin and eternal life. According to this second version of supersessionism, God elected Israel as a kind of "dry run" on His way to the church, like a sculptor who first molds a design in clay before committing it to marble. Once the spiritual church appears, carnal Israel becomes obsolete. Like a clay model, it can be set aside and even destroyed, since the reality that it once prefigured is now present.

In my view, this second form of supersessionism is even more perni-
cious than the first, since it implies that God's covenant with the Jewish people is inherently obsolete and inferior, quite apart from
whether the Jewish people are faithful or not. Yet like many bad theological ideas, this one goes astray by distorting a genuine feature of
biblical reality, one on which both Christians and Jews can agree.
There really is an important difference between Judaism and Christianity regarding how one becomes a Jew or a Christian, respectively.
Christians can free themselves from the spell of supersessionism in its
second form by coming to a more sound appreciation of this difference and by interpreting it in a nondualistic way.

Traditionally, Jews have understood themselves as God's chosen
people descended from the patriarchs and matriarchs. Hence the ordinary way of becoming a Jew is to be born of a Jewish mother. Even
converts, who are not Jews by birth, become members of the chosen
family through the appropriate ritual. This, of course, does not mean
that Jews share a common ethnicity or belong to a common race, another grotesque distortion. But, to use the language of the Jewish theologian Michael Wyschogrod, it does mean that God's election of the
Jewish people is like the election of a natural family. Of course, there
are segments of Judaism today that wish to downplay this aspect of the
tradition by putting the emphasis on a person's freedom to choose his
or her own religious identity. Still, the dominant interpretation remains. Most Jews are members of the chosen people by birth, and the
privileges and obligations of the covenant fall to them accordingly.

Christians, on the other hand, understand themselves as a fellowship that can be entered only through repentance and rebirth into the
messianic community (that is, by getting washed!). Hence, no one can
be born a Christian. Once again, there are segments of the Christian
community that blur this reality, especially by confusing Christian
identity with ethnic or national history, or by the practice of indiscriminate infant baptism. Yet the dominant interpretation remains:
one becomes a Christian through faith in Jesus as Messiah and Lord,
and through baptism in the name of the Father, and the Son, and the
Holy Spirit.

When Christians yoke this genuine difference between Judaism and
Christianity to an unbiblical dualism of flesh and spirit, supersessionism and other distortions result. As I noted, Christians become
tempted to view Judaism as spiritually inferior and destined to disappear. They overlook the importance of repentance, faith, obedience,

and forgiveness in Jewish life. Moreover, Christians become alienated from Jesus and the first disciples, who all lived and died as Jews. Christians often forget that Jesus' first Jewish followers continued to observe the Torah even while they dispensed with the requirement that Jesus' Gentile followers do the same (in keeping with the belief that Jesus had inaugurated the age when the nations would at last worship the God of Israel). Finally, the dualism of flesh and spirit tempts Christians to locate the reality of the church in an invisible realm cut off from the material world.

In my view, Christians need to dismantle this second theory of supersessionism for the sake of a better understanding not only of Judaism but of the church itself. In this connection, I and many other Christian theologians have found the work of Jewish thinkers especially helpful. Jewish thinkers such as Michael Wyschogrod have argued, for example, that Israel's "carnal" election makes it superior in certain respects to the church, whose membership is based on baptism and faith. When the costs of witnessing to God become too high, Christians find it relatively easy to disavow their baptismal identities, whereas Jews are not so easily quit of their carnal identity as God's covenant people. Therefore, Jews may remain witnesses to God in situations where Christians have melted from the scene.[5]

True, claims of superiority and inferiority are probably beside the point, even when reversed. The crucial point is that Christians can learn from Wyschogrod and others that God's election of Israel as a human family is not a temporary expedient on the way to the church. God's choice of the Jewish people, and the distinction between Jew and Gentile that it entails, are an abiding part of God's positive purpose in the world, irrespective of the posture that Jews may take toward the church's claims on behalf of Jesus of Nazareth. For its part, the church must understand itself as a messianic community of Jew and Gentile that arises through rebirth into fellowship with Jesus Christ, the one who has come and who will come again. But Christians do no honor to this confession by suggesting that fellowship in Christ replaces or brings to an end God's covenant with Abraham's chosen children after the flesh. As Paul declared in another of his letters, Christ means the confirmation rather than the invalidation of God's promises. "For all the promises of God find their Yes in him" (2 Cor. 1:20).

In short, whereas Christian theology traditionally cited the church's character as a community of rebirth in order to deduce the obsolescence of carnal Israel, I believe the correct conclusion is just the opposite. Because the church is a community of rebirth, it does not compete with the Jewish people as God's covenant people "according to the flesh" and therefore cannot supersede them. I believe this corrective to traditional Christian teaching is necessary in addition to the one noted earlier, according to which Gentile Christians should confess that Judaism's "no" to Jesus Christ in no way detracts from God's fidelity to his promises to Israel. Moreover, the church should accommodate its missionary practice to these insights. Gentile Christians should proclaim their faith in Christ before Jews by the quality of their communal life, and not by organized missionary activity. In my view, anything that erodes the capacity of the Jewish people to maintain itself as a distinct community from generation to generation is ultimately antithetical to the interests of Christian faith.

By way of conclusion, let me state that I do not think the views that I have proposed here would result in agreement between Jews and Christians even if every Christian on earth were eventually to adopt them. In my view, the relation between Jews and Christians includes an irreducible element of dispute and even rivalry. Above all, Christians and Jews will continue to disagree about whether God's promises have been "filled up" in Jesus of Nazareth, and hence about whether the church is in fact the genuinely messianic fellowship that it claims to be. But, from the Christian point of view at least, the dispute will no longer be about *whether* the other community enjoys a rightful and indispensable place in God's economy, but about *how* this is so. On these terms, I do believe that even the remaining element of rivalry between Jews and Christians can serve the faithfulness of both communities and the glory of God.

8

WORSHIP

Jewish and Christian Liturgy

LAWRENCE A. HOFFMAN

Obvious Parallels

Jewish and Christian liturgy emerged at roughly the same time and from a common heritage. We should therefore expect some obvious parallels, easily explainable by their shared provenance. But origins are one thing, and development is another. Jewish liturgy "peaked" by the time of the Mishnah's promulgation (c. 200), in the sense that its basic structure and calendrical formulation were already in place by then. Christian liturgy did not reach that state until the wake of the Council of Nicea (325) and beyond. So the surface similarities are spotty and not altogether self-evident. Also, Christian liturgy conflated the old Jewish mealtime prayer practice with the synagogal liturgy of the word, making them both over into the Eucharist, whereas table and synagogue prayer remained separate for Jews. Still, a Jew who visits church worship on an average Sunday will nod in knowing recognition.

Both Jewish and Christian services look forward and backward simultaneously, collapsing time into a single worship moment—that is, they remember time past when a covenant was initiated and look ahead to a messianic future when the covenantal promise will be realized. Both demand a certain structural order—in fact, Christians describe their worship as an *ordo*, the Latin equivalent for *seder* or *siddur* (order), the word customarily used for the Jewish service.[1] Both rely heavily on the Hebrew Bible, especially psalms. They both open with a call to prayer; then lead up to the reading of scripture that prompts a sermon. Both contain heavy doses of praise for God, and both carry petitions for the welfare of those to whom worshipers wish to draw God's attention. Both climax in prayer for a speedy arrival of the Dominion of God that is yet to come in all its fullness. For Jews, there is the *Kaddish* (*ve-yamlich malchuteih* = "May His kingdom come") and for Christians, the Lord's Prayer ("Thy kingdom come").

Despite all these similarities, however, a Jewish visitor to a Christian service is apt to feel lost as the worship unfolds. However similar Christian liturgy might once have been to its Jewish prototype, both Judaism and Christianity quickly developed their own distinctive shape and character. Lent, for example, was in all probability related originally to the preparatory period for Passover, marked in the synagogue by special readings of Torah (*Parashat Parah* and *Parashat Hachodesh*, which urge ritual purification and then announce the month of Nisan). Easter was the Christian Passover, kept (originally) on Passover day, the fourteenth day of Nisan. By the fourth century, however, Easter had been moved to the first Sunday after the first full moon after the spring equinox—which is to say after the onset of Passover, which occurred on the full moon itself; and Lent was determined to be forty days long (via various counting methods) and separated from any Jewish origins.

Similarly, less and less did Jews see themselves as having anything whatever to do with Christianity, which seemed increasingly foreign to them, especially in its primary liturgical practice, the Eucharist. The Eucharist makes Christianity what it is. All Christians either celebrate it or take their stand as the unique Christians they are by not celebrating it. ("Celebrate" is a Christian term, defining the action of the person who officially performs the ritual. It parallels what Jews mean when they say that someone "leads services" or, in Hebrew, acts as *sheli'ach tsibur*).[2]

Christians developed the Eucharist as a response to their tradition that, as Paul put it:

The Lord Jesus, on the night that he was betrayed, took a loaf of bread, and when he had given thanks, he broke it and said, "This is my body that is for you. Do this in remembrance of me." In the same way, he took the cup after supper, saying, "This cup is the new covenant in my blood. Do this as often as you drink it, in remembrance of me."

Paul then adds, "For as often as you eat this bread and drink the cup, you proclaim the Lord's death until he comes."[3]

The essence of Christian worship, the Eucharist, remains distinctively Christian, whatever its Jewish origins might once have been. Since the Eucharist is at the core of Christian faith, it is the Eucharist that demands the attention of Jews who want to understand what Christianity is all about.

A Deeper Analysis

Studying the Eucharist forces us into a deeper analysis. We need to contend with the fact that Christians think explicitly about the theological meanings of their liturgy, whereas Jews do not, even though Jewish liturgy does have underlying theological assumptions. A deeper analysis of Christian worship in Jewish terms requires that we elicit the implicit theological meanings that Jewish worship contains and then compare them to the parallel theological notions that the commentators on Christian worship explicitly profess. This is an exercise in comparative liturgical theology, akin to what anthropologist Clifford Geertz calls "thick description," the search for deeply rooted cultural meanings. Geertz cites Paul Ricoeur, who wants to go beyond the "speech event" to the "meaning of the speech event."[4] So, too, I want to go beyond the "liturgical event" (a Christian prayer that looks like a Jewish one) to the "meaning of the liturgical event"—what the liturgical act or prayer in question means in terms of the way Jews and Christians locate themselves in the world. The first thing to ask is, "What does Christian worship imply about the categories in which Christians think?" Looking then at the Jewish parallel, we can ask, "To what extent does Judaism (at least implicitly) think in the same categories?" and "Within the common categories, how are Judaism and Christianity similar and how different?"

In large part, Christians think of the Eucharist in terms of sacrifice, remembrance, and thanksgiving. We want to know the extent to which Jewish liturgy operates, at least implicitly, with the same three concepts at its center.

Sacrifice

Sacrifice is the concept about which Christians have had the most internal debate. At least since Luther, the question has been whether at the Eucharist an actual sacrifice is taking place. Modern Jews and Christians have domesticated the idea of sacrifice, thinking of it only in moralistic terms, for instance, so that we speak easily of self-sacrifice or of sacrificing valuable time to do a good deed. But that is distinctly not what first- or second-century Jews and Christians meant by the term. Until 70, when it was destroyed, the dominating institution in Jewish life had been the Temple, which boasted the only liturgy that most people would have said mattered: sacrifice. Fully one-sixth of the Mishnah is devoted expressly to Temple sacrifice, and even sections that are not, like descriptions of holidays, allot inordinate space to the sacrificial marking of sacred time. Passover, for instance, is indeed a time of prayer, but the prayers described in the Mishnah are mostly psalms said by the Levites as part of the offering of the paschal lamb. The home liturgy for the Seder is allotted only one chapter in ten. Of the other nine, four describe food regulations, and five are given over to sacrifice.

When the Temple fell, sacrifice ceased, since Deuteronomy had banished sacrifice anywhere but in the Temple complex. The rhetoric of sacrifice, however, was retained and applied to the alternative areas of sacred ritual: the home and the synagogue. Nowadays, it is common to think of the synagogue as primary, but at the time, it was still the home that ranked foremost in terms of ritual significance. An institution that paralleled the Temple was the *chavurah*, or table group: a Jewish version of the Greco-Roman symposium tradition.[5] Early on, the *chavurah* attracted cultic terminology: the table was seen as an altar and the participants who ate there as its priests. To the extent that Jesus' Last Supper with his disciples was such a *chavurah* meal, we can understand his references to himself as sacrificial victim as a rhetorical free play on a Jewish sacrificial theme.

Indeed, the eucharistic linkage of bread and wine with the body and blood of Christ, the new paschal lamb for Christians, arises out of a symbolic similarity to Jewish practice at the time. Jesus spoke as a Jew; his disciples heard him through Jewish ears. Much as it sounds Christian today, what Jesus said and did at that fateful gathering was rooted in normative Jewish liturgical practice. Bread was already a Jewish symbol of salvation that paralleled and then took the place of the paschal lamb as the primary symbol of God's deliverance of Israel in Egypt, and, by extension, of the ultimate deliverance with which history would someday end. The Talmud tells us, for instance, that the normal blessing over bread, "Blessed art thou . . . who brings forth bread from the earth," denotes not just the ordinary bread one holds in one's hand, but the eschatological promise that God will someday really bring forth bread from the earth, a return to the paradise that was Eden, when human beings did not have to work for their bread because bread trees grew abundantly in the garden. Similarly, the Christian Lord's Prayer—an eschatological parallel to the Jewish *Kaddish*—requests, "Give us this day our daily bread"; church fathers identify the bread in question not just as ordinary bread but as "bread of the kingdom."[6]

Wine, too, was widely assumed to be symbolic of blood. The Bible itself calls wine *dam anavim* (the blood of grapes). By rabbinic times, Jews identified two types of blood as especially apt to bring deliverance: the blood of the paschal lamb and the blood of circumcision. A midrash assumes that both of these blood types were smeared on the lintels of Jewish homes in Egypt to warn the angel of death to "pass over" them and kill only the first born of families who lacked the telltale blood sign.[7] The symbolic use of wine appears liturgically, therefore, in both the Seder and the rite of circumcision. The Palestinian Talmud calls *charoset*, the mixture made variously throughout time but always with a wine base, *zecher la-dam* (in remembrance of the blood [of the paschal lamb]).[8] As for circumcision, wine is applied to the lips of the baby boy just at the point where the operation causes blood to flow. Though widely regarded nowadays as just an anesthetic for the infant, the original use of wine was symbolic, as if to say, "Blood out; wine (as blood) in." As the wine is administered, the ritual script calls for a citation from Ezekiel: "I saw you wallowing in your blood and I said to you, 'By your blood, live; by your blood, live.'"[9]

The symbolic system that uses wine for blood and bread for the paschal lamb is, therefore, preeminently Jewish. Christianity applied the Jewish system to the crucified Christ, seen as the new paschal lamb whose body and blood were offered up on the cross.

It is helpful to think of liturgy as a sacred drama and of liturgical symbols as props that are paired with identifying words from the liturgical script. The result is a sort of exegetical, rather than systematic, theology. Even Christians who know little about Christian belief know that the host is "the body of Christ," or that the sunrise following the Easter vigil means that "Christ has risen." The ritual tells them so. For similar reasons, Jews know that the unleavened bread is "the poor bread that our ancestors ate in the Land of Egypt," or that the scroll of Torah is "the Torah which Moses set before the Israelites, by the mouth of God and by the hand of Moses." Sometimes the ritual meaning is understood literally, sometimes not. Some medieval Jews, for instance, changed "This is the poor bread" to "This is *like* the poor bread," probably because they did not want participants in the Seder rite to bestow the same degree of sacramental realism upon bread that Christians did during the Eucharist. Some modern Jews did away with "by the mouth of God and by the hand of Moses" because their nineteenth-century science had convinced then that the Torah was a human document that had evolved through time. In any event, ritual symbolism requires that the symbol be at hand and that there be a ready identification somewhere in the religious script.

In that regard, both Judaism and Christianity had to contend with the absence of paschal sacrifices after the Temple's fall. In addition, Christianity rejected circumcision. Christian exegesis, therefore, could hardly identify wine as circumcision blood. It could, however, replace paschal lamb blood with the blood of Jesus, who was identified as the final paschal sacrifice. With Judaism, it was the other way around. It had no alternative paschal lamb interpretation, but it retained circumcision. The result is that where ancient Judaism had once offered two kinds of saving blood, each of the two religions that emerged from that period was left with only one, and a different one at that: for Christian liturgy, the blood of the lamb; for Jewish liturgy, the blood of circumcision.

Sacrificial rhetoric went deep within the Jewish psyche. Even with the Temple destroyed, the language of sacrifice remained as a rationale for other forms of worship. We saw how it was transferred to the meal table at home. It also entered the synagogue service. Judaism's primary prayer, the *Tefillah* (or *Amidah*), was likened to the ancient *Tamid*, the public sacrifice offered daily, mornings and afternoons. Some authorities even declared the evening *Tefillah* (which was already in place) optional, since there had been no evening sacrifice for it to replace. Prayer was called "the offering of our lips." The final blessing of the *Tefillah* was the priestly benediction that had once concluded the Temple offering. The morning service was outfitted with biblical readings about offerings, and these were named *korbanot*, "sacrifices," to imply that if we cannot perform the sacrifices, we can at least read about them. Prayers for a restoration of the cult were introduced. Yom Kippur liturgy attracted a lengthy poetic description of the Temple offering that had characterized the Day of Atonement. Again, unable to offer it, we can read about it.

Everywhere we look, then, although the fact of sacrifice was gone, its rhetoric was retained as a running interpretation of prayer's efficacy. And here again Christianity borrowed the Jewish theme, but applied it in its own way. In the Epistle to the Hebrews, Jesus appears as the final high priest appointed by God as a sign of the new covenant heralded by Jesus' death. In the old covenant, the high priest offered sacrifices for his own sins and for the sins of the people. But Jesus is sinless. He sacrifices himself anyway, however, for the sins of the people. He is, therefore, both the last and final priest and the last and final sacrifice. In sum (Heb. 10:10), "By God's will, we have been sanctified by the offering of the body of Jesus Christ once and for all."

With this Epistle as scriptural precedent, Christian liturgy developed the theme of sacrifice in ways that Judaism did not. Gordon Lathrop reminds us just how deeply the rhetoric goes in the Eucharist. The table is an "altar" where "priests serve." Greek Christian traditions call for a prayer called the *anaphora*, meaning "offering" or "something carried up" in sacrifice. In the Roman Catholic Church, the bread and wine are called *oblata*, "things offered." And even in Protestant churches, which shun much of this language, the collection plate is usually called an "offering," as are certain prayers spoken at its presentation.[10] Christian commentators sometimes speak of actually participating (through the Eucharist) in the final sacrifice.

Sacrificial eucharistic theology is not shared universally by each and every Christian author. It became and remains a matter of contention among Christians. Joseph A. Jungmann's 1976 treatise on the Mass, for instance, is in part a polemic against the Protestant denial of Catholic sacrificial doctrine. He is careful to cite Cyprian (200–258) and Augustine (354–430) as emphatically demanding the sacrificial element in the Eucharist. He concludes that "in Catholic theology, the Mass is definitely a sacrifice under a two-fold aspect: it is the sacrifice of Christ re-presented or made present anew; and as re-presentation it is also itself an offering, an *oblatio*, a sacrifice."[11]

Jews are likely to find this internal theological debate baffling, but that is only because what talmudic niceties are to Jews, theological precision is to Christians. When, for instance, Alexander Schmemann says, "The Eucharist is a manifestation and actualization of the sacrificial character of the Church," or that Christ is "the complete, only, and consummate sacrifice of all sacrifices," he is speaking in Christian language.[12] But the essence of the Christian claim is Jewish to its core. As Jews had a paschal offering, so, too, do Christians. Jesus is to the new covenant what the paschal lamb had been to the Jewish covenant on Sinai. What Jews and Christians have in common is root metaphor. Where they differ rhetorically is in the set of questions they ask of the metaphor. Jews are distinctively Jewish when, as in the Talmud, they engage in halachic debate about the way in which a sacrifice took place when the Temple stood. Christians become distinctively Christian when they debate the theological significance of the sacrificed Christ.

All of this leads us to a critical general observation. Jews experience Christian theological dialogue as dense, just as Christians find talmudic debate impenetrable. The language of Jewish law is an internal Jewish code, and the language of theology is a Christian one. Halachah eventually becomes *pilpul*, just as theology evokes scholasticism. These respective developments should be seen as "poetic" versions of the internal codes taken to their extreme, used (that is to say) for their own sake, rather than to solve real problems in the world.

But that does not mean that Jews and Christians cannot dialogue at a very deep level. We can understand each other's liturgies if we return to our shared conceptual bedrock.

Remembrance

Christian eucharistic liturgy arises as a consequence of Jesus' command, "Do this is in remembrance of me." But it is hard for modern readers to grasp what remembrance meant back then.

Moderns think memory is simply the calling to mind of an event that occurred in the past. Unlike the original event, the recollection is in the mind alone. It does not actually reenact the past. It is not "real." As Annie says in her Broadway musical, "That's then; not now."

Christian theology of the Eucharist, however, makes no such sharp division between then and now. Christian remembrance is described as *anamnesis*, about which a dictionary on sacramental worship comments: "This Greek word is practically untranslatable in English. 'Memorial,' 'commemoration,' 'remembrance' all suggest a recollection of the past, whereas *anamnesis* means making present an object or person from the past. Sometimes the term 'reactualization' has been used to indicate the force of *anamnesis*."[13]

The classical Christian liturgy of the Eucharist contains a section known as the *anamnesis*. It precedes the actual offering of the bread and wine and, via prayer, establishes the nature of the moment by saying something about the remembrance that is called to mind and made present. The prototype is a eucharistic prayer by the third-century church father Hippolytus, who makes explicit how the offering is "in memory" of Christ by saying: "Having, therefore, in remembrance His death and resurrection, we offer unto Thee the bread and the cup."[14] Christian literature is filled with debate over the nature of this "remembrance," the best known instance being the lengthy argument on whether—and, if so, how—the "real presence" of Christ occurs in the wine and bread of communion.[15]

Once again we have an instance of an internal conversation among Christians, but built on a bedrock conceptual foundation that Jews and Christians share. For Jews, the apt equivalent terms for *anamnesis* are the Hebrew *zecher* and *zikaron*, both of which mean "remembrance" in the context of the liturgy.

The examples are legion, but of them all, Jews are most likely to recognize *zecher litsi'at mitsrayim* (in remembrance of the Exodus from Egypt) and *zikaron le-ma'asei vereishit* (in remembrance of the work of creation)—two formulas that occur in the *Kiddush*, the prayer that inaugurates the Sabbath and festivals. Though Jews today may think of these words just as wistful glances back in time, the rabbis saw *zecher* (or *zikaron*) as *anamnesis*: making the past present.

It helps to think of *zecher* (remembrance) as a "pointer" through time, connecting the present to the past. If we adopt the notion from physics of a time/space continuum, the problem of making the past present goes away. Since time and space are actually a single unit, we can transform one into the other by just changing the metaphors in which we think. Imagine, then, that all things that ever happened co-exist at different points in space. They may be connected by pointers. *Zecher* and *anamnesis* are liturgical pointers connecting events in the time/space continuum.

What makes the matter fascinating is that Judaism describes God, too, as remembering. Unlike human beings, however, God is omniscient: God sees everything all the time, a nice way of combining the two: "everything" (space) and "all the time" (time). There should be no need to remind an omniscient God of anything, even though Jewish liturgy regularly does just that, so we should reconceptualize "reminding" God as "claiming God's attention." A *zecher* or *zikaron* with regard to God is not so much a reminder or remembrance as it is a pointer that directs God's thoughts along the proper path.

Now we are in a position to understand Jesus' words from a Jewish perspective. We saw above that bread was a Jewish symbol of salvation that paralleled and then took the place of the paschal sacrifice. More specifically, it was *zecher la-pesach* (a remembrance of [or pointer to] the paschal lamb) offered in the Temple. But that lamb was a reenactment of the original lamb that the Israelites slaughtered to smear its blood on their doorposts as a signal for the angel of death to pass over them on the night when the Egyptian firstborn were slain. When Jesus says of bread and wine, "in remembrance of me," he means the same thing that Jewish tradition does when it calls bread "a remembrance of [or pointer to] the paschal lamb." Eating it will point to Jesus, who, like the paschal sacrifice, reenacts the original lamb's slaughter and points God's way toward merciful redemption. In both cases, we have liturgy as *zikaron*, liturgy as remembrance, or better, as a pointer, drawing God's attention to what matters.[16]

Thanksgiving

Of all the themes we are likely to encounter in Christian interpretations of the Eucharist, the most prominent is thanksgiving. The very title "Eucharist" is from the Greek *eucharistein* (to give thanks). The four earliest accounts of the Last Supper (1 Corinthians by Paul; Mark, Matthew, and Luke) all portray Jesus giving thanks. The accounts are not identical, however. Luke and Paul have Jesus giving thanks over the bread with which the meal began; Mark and Matthew have him saying a blessing over the bread and then giving thanks over a cup of wine. Luke and Paul identify the wine as a cup that was drunk after dinner, but they do not have Jesus giving thanks then.

As one would expect, an enormous literature tries to specify what kind of meal this was and exactly what Jesus was doing at it. Since the primary accounts were written so many decades after the fact, and because they are selectively perceived and delivered to us, we may never know precisely what transpired, but rabbinic literature allows us to speculate with some degree of probability. A festive meal at the time would have begun with the *motsi* (a blessing over bread) and concluded with a grace after meals (*Birkat Ha-mazon*), accompanied by a cup of wine. That final cup of wine is no longer the norm in Jewish homes, except at the Passover Seder where it remains as one of the four cups.

If this is the background of the Last Supper, then the Luke/Paul accounts correctly place the cup after dinner; but the Mark/Matthew accounts are more accurate regarding what happened over the bread. Jesus would have said a blessing over it, not given thanks at that point in the meal. He would have expressed gratitude only when the meal was completed, in the form of the *Birkat Ha-mazon*.

It is worth noting the extent to which Christianity elaborated the theme of gratitude at the expense of "blessing." As early as the Paul/Luke accounts, the notion of "blessing" (over the bread) had fallen out and been replaced by "giving thanks." Thanksgiving then became the theme on which the technical term "Eucharist" was built. Theological interpretation of the Eucharist frequently returns to the theme of gratitude, to the point where a reader is apt to think that the very essence of the Eucharist lies in expressing gratitude to God. Jungmann waxes eloquent on the subject:

> The prayer of thanksgiving is the appropriate garb for the Christian sacrifice because our Lord's command has to be fulfilled, and that command was not just "Do this," but "Do this for a commemoration of me." . . . But remembering and reminding are closely allied to being mindful and thankful; "to think" and "to thank" are cognate words derived from the same root. In thinking about benefits received, in calling them to mind, recollection spontaneously becomes a thanksgiving. Therefore, our Christian sacrifice is enclosed in a prayer of thanksgiving, in a prayer whose main subject is that salvation we have received through Christ. . . . And such it is still at present—a Eucharistic celebration beginning with the invitation, *Gratius agamus* [Let us thank]. It would be a beautiful task for us . . . to learn from the liturgy of the Mass that fundamental attitude of mind which animated the Christians of those heroic ages long ago . . . incessant thankfulness before God, the sentiment of undying gratitude.[17]

What Jungmann says seems unexceptional. Who would argue against proper gratitude to God for all our gifts? American culture is sufficiently saturated with this notion as to celebrate an annual Thanksgiving Day. Thanksgiving Day became an official holiday only in 1863, but it was initiated by the Pilgrims in 1621 to celebrate the first harvest at Plymouth. We should see it, then, not as the all-American holiday that it is today (part of what is known as American civil religion), but as a strand of Christian piety. It eventually shaped American consciousness so successfully that Americans, both Christian and otherwise, now think thanksgiving is a religious sentiment that is not only natural in human beings but also primal in the sense that all religions must necessarily be built upon it.

That may not be the case, however. Certainly Judaism urges gratitude, but there is reason to believe that the primal religious sentiment in Judaism is not thanksgiving but (to coin a phrase) "praisegiving." In Jewish prayer, the invitation to communal worship is the imperative *barechu*, literally, "say blessings [to God]," and the rabbis' favorite worship genre is a *berachah*, "a blessing." To some extent, blessings incorporate an aspect of gratitude, but only secondarily. The primary function of blessings is the praise of God. The infinitive *le-varech* (to say a blessing) is frequently found in apposition to a series of synonyms that mean "to praise," not "to offer thanks."[18]

I think we are dealing with two somewhat different modes of spirituality. The Christian emphasis on gratitude flows logically from the Christian doctrine of grace, defined broadly as divine love or favor offered to us even though we do not merit it. In general, Christian theology has emphasized human sinfulness. It follows that, as sinners, we deserve nothing. If, then, we find God reaching out to us anyway, we must be the recipients of God's grace, and the proper response cannot be anything but gratitude for a gift we do not merit.

Jews also have the notion of grace, namely, God's covenantal choosing of Israel, first through Abraham and then with the gift of Torah. In its precovenanted state, Israel did not merit Torah. God gave it as an act of grace, in the same way that (for Christians) God sent Jesus. But once the Torah has been given, Jews enter into a covenant with God. If Jews keep their part of the covenant, they are worthy recipients of God's reciprocal care, so Judaism does not emphasize gratitude in quite the same way Christianity does. Psychologically speaking, Jews feel grateful, just as Christians yearn to offer God praise. Jewish and Christian favored forms of liturgical spirituality are not mutually exclusive. But liturgically, we find very little expression of thankfulness in the Jewish service, relative to the excessive emphasis on praise. Put another way, we can say that what the Eucharist is to Christians, the blessing *(berachah)* is to Jews. The Christian Eucharist is a supreme act of gratitude. The Jewish blessing is a supreme act of praise.

Jewish liturgy preserves a prayer that contrasts Israel's state of being prior to the covenant (when, deserving nothing, Israel counted on God's grace to establish a covenant in the first place) and afterward (when, fully covenanted, the people might rightfully receive God's beneficence in return for their keeping the commandments). The prayer introduces a morning recitation of the *Shema* and is a meditation in two parts, separated by a disjunctive "But." We are first portrayed in the state of unmerited dependency; then (after the "But") we are rescued by the covenant. For heuristic purposes, I have labeled the sections numerically and thematically:

1: Unmerited Dependence on God's Grace

Master of all worlds, we cast our supplications before You, not on account of our own righteousness, but because of your great mercy. What are we, what is our life, what is our compassion, what is our righteousness, what is our strength? What can we say before You, Eternal our God? Are not all the mighty as nothing before You, and those of renown as though they had never existed, the sages as if without knowledge, and the discerning without insight. For whatever we do is primeval chaos *[tohu vavohu]*, and the days of our lives as vanity before You. As scripture says, "Humans are no better than animals, for all is vanity" (Qoh. 3:19).

2: State of Covenantal Merit

But we are your covenanted people, children of Abraham who loved You, with whom You made a sacred oath on Mt. Moriah; descendants of your precious Isaac who was bound on the altar; the congregation of Jacob, your firstborn son, whom You named Israel and Jeshurun on account of your love for him and your joy in him. Therefore, we are obliged to acknowledge You with praise and to glorify You by giving acknowledgment and praise to your name, saying daily before You: How happy we are, how good is our portion, how lovely is our lot, how fine is our inheritance, whereby, regularly, every morning and evening, we say, "Hear O Israel, The Eternal is our God, the Eternal is One!" (Deut. 6:4)

What could be clearer than this stark contrast between (1) utter dependence as a universal human being, in which we are as nothing, our deeds are like the precreation void, and we can do no more than cast supplications before God who listens out of grace; and (2) the status of covenant, whereby we may approach God through inherited tradition, no longer with supplication but with praise on our lips? God's original act of grace is the giving of that covenant to us while we still were in the state of nature. After receiving it, we enter the new state of partnership with the divine, which we affirm in the *Shema* that follows.

In sum, Judaism does indeed know the concept of grace. As in Christianity, God's grace consists paradigmatically of the gift around which the covenant is established. But for Jews this gift is Torah, whereas for Christians it is Jesus. And I think Christianity further developed the sense of human inadequacy even after the gift of Jesus, thereby focusing attention on gratitude as the primal spiritual sentiment, whereas for Judaism, the gift of Torah provided the potential for becoming worthy, a state that had been impossible when there were no commandments to perform. Jewish liturgy, therefore, is built on the *berachah*, the blessing, which accents praise; Christian liturgy focuses on the Eucharist, an act of thanksgiving.

Conclusion

Can Jews understand Christianity in Jewish terms? Is such a translation even possible? The answer is, yes and no. Surface similarities alone do not constitute understanding, but a comparison is possible at the deeper level of bedrock theological concepts. I have taken three of these—sacrifice, remembrance, and thanksgiving—and tried to make explicit what Jewish liturgy at least implies about them. Classic Christianity can be filtered through the prism of these concepts to see how Christian and Jewish views are either similar or different.

Grace is an especially good example of this comparative method at work. The Hebrew for "grace" (from the root *ch.n.n*) is translated in Jewish prayer books as a variety of things but almost never as grace, because Jewish translators systematically avoid using theological language that they mistakenly think is purely Christian. The famous prayer of the High Holy Days, however, *Avinu Malkenu* (Our Father, our King), gives us this memorable line that almost all Jews who attend synagogue know by heart: *Avinu malkenu, choneinu va'aneinu ki ein banu ma'asim / Asei imanu tsedakah va-chesed ve-hoshi'einu*. Here is that annual calendrical period when Jews come closest to the Christian anthropology of sin. Aware of our sins, we wonder, liturgically, if the covenant will be withdrawn. Standing naked before God, awaiting judgment of whether we shall live or die next year, and dressed in shrouds (according to traditional custom), Jews say these words, which can mean nothing but: "Our Father, our King, respond to us with grace, for we have no good deeds to our credit. / Deal charitably and lovingly with us and save us." Bereft, we imagine, of all good deeds, so undeserving of salvation, we depend on grace to provide the divine charity and love that we require.

Comparing bedrock conceptions helps Jews understand Christianity and Judaism at the same time. Even as they discover classic statements of Christian thought as liturgical theologians explicitly express them, Jews grasp the depth of the same concepts as they are embedded implicitly in Jewish liturgy. And in this relationship between concept and liturgical practice, both Jews and Christians should be able to see where we differ and where we are the same.

Liturgy and Sensory Experience

RUTH LANGER

The new era in Jewish–Christian relations has set before the Jewish community the challenge of coming to an appreciation of Christianity as a religious system that plays a positive role in God's designs for the world—a role that no longer takes supersessionist and persecutory stances toward Jews and Judaism. This renewed relationship challenges Jews and Christians to understand each other, not to minimize their differences but to appreciate them and even to use them as vehicles to greater self-understanding. The worship life of a community is one of the most public manifestations of its identity, and historically Jews have had negative images of Christian worship. I would like to suggest some approaches, not to the issues of Christian liturgical theology that Lawrence Hoffman discusses, but to a few matters of perception and historical memory. I deliberately focus on issues of popular religion, that living religion of the masses with which a healthy theology must ever be in dialogue. Thus, my emphasis here will not be on the words of the liturgy but on the sights, sounds, and smells that accompany it.

The sensory experience of a "high liturgical" church such as the Roman Catholic, Episcopalian/Anglican, or Orthodox (but not most Protestant churches) is radically foreign to most Jews and is something worthy of contemplation and deeper understanding. Sensory experience includes things like the sounds of the liturgy, its smells, and its visual environment, as well as its verbal elements. Jewish worship is intensely verbal, a literal flood of words interrupted by the occasional change in posture or use of a ritual object. Symbolically laden ritual objects are sparse in the synagogue. Most synagogues center around the Torah scroll and its ark. Building a beautiful synagogue as a communal expression of love of God and God's Torah is a desideratum. Yet even the most ornate synagogue is still austere in comparison to the total experience of a church, and especially of a cathedral. This is true even in today's world, which places no overt restrictions on the grandeur of Jewish public buildings.[1]

Incense and Music

Some of the sensory deprivation of the traditional synagogue is deliberate. Incense and musical instruments had roles in the worship activities of the Jerusalem Temple, and by not incorporating these activities in its new worship system, rabbinic Judaism carefully marked its liturgy as different from, and lesser than, the biblically mandated Temple worship. Although many elements of rabbinic liturgy did have significant continuity with the Temple, the sounds and smells of the rabbinic synagogue, utterly familiar to us today, were at first radically different from the Temple and created an effective affective distinction. In the synagogue, for example, all sacrifices, including that of incense, could only be *remembered* and "virtually" performed by study of the relevant biblical and rabbinic passages prescribing them.[2] Although Christianity also redefined the biblical (and pagan) concepts of sacrifice, its dialogue with the major worship systems of antiquity operated on different terms and eventually reached different resolutions, as Hoffman has discussed. In Christian circles, sometimes on the basis of biblical precedent, the use of incense as an act of adoration, as an honorific act, and eventually, in some times and places, as a sacrificial act is well documented from the fourth century on, as Christianity became the dominant religion of the Roman world and incense was no longer associated with pagan practices.[3] Thus, although both Judaism and Christianity recognized that sensory enhancement of the worship of God enriches the worship experience, Christianity was free to appropriate these aspects of Temple worship, whereas Judaism mourned their loss.

The modern liberal branches of Judaism rejected mourning for the Temple as a determinative basis for Jewish practice and thought. But perhaps because they found their richest development in Protestant Europe and America, among Christian communities where incense played little or no role in worship, there were not more than occasional, marginal attempts to recover its use.[4] The situation is quite different with regard to instrumental music on the Sabbath and holidays. Indeed, the use of an organ and mixed choir in deliberate imitation of church aesthetics was one of the early hot-button issues of Jewish liturgical reform in the nineteenth century.[5] Traditional Judaism permitted instrumental music on the Sabbath and holidays only within the context of the no-longer-functioning Temple and prohibited it in the synagogue as an act of memory and mourning. As a result, traditional Jews will find the elaborate musical traditions of the church foreign (at least for a worship situation); more liberal Jews, however, living in the wake of nineteenth-century reforms, feel much more at home.[6] In any case, Jews and Christians (with exceptions in both camps) share the sense that full celebration of God's presence is greatly enhanced by musical embellishment. The difference lies in the question of whether full celebration is a desideratum in our current situation.

Images and Idolatry

A more serious issue is the visual experience of worship. Jewish children, early in their religious education, learn that "we don't make pictures of God." Jews neither visualize God nor pray to any image. Even the greatest of prophets, Moses, was allowed to glimpse only God's back and not the divine countenance (Ex. 33:17–23). With this foundation, it becomes extremely easy for Jews who walk into a church (es-

pecially one of a "high liturgical" tradition) to feel immediately uncomfortable because of a sense that they stand in the presence of what
seems to be idolatry. The lighting of candles before statues and pictures, the kneeling and praying before them, the kissing of icons in the
Orthodox Church—all are ritual actions that Jewish law explicitly
forbids.

Yet there is, I believe, an avenue to understanding this aspect of
Christianity. Although halachah strictly prohibits the picturing of
God, Jews throughout the ages, in seeking to experience the divine
presence, have echoed the desire behind Moses' plea, "Show me,
please, Your glory." Different Jewish mystic traditions have described
this quest: as physical ascent (or descent) to the divine chariot; as an
act of unification; as clinging or cleaving to God. The rabbinic concept of the *Shechinah* as the indwelling presence of God who joins
Jews when they pray with a quorum *(minyan)*, learn Torah (ideally
with a study partner), or form a law court *(beit din)* answers this same
desire.[7] We need to feel God's presence in our lives, and we seek for
reliable ways to access it.[8]

Christianity, once it had established doctrinally that Jesus was simultaneously fully divine and fully human, had a comparatively simple answer to this need. In human history, God had become human
and lived a human life—had been heard, seen, and touched by significant numbers of people. Because this revealed presence was physical,
it could appropriately be replicated, remembered, and relived through
physical means, including artistic renditions. Revelation could be preserved not only verbally but also visually. Particularly in the eastern
churches, but with significant parallels in the West, too, this visual
preservation led to traditions of iconic art. Pictures of Jesus, Mary,
and, secondarily, the saints were and are venerated. This worship is
not directed to the artwork itself (which would be idolatrous) but
rather to the revealed reality to which it points. These depictions fill-
ing churches are part of ritual memory; they enable faithful Christians
to experience anew for themselves the immanent presence of God on
Earth.[9]

Some medieval rabbis understood that Christianity was not an idolatrous religion in spite of its use of visual imagery in liturgical settings.
They accepted that Christian prayers were directed to God, albeit in a
mediated fashion.[10] We need to remember also that this concept of
mediated prayer was not so foreign to many Jews as it might seem to
us today. Jews, too, have, in various times and places, directed per-

sonal prayers to biblical figures and even to their own deceased ancestors, asking for their intervention with God.[11] The primary difference, then, lies in the use of visual instead of exclusively verbal imagery. Christian theologians justify this seeming controversion of the Ten Commandments by asserting that it comes at God's own behest. Once God made His presence felt on Earth in approachable and tangible physical form, restrictions on reproducing this visible revelation made no sense.

The Cross

In many ways, for Jews, the most difficult symbolic and physical image of Christianity is the cross (and the crucifix with its figure of Jesus).[12] Unlike most other Christian ritual objects, the cross has a presence in the Jewish mind and has taken on symbolic meanings of its own. What for Christians today is a sign of God's saving love and self-sacrifice is for Jews a reminder of myriad anti-Semitic acts, large and small.[13] Jews who have any identification with the past two millennia of their people's history see the cross as a sign of that which is utterly and threateningly other, as a symbol of attempts to annihilate and subjugate their people. The utter disconnection between Jewish and Christian meanings for this symbol is a significant element of the ongoing controversy over the erection of crosses at Auschwitz, the memorial shrine par excellence to the victims of the Holocaust.

Of course, contemporary Christians engaged in repairing the relationships between Jews and Christians would not hesitate to claim that those extra-liturgical uses of this ritual object that led directly or indirectly to persecutions, forced conversions, and death for so many Jews (and other non-Christians) were abuses of the central symbol of Christianity.[14] But although symbols generally carry multiple meanings depending on their context, these meanings tend to be deeply embedded and organic. Symbolic meanings do change, but only through gradual historical experience, not by decree. Hence addressing Jewish perceptions of the cross is necessarily complex. An analogy might be the Star of David: after emerging as a symbol of Jewish self-identification in the seventeenth century, it gained one new set of meanings as a Zionist symbol and the dominant element on the Israeli flag and another as the Nazi "Jew badge."[15] Furthermore, although this star is immensely positive for most modern Jews, it is intensely negative for many Palestinian and Arab opponents of Israel. Just as part of the peace process must include transforming this negative image, part of the Jewish–Christian rapprochement will require Jews to learn to gaze on a cross, minimally, with the same neutrality with which we look at other religious symbols that do not belong to us. Essentially, then, for Jews to appreciate the meaning of the cross for Christians, Jews must find a way to transform the meanings they associate with this object. Does this mean forgetting the past? No, for to do so would be contrary to the very being of Judaism. But it does mean accepting the self-transformation of so many contemporary Christians and looking together with them toward a better future.

How might Jews approach this complex job of transforming their understandings of the cross? One primary task is to understand the role of this symbol in Christian liturgy, a task that is complicated by the fact that there is no direct Jewish equivalent to the cross. The cross points to the most fundamental elements of Christian doctrine—from creation and the fall, to the sacrificial death of Jesus, to the cosmic and future consequences of his resurrection—and it is precisely these moments that the mass celebrates and makes present in the assembled church. In contrast, the Star of David marks national identity and plays no ritual role. More similar to the cross, in ritual terms, is the Torah scroll itself, for it replicates and embodies God's revelation to the Jewish community and, in the eyes of many, is, like the cross for Christians, a marker of God's presence in the assembled community.[16] Moreover, when we examine the ritual treatment of the Torah scroll, we find that it is parallel not just to the cross but to the entire complex of symbolic objects and actions to which the cross belongs.

Jews' veneration of the Torah scroll—the extreme care with which it is handled, the love with which it is hugged and kissed—finds parallel in the way some churches interact both with the ornately decorated Gospel book as it is processed through the community and with elements of the Eucharist. The cross—as an object both carried at the front of the procession and placed in a prominent location on the altar, as a gesture, and, sometimes, as something integral to the very architecture of the church—accompanies and enriches other elements of the liturgy as a sort of "meta-symbol" for them all. A full Jewish parallel would require that a symbolic representation of Torah infuse every aspect of Jewish liturgical life. To a certain degree, this infusion does occur. The focal points of synagogue architecture are the Torah's ark and reading desk; and we find the overarching presence of the

Torah more subtly in the composition of Jewish prayer in a Hebrew heavily influenced by biblical idiom, in the decoration of synagogues with biblical texts, and in the consciousness in nonliberal synagogues that halachah, "Torah law," dictates the liturgy. The symbolic role of the Torah in Judaism is more verbal and less visual than that of the cross in Christianity, but the pervasiveness of the message about the presence of God's revelation is similar. And just as the contents of Torah ideally pervade every aspect of the life of a Jew, so, too, should the message of the cross inform and shape all of Christian life.

Conclusion

An important step in the transformation of the meaning of the cross for Jews is embodied in this book itself, insofar as the essays collected here exhibit an appreciation of Christianity as a whole. Can this appreciation go beyond being a positively oriented but necessarily insufficient understanding of Christianity? Perhaps not, for a true understanding of Christian mystery requires acts of faith that only Christians may take.

A Jewish theological understanding of Christian worship requires not only the engagement with Christian liturgical theology begun by Lawrence Hoffman in his essay, but also an attempt to understand the experience of Christian worship. I have tried here to place into context a few of the primary experiential differences between Jewish and Christian worship. Topics for future study that are necessary for the accomplishment of our task include, minimally, an understanding of the liturgical use of the Hebrew Bible by the church (in the context of the Mass and in other settings); a discussion of the nature of the gathered community and of those playing specific roles in the liturgy; and, most significantly, an exploration of the meaning of sacrament. Approached creatively and constructively, such a task can not only improve relationships with our Christian neighbors, but also strengthen our understanding of our own tradition and our rootedness in it.

Christian Worship:
An Affair of Things as well as Words

ROBERT LOUIS WILKEN

As a Catholic Christian, I found Lawrence Hoffman's essay particularly illuminating. Although he is aware of the different forms of worship one can find within the Christian community, he knows that along with baptism (the rite by which one enters the church) the most ancient and most distinctive Christian ritual is the Eucharist (or Mass)—a ritual eating of bread and wine. From earliest times, the Eucharist has been at the center of Christian worship, and to this day when most Christians come together on Sunday they participate in this ritual meal. What is more, Hoffman realizes that since the early centuries of the church's history, Christians have understood the Eucharist as a sacrifice, indeed as *the* sacrifice or "oblation." Hoffman's essay reaches out in two directions: on the one hand to Christians, by focusing on a central feature of Christian worship (emphasized particularly by Catholics and Orthodox); and on the other hand to Jews, for whom the language of sacrifice is familiar from the Scriptures, the rituals in the ancient Temple, and the *siddur*.

In this essay I want to suggest why Hoffman's approach is fruitful for the dialogue between Jews and Christians, but I will begin by talking more personally about the Eucharist as celebrated today.

Often as I sit in church waiting to approach the altar to receive communion (consuming the consecrated bread and wine), I am drawn to the faces of my fellow communicants. In the Christian service there comes a time when the action shifts from the altar to the congregation. After the priest has completed the prayer of blessing over the offerings of bread and wine, the congregation recites together the Lord's Prayer ("Our Father Who art in Heaven, hallowed be thy name . . . "). Then the faithful greet each other with the words, "The peace of the Lord be with you." As the priest prepares the consecrated bread and wine to be distributed to the faithful, the congregation sings: "Lamb of God who takes away the sins of the world, have mercy on us. Lamb of God who takes away the sins of the world, have mercy on us. Lamb of God who takes away the sins of the world, grant us peace." At this point, the priest holds the consecrated bread up and says: "Behold the Lamb of God who takes away the sins of the world." And the people say: "Lord, I am not worthy to receive you, but only say the word and I shall be healed."

After this prayer, the members of the congregation begin to file forward toward the front of the church. In most congregations during the distribution of communion, the communicants form several lines as they wait their turn to receive the body and blood of Christ. As they come forward, there is no chatter, no relating to the person in front or behind, indeed no sound except perhaps a hymn sung by those who have already received or who are still to receive. There is only a line of people, old and young, hearty and infirm, parents holding on to young children, others carrying infants, all waiting quietly and expectantly to reach the head of the line, to stretch out their hands, palms upward, to receive what is given. When the communicant receives the consecrated bread, the priest or lay minister says, "The body of Christ," and the communicant responds, "Amen." When he or she receives the consecrated wine, the priest or lay minister says, "The blood of Christ," and the communicant again responds with an "Amen" and returns quietly to his or her seat to kneel and pray.

Books and essays on the Christian Eucharist often say that the high point of the liturgy comes when the priest recites the prayer of blessing over the bread and wine, raises aloft the bread and then the chalice of wine for the congregation to adore, and then kneels himself in an act of devotion and veneration. At this point in some churches tiny bells are rung to alert the faithful to what is happening at the altar. Yet the action of the liturgy is not completed until the priest and people consume the consecrated bread and wine. Usually when we stand in line, we carry something with us, an item to be purchased, a check to be deposited, a form to be handed over, even a question to be asked. But in this line one says nothing and offers nothing except outstretched hands, and what one receives is an apparently insignificant thing, a tiny piece of bread and a sip of wine. Yet those who come approach with solemnity and reverence as persons expecting a gift.

Christian worship is sacramental, an affair of things, not only of words. The most common definition of "sacrament," formulated by

Augustine centuries ago, is a "a visible form of an invisible grace." In a sacrament, a spiritual reality is conveyed through a material object. The object can be bread and wine as in the Eucharist, water as in baptism, the hands of a bishop in ordination, oil in the anointing of the sick or dying. In the eastern church, icons, those pictures found on the screen at the front of the church or on stands are "sacramental." They are not simply pictures to admire; through them the believer has access to the spiritual reality they depict. Hence the faithful kneel before them, kiss them, or light a candle in front of them. In the Christian Eucharist, the bread and wine are visible forms that convey an invisible blessing. What one sees is bread and wine, but what one receives is Christ.

In the middle of the second century, Justin Martyr, a Christian philosopher, wrote a little essay to the emperor, Antoninus Pius, explaining and defending the new religion that had begun in Palestine a century earlier. Toward the end of the treatise, Justin described what Christians do when they gather together for worship:

> On the day called Sunday there is a meeting in one place of those who live in cities or the country, and the memoirs of the apostles or the writings of the prophets are read as long as time permits. When the reader has finished, the person who is presiding gives a talk urging and inviting us to imitate the noble things that were read. Then we all stand up together and offer prayers. . . . When we have finished the prayer, bread is brought, and wine and water, and the president similarly sends up prayers and thanksgiving to the best of his ability, and the congregation assents, saying the Amen. This is followed by the distribution and reception of the consecrated bread and wine to each one present; afterward what was consecrated is taken by the deacons to those who are absent.

In some form, this simple rite, variously called the Eucharist, the Mass, Holy Communion, the Divine Liturgy, has been practiced by Christians from the beginning until today. The first part of the service, the service of the word, as it is sometimes called, is derived from the synagogue. A Jewish visitor to a Christian church would recognize the lineaments of the synagogue service: reading from the Scriptures, recitation of psalms, songs, prayers, and a sermon. There is even a parallel in the hierarchy of readings. Just as in the synagogue the reading from the Torah is the most important reading, so in the church the reading from one of the Gospels, the books that narrate the life of Jesus and present his teachings, is the high point of the service of the word. When the reading of the Gospel is announced, the congregation stands to sing a brief verse and remains standing for the reading. Then follows a sermon or homily. After the homily, the people recite the confession of faith in the words of the Nicene Creed, an ancient creed that originated at the Council of Nicaea in the fourth century and that sets forth Christian belief in God as triune. The service of the word ends with prayers for people of all sorts in conditions of all kinds.

Since the Reformation in the sixteenth century and developments that came in its wake, some Christian communions celebrate only the "service of the word" on Sunday. If one visits a Baptist or a Presbyterian church, for example, the service will be composed of readings from the Scriptures, psalms, hymns, prayers, and a sermon. But even those Christians who limit their Sunday celebrations to the service of the word do, occasionally or periodically (once a month, for example), celebrate the second part of the liturgy much as Justin described it. Whatever the practice, and however it is understood, the ritual consumption of bread and wine in some form is a universal Christian practice.

The second part of the Christian Eucharist has parallels to the sacrifices in the Temple in Jerusalem in ancient times. From the beginning of Christianity, the death and resurrection of Christ have been understood as a sacrifice. In the Epistle to the Hebrews, an early Christian letter in the New Testament, the author writes: "When Christ appeared as a high priest of the good things that have come . . . he entered once for all into the Holy Place, taking not the blood of goats and calves but his own blood, thus securing an eternal redemption" (Heb. 9:11–12). In the ancient prayers spoken over the bread and wine, the priest said: "We offer to Thee O Lord this fearful and unbloody sacrifice, beseeching Thee that thou deal not with us after our sins nor reward us after our iniquities, but according to thy leniency and thine unspeakable love towards mankind overlook and blot out the handwriting that is against us thy suppliants." It is clear from this prayer that Christian worship has deep roots in the sacrificial worship of the ancient Jewish Temple, but in Christian belief there is only one sacrifice, one offering, the offering of Christ's life.

What binds Christian worship to Judaism is the language and imagery of Christian prayer; what sets it apart is the person of Christ, who is present in both parts of the Christian liturgy. First the reading from the Gospels tells the story of Christ's life and death and presents his sayings and parables, and then the consecrated bread and wine become the body and blood of Christ. Here, too, Justin is helpful. "This food we call Eucharist. . . . For we do not receive these things as common bread or common drink, but as Jesus Christ our Savior who became incarnate when God's word took flesh and blood for our salvation, so also we have been taught that the food consecrated by the word of prayer which comes from him . . . is the flesh and blood of that incarnate Jesus." In its classical form, Christian worship is always centered on the sacrifice of Christ, which brings me to Hoffman.

The language of sacrifice comes directly out of Jewish tradition, and the prominence of a term such as "lamb of God" (as in the canticle mentioned above, "Lamb of God who takes away the sins of the world have mercy on us") has broad symbolic links to Jewish practice at the time of Christian beginnings. In calling the Eucharist a sacrifice, Christians wish to say that their liturgy is not a memorial meal recalling what happened centuries ago, but a re-presenting of what happened once for the benefit of the present community.[1] Hoffman captures this aspect of Christian worship when he discusses "remembrance" and says, "Christian eucharistic liturgy arises as a consequence of Jesus' command, 'Do this in remembrance of me.'" In common use, remembering has to do with recalling something that happened in the past but that is no longer actual. But in the Christian liturgy, the term "remembrance" means re-presenting, re-actualizing, making present what happened in the past.

Hoffman cites some parallels from Jewish tradition, for example, the phrase "in remembrance of the Exodus from Egypt" that occurs in the *Kiddush*. One might also note the passage in Mishnah Pesachim, which is incorporated into the Haggadah. Rabban Gamaliel says, "In every generation a man must so regard himself as if he came forth himself out of Egypt, for it is written, 'And thou shalt tell thy son on that day saying, "It is because of that which the Lord did for me when I came forth out of Egypt."'" Here "remembrance" is not simple recall. The person who celebrates Pesach is not a distant spectator. He or she is a participant, for what happened then is now being re-presented in the Seder. As Gamaliel says, "It is I who came forth out of Egypt." What God did in the past, he continues to do in the present, not in a general way, but through the Seder ritual.

The parallels here between Jewish and Christian understanding are very close, and the words that follow immediately after Gamaliel's statement in Mishnah Pesachim are striking: "Therefore we are bound to give thanks, to praise, to glorify, to honor." Given Hoffman's account of thanksgiving, the term that jumps out, of course, is "give thanks." As Hoffman notes, "Eucharist"—the term most commonly used to designate the Christian passover—comes from the Greek word meaning "to give thanks." The great prayer over the gifts of bread and wine is a prayer of thanksgiving. But this thanksgiving is not simply a word of thanks, an expression of gratitude, but also a thanksgiving that takes place through the offering, the sacrifice, itself, hence the importance of eating and drinking.

In ancient sacrifices, whether in the Temple or in the cities of the Roman world, the animal that was offered was eaten. Though Jews would not use the Christian term "sacramental," they would recognize something distinctive about giving thanks through the ritual of eating and drinking. The Passover Seder, for instance, is a more profound way of giving thanks than a purely verbal expression. It is one thing to say a prayer of blessing over a meal, something else to eat a piece of bread as one speaks the prayer, which suggests that Jews have a capacity to understand Christian worship in terms that Christians use and understand. The language, the images, the framework of ideas of Christian worship, even its sacramental form, are intelligible to Jews, not simply as interesting religious conceptions but as ways of thinking and practice that resonate in Jewish life.

In his essay, Hoffman highlights three aspects of Christian worship—sacrifice, remembrance, and thanksgiving. I have introduced a fourth: sacramental. For what gives sacrifice, remembrance, and thanksgiving their distinctive character in Christian worship is the fact that they occur in relation to things, bread and wine. The reason for this is that Christians believe that God comes to us not only through words but through a human being, someone who could be seen and touched. One of the writings in the New Testament begins as follows: "That which was from the beginning, which we have heard, which we have seen with our eyes, which we have looked upon and touched with our hands, concerning the word of life . . . we proclaim to you." This is a reference to the Incarnation, the Christian belief that in the person of Jesus of Nazareth God was made known. In the Eucharist, according to Christian teaching, the Christ who lived in the first century is now present in the blessed bread and wine. A spiritual grace is conveyed through sensible material.

There was a time not too long ago when Jews and Christians thought the most constructive way to relate to one another was to focus on moral questions or perhaps to join together in defense of religious freedom. But in recent years, and this is reflected in the "Jewish Statement on Christians and Christianity" that prompted this volume of essays, one senses a move toward the center, toward a focus on those things that are the source of life for Jews and Christians. Surely worship belongs in this category, for it is the one aspect of religious life in which one speaks, as it were, in a native language where translation is most difficult. How, for example, can one translate the Shema or transpose the invocation that stands at the beginning of the Christian Eucharist—"In the Name of the Father and of the Son and of the Holy Spirit"—into another idiom? There is something irreducible here. In worship, Christians and Jews are most uniquely themselves, and it is gratifying that the present symposium challenges Jews and Christians to move from the periphery to the heart of Jewish and Christian life.

9

SUFFERING

On the Suffering of God's Chosen: Christian Views in Jewish Terms

LEORA BATNITZKY

The notion that Jesus Christ suffered and died for the sins of all humanity is unarguably central to all strands of the Christian religion. For the Christian tradition, Isaiah 52:13–53:12 captures the meaning of the suffering Christ: "By his sufferings shall my servant justify many, taking their faults on himself" (53: 11). The Christian view of suffering holds that Christ suffered vicariously for the sake of others. From a Christian perspective, one both experiences and transcends human suffering through suffering with Christ. Christ is God's servant who suffers for others and offers consolation to others for their suffering, as we read in 2 Corinthians:

> Christ's cup of suffering overflows, and we suffer with him, so also through Christ our consolation overflows. If distress be our lot, it is the price we pay for our consolation, for your salvation; if our lot be consolation, it is to help us to bring you comfort, and strength to face with fortitude the same sufferings we now endure. And our hope for you is firmly grounded; for we know that if you have part in the suffering, you have part also in the divine consolation. (2 Cor. 1:3–7)

This essay reflects on these three dimensions of the Christian interpretation of Isaiah 52:13–53:12 as they might be understood in Jewish terms: the first that Christ is God's chosen servant, the second that Christ suffered for the sake of others, and the third that redemption is found through suffering with Christ.

Isaiah 52:13–53:12 in Its Biblical Context

Implicit in Isaiah 52:13–53:12 is a transformation of a retributive notion of suffering, the principle that there is a direct correlation between the sins we have committed and the suffering we bear. We need but recall 53:3, made famous by Handel's *Messiah*, "He was despised, shunned by men, a man of suffering, familiar with disease. As one who hid his face from us, he was despised, we held him of no account." The assumption of this verse is that the suffering servant is despised because people presume that he is a sinner who deserves his punishment. But note what follows:

> *Yet it was our sickness that he was bearing,*
> *Our suffering that he endured.*
> *We accounted him plagued,*
> *Smitten and afflicted by God;*
> *But he was wounded because of our sins,*
> *Crushed because of our iniquities. (53:4–5)*

In effect, these words reverse the retributive view of suffering, suggesting that it is we who are not suffering who have sinned, not the suffering servant. We are told, moreover, that "he bore the chastisement that made us whole, and by his bruises we were healed. . . . My righteous servant makes the many righteous. It is their punishment that he bears." Not only do we bear responsibility for the suffering of the suffering servant, but also only the servant's suffering has the capacity to redeem us. His suffering is representative of both our sins and his ability to heal us.

It is not possible to understand this view of the dynamics of suffering without appreciating the dominant (though not the only) biblical perspective on suffering; namely, those who obey God will be blessed; and those who don't obey will be cursed. We need but recall Proverbs 3:33: "The curse of the Lord is on the house of the wicked, but He blesses the abode of the righteous." The list of blessings and curses in

Leviticus 26 is also predicated on a simple arithmetic of retribution, and even in the Book of Isaiah we encounter this view:

> *Assuredly,*
> *As straw is consumed by a tongue of fire*
> *And hay shrivels as it burns,*
> *Their stock shall become like rot,*
> *And their buds shall blow away like dust.*
> *For they have rejected the instruction of the LORD of Hosts,*
> *Spurned the word of the Holy One of Israel.*
> *That is why the LORD's anger was roused against His people.*
> (5:24–25)[1]

    This view of suffering as punishment for sin is the most pervasive view of the Hebrew Bible, but it is not the only one. In Deuteronomy we read, "You alone have I singled out of all the families of the earth—that is why I will call you to account for all your iniquities" (3:2), and further on, "As a man chastens his son, so does the Lord, your God, chasten you" (8:5). Here the notion that suffering is intimately connected to chosenness is emphasized. Proverbs makes the analogy between a beloved son whose father expects more from him than from his less-favored children: "For whom the Lord loves, He rebukes, as a father the son whom he favors" (3:12). Suffering, from this perspective, results not from a moral inferiority but from a kind of superiority. The chosen suffer not because they are worse than others, but because they are in fact capable of being better than others. The representation of vicarious suffering in Isaiah 52:13–53:12 is consistent, then, with other strands in the Hebrew Bible that also emphasize the connection between suffering and chosenness.

    This point is important because it shows that aside from the obvious fact that Isaiah 52:13–53:12 is part of the Hebrew Bible, its content is consistent with the Hebrew Bible itself. Far from being a Christian innovation, the notion that suffering reflects a kind of moral superiority, not inferiority, and that, moreover, there is theological and ethical value in suffering for others is basic to the Jewish tradition in its rabbinic, medieval, and modern forms. For important strands of both the Jewish and Christian traditions, Isaiah 52:13–53:12 offers a transformation of (though not the complete rejection of) a straightforward arithmetic of suffering and sin. Isaiah 52:13–53:12 emphasizes the innocence of the suffering servant in contrast to others and suggests that

God's chosen suffer for the sake of others. The central difference between the Jewish and Christian traditions is that the Jewish tradition understands the people of Israel to be the suffering servant, whereas the Christian tradition associates the suffering servant with Jesus Christ. This difference is compounded, as we will see, by the question of whether suffering itself is intrinsically valuable and necessary.

Suffering and Chosenness

Biblical scholars have had much to say from a source-critical point of view about Isaiah 52:13–53:12 and about the identity of the intended servant.[2] Textual evidence within Isaiah itself suggests that, indeed, Israel is the servant.[3] Our concern, however, remains the importance that this text has taken on within the Jewish and Christian traditions, not only for understanding suffering but also for understanding the unique, world-historical roles of the Jewish and Christian peoples, respectively.

In both the Jewish and Christian traditions, the notion of vicarious suffering expressed in Isaiah 52:13–53:12 is interpreted together with an equally famous and contentious chapter of Isaiah 42, which describes God's servant as "My chosen one, in whom I delight . . . a light of nations—Opening eyes deprived of light" (42:1–7). For both traditions, suffering, chosenness, and a theological and moral mission to the nations of the world are intimately connected; therefore, suffering is not an isolated issue that can be separated from the meaning of each faith community. Each community finds this meaning by interpreting its historical reality through the lens of a scriptural tradition.

For the Christian tradition, the central historical and scriptural event is the life, death, and resurrection of Jesus Christ, who died, according to this tradition, for the sins of all others, thereby redeeming them. For many strands of the Christian tradition, this redemption involves participating in the suffering of Christ, the light and redeemer of humankind. For the Jewish tradition, in contrast, the central historical and scriptural event is God's choice of and covenant with the people of Israel, a choice and covenant that remain unbroken. The Jewish people are the light unto the nations that can bring the nations out of their darkness. Suffering plays a central role in this narrative because, as God's elect, the people of Israel suffer throughout history, both for their refusal to live up to their potential and for the inability of the nations of the world to follow Israel's example.

For both the Jewish and the Christian traditions, suffering as God's chosen includes several possible kinds of suffering, including the just chastisement of the beloved child gone astray and the wholly innocent suffering of the chosen son who suffers vicariously for the sins of others. Many strands of the Christian tradition emphasize the latter view. Only Christ, they say, is innocent of sin and thus capable of redeeming the world; all other human beings are intrinsically sinful. As we read in Romans, "since all have sinned . . . they are justified by his grace as a gift, through the redemption which is in Christ Jesus, whom God put forward as an expiation by his blood, to be received by faith. This was to show God's righteousness, because in his divine forbearance he had passed over former sins; it was to prove that . . . he himself is righteous" (3:23–26). Following Isaiah 52:13–53:12, this Christian understanding is a rejection of a straightforward retributive view of suffering because here suffering is not the punishment for particular sins committed but a sign of human fallenness more generally. In contrast, much of the Jewish tradition stresses the view of suffering as the just chastisement of the beloved child gone astray, but here the connection between suffering and sin is far more ambiguous. Although the favored son is no doubt held accountable for the wrong he has committed, his suffering marks not his intrinsic fallenness but his freedom to follow and fulfill God's laws if he would choose to do so. In the modern period, and especially after the Holocaust, many Jewish thinkers reject even this connection between suffering and sin; indeed, they reject the connection between suffering and sin altogether, while nonetheless retaining the intimate connection between suffering and chosenness.

An early rabbinic text allows us to appreciate aspects of Judaism's movement away from a notion of retributive suffering toward an emphasis on the connection between suffering and chosenness in light of historical circumstance. The text begins by discussing the verse that concludes the Ten Commandments: "With Me, therefore, you shall not make any gods of silver, nor shall you make for yourselves any gods of gold" (Exodus 20:20). R. Akiba interprets this verse as a rejection of a retributive view of suffering. He states that the verse teaches "that you should not conduct yourselves with respect to me as others conduct themselves with respect to those [gods] that they fear. For when good comes upon them, they honor their gods . . . but when suffering comes upon them they curse their gods." R. Akiba continues with the following, and is joined by R. Eleazar b. Jacob and R. Meir:

And moreover [it teaches] that *a person should be happier with suffering than with the good,* for even if a person experiences good all of his days, he is not forgiven for his sins. And *what causes his sins to be forgiven? Say: suffering.* R. Eleazar b. Jacob says, "Behold, it says, 'Do not reject the discipline of the Lord'. . . For what reason? 'For whom the Lord loves, He rebukes [as the father the son whom he favors]' (Prov. 3:11–12). You say: come and see, what caused this child to be pleasing to his father? Say: suffering."

R. Meir says, "the Lord your God disciplines you just as a man disciplines his son (Deut. 8:5). [According to the instruction of this verse] your heart should know: the deeds that you have done and the suffering that I have brought upon you, not according to your deeds have I brought suffering upon you."[4]

Here we find R. Akiba, R. Eleazar b. Jacob, and R. Meir concurring that the historical condition of the Jewish people—the destruction of the Second Temple and the exile of the Jewish people from the land of Israel—is not the direct result of the sinfulness of the people but of their favored status. The suffering of the Jewish people is in fact a sign of their chosenness and future redemption, as well as of God's love for the people.[5] R. Akiba, R. Eleazar b. Jacob, and R. Meir suggest, however, that the Jewish people suffer not only because God loves them most but also because they are, and have the capacity to be, better than others are.

The early Christian and early Jewish traditions inherited a similar problem: how to make sense of the connection between the reality of their suffering and their chosen status. Significantly, they responded to this problem in a similar way, which was to disconnect, though not to reject completely, a direct arithmetic of suffering and punishment for sin. The identification of the suffering servant with Jesus became central to early Christianity and served to define its message about the saving grace of Christ (see, for example, Acts 8:26–35). At the same time, the disconnection of a direct correlation between punishment for one's own sin and suffering became an important way for early rabbinic Jews to make sense of the connection between their suffering and their chosen status. The notion of vicarious suffering became increasingly important for the Jewish tradition as it responded to the suffering of the Jewish people in the medieval period.

Isaiah and Isaac in the Middle Ages

The Christian interpretation of Isaiah 52:13–53:12 parallels in significant ways the portrait of Isaac in various early Jewish sources.[6] The themes of the death and resurrection of the beloved son (Isaac and Jesus, respectively) play crucial roles in the formation and development of both the Jewish and Christian traditions. The Christian interpretation of Isaiah 52:13–53:12 is in keeping with Jewish interpretations of the binding of Isaac throughout the rabbinic and medieval periods. Both narratives describe the sacrifice of an innocent, beloved son who is sacrificed on account of the father's love for a God who demands such sacrifice.

Interpretations of the story of the sacrifice of Isaac became one way that Jewish communities throughout the medieval period understood their suffering. Like the early Christian interpretation of Isaiah 52:13–53:12, Jewish communities in the Middle Ages understood their suffering as intimately linked to the suffering of God's beloved son, in this case Isaac. The Jewish community's suffering under this interpretation is not retributive. It is not a sign of God's rejection of the Jewish people. Rather, like Isaac, the Jewish community is the favorite of the father, who, for the sake of the will of God, is sacrificed precisely because of its beloved status.

The notions of sacrifice and vicarious suffering as they are embodied in the story of Isaac played a significant role in Jewish responses to the Crusades. Consider the poem by Rabbi Ephraim of Bonn, written in 1146:

> *He made haste, he pinned him down with his knees,*
> *He made his two arms strong.*
> *With steady hands he slaughtered him according to the rite,*
> *Full right was the slaughter.*
> *Down upon him fell the resurrecting dew, and he revived.*
> *(The father) seized him (then) to slaughter him once more.*
> *Scripture, bear witness! Well-grounded is the fact:*
> *And the Lord called Abraham, even a second time from heaven.*[7]

Here, as distinct from Genesis 22, Isaac is actually sacrificed by Abraham. God did not save the Jewish people from death as an angel of God saved Isaac from his father's sword. Indeed, Rabbi Ephraim of Bonn calls scripture to bear witness to this fact. The innocence of the Jewish victims of the Crusades seems to be all the more confirmed in relation to the binding of Isaac. It is God's most beloved who suffer and who sacrifice themselves for the sake of God. This text goes further than the rabbinic text we discussed above by emphasizing, as the Christian interpretation of Isaiah 52:13–53:12 suggests in regard to

Jesus, that as suffering increases so does the presumption not only of God's love but of the innocence of the sufferer.

The notion that suffering was not a sign of rejection but of chosenness also played a significant role in Jewish–Christian disputations in the Middle Ages. Significantly, medieval Jews often used Isaiah to respond to the most dominant Christian claim against Judaism. Christians argued that the degraded status of the Jewish community and the exalted status of the Christian community were proof of Christianity's triumph over Judaism and of God's preference for the Christian people. Medieval Jews quoted Isaiah explicitly to prove to Christians that the degraded status of the Jewish community was in keeping with Jewish chosenness. For example, in the thirteenth century, Rabbi Meir ben Simon of Narbonne remarked, "The prophet said, 'Fear not the insults of men, and be not dismayed at their jeers [Is. 51:7].'"[8]

Judah Halevi and Thomas Aquinas
on the Suffering of the Chosen

The medieval Jewish philosopher Judah Halevi (1074—1141) explored more fully the theological and ethical dimensions of Jewish suffering in light of Israel's chosenness. Halevi's magnum opus, the *Kuzari*, is a dialogue between the king of Khazar and a Christian, a Muslim, and a Jew, each of whom tries to convince the king that his way is the true one.[9] The king is convinced by a Jewish sage to convert to Judaism. The subtitle of Halevi's text—"In Defense of the Despised Faith"—indicates that one of the pressing questions to which a defense of Judaism must respond is how to account for Judaism's degraded status. Significantly, one of the ways in which Halevi does so is through an interpretation of Isaiah 52:13–53:12.

The king presses the rabbi to explain how the Jews could possibly be God's elect when they suffer so. It is useful to quote the rabbi at length as he responds to the king's claim that "the Jews have sustained what they have only because of their own sins!" Halevi writes:

> We [the people of Israel] are . . . not at the level of a corpse, but rather at the level of a sick man who has wasted away. . . . This is what Scripture means in saying, "Can these bones live?" [Ezekiel 37:3] It is detailed further in the section of "Behold, my servant shall prosper," specifically from the verses "He has no form nor beauty. . . . It was as if we hid our

faces from him, he was despised, and we did not esteem him." [Isaiah 52:13–53:12] This [turning away] is because of the sick person's visible deterioration and poor appearance, much like a fastidious person will turn away from dirty things—"Despised and rejected by people, a man of pains and well acquainted with illness." . . .

Israel amongst the nations is like a heart amongst its organs—[the heart is a very sensitive organ, in that] it becomes considerably ill from the influence of the other organs and also considerably healthy from their influence. . . . The Divinity in relation to us is like the soul in relation to the heart, [just as the soul first connects to the heart and then spreads to the rest of the body, so does God's influence in the world connect first to Israel and then spread to the rest of the world. . . . Just as the heart's inherent equilibrium and pure makeup allows the soul to attach to it, so, too, does the Divinity attach Itself to Israel because of their inherent nature. But [despite the heart's inherent purity,] it still becomes tainted at times because of the other organs. . . . Similarly, Israel becomes tainted from their assimilation with the other nations, as it says, "And they assimilated with the nations, and they learned from their ways." [Psalms 106:35][10]

Halevi suggests that Israel becomes ill from the influence of the other nations for two, interrelated reasons. First, when Israel assimilates into the other nations, Israel relinquishes its chosen status. Here Halevi suggests, in keeping with the notion of the just chastisement of the beloved child gone astray, that the Jewish people suffer for not being as good as they could and should be.

At the same time, however, the analogy of Israel as the heart among the nations suggests a view of innocent, vicarious suffering. Halevi argues that although the Jewish people have a unique status, their fate is not divorced from the fate of the nations. Without the heart, the body has no link to the soul, just as without Israel, the world has no link to God. And yet, it is also true that in spite of its link to the soul, the heart is dependent on the other organs of the body and on their ability to receive what the heart has to give, and so Israel's health is dependent on the ability of the nations of the world to come closer to God's true teaching. To the extent that the nations fail to receive what Israel provides, the Jewish people become weak. Here Halevi rejects explicitly the view that the Jewish people suffer because of their sins, arguing instead that the Jewish people suffer for the sake of others.

Halevi's interpretation of Jewish suffering bears an important similarity to the Christian view of Isaiah 52:13–53:12. The difference is that Halevi, in the face of a debate about which religion is superior—Judaism, Christianity, or Islam—asserts that the Jewish people are God's suffering servant. Halevi is well aware of Christian arguments to the contrary. But the king is in fact won over to Judaism after the first chapter of the *Kuzari* precisely because he accepts the rabbi's argument that any favorable arguments made by the representatives of Christianity or Islam originated in Judaism. Halevi's analogy that Israel is like the heart among the nations combines the two notions about the relation between suffering and chosenness that we have been exploring—first, the just chastisement of the beloved child gone astray and, second, the innocent suffering of the chosen son who suffers vicariously for the sins of others. When Jews assimilate to the ways of other nations, they suffer just chastisement. But as the heart of the world, as the all-important link between God and the nations, Jews suffer for the sins of others.

St. Thomas Aquinas (1225–1274), arguing from a Christian perspective and using a different analogy, shares Halevi's view that the unique status of God's chosen exposes them to suffering:

> It is plain that the general of an army does not spare [his] more active soldiers dangers or exertions, but as the plan of battle requires, he sometimes lays them open to greater dangers and greater exertions. . . . So also the head of a household assigns greater exertions to his better servants, but when it is time to reward them, he lavishes greater gifts on them. And so neither is it characteristic of divine providence that it should exempt people from the adversities and exertions of the present life, but rather that it reward them more at the end.[11]

We see, then, a striking similarity between the Jewish and Christian views of the relation between suffering and chosenness, one that, significantly, each tradition at various historical stages used as an argument against the validity of the other tradition. For both traditions, God does not spare those whom God loves most, but recognizes that it is they who can and must bear suffering. For Halevi and Aquinas, respectively, Jews or Christians suffer uniquely because of their respective special aptitudes for service to God.

Despite this significant similarity, there is also an important if subtle difference between many strands of Jewish and Christian views of the relation between chosenness and suffering. Although many Christian thinkers, including Thomas Aquinas, emphasize the role of human freedom in creating human suffering, many strands of Christianity also emphasize the sinful nature of humanity that makes suffering a necessity and in this sense intrinsically valuable. From this perspective suffering cannot eradicate sin, as God's grace can, but suffering is a necessary, though not sufficient, step toward grace, or spiritual health. As Eleonore Stump puts it in the context of Aquinas's thought, "If suffering is the chemotherapy for spiritual cancer, the patients whose regimen doesn't include any are the only ones for whom the prognosis is really bad."[12] From Aquinas's and much of the Christian tradition's point of view, sin is a disease that needs eradicating. If suffering is a terribly horrible medicine, it is only because the disease of sin is that much worse.

Returning to Halevi, we might say that the difference between these representatives of the Jewish and Christian traditions is that in contrast to Aquinas, Halevi's assumption is that though the body of humanity (with the Jewish people as its heart and the nations of the world its other organs) may become severely ill and even die, health is a possibility, if all the organs, including the heart, do their proper jobs. So, too, spiritual health is attainable so long as the nations of the world, again including Israel, recognize and worship the God of Israel properly. The premise of Aquinas's view, on the other hand, is that the body of humanity is intrinsically diseased. The proper recognition and worship of God is predicated on an eradication of the sinful disease intrinsic to humanity, and suffering is the only medicine strong enough to begin to accomplish this task.

To quote Stump on Aquinas once again, for much of the Christian tradition "Christ not only makes atonement for sinners but also sets them an example, so that they will understand that the path to redemption goes through suffering."[13] In contrast, for many strands of the Jewish tradition, the connection between suffering and chosenness is more an effect of the human freedom (both Israel's and the nations of the world's) to reject (and also therefore to accept) God than it is a necessity required by human nature.[14] In both cases, the suffering of God's chosen is the result of a rejection of God. But in the Christian case this rejection is caused ultimately by human nature, whereas in the Jewish case it is caused ultimately by human choice. For this reason, suffering can be averted in the Jewish case, if only people would choose to follow God's law (which is possible, if unlikely). In the Christian case, on the other hand, suffering is inevitable.

Modern Jewish Views of Suffering

Halevi's argument about the vicarious capacity of the Jewish people to suffer because of the sins of others is one that we see increasingly when we turn to the modern context. It may be surprising to realize that the notion of representative suffering is central not just to traditional Judaism but also to the formation of modern liberal Judaism. Abraham Geiger, the German-Jewish founder of the Reform movement, drew on the notion of the Jewish mission to the nations described in Isaiah 42:1–7 to make an argument that became the core of modern liberal Judaism: the claim that the essence of Judaism is ethics. Geiger and those who followed him claimed that Isaiah's description of a chosen one who will teach the nations indicates that the Jewish people act as a kind of moral exemplar to the rest of the world.[15] Furthermore, Geiger interpreted Halevi's metaphysical view of the Jewish people as an argument about the ethical contribution that Judaism makes to universal culture, and he then extended the argument to support the legitimacy of the Reform movement: "Judah Halevi stresses that revelation is a tendency that was alive in the people as a whole. Israel, he says, is the religious heart of all mankind. As a group, Israel always maintained this higher susceptibility, and the great individuals who stood out in Israel's midst were the heart of that heart, as it were."[16] The Reform movement is to "contemporary" Jewry as the Jewish people are to the nations: both are a light shining in the darkness. Israel is the heart of mankind, and, Geiger argues, the Reform movement is the heart of that heart.

Increasingly, modern liberal Judaism came to see Jewish suffering, and specifically anti-Semitism, in connection with the inability of the nations of the world to accept Judaism's contribution to universal culture. Jewish suffering, then, only reinforced the Jewish mission to the nations, for this suffering showed the distance the nations of the world were from the pure monotheism that Judaism taught. The German-Jewish philosopher Hermann Cohen (1842–1918) argued perhaps most explicitly that Judaism was defined in terms of its vicarious capacity to suffer for others. According to Cohen, this view is the proper interpretation of the suffering servant: "As Israel suffers, according to the prophet, for the pagan worshipers, so Israel to this very day suffers vicariously for the faults and wrongs which still hinder the realization of monotheism."[17] Underlying Cohen's argument about the suffering servant is his attempt to maintain that Judaism does not ascribe an independent value to suffering. Jews suffer for the sake of and indeed because of the failures of others, but this suffering has no intrinsic value. Cohen argues that in contrast to Judaism, Christianity ascribes an intrinsic value to suffering through its view of original sin.[18] The Jewish view of suffering, on the other hand, is wholly devoid of a notion of sinfulness. According to Cohen, this distinction between the two traditions captures the essential ethical and theological error not only of Christianity's interpretation of Isaiah 52:13–53:12 but of Christianity more broadly.

Cohen certainly overemphasizes the view that Judaism has no notion of human sinfulness. We need but recall God's view of humanity both before and after the flood: "And the LORD saw how great was man's wickedness on earth, and how every plan devised by his mind was nothing but evil all the time" (Gen. 6:5) and how "the devisings of man's mind are evil from his youth" (Gen. 8:21). The view that Judaism does not have a notion of sin is a modern misconception.[19] The Jewish tradition for the most part does see the human being as at least tending toward sin. In the context of Jewish views of suffering as they relate to Christian views, I would suggest that much of the Jewish tradition understands sin as a deviation from God that results from human freedom. Sin is not, however, akin to a disease that requires excess suffering as a necessary but not sufficient cure. In this sense, Cohen's distinction between Jewish and Christian views is accurate, if overdrawn. From a Jewish perspective, sin marks not human fallenness but the sometimes difficult task of following God's law. Many strands of Judaism, increasingly in the modern period, suggest that although vicarious suffering has an ethical and theological value, suffering is not a value in and of itself. It would be better to do without suffering, and humanity as a whole has the capacity, though certainly not the tendency, to do without it.

Suffering and Chosenness After the Holocaust

The tension between recognizing the ethical and theological value of suffering without assigning it an intrinsic value is especially important for many Jewish thinkers, both liberal and traditional, after the Holocaust. Many Jewish thinkers have increasingly moved away from ascribing any sort of value to suffering. Although Jewish thinkers have not for the most part rejected the notion of chosenness after the Holocaust, many have rejected the notion that suffering, even in the context of chosenness, has any intrinsic worth. Consider the arguments of Richard Rubenstein in *After Auschwitz* and of Eliezer Berkovits in *Faith After the Holocaust*, keeping in mind that these thinkers represent opposing ends of the liberal/traditional spectrum.

Rubenstein and Berkovits differ most fundamentally on the issue of the meaning of chosenness. Rubenstein rejects explicitly any notion of Jewish chosenness after the Holocaust, whereas Berkovits distinctly embraces Jewish chosenness. Both thinkers agree, however, that the suffering that defines the Holocaust cannot be justified theologically or otherwise. Let us begin with Rubenstein:

> How can Jews believe in an omnipotent, beneficent God after Auschwitz? Traditional Jewish theology maintains that God is the ultimate, omnipotent actor in historical drama. It has interpreted every major catastrophe in Jewish history as God's punishment of a sinful Israel. I fail to see how this position can be maintained without regarding Hitler and the SS as instruments of God's will. . . . To see any purpose in the death camps, the traditional believer is forced to regard the most demonic, anti-human explosion of all history as a meaningful expression of God's purposes.[20]

Rubenstein's characterization of traditional Jewish theology is strange, given our brief discussion of traditional Jewish views of suffering, which do not see every instance of Jewish suffering "as God's punishment of a sinful Israel." Nonetheless, Rubenstein's point is well taken: the atrocities of the Holocaust cannot be justified from any theological point of view that is not deeply offensive.

Berkovits's thought, in contrast to Rubenstein's, revolves around an embrace of the notion that the God of Israel is, and remains after the Holocaust, the God of history who interacts with his people in time. In fact, contends Berkovits, even, and perhaps especially, after the Holocaust, the Jewish people bear witness to God's intervention in history. Berkovits is unique among a number of other influential post-Holocaust Jewish thinkers in his denial of the claim that the Holocaust brings about a complete paradigm shift in Jewish thinking about God.[21] He maintains that even after the Holocaust, it is possible to find meaning in the notion of *kiddush ha-shem*, the sanctification of God's name in the innocence of martyrdom. Nonetheless, Berkovits, who self-consciously takes an Orthodox position in his arguments about suffering, maintains that "the sacrificial way of the innocent through history is not to be vindicated or justified! It remains unforgivable. . . . Within time and history God remains indebted to his people."[22] Berkovits makes this argument with recourse to the traditional notion of God hiding his face *(hester panim)* in order to make room for human freedom. We see, then, that even for Berkovits, who maintains that after the Holocaust innocent suffering still has a theological value, the notion that human suffering is necessary from a theological perspective remains anathema. The suffering of the Holocaust does not display the link between the sickness of sin and the necessary (but not sufficient) healing medicine of suffering, as it might for much of the Christian tradition; rather the Holocaust displays God's debt to humanity for bearing this unjust suffering.

Two rather diverse twentieth-century Christian figures who proclaim, especially in light of the horrors of the twentieth century, the meaningfulness of suffering are Simone Weil and C. S. Lewis. Both Weil and Lewis in fact define Christianity and the relevance of Christianity for the modern person in terms of its valuation, and indeed valorization, of suffering.

Simone Weil (1909–1943) repudiated her ancestral Judaism as overly life-affirming in order to embrace Christianity's view of suffering. "The extreme greatness of Christianity lies in the fact that it does not seek a supernatural remedy for suffering but a supernatural use for it."[23] The supernatural use of suffering that Weil points to is the Christian view that only suffering—what she calls elsewhere "affliction," to designate suffering that is at once physical, mental, and social—can begin to purge us of our sin. Like Aquinas, as well as a number of Jewish texts and thinkers we have explored so far, Weil holds that those closest to God suffer the most. Unlike a number of Jewish views we have encountered, however, Weil argues for the necessity of affliction: "God is not satisfied with finding his creation good; he wants it also to find itself good. . . . It is the purpose of affliction to provide the occasion for judging that God's creation is good."[24] Weil holds that only human affliction can begin to make God's creation good and prepare the way for grace, because affliction "de-creates" the human being.

Though temperamentally and philosophically at odds with the tenor of much of Weil's thought, C. S. Lewis (1898–1963) concurs with Weil's affirmation of this Christian view of suffering and its relevance for the modern world. Note the epigraph Lewis chose for his book *The Problem of Pain:* "The Son of God suffered unto the death, not that men might not suffer, but that their suffering might be like his."[25] Like Weil, Lewis holds that Christianity is defined by affirming the role and necessity of suffering for human beings. Christ does not end suffering but is a model for it. Such an account echoes some Jewish views of the suffering servant and the Jewish mission to the nations, but, again, the difference is that Lewis's view of vicarious suffering, like many Christian views, also becomes an affirmation and valorization of suffering.

The Jewish tradition often maintains a difficult balancing act when it affirms both the theological and ethical value of suffering for others, while denying the necessity of suffering itself. Weil, Lewis, and much of the Christian tradition avoid this difficulty by simply insisting on the intrinsic value to suffering. The late French, Jewish philosopher Emmanuel Levinas attempts to capture the proper balance between the affirmation of the ethical value of vicarious suffering and the declaration that suffering can never be justified.

Levinas argues, first, that the right response to the atrocities of the twentieth century is an end to all theodicy, to all attempts, theological or otherwise, to justify suffering. He then asks a question: "But does not this end of theodicy, which obtrudes itself in the face of this century's inordinate distress, at the same time in a more general way reveal the unjustifiable character of suffering in the other person, the scandal which would occur by my justifying my neighbour's suffering?"[26] Levinas argues that any attempt to justify my neighbor's suffering would be a scandal indeed, and that in fact my neighbor's suffering is beyond justification; it is, in a word, meaningless. Recognizing suffering's meaninglessness is, for Levinas, an ethical imperative. However, this imperative leads to a recognition of the ethical value of suffering for and with others. Suffering in and of itself is meaninglessness, but my neighbor's suffering takes on meaning *for me* as its very meaninglessness becomes an imperative that I care for my neighbor. In Levinas's words, "the suffering of suffering, the suffering for the useless suffering of the other person, the just suffering in me for the unjustifiable suffering of the Other, opens upon suffering the ethical perspective of the inter-human."[27]

Levinas articulates in philosophical (and admittedly difficult) language the tension that we have encountered in various Jewish interpretations of vicarious suffering. Vicarious suffering has a value insofar as I recognize my obligation to God and to other people by way of it; at the same time, however, I cannot affirm the value of suffering in and of itself, for to do so is both morally and theologically offensive. Levinas in fact calls suffering "useless" to emphasize both the moral inappropriateness and philosophical impossibility of ascribing an intrinsic value to suffering itself.

Although the attempt to affirm suffering while also denying its necessity and hence its intrinsic value is more pronounced in the modern period, especially after the Holocaust, it has its precursors, as we have seen, in earlier Jewish literature.[28] The following rabbinic text is an antecedent, I believe, for Levinas's philosophical formulation of the ethical dangers of valorizing suffering: "Just as there is overreaching in trade, so too is there oppression in words, and moreover, oppression by words is [a] greater [wrong] than oppression with money. . . . If illness and sufferings were coming upon him, or [if] he buries his children [who have died prematurely], one should not speak to him as Job's colleagues spoke to him."[29] Much of the Jewish tradition suggests that we find God's love for us and our love for others through the experience of suffering, but, as this text indicates, much of the tradition also suggests that justifying suffering is a spiritual robbery, an overreaching, in which we steal other people's dignity.

We have found, then, a subtle but important difference between Jewish and Christian thought—a difference that is particularly relevant after the Holocaust. The notion of the ethical and religious value of vicarious suffering is central to both the Jewish and Christian traditions, but many strands of the Jewish tradition, from the early rabbis to Levinas, do not embrace the intrinsic value of suffering. It is not impossible to find strands of the Jewish tradition that do find suffering necessary and thus intrinsically valuable. But especially after the Holocaust, and in the modern period more generally, many if not most strands of the Jewish tradition find it theologically and ethically difficult to embrace the intrinsic value of suffering. At the same time, it is possible to find post-Holocaust articulations of Christian tradition that shy away from the perspective that suffering is necessary and intrinsically valuable. Much of Christian liberation theology, for example, moves away from ascribing an intrinsic value to suffering and focuses instead on issues of social justice.[30]

After the Holocaust a number of important Christian thinkers have tried to avoid justifying suffering; at the same time, some continue to find a central core of Christian meaning in and through suffering. A recent statement by Pope John Paul II captures this tension in post-Holocaust Christianity:

The scandal of the Cross remains the key to the interpretation of the great mystery of suffering, which is so much a part of the history of mankind. . . . Everything is contained in this statement. All individual and collective suffering caused by the forces of nature and unleashed by man's free will—the wars, the gulags, and the holocausts: the Holocaust of the Jews but also, for example, the holocaust of the black slaves from Africa.[31]

The pope's use of the phrases "the *scandal* of the Cross" and "the great *mystery* of suffering" seems to reflect an attempt not to justify suffering. His suggestion is that suffering is at once scandalous and mysterious. But then the pope begins to attribute an intrinsic value to suffering when he conflates "all individual and collective suffering"—including "the wars, the gulags, and the holocausts: the Holocaust of the Jews . . . [and] . . . the holocaust of the black slaves from Africa"—with the suffering of Christ on the cross. Here the pope's statement bears an important similarity to Lewis's epigraph, quoted above: "The Son of God suffered unto the death, not that men might not suffer, but that their suffering might be like his."

If there is indeed a tension in the pope's understanding of suffering, it is a tension with a long history, as I have tried to indicate in this essay. That history has delivered us into the present. The issue of suffering has two fundamental roles to play in contemporary Jewish–Christian dialogue. First it points toward the similarity of the two traditions, since Judaism and Christianity share overlapping stories about the relation between suffering and chosenness. Second, it points toward a profound difference between Jews and Christians: even religious Jews, as opposed to secular ones, cannot always find meaning in suffering. Significantly, *both* the similarities *and* the differences between Jewish and Christian views of suffering complicate Jewish and Christian dialogue after the Holocaust.

Suspicions of Suffering

ROBERT GIBBS

In the Jewish community today, there is little patience with a theology of suffering. Our communal suffering, particularly the Shoah, makes us intolerant of any description or theological justification of suffering. Indeed, we turn our backs on justifications of the suffering of our people, and all the more on a theology of the redemptive value of an individual's suffering. But the word "today" may be a little overemphasized. Despite the pleas of the prophets and the interpretations of the sages, the theories of the medieval philosophers, or the charismatic leadership of the Chasidim, it is not clear that Jews have ever had patience with suffering and its theology. I am not a historian of Jewish popular attitudes, but I suspect that in every generation, Jewish suffering has met with despair, anger, and a refusal to dignify it with redemptive theories. What I do know is that in synagogues when I try to present contemporary accounts of suffering by leading Jewish thinkers, I am met with at least the suspicion that those thinkers are betraying our experiences in this century.

I am thinking most of all of Emmanuel Levinas (but we could substitute Hermann Cohen, or Martin Buber or Franz Rosenzweig, or others) and his discussion of how my responsibility for the other person, the one nearest to me, makes me hostage for the other, persecuted for the other, and responsible for the other, to the point of atoning for the other.[1] When most Jews hear such views, they object that such a theory of suffering and responsibility is Christian, *and not Jewish*. It does not seem to matter that such a theory of suffering for the other arises from Isaiah, or that the long tradition of Jewish exegesis and reflection on martyrdom lies behind it. Today (and again I hesitate to see our time as an anomaly) an elevation of suffering, even a reflection on suffering, seems un-Jewish. It would be, we Jews often think, something that Christian thinkers do. They praise suffering; they imagine expiation. We have had enough of it.

As a Jewish thinker who makes far-reaching claims for ethics, I line up with those Jewish thinkers who understand that what is right requires a vulnerability that must include the possibility of suffering. But in this essay I wish to pause and reflect on why "today" Jews are so reluctant to recognize this Jewish tradition of running the risk of suffering and, instead, relegate it to Christian thought. At first glance, this reluctance seems to be a reflex of anger and insecurity: "We must never again be lambs led to the slaughter." "We have suffered enough and should never have to suffer again." "We are destroyed by the suffering they wreak upon us, not redeemed by it." Beneath those visceral reactions, however, lies a deeper justified complaint. We have exposed ourselves in the world's eyes, stayed true to a particularity that was despised, and we have suffered for it—our families murdered, our culture obliterated and world dislocated. For nonreligious Jews, this seems an adventitious moment to quit, to stop running the risk and exposing our children to the world's hatred. But even for those of us who stay, who stay Jewish, who maintain a religious affiliation, liberal or traditional, we are inclined to think that our suffering is not the stuff of theology. Surely whatever God wants, God does not want Jews to suffer again, to suffer more. That was enough.

The Jewish Refusal to Reflect on Suffering

But why do Jews identify thoughts about suffering with Christians? I think that identification happens at two levels of reflection—both of which provide unsatisfactory but not untypical justifications for the Jewish refusal to reflect on suffering. First, Jews often think that Christians value suffering itself because Christian theology depicts God suffering. Jews would be uneasy with the spirituality of Philippians 2:5–8: "Christ Jesus, who, though he was in the form of God, did not count equality with God a thing to be grasped, but emptied himself, taking the form of a servant, and being born in the likeness of men. And being found in human form he humbled himself and became obedient unto death, even death on a cross." For many Jews, such suffering unto death and, even worse, exposure to the pain of crucifixion are extreme, not merely because it is God suffering, but because death on a cross is too passive, too accepting, too much a willed suffering. At this level of reflection, a thinker like Levinas refuses to let me fight back and seems to tell me to revel masochistically in the pain and violence done against me. Christianity preaches that masochism, or at least that is what many Jews now think.

The second unsatisfactory level of reflection is still more charged: Christians are the basic cause of Jewish suffering—they preach a kind of individual self-abasement but practice communal violence against us. Thus to adopt an ethics like Levinas's, to understand my responsibility to extend to my persecutors, would be not merely to expose myself to their violence but to encourage it.

These reflections, these hesitations of Jews to think about suffering and this readiness to blame Christianity for a theological interpretation of suffering, are painful. They mark a real wound in the Jewish people—a wound that blocks both a renewal of Jewish tradition and a direct engagement with Christianity. The problem, then, is not how to make my cherished ideas about responsibility palatable for Jews, but rather how to treat this wound. We cannot ignore the wound, nor are the scars and fears that arise from it false; rather, we must diagnose the wound, sorting its sources via various distinctions. Such distinctions will allow us to separate offensive views of suffering from other views that can in fact renew both Jewish and Christian thought.

Three Views of Suffering

A first step toward diagnosing (and healing) the wound requires that we distinguish three ways of viewing suffering: representative suffering, subordinating suffering, and totalizing suffering. The privileged view is representative suffering, where someone suffers for the sake of others. The subordinating view understands that each sufferer is only part of a whole, and so each suffers for his or her own self, but always within a larger whole. The totalizing view extends subordination, such that each self plays its own role but must also surrender itself to combine with others and become something larger—ultimately a totality.

As Jews, we are jealous of our own history, of our particular forms of exile, of our own people's suffering, and so we resist theories that dissolve our existence, which is not to say that our insistence on our particular suffering cannot be framed in a relation to the meaning it has for a wider world. Consider Isaiah 53:4–5, the main passage on suffering in Leora Batnitzky's essay: "Yet it was our sickness that he was bearing, our suffering that he endured. We accounted him plagued, smitten and afflicted by God; but he was wounded because of our sins, crushed because of our iniquities. He bore the chastisement that made

us whole, and by his bruises we were healed." Even without clarifying
the identity of the sufferer, we cannot fail to notice that one suffers for
others. Jews have usually read this text as an account of our suffering,
of the fact that the Jews have suffered for the world, for the sins of
others.

The representative view of suffering differs from the subordinating
and totalizing views, both of which are suspect. The subordinating
view makes our suffering merely part of all the suffering of the world.
Compared to the suffering of other groups and communities in world
history, ours is a small fraction, and, therefore, it loses any meaning
without reference to the whole. In a totalizing view, however, each
group is only an organ in a set of systems—like the heart in the circu-
latory system, to invoke Judah Halevi's view of the Jews. In this case,
Jewish suffering is part of religious suffering, maybe even a vital organ, and it is justified when we grasp how the whole world forms a totality and needs suffering in order to achieve its unity. Batnitzky
warned us against this reading, a reading that demands Jewish suffering in order to make the system work. I suspect that Halevi's analogy,
while flattering Jews as the heart, is held in suspicion because we
refuse to let our blood be the oil that makes the machine of history
run smoothly. Our suffering is not simply absorbed in a big picture,
nor is it required for the system.

For some Jews, the refusal to value suffering arises from the offense
of accounts that subordinate or totalize the particularity of Jewish experience. The representative view of Isaiah's text, however, does not
discount our particular suffering, and thus offers us a way to think
about our suffering without offense. This view opens a possibility for
an ethical or theological interpretation of our suffering. It preserves
our suffering in the midst of all other suffering, and it offers an important relation to the suffering of others, too. As representatives, we are
called to fight against others' suffering, as well against our own. We
are called to treat the stranger fairly, even to prevent genocide against
other peoples.

Such a representative view of suffering, moreover, is repeated in
Christian theology: the Christ is understood to suffer for all, to be the
representative for all the world, and so to redeem everyone through
his singular suffering. The refrain is common, and well represented by
Romans 5:15: "For if many died through one man's trespass, much
more have the grace of God and the free gift in the grace of that one
man Jesus Christ abounded for many." Christian theology can no

more think about suffering in general without reference to Christ than Jewish thought can approach suffering by forgetting the specificity of Jewish suffering. And despite the appearances of certain intricate reasonings, Christian theology need not understand suffering as required in a total system of redemption. The understanding of God's freedom in taking on suffering stands against the reasoning of calculable necessity.

The Asymmetry of Suffering

A second and even more significant step in diagnosing the wound that has been inflicted upon Jews by reflections on suffering involves acknowledging that suffering is asymmetrical (my suffering is different from your suffering). It is not just particular suffering that represents the suffering of the whole world, but *our* particular suffering. *Who* suffers is a vital aspect of interpreting representative suffering, a point most evident in Jewish prophetic self-critique. The prophetic message is often double-voiced, requiring an interpretation of who the sinner is and of who shall suffer. A straightforward example is Isaiah 2:5–6: "O House of Jacob! Come, let us walk by the light of the LORD. For you have forsaken [the ways of] our people, O House of Jacob!" Clearly the second verse identifies Israel as sinful and abandoning God. But the first verse calls the people back. The deep problem such critical texts present for Jewish and Christian interpretation is the way they shift from first person to second (or third) person, from an internal critique (let *us*) to an external one (*you* are). To return to Isaiah 53, "Yet it was our sickness that he was bearing. . . . My righteous servant makes the many righteous. It is their punishment that he bears." The text switches from our discourse about our sins to a divine discourse about "their" sins. We must attend to this confusion, for the asymmetry of suffering raises the question of whether our suffering redeems others' sins. Or must we condemn others to suffer either for our sins or for their own?

I might be willing to suffer so that my child will not, and that might not merely be nice but right. But to reverse that relation, to say that someone else (my child or my neighbor) should suffer so that I will not—that is the primordial violence of thought. Batnitzky cites a text by Levinas that describes "the scandal which would occur by my justifying my neighbor's suffering." To justify another person's suffering, as do Job's comforters, is offensive and provokes anger. Indeed, the problem is so acute, the suspicion that another is making sense of our suffering so bitter, that we often would rather make the more blanket claim that no one can make sense of any suffering. If my claims about what suffering means automatically become statements about what *your* suffering means, then you are offended.

But if I can't make statements about your suffering, can I find any meaning in my own? Can I say that my suffering is for someone else's sake when I will not condone or give meaning to someone else's suffering? If we can maintain this asymmetry, we will find that Jews are in the position to make what sense we can of our own suffering, and that Christians, similarly, can make what sense they can of their own suffering. If we understand our suffering to be the result of our sins or to arise out of God's special love and desire to chasten us, that does not mean that we must understand the suffering of others in the same way. Jewish suffering through the ages has been subject to various interpretations. One is cautious even with these interpretations, but our tradition explores them in order to make sense of, and to respect, our suffering. The conflict with Christian theology arises when these same interpretations become justifications of "your sufferings." When the prophets' words are turned against the Jews by those who stand opposed to the Jews, they function in a remarkably different way than when they arise as explanations of our suffering. The "dialogue" of judgment upon the other is a violence.

Rosemary Ruether examines how Christian interpreters broke apart the complexity of Jewish prophecy:

> The meaning of the prophetic dialectic of judgment and promise is destroyed when its cohesion in a single people is pulled apart. By applying prophetic judgment to "the Jews" and messianic hope to "the Church," Christianity deprived the Jews of their future. They also denied to the Jews the record of their greatest moral accomplishment, the breakthrough from ideological religion to self-critical faith. By the same token, the Church deprived itself of the tradition of prophetic self-criticism.[2]

As extreme as her interpretation is, Ruether writes about the historical record, following out the point I have been making more abstractly. The Jewish texts subject our people to severe criticism and interpret our suffering as suffering for the sake of others, precisely by accentuating self-criticism and by holding out hope for redemption through suffering. But to use the others' suffering as a proof of their sin and of their deserved punishment is to misread these texts. Such justification of Jewish suffering by Christians has made it almost impossible for Jews to continue to recognize any meaning in our own suffering.

Not all Christian theologies of suffering serve to justify others' suffering. Indeed, at the heart of Christian thinking about suffering is precisely the asymmetry in Jewish thinking: why do we (Christians) suffer? In both traditions, there are resources for cultivating this asymmetry: a respect for our own suffering and for others' suffering as something not to be justified through our reasoning. The task, then, is to discover how the two traditions interpret their own suffering and, indeed, to what extent either is capable of respecting this asymmetry.

Communal Suffering

If I return again to Isaiah's Suffering Servant, I can add a third step toward diagnosing the wound that plagues Jewish reflection about suffering. The servant is personified as a singular man, who in Jewish tradition represents the people—the singularity of the community. Jewish suffering is first and foremost communal, in contrast to merely personal suffering. As a fact of life, individuals suffer—from death, illness, heartbreak, and even morally and spiritually. But the description in Isaiah ("We accounted him plagued, smitten and afflicted by God") describes not the characteristics of an individual but of a community's suffering in war and exile, in famine and destruction. Communal suffering takes the form of genocide, exile, torture, and poverty. Of course, communal suffering has some intrinsic relation to the suffering of individuals. If it were not for the individuals who had to move, to leave behind their home and their belongings, then exile as a communal experience would not be real. But part of the cruelty of communal suffering is precisely the multiplication of loss—losing not only a parent but also uncles and aunts, friends and their parents, and so on. Such loss is not simply a summation but an exponential weight, and so the loss of a village, the destruction of the Temple, the annihilation of culture exceeds the losses and deaths of individuals.

In the Jewish tradition this distinction between individual and communal suffering is in play in articulated allegories. Isaiah portrays a Suffering Servant, an individual, who also is an allegory for the people. Much of Jewish thought about suffering and about Jewish experience in general is about our communal experience of slavery in Egypt, of exile in Babylon, of the Inquisition, and so on. We suffer individually (in North America, almost every single Jew moved here to escape some kind of suffering, with some hope of freedom from suffering), but always together. The accentuation of individual suffering in Levinas's thinking about responsibility strikes many Jews as Christian, because for the Jews, Christianity focuses only on individual suffering. One individual suffering on the cross redeems all humanity. Hence the question of whether the church suffers in the way that the Jewish people suffer is a sharp issue of difference.

This difference has a historical moment of similarity. The Roman Empire persecuted each religion in turn. Jews recite the stories of the martyred rabbis; and Christianity was built on the witness of the martyrs. For each group the individual narratives stand for the misery of the respective communities, in a way parallel to the prophets' extreme individuality in times of destruction and devastation. A theory of martyrdom would help Jews understand both their own suffering and that of Christians, for a martyr does not desire death but accepts suffering for God's sake. But martyrdom has a different track record in the two traditions. Since Constantine, Christians have rarely been martyrs, particularly not at the hands of non-Christians, and almost never at the hands of Jews. Jews, alas, have been martyred at a disturbing rate throughout the centuries, most often at the hands of others, and especially at the hands of Christians. The way a martyr represents the whole community, suffering with the community's suffering and accepting but not desiring that suffering, even unto death, is alive throughout the Jewish tradition.

Batnitzky cites the poems of the Crusaders' victims, who yet again liken their communal suffering to the figure of Isaac. For Christians, secure from other religious communities (although not always from other churches and sects), the martyrs become an inspiration for asceticism, both for individuals and for religious communities. I would hesitate to equate thinking about asceticism with thinking about suffering, largely because of the contrast between a self-chosen discipline and suffering undergone at others' hands against or beyond my will. Judaism is not free of asceticism, but the ongoing suffering of persecution, always fresh at least in memory, provides a different emphasis on suffering. Here lies the root of the sense that Jewish suffering is about *our* suffering and not only about my singular suffering.

Conclusion

For Jews, suffering is a communal experience, visited upon us at the hands of other people. The struggle in Jewish thought has been how to respect that suffering and yet offer some sense even to the senselessness of our suffering. The ethically and spiritually strongest vision has been one of representative, asymmetrical, communal suffering: we expose ourselves to suffering for the sake of others. The martyr does not will suffering but suffers for the sake of God's name. And in many strands of this theme, God suffers with the suffering Jews. Such an understanding of suffering is not foreign to Christianity, even though God is seen to suffer for the Christian and even though the imitation of God's suffering is often understood to be that of an individual. The decisive conflict between Jews and Christians lies in the asymmetry of suffering and in the immorality of justifying another's suffering. However, attention to the threefold character of suffering, as I have portrayed here, can treat the wound in the Jewish mind. We do have ways of speaking about suffering, of taking responsibility for our suffering and, even more, for the suffering of others. The protest against suffering and against the justification of suffering is not foreign to either Jewish or Christian thinking. Both traditions teach us the responsibility to work to stop both our own suffering and the suffering of others.

The Meaning and Value of Suffering: A Christian Response to Leora Batnitzky

JOHN C. CAVADINI

Leora Batnitzky's essay depicts the richness of Jewish and Christian theological traditions on the subject of suffering. It is a richness that belies the simplistic views one often finds at the surface of opinion.

She finds a tension running through both traditions, a tension that thus constitutes a similarity between the two traditions. Both are equally formed by a biblical theology of retributive suffering, in which suffering is seen as divine chastisement of the chosen, beloved people for their sins. On the other hand, both traditions hold that view in tension with another, equally biblical notion of suffering, namely, the contrasting and more complex notion that suffering divinely sent to the beloved and chosen people is not something they deserve at all. Rather, their bearing of the suffering becomes a light of redemption, as they reveal, by their faithful endurance, the freedom human beings were created with. The vicarious suffering of the chosen redeems the sins of all the nations. By holding in tension the two notions of suffering, one as retribution for sin and the other as vicarious, redemptive suffering, both traditions "disconnect, though [do] . . . not reject completely, a direct arithmetic of suffering and punishment for sin."

On the other hand, Batnitzky goes on to characterize the Jewish theological tradition as the bearer of another tension, namely, the tension of affirming "the theological and ethical value of suffering for others, while denying the value of suffering itself." This tension is especially glaring after the Holocaust, since to assert the value of suffering as punitive retribution seems altogether repugnant, and even to assign any value at all, vicarious or otherwise, to suffering would seem to amount at least implicitly to the approval of an atrocity. Batnitzky argues, however, that the Christian tradition is beset by no similar worries regarding the intrinsic value of suffering. Christians "valorize" suffering as "intrinsically valuable and necessary." The doctrine of original sin means that humans are "intrinsically sinful," possessed of a "sinful nature," which thus necessitates suffering as a kind of medicine (stating Eleonore Stump's reading of Thomas Aquinas), and so "Christianity ascribes an intrinsic value to suffering through its view of original sin" (reflecting Hermann Cohen's view).

I would like to argue that in fact the tensions within the Jewish theological tradition that Batnitzky has displayed so persuasively are equally characteristic of the Christian tradition, and that here, too, is a similarity in the two traditions as they struggle together with this complex issue. At the outset, I would agree with Batnitzky to this extent: Christians are more likely to resolve the tension on the side of valorization. The view that most tempts Christianity is the valorization of suffering; given the material Batnitzky cites, it may be that Jews are more tempted to say that suffering is meaningless unless it is undertaken for others. Still, these are only temptations to dissolve what in each tradition remains a real tension. My argument is simply that this ongoing tension is as much a feature of the Christian tradition as it is of the Jewish tradition.

Suffering in the Augustinian Tradition

Most of western Christianity is indebted in some way to the thought of Augustine (353–430), and so it is good to begin with a brief consideration of what the Augustinian tradition has to say about suffering. Augustine, and those thinkers most indebted to him, offer perhaps the severest version of original sin in the whole Christian tradition, the closest one gets to a notion of "intrinsic" sinfulness without lapsing beyond the bounds of orthodoxy. For Augustine, human nature is intrinsically good but corrupted by original sin. In this sense, the notion of original sin as the cause of an infirmity in human nature is correct. For Augustine, original sin begets a tendency to sin that is inherited by each person. Each individual, personal act of sin is a kind of obsessive reenactment of the original sin of preferring some good of one's own choosing to the Highest Good, which is God. Suffering comes inevitably in the wake of sin. Sin is the cause of suffering, and suffering the punishment of sin. Original sin thus serves as Augustine's theodicy. The evil that occurs to us in this life—death, mortality, and all of the suffering associated with them—is the punishment due original sin, not a meaningless, irrational current at work in the cosmos, nor the work of an original evil principle.[1] There is a direct arithmetic between punishment and sin on this level.

Yet the doctrine also functions in an opposite direction. Original sin is not the *personal* sin of any one of us, and so there is no direct connection between any of our personal sins and any suffering we may incur. One's liability to sickness is not due to any evil one has personally committed. The doctrine of original sin allows no room for "blaming the victim" of disease or persecution and is meant in fact to deflect the individual's susceptibility to blame. Augustine's answers (in Book 1 of the *City of God*) to questions about why good Christians' houses were burned with those of the worst pagan sinners by Alaric in 410 make it clear that there is no direct connection between good behavior and divine favor, or personal sin and divine retribution. Original sin makes us all equally liable to suffering, but not personally liable. Thus the "disconnection," but not entire rejection, of a direct arithmetic between sin and retribution is present right at the heart of the doctrine of original sin.

The corollary doctrine is that suffering, caused by and in retribution for original sin, is evil, and nothing can make it good. Not even God can make it good. Death—and the whole train of suffering consequent upon mortality—is the punishment of original sin, a corruption of human nature. It is not a good and can never be made into a good (see *City of God* 13.1–7). In this system, at the root of most of western Christianity, suffering, far from having "intrinsic value" of its own, has no utility whatsoever. Augustine asserts, however, that faith in Christ enables one to put suffering to a "good use."

In the Christian view, suffering is indeed a "necessity," as Batnitzky asserts, but it is not a necessity in the sense that it is a divinely prescribed good. Rather, it is simply a fact of mortal life, intrinsically evil if it is intrinsically anything. But faith in Christ enables the believer to "use" something that has no inherent utility. Those who believe that Christ is the Word made flesh see his suffering as wholly voluntary, since as the Word he does not have original sin and is thus not liable to death. His choice to share our life, and not even to balk at death, is an act of solidarity with us, undertaken out of love for us. Those who believe are enabled to imitate the Word made flesh, to freely embrace suffering in circumstances where not to do so would mean that sin is the only alternative. We can die a martyr's death rather than sacrifice to the emperor, and such a death is indeed meritorious, but it is Christ that is the good here, not death. If I am sick, I can make that a "sacrifice of praise" in faith, not valorizing my suffering, but making it the occasion for greater insight and identification with the love of Christ. Again, it is not the suffering that is the good, but Christ.

This Christian scheme does, then, display the tension between recognizing the value of suffering and denying that that value is intrinsic—the "difficult balancing act" of affirming "both the theological and ethical value of suffering for others, while denying the value of suffering itself." In fact, with these words, Batnitzky provides an exact description of the Augustinian view, the foundational background against which most western Christianity discusses suffering. But what, then, of Batnitzky's argument to the contrary, of her portrait of Christianity as a tradition that simply valorizes suffering and thus avoids the difficulties of a balancing act? In part, the answer has to do with Batnitzky's selection of sources.

Weil, Lewis, the Pope, and St. Francis

First, Simone Weil is an odd choice to represent the Christian tradition, since she was not a Christian (she refused to be baptized). Her view of "affliction" and its utility is in fact an exaggeration of the traditional Christian understanding of putting suffering to use without granting it intrinsic value. As for C. S. Lewis's *The Problem of Pain*, I agree with Batnitzky's worries that in general *The Problem of Pain* tends to valorize suffering, but it is effectively balanced by Lewis's later work, *A Grief Observed*. And in any event, the passage that Batnitzky quotes, which argues for the conformation of individual suffering to that of Christ, is fully compatible with the Augustinian view. "Conformation" of one's sufferings to Christ is a "use" of suffering that faith in Christ permits without turning the intrinsic evil of suffering into something good or useful in itself. Finally, John Paul II's statement, as Batnitzky's own analysis indicates, for the most part displays the presence within the Christian tradition of the very tensions that Batnitzky reserves for the Jewish tradition alone.

From the pope's Christian perspective, there is no value whatsoever in slavery or genocide, and not even God can make them good. If God suffered for all our sins in Christ, then none of these events are grounds for the assertion that these groups were singled out for punishment for any particular sins or evils they may have committed, any more than Christ was singled out and punished for any sins he committed, since in Christian tradition Christ is sinless. Christians are called to see the sufferings of their Savior in the sufferings of these people, and to treat them as they would him. They have the same claim on Christian attention as the Word incarnate does. That Christians have so often failed miserably to react to the suffering of others in this way is something for which we must beg forgiveness. Faith in Christ should give me the ability to "use" my own sufferings so that I have a loving empathy for the sufferings of others, who have the same claim on me that Christ has. Still, in the Christian tradition, unlike the Jewish tradition as Batnitzky presents it, the temptation is to valorize suffering rather than to regard it as wholly meaningless. Someone who is represented as riding the razor's edge of this balance is St. Francis.

Francis received the Stigmata, the wounds of Christ, which, as the third *Consideration on the Holy Stigmata* tells us, transformed him "into the direct likeness of Christ Crucified, not by physical martyrdom, but by enkindling of the mind." In the *Considerations*, this transformation is the result of a prayer of St. Francis:

> My Lord Jesus Christ, I pray You to grant me two graces before I die; the first is that during my life I may feel in my soul and in my body, as much as possible, that pain which You, dear Jesus, sustained in the hour of Your most bitter Passion. The second is that I may feel in my heart, as much as possible, that excessive love with which You, O Son of God, were inflamed in willingly enduring such suffering for us sinners.

Here St. Francis requests the suffering of God, though he requests it not for its own sake, but so that he might come to feel the same love that Christ had for all. The prayer is not a statement about the intrinsic value of suffering, especially of the suffering of other people. Rather, it is a statement about Christ and, one could say, about a "use" of suffering that is granted by faith in Christ but not contained in suffering itself. Nevertheless, if one is not St. Francis, ready to spend one's life binding up and treating with affection the sores of lepers, then one probably is ill-advised to pray for suffering. And one can readily see how lesser attempts to imitate Francis here would end up (and have ended up) as crude valorizations of suffering in and of itself. Unless one is used to hearing such stories in an Augustinian "key," one will miss the tension they embody—the "difficult balancing act" of affirming "both the theological and ethical value of suffering for others, while denying the value of suffering itself."

When discussing Levinas and the rabbinic roots of his view of suffering, Batnitzky casts this balancing act in terms of the ethical responsibility that we have to find meaning in the specific suffering of others while also declaring that suffering in itself is meaningless and thus unjustified. To justify others' suffering is to adopt the role of Job's friends and to commit "spiritual robbery." I am sure this is a point of agreement between Jews and Christians. We are called to affirm the value of a person, even one whose life is consumed by suffering, but not to affirm the suffering itself by saying "your suffering is good for you." In other words, suffering does not render human life meaningless, no matter how severe the suffering may be.

In Christian terms, this view is exhibited in John Paul II's encyclical letter *Evangelium Vitae* (The gospel of life), where his arguments against euthanasia are especially relevant:

Here we are faced with one of the more alarming symptoms of the "culture of death," which is advancing above all in prosperous societies, marked by an attitude of excessive preoccupation with efficiency and which sees the growing number of elderly and disabled people as intolerable and too burdensome. These people are very often isolated by their families and by society, which are organized almost exclusively on the basis of criteria of productive efficiency, according to which a hopelessly impaired life no longer has any value. (p. 65)

The pope's alarm at the fate of the disabled and the elderly in our society suggests that he sees no *intrinsic* value in their suffering. Indeed, the pope goes on to explain that euthanasia must be distinguished from the refusal of aggressive medical treatments that would unduly prolong life, and he spends a paragraph explaining why pain-killing drugs are a desirable benefit:

While praise may be due to the person who voluntarily accepts suffering by forgoing treatment with painkillers in order to remain fully lucid and, if a believer, to share consciously in the Lord's Passion, such "heroic" behavior cannot be considered the duty of everyone. Pius XII affirmed that it is licit to relieve pain by narcotics, even when the result is decreased consciousness and a shortening of life. In such a case, death is not willed or sought, even though for reasonable motives one runs the risk of it: there is simply a desire to ease pain effectively by using the analgesics which medicine provides. (p. 65)

Here, using the pronouncement of one of his predecessors to support his case, the pope makes it clear that the alleviation of suffering is legitimate, which would not be the case if suffering had an "intrinsic" value. And yet the pope also acknowledges the praise due to those "heroic" individuals who, not unlike Francis, consciously accept suffering and thus share in the suffering of Christ.

One can see in the pope's views an attempt to strike a balance between holding human life intrinsically valuable, even in irreparable suffering, and ascribing intrinsic value to suffering itself. One can see the Augustinian view in the background, too: suffering can be "used" as the occasion for participation in the Passion of Christ, but it is Jesus who is good, not the suffering per se, either of the individual or of Christ; suffering per se is evil. In the peculiar language of encyclicals, the term "heroic" is as much warning as it is admiration.

Weil Revisited

In closing, let me return briefly to Simone Weil, since even in her exaggerated understanding of "affliction," she did not ascribe "intrinsic" value to suffering: "He whose soul remains ever turned toward God though the nail pierces it finds himself nailed to the very center of the universe" ("The Love of God and Affliction," 135).[2] In other words, any value that suffering has it acquires from its relationship to God's own enduring of suffering and death in Christ and not from its own "intrinsic" qualities. It is also worth noting that one of the reasons Weil refused to be baptized was that she was reluctant to identify herself with a church that had a totalitarian past, as she put it, and that had not publicly disowned that past along with the suffering it had caused. Weil did not wish suffering on other people, as one would if it were an "intrinsic" good ("Spiritual Autobiography," 81–83). Even for Weil, then, it is not affliction per se that is useful, but the occasion it presents for a believer to endure in the love of God. She puts it this way in a letter written from Casablanca:

> If still persevering in our love, we fall to the point where the soul cannot keep back the cry, "my God, why hast thou forsaken me?" if we remain at this point without ceasing to love, we end by touching something that is not affliction, not joy, something that is the central essence, necessary and pure, something not of the senses, common to joy and sorrow: the very love of God. ("Last Thoughts," 89)

Suffering presents the occasion for heroic endurance in the love of God. That endurance is good, but there is no question of the suffering that is its occasion being intrinsically good.

Every tradition has, I would imagine, both characteristic strengths and also characteristic pathologies; the latter are often disfigurements of a strength. I would submit that it is a shared strength of Judaism and Christianity that they both attempt to ascribe meaning to suffering. At the same time, while insisting that suffering does not render the life of the sufferer meaningless, they also both insist that this conviction should never transmute into a glorification of suffering as an intrinsic benefit that is "good for you." I agree that Christianity has shown itself more prone to this transmutation than Judaism has, yet I would caution that we all acquire more Augustinian ears so that we recognize the distinctions implicit in certain Christian statements about suffering. I would also pose as a question for Batnitzky whether she thinks, as her essay seems to imply, that if Jews were tempted to err on this question, it would be a temptation complementary to Christian error, namely, the temptation not only to deny the intrinsic value of suffering but to declare it meaningless. This I pose only as a question, perhaps to stimulate further dialogue on the matter.

10

EMBODIMENT

Judaism and Incarnation: The Imaginal Body of God

ELLIOT R. WOLFSON

The impression one gets from historians of religion is that Judaism has officially rejected incarnation as a legitimate theological position.[1] As the historian of early Christianity, Hans Joachim Schoeps observed: "Christological doctrine in itself—the belief that God has become man and has allowed his only-begotten son to suffer sacrificial death as a propitiation for the sins of mankind—has remained, as Paul rightly says, a 'stumbling block' to the Jews. It is an impossible article of belief, which detracts from God's sovereignty and absolute otherness—an article which, in fact, destroys the world."[2] Even the contemporary theologian Michael Wyschogrod, in his attempt to reinscribe Israel as the site of God's concrete dwelling, insists that Judaism has categorically rejected the Christian theology of incarnation. To say that God dwells in the Jewish people does not imply the deification of the Jewish people, which would be implied by an acceptance of incarnation.[3] In a more recent discussion of the Jewish attitude toward the Christian doctrine of incarnation, Wyschogrod has reiterated his view that Judaism is not inherently non-incarnational and thus it is

not diametrically opposed to the notion of a transcendent God entering space and time. However, the immanentism of the Jewish experience of God notwithstanding, there is still a categorical rejection of
the incarnational theology predicated on the view that Jesus is both
human and divine. From the Jewish perspective (at least as it may be
reconstructed from classical sources), God may be spatially present in
a holy place or even in the congregation of the holy people, but he is
not embodied in any particular human being.[4]

It may be valid to conclude (and even this is by no means beyond
critical assessment) that the particular expression of incarnation in
Christianity, the union of the divine and the human in the body of Jesus, is an idea that has neither precedent in the ancient Israelite religion nor parallel in any of the varieties of Judaism in late antiquity
that were contemporaneous with the emerging religion.[5] This does
not mean that the doctrine of incarnation in general is antithetical to
Judaism. On the contrary, the idea of incarnation unique to Christianity should be viewed as a "particular framing" of the conception of incarnation that was idiomatic to a variety of Judaic authors who represented God as a person.[6] The evolution of the Christological doctrine
of the incarnation of the Son is undoubtedly indebted to the scriptural
tradition regarding the corporeality of God, a legacy that clashed with
the Greek philosophical emphasis on the incorporeality and transcendence of ultimate reality.[7] By reclaiming the significance of incarnation in the history of Judaism, therefore, one can simultaneously acknowledge the common ground between Judaism and Christianity
and the uniqueness of this doctrine in each religious culture.

The task set before me is to explicate the role of incarnation in the
case of Judaism. Simply stated, my thesis is that classical Jewish
sources yield a philosophical conception of incarnation (which I will
render by the Hebrew: *hitgashmut*) that refers specifically to the imaginal body of God, a symbolic construct that allows human consciousness to access the transcendent reality as a concrete form manifest primarily (if not exclusively) in the sacred space of the two major forms
of worship of the heart: prayer and study.

The Imaginal Body of God

The embodiment of God in Judaism is not merely a rhetorical matter,
a way to speak of the divine that complies with our limited intellects;
rather, it implies an ontological investiture experienced concretely, al-

beit in human imagination. To say that God is incarnate is to claim something more than that God can be represented metaphorically in images derived from human experience.[8] Obviously, the statement that God assumes human form presupposes the corollary that God may be represented in human terms, but the reverse is not so, for it is entirely plausible to argue that God may be represented in human terms without necessarily implying that God assumes human form.[9] The ontological dimension implied by the doctrine of incarnation is not reducible to linguistic anthropomorphization. To posit as theologically viable an incarnate God, therefore, is not merely to portray God in figurative terms; it is to say that God is configured phenomenally as "body," whether we understand that configuration veridically or docetically, an epistemological issue that divided Christian interpreters from an early period.

For Jewish thinkers the configuration is docetic in orientation, by which I intend not the apparition-like quality of physical events, but the somatic feature of mental images that have as their objective correlative a spiritual entity. It will be recalled that the original issue for the so-called Docetists in the early history of Christianity was precisely how one explains the seemingly corporeal incarnation and/or crucifixion of an incorporeal reality. Consider Kurt Rudolph's account of docetism: "What is meant is . . . that Christ appeared only in semblance (Greek: *dokesei*) as a man or in the flesh, and correspondingly neither suffered nor was really crucified."[10] God appears in semblance as human; the redeemer shows himself as if in the flesh to those of insight. Naturally, the physical event is treated as an apparition, not, however, because there is nothing real, but only because the physical manifestation is an appearance of something real in the spiritual plane. The corporeal nature of the phenomenon is thus located in the image or the "phantasm"—a term I use to refer to a tendency in rabbinic Judaism and medieval forms of Jewish mysticism to explain the apparitions of God as warrior, elder, lover, and so on as modes of being that God assumes when appropriate in the context of either a historical or a liturgical event.[11] Incarnation of the divine body in Judaism relates to theophanic images that are localized in the imagination.[12]

Do we have evidence in the canonical texts of biblical and rabbinic Judaism for the phenomenon of incarnation along the lines that I have charted? According to a growing consensus in biblical scholarship, the textual evidence indicates that for the ancient Israelites the burning issue was not God's corporeality per se, but the problem of iconically representing the divine in corporeal images.[13] Even archaeological evidence that attests that YHVH was represented iconographically indicates that this representation complied with the prohibition against representing the God of Israel. For example, in one of the more significant discoveries, a tenth-century cult stand from Taanach with representations of Asherah as the Lion Lady, YHVH is depicted as the invisible deity posed between the cherubim, an iconic motif that parallels the biblical description of God: *yhwh tseva'ot yoshev ha-keruvim.*[14] Thus we are led to the conclusion that the official cult, already in the early monarchic period, was aniconic. The phenomenon of the empty throne in the temple of Jerusalem confirms the paradoxical idea that the God of Israel is enthroned in unseen majesty.[15] This aniconism, however, did not imply the incorporeality of God, an inference made repeatedly by rationalist interpreters of Judaism from Philo of Alexandria to Hermann Cohen. One must distinguish between the prohibition of depicting God in images and the claim that God cannot be manifest in a body. One may presume, as indeed the evidence from the Bible seems to suggest, that God is capable of assuming corporeal form, although that form should not be represented pictorially.

Needless to say, many passages in Hebrew Scriptures presuppose an anthropomorphic conception of God. This conception, moreover, is predicated on the notion that God can assume an incarnational form that is visually and audibly available to human perception.[16] There is no reason to suppose, as have apologists of Judaism in both medieval and modern times, that the anthropomorphic characterizations of God in Scripture are to be treated figuratively or allegorically. I will cite here one example of what I consider to be a striking illustration of incarnational thinking in biblical religion. In the narrative concerning Jacob's struggle with the mysterious "man," who is explicitly identified as *Elohim* and on account of whom Jacob's name is changed to Israel, Jacob is said to have called the place of the theophany *"Peniel,"* for he saw Elohim face-to-face, *va-yikra ya'akov shem ha-makom peni'el ki ra'iti elohim panim el panim* (Gen. 32:30). The anthropomorphization of God in this biblical text suggests that in ancient Israel some believed that the divine could appear in a tangible and concrete form. The issue, then, is not how one speaks of God, but how God is experienced in the phenomenal plane. In this light, it becomes quite clear that in some cases the anthropomorphisms in Hebrew Scripture do imply an element of incarnation.

The literary evidence does not indicate that the ancient Israelites affirmed the notion of incarnation evident in other Near Eastern cultures, predicated on the idea that a particular royal person is the embodiment of the divine.[17] There is ample evidence, however, that the biblical conception (at various stages reflected in the redactional layers of Scripture) maintained the possibility of God manifesting himself in anthropomorphic form. For example, God is frequently depicted in regal terms: in the theophany related in Exodus 24:10–11, in Isaiah's vision of God enthroned in the temple (6:1–3), in Ezekiel's vision of the glory enthroned upon the chariot (chapters 1 and 10), and in Daniel's apocalyptic vision of the Ancient of Days (7:9–10). These epiphanies of the divine in human form have the texture of a tangibility that one would normally associate with a body of flesh and bones. Clearly, the God of Israel is not a body in this sense, but this does not diminish the somatic nature of the divine appearance attested in various stages of the history of the biblical canon. On the contrary, the ostensibly paradoxical notion of the visible manifestation of the God who is hidden provides us with a different notion of embodiment. The "real" body is the imaginal body that is configured in the heart of the prophet. As I shall discuss in greater detail below, in subsequent rabbinic literature, the matter is extended to the pious believer who stands in God's presence through doing good deeds, especially prayer and study, the two devotional acts that facilitate the attainment of an experience that approximates the visionary ecstasy of prophecy.

The possibility of God occupying space as an incarnate form (although not specified as anthropomorphic in nature) is also implied in the depictions of the indwelling of the glory in the tabernacle (Ex. 40:34–35) and in the temple (1 Kgs. 8:13). An important stage in the evolution of the incarnational orientation occurs in several verses in the book of Deuteronomy, wherein the divine name is described as dwelling in the sanctuary (12:5, 11; 14:23–24; 16:11). The glory of God thus inhabits the earthly temple through the agency of the name. The Deuteronomistic conception of the name inhabiting the sacred space of the community of Israel must be seen against the widespread belief in the magical power of divine names that characterized the religious cultures of the ancient Near East. In the biblical context, the occult power of the name is expressed especially in terms of the revelatory and salvific nature of God's relationship to Israel (Ex. 3:13–15; Ps. 20:2, 54:3; Is. 45:3; Zech. 14:9; Prov. 18:10).[18] There is no reason to suppose that in the biblical context the divine name assumes a personified character. However, the localization of the name in the temple served as the exegetical springboard for subsequent conceptions of the incarnation of God in the letters of the name: the hypostasized power that is both the instrument of creation and the object of revelation.[19] In some sources, both the semiotic form of the name and the angelic hypostasis that bears the potency of the divine glory are identified.[20]

God as an Angel

The textual roots for the incarnation of the divine in the angelic figure are found in passages where there is a deliberate confusion between the angel of God and divinity itself (Gen. 16:9–13, 18:2, 21:7, 22:11, 31:11, 33:11–13; Ex. 3:2ff., 14:19, 23:21, 32:34; Jos. 5:13–15; Jud. 2:1, 4, 5:23, 6:11ff., 13:3ff.; Is. 63:9; Ps. 34:8).[21] In such instances, the shift in the narrative from God to the angel points to the fact that God appears in the guise of the angel. One scriptural verse that is extremely significant for understanding this ancient Israelite conception is God's statement that the Israelites should give heed to the angel whom he has sent before them and not rebel against him, for his name is in him (Ex. 23:21). The line separating the angel and God is substantially blurred, for by bearing the name, which signifies the power of the divine nature, the angel is an embodiment of God's personality. To possess the name is not merely to be invested with divine authority; it means that ontologically the angel is the incarnational presence of the divine manifest in the providential care over Israel. Interestingly enough, the ontological blurring of the divine presence and the highest of the angels—designated variously as "Michael," "Yahoel," "Jacob-Israel," and "Metatron," to mention some of the better known names—is a cornerstone of esoteric doctrines promulgated most explicitly by various medieval Jewish mystics.[22] This notion, attested in older Jewish mystical texts as well, is consistent with what one finds in the biblical texts themselves;[23] that is, the ancient Israelite belief was that God could appear as an angelic presence to human beings, and the shape that this presence took was that of an anthropos. The angelic form, therefore, is the garment (as later kabbalists expressed the matter) in which the divine is clad when it is manifest in the world in the shape of an anthropos. Clearly, this phenomenon, which is notably similar to the Christological identification of Jesus as the glorious angel, should be classified as an example of incarnation as distinct from anthropomorphization.[24]

What is critical is that we not only appreciate the presence and enduring influence of the symbol of the glorious angel within Judaism, but that we resist the temptation to dismiss this critical issue of religious phenomenology as something derived from Christian sources. I would argue that the possibility of God assuming the form of an angel is one of the ground myths that informs the liturgical imagination in rabbinic praxis. The implication of the biblical conception is made explicit in several midrashic sources. Thus, in one context, the matter is related exegetically to the expression "captain of the Lord's host" (Jos. 5:14): "I am the captain from above, and in every place that I am seen the Holy One, blessed be he, is seen."[25] The particular angelic being who serves as the chief of the celestial host is not identified in this text, but the implication of the passage is clear: from a theophanic perspective, the highest angel and God are phenomenally interchangeable, for in every place that the former appears the latter appears. It is not only that the two belong together, but that they resemble one another to the point that the ontological difference between the two is obscured. The idea is repeated from a different exegetical standpoint in a second source: "In every place that the angel is seen, the *Shechinah* is seen, as it says 'An angel of the Lord appeared to him in a blazing fire out of a bush' (Exod. 3:2) and immediately 'God called out to him [out of the bush]' (Exod. 4)."[26] The idea is reiterated in a third passage, but in this context an attempt is made to identify the angelic being who is in the image of the divine: "'An angel of the Lord appeared' (Exod. 3:2). R. Yohanan said, 'This is Michael.' R. Hanina said, 'This is Gabriel.' . . . In every place that he appeared there is the glory of the *Shechinah*."[27] The subject of the last sentence is deliberately ambiguous. According to the first printed edition (Constantinople, 1512), the reference is to Michael, but according to at least one manuscript (Jewish Theological Seminary of America of New York 5014), the reference is to Gabriel.[28] Whether we interpret the reference to Michael or to Gabriel, the significant point is that the demarcation of identity separating the angel and the glory is obfuscated. I suggest that this obfuscation of the difference between God and the angel is related to the belief that God is incarnate in the form of the angel and thus we can speak of the angelic glory that is the glorious angel.

I will mention one other passage, transmitted by R. Samuel ben Nahman in the name of R. Jonathan, for it seems to me to embrace an incarnational doctrine related to the angelic manifestation of God. "From each and every word that comes out from the mouth of the

Holy One, blessed be he, one angel is created, as it says, 'By the word of the Lord the heavens were made, and by the breath of his mouth, all their host' (Ps. 33:6)."[29] The third-century rabbi to whom this tradition is attributed, Jonathan ben Eleazar, was born in Babylonia but lived the better part of his life in the land of Israel, especially in the Galilean city of Sepphoris.[30] I cannot determine definitively if his dictum was influenced by a Christological doctrine of the incarnation of the Logos in the angelic form of Christ, although his particular location and time would certainly not preclude such a possibility.[31] Perhaps R. Jonathan's comment polemically undermines the Christian view by adapting it and giving it a new spin. The belief that God's word is incarnate in the one person of Jesus is undermined (or upstaged) by the claim that each word that issues from God's mouth produces a distinct angelic being.[32] Again I will bracket the question of historical connection, for the more important issue is the conceptual underpinning of R. Jonathan's statement. It seems to me entirely appropriate to use the word "incarnation" to refer to the hypostatic angel created from the word of God.[33]

God as Torah

In my view, there is much evidence in the rabbinic corpus of an incarnational theology, albeit modified in light of Judaism's official aniconism. Of course, I do not wish to ignore the fact that within rabbinic literature itself one finds statements that unequivocally reject the Christological doctrine of incarnation. Does that mean, however, that there is no justification for using the word "incarnation" to characterize ideas espoused by the rabbis themselves? I do not think so, and, as the cluster of motifs to be discussed below will illustrate, incarnational theology is vital to the rabbinic worldview. I am not suggesting that every single rabbinic figure would have accepted the doctrine of incarnation as an appropriate theological posture. With respect to this topic, as one finds in the case of most issues of religious phenomenology, rabbinic literature demonstrates a diverse range of opinions. But within that range one can assuredly find expressions of some form of incarnation.

Of late, a variety of scholars have reexamined the centrality of anthropomorphic representation in the mythic imagination of the rabbis.[34] Although it is premature to speak of a scholarly consensus in this area, we may refer to a new paradigm that is emerging with respect to our appreciation of the mythopoeic nature of rabbinic theological pronouncements. A key element of the rabbinic theological imagination is the supposition regarding the incarnate form of God. More specifically, this form is rendered accessible through the liturgical imagination, which is expressed in Torah study and prayer, the two primary ways of worshipping God in the absence of the temple and the sacrificial cult.[35] These two equally significant ritual acts that sustain rabbinic religiosity present distinct modes of divine incarnation.

Just as early Christian exegetes saw in Christ, God made flesh, so the rabbis conceived of the Torah as the incarnation of the image of God.[36] In the rabbinic imagination, moreover, the sage is a personification of the Torah. It follows, therefore, that insofar as the Torah is the embodiment of the divine image, the sage can be considered the incarnational representation of God.[37] To be sure, rabbinic figures of the formative period fell short of identifying Torah and God in the manner that we find explicitly in medieval kabbalah. The depiction of Torah in mythic form, especially in feminine images, is well attested in rabbinic literature, but in the relevant passages, there is no explicit identification of Torah as divine, let alone as the body of God.[38] The daring idea that prior to the creation of the world the Torah was written on the forearm of God indicates that rabbinic figures were cognizant of the esoteric tradition wherein the Torah is associated with the limbs of the divine body.[39] At the same time, these isolated passages reinforce the conclusion that for the most part the rabbis did not identify God and Torah.

I would like to concentrate on an incarnational tendency discernible in the rabbinic view that the study of Torah is the means by which one lives in the immediate presence of God. Far from being merely rhetorical in nature, these pronouncements are predicated on the presumption that Torah embodies the divine glory. A classic formulation of this sentiment is found in a dictum of Rabbi Halafta:

> The *Shechinah* dwells amongst ten men who sit together occupied with the Torah, as it says, "God stands in the divine assembly" (Ps. 82:1). Whence do we know even by five? As it says, "the foundation of his group is on earth" (Amos 9:6). Whence do we know even by the three? As it says, "among the divine beings he pronounces judgment" (Ps. 82:1). Whence do we know even two? As it says, "Thus those who fear the Lord have conversed one with another and the Lord has heard and listened to it" (Mal. 3:16). Whence even one? As it says, "In every place

where I cause my name to be mentioned I will come to you and bless you" (Ex. 20:21).[40]

The study of Torah, as it is presented here, occasions living in the direct presence of God. The rabbinic emphasis on the indwelling of the *Shechinah* should not be taken as a mere figurative expression but as a signification of an encounter that approximates the intensity of mystical experience.[41] What is especially noteworthy is the concluding part of this passage. The notion that the *Shechinah* dwells even with a man who studies Torah by himself is supported by the proof text "In every place where I cause my name to be mentioned I will come to you and bless you" (Ex. 20:21). Implicit in the homiletical use of this verse is the presumption that the name of God is symbolically interchangeable with the Torah, an idea that later became a cornerstone for various forms of medieval Jewish esotericism.[42] The symbolic identification of the divine name and Torah is attested in another pronouncement transmitted in the name of Rav Judah: "Whence do we know that the blessing before [the reading of] the Torah is [obligated on the basis of a verse] from the Torah? As it says, 'For the name of the Lord I proclaim, give glory to our God!' (Deut. 32:3)."[43] It makes little sense to derive the ritual of reading Torah from the verse about proclaiming the name of God unless the name is identical with the Torah. If we assume, moreover, that the name comprises within itself all the letters of the Hebrew alphabet, and that the letters represent the Torah in its most elemental form, then we can conclude that the demiurgic role assigned to the name is implied in the rabbinic claim that the Torah is the instrument through which God created the world.

The incarnational notion of Torah has major implications for understanding the attitude of the rabbis with regard to the study of Torah. Study is not primarily an intellectual activity but an imaginative process through which the imaginal body of God is conjured. Insofar as the body that is configured in the imagination of one who studies Torah is the name, the hypostasis composed of the graphemes through which the world was created and is perpetually sustained, one may conclude that textual interpretation is itself a form of constructing the anthropomorphic figure of the divine. To be sure, in the rabbinic texts, the body of God is not depicted in the colossal numerical measurements that one finds in the *Shi'ur Komah* fragments, the sources that delineate in explicit fashion the dimensions and names of the stature of the Creator.[44] Nevertheless, the somatic form of God discovered through midrashic hermeneutics and the anthropomorphic God of the esoteric *Shi'ur Komah* speculation are not radically distinct.[45] In either case, there is a convergence of anthropomorphism and letter symbolism that is related more specifically to the identification of Torah and the name.

The equation of Torah and YHVH suggests a form of incarnation predicated on the assumption that the nature of corporeality in its most fundamental sense is linked to letters. To speak of the Torah as the name not only has magical implications; it entails a metaphysical claim (even if expressed mythopoetically) regarding the ultimate nature of reality that is apprehended by mystical insight;[46] that is, in the mind of the rabbis, the physical universe is constituted by the letters of the Hebrew alphabet, which are comprised within the Tetragrammaton. An allusion to this esoteric tradition is attested in the saying attributed to Rav and transmitted by Rabbi Judah, "Betsalel knew how to combine the letters by means of which heaven and earth were created."[47] As a number of scholars have suggested, implicit in this statement is the archaic belief that heaven and earth were created by means of the name of God, an idea attested in apocryphal, rabbinic, and mystical sources as well, specifically in terms of *yod* and *he*, the first two letters of the Tetragrammaton used to signify the complete name.[48] According to the statement of Rav, Betsalel could construct the tabernacle, a microcosm of the universe, for he knew the hidden gnosis of combining the letters of the name whence emerge all the other letters that make up the nature of what exists. The full implication of the semiotic nature of divine creativity is drawn explicitly in the second part of *Sefer Yetsirah*, the ancient work of Jewish cosmogony:

> Twenty-two foundational letters *(otiyot yesod)* are fixed in a wheel in 231 gates. The wheel rotates forward and backward. . . . Twenty-two letters: He engraved, hewed, weighed, permutated, and combined them, and he formed through them the soul of every creature and the soul of everything to be formed. How did he weigh and permutate them? *Alef* with all of them and all of them with *alef*; *bet* with all of them and all of them with *bet*; *gimmel* with all of them and all of them with *gimmel*. All of them rotate in a cycle and go forth in 231 gates. Thus every creature and every word goes forth in one name.[49]

Building upon an ancient cosmological belief, the author of this section of *Sefer Yetsirah* maintains that creation comes about by divine fiat. More specifically, God creates the world through a complex process of combining and permutating the twenty-two letters of the Hebrew alphabet through 231 gates (each gate *(sha'ar)* is a combination of two letters).[50] The consequence of the permutation is that all that exists comes from one name. It is reasonable to assume (as several kabbalistic commentators explicitly affirm) that the implication here is that the twenty-two letters collectively constitute the one name of God, the Tetragrammaton, which is the instrument and substance of creation. If this surmise is correct, then attested here is the notion that the letters are contained in the most sacred of divine names. In a second passage from *Sefer Yetsirah*, God is similarly described as transforming and making "every creature and every word one name, and a sign for this matter is the twenty-two objects in one body."[51] All that is created constitutes one name, which is the name of God formed out of the twenty-two letters that correspond to twenty-two parts of the human body.[52] There is thus a correlation between letters, the divine name, and an anthropomorphic figure. This triadic structure is essential to the incarnational theology of Judaism: the body of God is composed of letters that make up the name. I would contend that this triadic structure underlies the rabbinic belief that study of Torah affords one access to the divine. No gap separates the hermeneutical enterprise and religious experience: engagement with the text facilitates the indwelling of God's presence, which is experienced as the textual body of Torah.

The linkage of Torah study and the experience of the *Shechinah* in the rabbinic imagination raises another crucial aspect of incarnational theology that is related more specifically to the role of the imagination in actively configuring the semiotic body of God. The key passage that articulates this dimension of the contemplative practice of envisioning is one talmudic text wherein the dictum "It matters not whether one augments or one diminishes if only one orients one's heart to heaven"[53] is applied to the study of Torah. As Max Kadushin noted long ago, this text reflects the view that the study of Torah requires that one have the proper intention *(kavanah)*—that one direct one's mind and heart to God.[54] To appreciate the philosophical intent of this view, we must ponder the precise meaning of the idiom *she-yechaven libo la-shamayim* (to direct one's heart to heaven.) The word *kavanah* is derived from *kiven* (from the root *kvn*), to turn or to face a particular direction, to orient oneself, to find one's bearings in space. Whatever layers of signification and hermeneutical transformations the term has assumed in rabbinic sources through time, something of its etymological foundation is retained, for at the core, *kavanah* involves an orientation in space, an intentional facing, a directing of the heart to the other. But what is it to face the other when the face of the other is invisible, to turn one's gaze upon that which cannot be seen? Here we arrive at the phenomenological mystery of the Jewish notion of incarnation: by directing the heart through study heavenward, the celestial habitation of the transcendent other (the word *shamayim*, which literally means "heaven," is one of God's appellations in rabbinic thought), the individual provides the mental space wherein the incorporeal God is embodied. The divine body is composed of the letters of the Torah, which is the name, but that body is apprehended only when the Torah is contemplated with the proper intention. Through the body of the text one accesses the text of the body.

Prayer and Incarnation

In a separate study, I have suggested that the rabbinic conception of *kavanah* in prayer, at least according to one trajectory, entailed the visual apprehension of the divine.[55] The term *kavanah*, therefore, refers to an internal state of consciousness by means of which the worshiper creates a mental icon of God, the function of which is to locate the divine presence in space. In this state of consciousness, the phenomenal boundaries of inside and outside dissolve, for only by means of the internal image does the worshiper experience the divine as external. This conception of mental imaging is epitomized in the teaching attributed to Simeon the Pious, reported by Hana ben Bizna: "The one who prays must see himself as if the *Shechinah* were opposite him, as it says, 'I have set the Lord always before me' (Ps. 16:8)."[56] Prayer requires a visualization of that which cannot be visualized, a process that is predicated on the assumption that God can assume incarnate form. The word "incarnation" refers to the ontic presencing of God in a theophanic image, rather than to the metaphorical figuration of God in a rhetorical trope. The specific form that this image assumes is suggested by the proof text cited by Simeon the Pious, *shiviti YHVH lenegdi tamid* (I shall place the Tetragrammaton before me constantly). The image that the worshiper must set in his mind is that of the ineffable name, the sign of that which cannot be signified, for only through that name is the invisible face of the transcendent rendered visible.

Rabbinic discussions on the intentionality in prayer are based on the notion of an imaginal body attributed to God, the somatic form that inheres in the human imagination as a symbolic configuration constituted by the letters of the unutterable name. Within the aniconic framework of classical Judaism, only such a body could be ascribed to God. This does not mean, however, that the rabbinic texts that speak of God's body ought to be deciphered as merely allegorical. On the contrary, the language of the texts points beyond the textual margins to an experience of God's imaginal body refracted through the prism of the name.[57] The intricate nexus between the name, prayer, and the sacred space of the sanctuary, wherein the envisioning of the imaginal body occurs, is implicit in the following talmudic passage:

> R. Eleazar said, "Great is the sanctuary for it is placed between two [divine] names,[58] as it says '[The place You made to dwell in] O Lord, the sanctuary, O Lord [which Your hands established]'" (Ex. 15:17). R. Eleazar said, "Every person who has knowledge, it is as if the temple were built in his day. Knowledge is placed between two names and the sanctuary is placed between two names."[59]

The pietistic mentality expressed in this passage reached its fullest expression in medieval kabbalah. Indeed, this literature even suggests that through their mystical intentions in prayer kabbalists adopted the role of high priests, as if the temple were built in their day. Of course, kabbalists did not relinquish their faith, hope, and conviction that the physical temple would actually be rebuilt in the messianic future. Still, in the absence of the temple, they spiritualized the sacrificial rites by identifying them with their mystical intentions in prayers that were focused on the appropriate names of God. In my judgment, this meditative ideal is already implied in the talmudic text. Support for my conjecture may be gathered from the following comment on the words of R. Eleazar offered by Moses ben Isaac of Prossnitz:

> The secret of knowledge is the secret of the sanctuary, for the matter of the building of the temple is explained and made sensible from understanding the verse[60] "and the House that King Solomon has built" (1 Kgs. 6:2). It says there, "Even the heavens to their uttermost reaches cannot contain You, how much less this House [that I have built]. Yet turn, O Lord my God, to the prayer and supplication of Your servant, [and hear the cry and prayer that Your servant offers before You this

day]" (1 Kgs. 8:27–28). He thus explained the purpose of his intention in the building of the temple, which was that He might heed the prayer and supplication. For this reason he said, "O Lord my God." . . . Therefore, regarding he who has knowledge to intend in his prayer . . . so that God, blessed be He, will turn to listen to the prayer and supplication, it is as if the temple were built in his day.[61]

The mystical secret of the sanctuary (*sod ha-mikdash*) is connected to the secret of knowledge (*sod ha-de'ah*), for he who has the proper knowledge of the divine names can have the correct intention so that his prayers will be heard. Since the ultimate purpose of the temple was that God might heed the prayers of Israel, it follows that, in the absence of the temple, the one who has the proper intention fulfills the task of building the temple in his time.

Conclusion

In the history of Judaism, unlike Christianity, belief in incarnation never attained the status of dogma. On the contrary, in rabbinic texts there are clear polemical statements rejecting the Christological doctrine, and in medieval philosophical literature one of the recurring tenets viewed as basic to Judaism was the claim that God is not a body. However, in rabbinic Judaism of the formative and medieval periods, based on biblical precedent, an anthropomorphic conception of God is affirmed. These anthropomorphic characterizations are not to be taken simply as figurative or metaphorical. Underlying the rhetoric of representation is the eidetic presumption that God can be experienced in a tangible and concrete manner. Prayer and study, according to the rabbis, are key ways that God is so experienced. Proper intentionality in these two acts of piety is predicated on the iconic visualization of the divine within the imagination. In the physical space circumscribed by words of prayer and study, the imaginal body of God assumes incarnate form. This is the intent of the statement attributed to R. Abbahu, "'Seek the Lord while He can be found' (Is. 55:6). Where is He found? In the houses of worship and the houses of study."[62] The rabbinic notion of incarnation embraces the paradox that God's body is real only to the extent that it is imagined, but it is imagined only to the extent that it is real.

The conception of God's imaginal body evident in different phases of Jewish thought can contribute significantly to Christian reflection on the doctrine of incarnation. Indeed, the Judaic perspective should induce us to alter our views regarding corporeality in general. Proper attunement to the idea of the divine body in ancient Israel (and subsequent periods of Jewish history) may lead one to appreciate that the body is a complex construct of the imagination rather than a material artifact that can be measured by the dimensions of three-dimensional space. The phenomenological parameters of embodiment must be significantly expanded if we are to comprehend the enigma of incarnation, the limitless delimitation of the delimited limitlessness. To place YHVH before one constantly is to confront the holiness of the Holy One in the otherness of his being, a confrontation that is both encounter and resistance. Facing the face that cannot be faced in hearing the name that cannot be pronounced—therein lies the secret of incarnation in Judaism, a mystery of transcendence that the imagination alone is capable of rendering imminent. As Gaston Bachelard put it, "To enter into the domain of the superlative, we must leave the positive for the imaginary. We must listen to the poets."[63] In the end, the Christological doctrine of incarnation is not, as Paul surmised, a stumbling block particularly to the Jews, but rather to anyone whose religious sensibility has not been properly nourished by the wellspring of poetic imagination.

The Christian Doctrine of the Incarnation

RANDI RASHKOVER

The belief in the incarnation, arguably the centerpiece of the Christian worldview, has often shocked and perplexed Jews. In his essay, Elliot Wolfson helps Jews appreciate the Christian belief in the incarnation by using classical Jewish sources to outline "a philosophical conception of incarnation that refers specifically to the imaginal body of God, a symbolic construct that allows human consciousness to access the transcendent reality as a concrete form." However, the Christian concept of incarnation is the more particular belief that "in the beginning was the Word, and the Word was with God, and the Word was God . . . and the Word became flesh"(Jn. 1:1, 14). In Christianity, incarnation refers directly to the embodiment or incarnation of the Word of God or of what is alternately considered God's eternal thought, speech, or order. In what follows, I will argue that Judaism also maintains a notion of the embodiment of the Word of God, insofar as Jews are elected to embody the Word of God and, by so doing, participate in a covenantal relationship with the God who elects them.

The Torah, the Word of God, and Corporeal Israel

In Judaism, God's Word is the Torah. Like the Christian concept of the Word, the Torah is identified as God's speech, God's thought, or God's blueprint for the world: "[T]he craftsman does not build according to his own wisdom, rather he sees plans and blueprints in order to know how to make rooms and corridors. The Holy One blessed is He did the same. . . . He looked into the Torah and created the world" (Gen. R. 1:1). Michael Fishbane states it nicely: "These narratives and laws are but a species of the divine Logos which radiates from the inmost center of divinity."[1]

According to the Bible, God speaks his Word to the Jewish people at Mount Sinai (Ex. 19:3–19:9). The revelation of the Torah at Sinai is the event of God's election of the Jewish people to follow God's ways and institute God's order on earth. The Jews are not only to follow God's laws but also to embody them: "For this commandment that I command you today—it is not hidden from you, and it is not distinct. . . . Rather, the matter is very near to you—in your mouth and your heart—to perform it" (Deut. 30:11–14). Elected to take responsibility for doing God's Word, the Jews are commanded to embody the Torah. In the *Shema*, one of the central prayers of the Jewish liturgy, we read:

> You shall love the Lord your God, with all your heart, with all your soul, and with all your resources. Let these matters that I command you today be upon your heart. Teach them thoroughly to your children and speak of them while you sit in your home, while you walk on the way, when you retire and when you arise. Bind them as a sign upon your arm and let them be tefillin between your eyes. (Deut. 6:5–9)[2]

As Michael Wyschogrod says, Israel is to inscribe God's Torah into every aspect of its life as a national body; "Israel's election is therefore a carnal election."[3]

That God elects the Jewish people to embody his Torah or Word is already established in the election of Abraham (Gen. 17:9–12). Through the *mitsvah* of circumcision—the mark of the covenant— God commands Jewish men to embody the Torah, to inscribe the law on to their bodies.[4] The Jews' embodiment of God's Torah has significance beyond obedience to God's will. Embodying God's Torah, the Jews become the corporeal sign of God's presence. Bearing the marks of God's Word, the people Israel become a sign or a testimony to God's reality here on earth.

By incorporating God's Word into their life as a nation, the Jews participate in a covenant with God. Not only the fulfillment of a responsibility, the embodiment of God's Word is a response to the biblical God's gesture of initial love toward the Jewish people: "It was only for your forefathers that YHVH took a passion, loving them, so that he chose their descendants after them—you!" (Deut. 10:12–15). Embodying God's Word, we take God's Word into our physical selves and draw nearer to the God who loves us. The embodiment of the Torah secures the covenant with God.

Embodiment of Torah and the Community of Scholars

The theme of embodying the Torah to secure the covenant with God continues throughout postbiblical Judaism. The sages detail how every aspect of a Jew's life, physical and mental, must be devoted to performing the law. But writing in a time of exile from the land, the rabbis understood the embodiment of Torah less in terms of the body politic and more in terms of the community of scholars who commit their lives to interpreting and inscribing Torah in their minds and memory.[5] Tradition tells us that the first sages committed the oral Torah to their memory. Like circumcision, which inscribes the Torah into the flesh, memory inscribes the Torah into the mind, embodying and humanizing it. Later, the commitment to memorize became the commitment to learn and interpret the Torah. The following famous midrash illustrates this point:

> There was a sharp disagreement between the majority of the sages and the mighty Rabbi Eliezer. . . . Upon the call of Rabbi Eliezer a number

of miracles occurred as signs that his opinion was the correct one. . . . His colleagues were not impressed. Finally a heavenly voice was heard: "What is it you want with Rabbi Eliezer? Wherever he expresses an opinion, the Halakha is according to him." This would seem to have settled the issue, but not for the rabbis. Upon hearing the heavenly voice, Rabbi Yehoshua stood up and, in response, called out: "It is not in the heavens." [The postscript of the story continues.] Rabbi Natan, once encountered the prophet Elijah . . . and asked him, "What was God doing at the time of that great discussion?" Elijah's reply was, "God was laughing and said: 'My Sons have defeated Me; My sons have defeated Me.'"[6]

The story illustrates three points: First, it confirms that God's Torah or Word is not in heaven; it is here with us on earth. Second, the story establishes that the Torah is not simply with the Jewish people but with the majority of the rabbis, the community of scholars. Third, this community of scholars embodies the Torah by interpreting and inscribing it in their minds.[7]

Like the embodiment of the Torah in the political life of the people, study of Torah is a central element in covenantal life with God. The community of scholars who learn Torah becomes a visible sign of the Word of God. The rabbis say, "If ten men sit together and occupy themselves with the words of the Torah, the Shechinah is in their midst" (M. Avot 3:7).[8]

The Word Made Flesh and the Election of Jesus

If the Torah is the Word of God for Jews, what is the Word of God for Christians? According to Christianity, the Word of God is God's own self-testimony, self-proclamation, or self-glorification. In the words of one Christian theologian, God's Word means, "God speaks and interprets God by God."[9] In Jewish tradition, God testifies to himself through the Torah or through law. In Christian tradition, however, God testifies to himself through a Son—the Word made flesh. In Judaism, God lovingly elects the Jewish people to embody his Word or Torah on earth. In Christianity, God "elects" the man Jesus to become the embodiment of his Word or self-testimony and to participate in his own self-proclamation.

Although a number of Christian theologians have drawn attention to the election motif within Christology, Karl Barth, in his *Church Dogmatics*, arguably provides the most detailed and systematic discussion of

God's act of election in Christ. Barth says that God's incarnation in the man Jesus is God's "self-giving. And that is how the inner glory of God overflows" (II.II, 121). Elsewhere he says, "Jesus Christ is the elected man" (II.II, 116). By electing Jesus, "[God] permits some one of His creatures . . . in the sphere and time of the world created by Him to speak for Him (II.II, 54). As the elected man, Jesus testifies to God through his words and his acts but most significantly through his suffering and death. Jesus testifies to God in his suffering and death because it is in these moments that he affirms his faith in God, saying, "Not my will, but thine, be done" (II.II, 177). In this way, Jesus so fully embodies God's Word that he sacrifices or offers his own body as a testimony to God.

Michael Wyschogrod points out that such embodiment unto death is not unique to the man Jesus but has a precedent within the Jewish people themselves.[10] Barth's account of Jesus allows us to identify other precedents as well. For instance, in their embodiment of the law, the Jews covenanted with God in his efforts to establish his name and presence on earth; so, too, Jesus' embodiment as the Word leads him to covenant with God and through his life to announce God's reality on earth: "Through the man Jesus we find the attestation of God" (*Church Dogmatics*, II.I, 54). Moreover, by proclaiming God's presence on earth, Jesus, like the Jews, achieves intimacy with God: "By these events God confirms that the Elect is the only-begotten Son of God (II.II, 125).

Jews and Christians:
Differing Conceptions of Embodiment

Clearly, the Christian conception of an embodied Word has precedents in Jewish tradition; indeed, it is not a concept radically divorced from Judaism. Nonetheless, the Christian concept of the Word made flesh ultimately alters the Jewish model of embodiment. In closing, let me outline three key differences between Jewish and Christian understandings of the incarnation of the Word.

First, in Christianity Jesus is both elected man and electing God. Although Judaism maintains that the embodiment of the Word can result in a covenant and even in a mystical union with God, it stops short of simply identifying those who embody the Word with God.[11] The Christian understanding of Jesus as both the elected man and the electing God is rooted in the notion of original sin. God created hu-

mankind as natural and righteous doers of God's will, but human beings have chosen instead to assert their own will and to disregard
God's sovereignty. In so doing, they estrange themselves from God
and live in a condition of sin from which they cannot extricate themselves. Consequently, the reality of sin precludes the possibility of participating in God's election. According to Christianity, only God
maintains power over sin, and only God can free us from it. It follows
that the man Jesus participates in God's election only insofar as he is
not exclusively the elected man but also the electing God. Thus in the
Nicene Creed Christians confess:

> We believe in one God, the Father, the Almighty, maker of heaven and
> earth, of all that is seen and unseen. And in one Lord, Jesus Christ, the
> only Son of God, eternally begotten of the Father, God from God,
> Light from Light, true God from true God, begotten, not made, one in
> Being with the Father. Through him all things were made.... For us
> and for our salvation he came down from heaven and was incarnate ...
> and became man. For our sake he was crucified ... suffered death and
> was buried. On the third day he rose again ... ascended into heaven and
> is seated at the right hand of the Father. He will come again in glory to
> judge the living and the dead.

Given that humankind cannot autonomously engage in covenant with
God on account of its sin, God's incarnation in the man Jesus establishes the conditions necessary for salvation, for human participation
in God's covenant.

How is it that Jesus as the incarnate God establishes the conditions
for covenant? First, in the man Jesus, God subjects himself to suffering, reveals the reality of his judgment over sin, and takes this judgment upon Himself. The human community who bears witness to this
suffering and judgment then awakens from its blind slumber and recognizes the sin that enslaves it. Second, Jesus, the incarnate God, is
not only the one who suffers and dies but also the one who, through
his life and resurrection, testifies to God, embodies the Word, and reveals God's will, namely, that humans testify to and participate in the
divine life of proclamation and covenant.

The notion of participating in the divine life brings us to the second
difference between Jewish and Christian conceptions of the embodied
Word. For Christians, participation requires faith. *Only* through faith
in Jesus Christ, and not, as is the case for Jews, through the obser-

vance of the law or through learning, can one participate in the embodiment of the divine Word. To elaborate, let me draw again on the work of Karl Barth.

According to Barth, the event of the incarnation is the *announcement* or revelation of the reality of the kingdom of God, or the eternal covenant between God and his children. However, the announcement of the kingdom is received by those who dwell in the time and place prior to the kingdom. The election of Jesus and his resurrection to eternal fellowship with God is an event available only to the man Jesus. As man, Jesus is the first of the creatures to have his creaturely reality redeemed from sin. Those who receive this revelation, on the other hand, await their redemption from sin. However, Christians may participate in God's election here and now insofar as they maintain *faith* in the promise of their future redemption as the promise that has been made visible in the event of the incarnation. To have faith is to believe in what God has done and revealed in Jesus Christ as the promise of one's own future redemption. And to have faith in what God has done is to testify to God. Faith in Jesus Christ is the way the community of the church testifies to God and participates in a covenant with God here and now.

The third difference between Jewish and Christian conceptions of the incarnation can be named in a word: Trinity. For Christianity, the incarnate Word is not only God but the God of the Trinity. To understand the incarnation one must understand the Trinity—the triune divinity of God as Father, Son, and Holy Spirit.

Recall that John's Gospel says of the Word that it was "in the beginning," that it was with God, and that, indeed, it was God, and that it was this Word that became flesh. Recall, as well, that the Nicene Creed begins, "We believe in one God, the Father, the Almighty, maker of heaven and earth, of all that is seen and unseen. And in one Lord, Jesus Christ . . . one in Being with the Father. Through him all things were made." The same Word, then, that was at the beginning and that created the world later became the Word incarnate, and later still, as the creed notes, "rose," "ascended," "is seated at the right hand of the Father" and "will come again to judge the living and the dead." As the electing God, Jesus Christ is not only the one who suffers and dies but also the one who creates, judges unto death, and bestows eternal life. Only a God who maintains power over human existence or who *creates* human existence is capable of taking it away and reinstating it.

In Judaism, a separation is generally maintained between God and his Word, or Torah, but as both John and the Creed make plain,

Christianity holds that the Word is identical with God, even before the event of the incarnation. Indeed, even before creation, God seeks to share his glory with another. God the Father begets or posits *himself* as another or Son, with his own eternal reality. As such, the Son is not a creature but is of the same essence as God the Father. Barth explains: "In the inter-trinitarian life of God the eternal generation of the Son or Logos is, of course, the expression of God's love, of His will not to be alone" (*Church Dogmatics*, I.I, 139). But to share in God's glory is to testify to it. The Son of God is the *Word* of God. Therefore, the incarnation in Jesus Christ is the embodiment of God as the Son or the Word. Through the incarnation, God extends his own eternal fellowship with the Son to humanity.

In addition to the Father and the Son, Christians speak of the Holy Spirit. In the words of the Nicene Creed, "We believe in the Holy Spirit, the Lord, the giver of life, who proceeds from the Father and the Son. With the Father and Son he is worshiped and glorified. He has spoken through the Prophets." As noted, the event of the incarnation of Christ culminates in the testimony of the church community to its belief in the promise of God's future redemption. As the electing God, Jesus Christ is the means through which the church community stands in a covenant with God. However, Jesus as the embodied Word is no longer here; as the creed states, he has ascended to be with the Father. In the absence of the Son, and in his name, the Father sends an "advocate"—the Holy Spirit (Jn. 14:16, 26). According to Barth, the Holy Spirit, is the "act of communion of the Father and the Son." (*Church Dogmatics* I.I, 470). The Holy Spirit enables the one to receive love from the other. Consequently, as electing God, Jesus Christ, now in his work as the Holy Spirit, enables the church community, here and now, to receive God's love and to testify to it.

With its notions of an embodied Word that is identical to God, of a God that is one and yet three, and of faith and not observance of the law and Torah study as the key to participation in this Word, Christianity departs significantly from Judaism. Nonetheless, as I stated at the start, Judaism also maintains a notion of the embodiment of the Word of God. Indeed, as Elliot Wolfson says in his essay, "the idea of incarnation unique to Christianity should be viewed as a 'particular framing' of the conception of incarnation" present in various strands of Judaism. Thus even on the subject of this most central and, in Jewish terms, perplexing of Christian doctrines, Jews and Christians have hope of mutual understanding.

Embodiment and Incarnation:
A Response to Elliot Wolfson

SUSAN A. ROSS

Elliot Wolfson identifies a tension at the heart of language about God: how is it that human beings, who are bound to the terms in which we live—enfleshed and embodied ones—can talk about and pray to God, the transcendent, the Holy One, the utterly Other? We confront, as Wolfson describes it, the task of "facing the face that cannot be faced in hearing the name that cannot be pronounced." Christians meet this difficulty by "seeing" God through the person of Jesus of Nazareth. Nonetheless, the inherent tension of religious language and the utter transcendence of God remain integral to the Christian tradition; they simply take on a different tone. In what follows, I discuss various ways in which both the tension of religious language and the utter transcendence of God persist in Christian discourse about incarnation As a way of introducing what I want to say about Christian conceptions of an incarnate God, let me make two general observations about Wolfson's essay.

The first thing that strikes me about Wolfson's essay is his initial approach. In the terms of Christian Christology (language about Christ), this is an approach "from above"; that is, the question of the possibility of incarnation begins with the affirmation of divine transcendence ("above") and moves ("down") from there: how can God, who is "above" us and eternal, be seen in, related to, experienced in, or even discussed in terms of the flesh? How can that which is *not* body be understood by those who *are* embodied? For at least the last two centuries or so, many Christians have approached the question of incarnation "from below"; that is, how does the human person Jesus of Nazareth reveal God to human beings? What is it about his life and death that convinced a group of first-century Jews that they had indeed encountered the Holy One in this human being? Such an approach begins where Wolfson ultimately suggests we should, with *experience*. For Wolfson, it is the *experience* of God in prayer and study that brings about the sense that God is really present in an image. For Christians, it is the *experience* of Jesus' message and life—sometimes in prayer, sometimes in hearing the scriptures, sometimes in the witness of a person's life to that same message—that suggests that one has encountered not just another human being, not even a quite extraordinary one, but the living God.

The Christian approach to the incarnation "from below" has not been developed without controversy. There is always the fear among some Christians that too great a focus on Jesus' humanity will detract from his divinity. When I went to see the film *The Last Temptation of Christ*, based on Nikos Kazantzakis's novel, about ten years ago, I encountered a noisy group of Christian (mostly Roman Catholic) religious protesters outside the theater. They were aghast that anyone should even think that Jesus Christ would have experienced sexual feelings. What they missed, of course, was the point, in both the novel and the film, that Jesus' temptation was *not* primarily sexual but, rather, was the temptation to "use" his divinity to escape the terrible (human) death of crucifixion and to die in bed, after a long and happy life. This nervousness about the humanity of Jesus goes back to the very earliest years of Christian reflections, when Gnostics ("knowers," in Greek) claimed that one could not reconcile the transcendent God with flesh and thus mortality. Jesus only "seemed" to be human (Docetism). Clearly, the radical implications of incarnation are a Christian as well as a Jewish concern, a concern that is, I think, part of a healthy and fundamental response to the problem of idolatry.

The issue of idolatry brings me to the second point that strikes me about Wolfson's essay, which is the absence of any discussion of the *moral* dimensions of embodiment. I hasten to say that this is by no means a *lack*; rather, it confirms for me the more evenhanded approach to flesh, sexuality, food, and the basic material stuff of life that characterizes the Jewish tradition. In other words, what is not present in Wolfson's discussion of incarnation is the body-soul dualism that has influenced (and, some would even say, infected) the Christian tradition for nearly all of its history. Christian nervousness about the body—which has manifested itself in the value given to celibacy over married life and in the focus on (some would say obsession with) sexual issues as the litmus test for one's Christian faith—does not seem to have the same influence in Judaism that it has in Christianity, although a discussion between Christians and Jews about the laws of ritual purity would be a worthwhile one. Ironically, then, the tradition that has raised incarnation to the status of a dogma is arguably more nervous about matters of the flesh than the tradition that has not done so.

Feminism and the Tension of Religious Language

In recent years, feminist theologians have taken the Christian tradition to task for its denigration of the body—more particularly, of women's bodies—and have argued that traditionally male language for God and the apparent appropriateness of the incarnation in the male sex have led to a number of questionable or even faulty beliefs, including the beliefs that women are inferior to men, that women cannot be ordained because the priest is an *alter Christus* (another Christ), and that God *is* more appropriately spoken of in male terms since the male is the "active" principle, whereas women are "receptive."

Standing behind these feminist criticisms of the Christian tradition is the assumption that our language about God arises out of our *experience* and that, more specifically, largely male language about God has in turn shaped the *experience of God* so that God's "maleness" has become a given. From this perspective, it is no surprise that a tradition dominated by celibate white men has talked of God in largely (white) male and asexual terms. However, voices that have gained theological expression in the last four decades—those of women, people of color, the poor—have raised serious questions about what it means to be created "in the image of God" for those who are not male, or white, or privileged.

This "anthropomorphic issue," which Wolfson summarizes nicely in his essay, has taken on its own distinctive shape and form in Christianity. The issue of "inclusive language" (that is, language that includes female as well as male imagery) for God has been a heated issue among Christians. The official Roman Catholic tradition has largely rejected "vertical inclusive language" (language having to do with God) and has approved "horizontal inclusive language" (language having to do with human beings) in only some cases—for example, the use of "children of God" rather than "sons of God." *The Inclusive Language Lectionary*, which was a largely Protestant effort to recast the traditional weekly readings in inclusive terms, aroused much controversy, especially among conservative Christians.[1]

Amid these controversies and criticisms, some feminist theologians have argued that taking incarnation seriously will result in a more balanced approach to the body and to women's participation in religious life.[2] As long as the body is seen as the "lower" part of the person and women are seen to be "more bodily" than men, the incarnation has not been taken seriously enough. Serious consideration of incarnation will also make Christians less reluctant to speak of God in female terms.[3] Jewish feminist theologians tend to be less eager to focus on female language for God, but they share the conviction that men have no religious priority before God and that women have not always been served well by religious traditions.

The Utter Transcendence of God

The incarnation has not allowed Christians to evade the difficulty of talking about God, nor has the Christian notion of God incarnate in human form overcome a profound sense of the utter transcendence of God. This transcendence is especially evident in three interrelated aspects of Christian thought: (1) the body of Christ; (2) the resurrection and ascension of Jesus; (3) the immaculate conception and assumption of Mary.

The Body of Christ and the Imaginal Body of God

The absence of the physical Jesus from the Christian community takes Christians, in a sense, back to the drawing board. I am reminded of Elie Wiesel's remark, "The Jew says, 'the world is filled with evil; why has the Messiah not yet come?' and the Christian says, 'The Messiah has come; yet why is the world still filled with evil?'" If the incarnate God once walked among humans, how do we experience God now, when Jesus is "at God's right hand"?

The Christian answer to this question takes shape in the community's witness to the Word (the Bible) and in the sacraments. In Roman Catholicism, the experience of both takes place in the church, and so the church itself, with all its members, constitutes "the body of Christ." "We are the body of Christ" say the words of hymns and prayers. Moreover, the mystical tradition is filled with examples of holy people being physically imprinted with the wounds of Christ (the stigmata). The body of Christ is affirmed as uniquely present, however, in the elements of communion—the bread and the wine. Through communion, believers come into contact with the continuing presence and "work" of Christ in saving the world; they become the body of Christ here and now, living out the Christian message in the world. This understanding of the body of Christ bears some resemblance to Wolfson's discussion of the "imaginal body attributed to God," which in Judaism is experienced not in communion but in prayer and study. For all their differences, both the imaginal body of God and the body of Christ rely for their expression on human intentionality. In Wolfson's terms, each is a "symbolic construct that allows human consciousness to access the transcendent reality as a concrete form."

I mention the analogy (and it is only an analogy) between the body of Christ and the imaginal body of God to suggest that the incarnation does not take Christians off the hook, so to speak. Indeed, the incarnate God is present in communion and in the church that gathers around the bread and the wine: both are the body of Christ, God incarnate, here and now. And yet it takes only a moment of reflection to realize that amid this presence there remains something utterly transcendent. Wolfson's statement that "the 'real' body [of God] is the imaginal body that is configured in the heart of the prophet" is not so distant from the idea that the Christian church, in its life of worship and prayer and fidelity to the gospel, is the "body of Christ"—a body at once real and imaginal, immanent and transcendent. This dual character of the body of Christ gains clarity when it is placed in the context of the resurrection and ascension of Jesus.

Resurrection and Ascension

The common misunderstanding of the resurrection is that Jesus' physical corpse was resuscitated, walked among his disciples for a time, and then "went up" to heaven in the ascension. However, there is broad scholarly agreement that the early church did not view the resurrected Jesus as a resuscitated corpse; rather, the first Christians understood the resurrection as a sign that Jesus of Nazareth was gloriously assumed into the life of God, as mysterious as this phrase sounds. Thus to say that Jesus "lives" is not to affirm that he came back to life in any ordinary sense, but that he now lives in God and that his message continues in the lives of his followers. That Jesus' "aliveness" is nevertheless "bodily" is expressed in the postresurrection stories in which Jesus eats with his disciples (Jn. 21:9–14) and in which one apostle puts his hand in Jesus' wounds (Jn. 20: 26–29). But, again, it is a mistake to equate this bodily presence with resuscitation. The meaning of the resurrection is more profound: in Christ, life has triumphed over death; and just as Jesus "lives" in God, so will the faithful, when they, too, are resurrected.

Like the resurrection, the ascension—"the definitive entrance of Jesus' humanity into God's heavenly domain"—is an event prone to misinterpretation.[4] If Jesus' body "ascended into heaven," then where did it go? The question is already a misunderstanding. Again, modern scholarship argues that this event displays the early Christian realization that Jesus was no longer immediately present among them but was *with* God. If Jesus had remained among the disciples, they would have "clung" to him (see Jn. 20:17) and thus would have stood in the way of his universal presence to the whole world. Ten days after Jesus' ascension, the Spirit of God came upon the disciples at Pentecost (Acts 2:1–4), and with that, the church was born, a birth made possible, oddly enough, by the absence of Jesus (Jn. 16:7). The church becomes the body of Christ, the presence of God here and now, only in the absence of the body of Jesus, who rose and then ascended to be with God. For Christians, the incarnation is like a rainbow: it makes God unmistakably present, and yet also inherently elusive and utterly transcendent.

Mary and Incarnation

The doctrines of the immaculate conception and the assumption, both of which concern Mary, the mother of Jesus (incidentally, the only doctrines the Roman Catholic Church has explicitly declared to be "infallible" dogmas), also deal with incarnation, embodiment, and transcendence. The doctrine of the immaculate conception declares that Mary was conceived without original sin in the womb of her mother. Traditional Christian understandings of original sin assumed that it was passed on from generation to generation—in the act of sexual intercourse. Because Mary was to be the mother of the son of God, and yet was conceived in intercourse, her "sinlessness" was important to establish, else she might have passed it on to her son, who, according to tradition, was without sin. The belief in the immaculate conception originated early in Christian thinking and continued to grow, especially in post-Reformation Catholicism. When the dogma was promulgated in 1854, it affirmed the "popular faith" of many ordinary Christians in the face of modern intellectual skepticism about such miraculous events. This dogma is not accepted by Protestant or Orthodox Christians because of its lack of biblical support.

The doctrine of the assumption, promulgated in 1950 (also a time of turmoil over "modern" tendencies in Catholic theology) maintains that Mary's body was "assumed" into heaven, thus guaranteeing that her body did not suffer physical corruption after death. Karl Rahner, the great twentieth-century German Catholic theologian, interprets this dogma as an affirmation of the importance of the body in Christian thinking.[5]

The immaculate conception and the assumption of Mary attest to the significance of incarnation in the Christian tradition: the mother of God is not unaffected by the event of incarnation. Yet these doctrines also suggest an ambivalence about the relation of the body—and its companions, sexuality and death—with the divine. God may have become flesh, but this flesh is unique. In the Christian tradition, Jesus' "full humanity" is affirmed repeatedly, in the face of Gnostic denials and Docetism, but his flesh and the immaculate and virginal flesh from which he came are uniquely human: sinless and pure.

As I said at the start, the radical implications of incarnation are a Christian as well as a Jewish concern, a concern rooted in fears of idolatry. In Christian understandings of the immaculate conception and the assumption, of the resurrection and the ascension, and of the body of Christ, one can see that even the most intimate depictions of the incarnate God are cast against the background of utter transcendence.

In closing, it might be helpful to mention the Eastern Orthodox Christian practice of the veneration of icons, a practice that came to mind when I encountered Wolfson's emphasis on intentionality, prayer, and study. Icons—pictorial representations of God and of the saints—are not meant to be literal pictures of the divine. Rather, they are intended to be images that focus the mind and heart on what lies beyond; indeed they represent the whole community of the church together, living and dead. They are "windows" to the transcendent. Perhaps where Jews and Christians come together is in the recognition that God's presence to us is always mediated through history and experience. Incarnation provides a fruitful way for both traditions to engage in conversation—a conversation that needs to continue.

11

REDEMPTION

How Ought a Jew View
Christian Beliefs About Redemption?

MENACHEM KELLNER

In this essay I take as my text Paul's letter to the Romans. My point of departure is Paul's use of Habakkuk 2:4, "the righteous shall live by his faith," to express the view that redemption comes through faith.[1] I will then discuss what I take as two Jewish alternatives to this reading:

A. that of Rav Simlai, who, in the talmudic tractate Makkot, apparently sees the faith spoken of by Habakkuk in terms of loyalty to the commandments

B. that of Maimonides, who apparently sees the faith spoken of by Habakkuk in terms of correct intellectual apprehensions

Paul focuses on the individual (what a person must do in order to be saved from damnation), whereas Jewish thinkers have traditionally focused on what the Jewish people must do corporately to achieve redemption.

The prophet Habakkuk said, *tsadik be-emunato yihyeh* (literally: "The righteous [individual] lives [or, will live] through [i.e., by virtue

269

of] his faith"). Two of the Hebrew words need explanation, as does their relationship. What is a *tsadik* (righteous person)? Is she defined as righteous by her faith or by her actions or by some combination? Is the life referred to life in this world, or perhaps in the world to come? Is the verse telling us how a *tsadik* lives (a life characterized by *emunah*, faith) or is it telling us that *emunah* is a prerequisite for achieving life in the world to come? Finally, and crucially, what is the nature of that *emunah* that characterizes the righteous life or through which the righteous individual earns life?

R. Simlai on Faith and the Commandments

The verse from Habakkuk is cited only once in the Talmud. It appears at the end of a discussion that begins when R. Simlai tells us that the Torah contains precisely 613 commandments. R. Simlai then notes: "David came and reduced them [the six hundred thirteen commandments] to eleven." Here R. Simlai cites Psalm 15, in which he finds eleven characteristics of the person who seeks "to sojourn in the Lord's tabernacle and dwell in the holy mountain." R. Simlai then says that Isaiah reduced the 613 to six; Micah reduced them to three; and Isaiah, again, reduced them to two. The passage ends as follows:

> Amos came and reduced them to one, as it is said: "For thus saith the Lord unto the house of Israel, Seek ye Me and live." To this R. Nahman ben Isaac demurred, saying [Might it not be taken as meaning,] Seek Me by observing the whole Torah and live? But it is Habakkuk who came and based them all on one, as it is said, "But the righteous shall live by his faith."[2]

As I see it, the Talmud teaches here that the faith *(emunah)* through which one achieves righteousness and life is expressed through the fulfillment of the 613 commandments of Judaism. To the extent that talmudic Judaism has a settled doctrine about how redemption is to be achieved, the route is through fulfillment of the commandments.

How does the Apostle Paul read Habakkuk? In Romans 1:16–17 we read: "For I am not ashamed of the gospel: it is the power of God for salvation to everyone who has faith, to the Jew first and also to the Greek. For in it the righteousness of God is revealed through faith for faith; as it is written, 'The one who is righteous will live by faith'." The salvific context is explicit here. Paul never connects the faith that makes for righteousness and that leads to salvation to fulfillment of divine commandments. We are dealing here with two very different religious sensibilities that lead to two different understandings of redemption.

Paul is consistent on this point:

> But now, apart from the law, the righteousness of God has been disclosed, and is attested by the law and the prophets, the righteousness of God through faith in Jesus Christ for all who believe, for there is no distinction, since all have sinned and fall short of the glory of God; they are now justified by his grace as a gift. . . .
>
> For if Abraham was justified by works, he has something to boast about, but not before God. . . .
>
> For the promise that he would inherit the world did not come to Abraham or his descendants through the law but through the righteousness of faith. . . .
>
> So it depends not on human will or exertion, but on God who shows mercy. . . .
>
> 'The word is near you, on your lips and in your heart' (that is, the word of faith that we proclaim); because if you confess with your lips that Jesus is Lord and believe in your heart that God raised him from the dead, you will be saved. (3:21–23; 4:2; 4:13; 9:16; 10:8–9)

These verses teach the following doctrine: All humans are sinners and as such have no right to salvation nor any reason to expect to be saved. No matter how many righteous deeds are performed, one cannot earn salvation.

It seems fair to read the talmudic passage cited above from Makkot as teaching that a righteous person is defined as such by his or her faith and that through that faith the righteous person lives.[3] The faith that defines a righteous person as such, moreover, finds expression in the fulfillment of as many of the 613 commandments as one can fulfill. Paul understands Habakkuk to mean that faith alone makes one righteous and leads to salvation.

Maimonides on Faith and Philosophical Assent

Moses Maimonides (1138–1204) presents a highly influential doctrine of salvation (of the individual) and redemption (of Israel and, through Israel, of the world). Maimonides believes that righteous individuals are both defined by their faith and achieve life in the world to come through it. He understands faith to be the affirmation of true claims (as opposed to an understanding of faith as trust in God as expressed through behavior). Maimonides was thus led to ask: Which specific beliefs constitute the faith of the righteous Jew and grant that Jew access to the world to come? He phrased the answer to that question in his famous Thirteen Principles of faith.[4] Acceptance of these principles is the key to individual salvation. Rejecting any of the principles, or even doubting them, costs one his or her share in the world to come.

How can a Jewish thinker say this? Maimonides is locked into this claim because, following Habakkuk, he defines righteousness as faith, and he then defines faith as assent to a set of propositions. If one denies (or even doubts or questions) any one of these propositions, one's faith is deficient, and so is one's righteousness. Maimonides even demands assent to these propositions as a prerequisite for being a Jew in the fullest sense of the term, regardless of one's actions.

But this is not the whole story. Individual salvation for Maimonides is a matter of holding a particular set of doctrines in a particular fashion. In order to hold these doctrines properly, one must attain a high level of moral perfection. As he says, "The moral virtues are a preparation for the rational virtues, it being impossible to achieve true, rational acts—I mean perfect rationality—unless it be by a man thoroughly trained in his morals and endowed with the qualities of tranquillity and quiet."[5] One must be trained, then, to be faithful. And moral training comes through the performance of the commandments.

But what about the redemption of the Jewish people and of the world? The situation is similar. Maimonides predicates the coming of the Messiah upon the worldwide acceptance of at least the philosophical underpinning of his Thirteen Principles and furthermore makes the necessary understanding of these principles dependent in most cases upon fulfilling the commandments of the Torah.[6]

For Maimonides salvation of the individual and redemption of the world both depend upon a complicated interaction between fulfillment of the commandments and true philosophical understanding.

Maimonides on the Messiah

Maimonides makes a remarkable claim in his description of the conditions necessary for the coming of the Messiah. In a passage censored from all premodern editions of the *Mishneh Torah*, his great law code, Maimonides writes:

> But if he does not meet with full success, or is slain, it is obvious that he is not the Messiah promised in the Torah. He is to be regarded like all the other wholehearted and worthy kings of the House of David who died and whom the Holy One, blessed be He, raised up to test the multitude, as it is written, "And some of them that are wise shall stumble, to refine among them, and to purify, and to make white, even to the time of the end; for it is yet for the time appointed" (Dan. 11:35). Even of Jesus of Nazareth, who imagined that he was the Messiah, and was put to death by the court, Daniel had prophesied, as it is written, "And the children of the violent among thy people shall lift themselves up to establish the vision; but they shall stumble" (Dan. 11:14). For has there ever been a greater stumbling than this? All the prophets affirmed that the Messiah would redeem Israel, save them, gather their dispersed, and confirm the commandments. But he [Jesus] caused Israel to be destroyed by the sword, their remnant to be dispersed and humiliated. He was instrumental in changing the Torah and causing the world to err and serve another beside God. But it is beyond the human mind to fathom the designs of the Creator; for our ways are not His ways, neither are our thoughts His thoughts. All these matters relating to Jesus of Nazareth and the Ishmaelite [Mohammed] who came after him, only served to clear the way for King Messiah, to prepare the whole world to worship God with one accord, as it is written, "For then will I turn to the peoples a pure language, that they all call upon the name of the Lord to serve Him with one consent" (Zeph. 3:9). Thus the messianic hope, the Torah, and the commandments have become familiar topics—topics of conversation (among the inhabitants) of the far isles and many people, uncircumcised of heart and flesh. They are discussing these matters and the commandments of the Torah. Some say, "Those commandments were true, but have lost their validity and are no longer binding"; others declare that they had an esoteric meaning and were not to be taken literally; that the Messiah has already come and revealed their occult significance. But when the true King Messiah will appear and succeed, be exalted and lifted up, they will forthwith recant and realize that they have inherited nothing but lies from their fathers, that their prophets and forbears led them astray.[7]

Here Maimonides explains that Christianity and Islam have a messianic role. By preparing the world to accept ideas concerning messianism, Torah, and commandments, they help pave the road on which the Messiah must travel. How so? Among the tasks of the Messiah will be "to prepare the world to worship God with one accord." This will be accomplished through natural means: "Let no one think that in the days of the Messiah any of the laws of nature will be set aside, or any innovation be introduced into creation. The world will follow its normal course."[8] But to convert the world to pure monotheism overnight (to say nothing of acceptance of the Torah and its commandments) would be an "innovation into creation," a miracle of unprecedented proportions, extending over the face of the entire world and persisting forever. Maimonides believes that the role of Christianity and Islam is to wean idolaters away from idolatry. It is their job to prepare the larger world to accept faith in God and in his Torah in order "to call upon the name of the Lord to serve Him with one consent" (Zeph. 3:9) when the true Messiah comes.

Conclusion

R. Simlai and Maimonides, for all their differences, illustrate that a Jewish view of redemption must emphasize a number of issues: this-worldliness, good works, and truth. Paul's view of redemption as expressed in Romans seems to be wholly other-worldly, divorced from good works, and focused entirely on truth. Paul seems to be answering the following question: What doctrine must a person accept as true in order to be saved? Maimonides is the first Jew to ask even a similar question (but for Aristotelian, not Pauline, reasons); still, he is drawn by the Jewish tradition to focus on good works in this world as well.

How are we to understand Paul's position, which seems so divergent from the faith of his fathers and mothers? The answer relates to the question of original sin. Since for Paul "all have sinned and fall short of the glory of God," they can now only be "justified by his grace as a gift" (3:21–23). Grace cannot be earned; it can only be bestowed by God as a gift and accepted as such by those who are happy enough to recognize it and receive it. On this question the Jewish view seems well expressed by the Mishnah (Sanh. 10:1): "All Israelites have a share in the world to come"—since humans by their nature do not fall short of the glory of God, they are by nature worthy of a share in the world to come.[9] Thus, by nature, humans are redeemed. The Jew's problem is not his or her individual salvation, but how to bring redemption to the world.

How, then, ought I as a Jew, and as an heir to the Jewish tradition, view Christian beliefs about redemption as expressed in Paul's letter to the Romans? The answer, I submit, is as follows: Because of his revolutionary, un-Jewish view of human nature as necessarily falling short of the glory of God, Paul was led to ask the wrong question. The question that Jews must ask is: What must we do in order to make the world messiah-worthy?

Redemption:
What I Have Learned from Christians

NANCY FUCHS-KREIMER

The Messiah finally arrives. Jews and Christians, after waiting for so many centuries, rush to meet him. The Jews cry out, "This is the first time You have come, is it not?" The Christians, raising their voices above the Jews, insist, "This must be Your second coming that we have been waiting for!" The Messiah smiles wearily and waits for the noise to subside. Then, in a quiet and gentle voice, long suffering, He says, "My dear, foolish children. I have come not once, nor twice. I have been here hundreds of times. But you have all been so busy fighting with one another you have never even noticed."

I first heard that story from Zalman Schachter-Shalomi almost twenty years ago at a gathering of Jews and Christians in Germany. He told it in the waning light of the departing Sabbath, and in that setting it had the feel of truth. One could almost dare to imagine that even if it did not really happen, at least the story was an authentic folk tale with some pedigree within Judaism. In the cold light of day, I suspect Reb Zalman may have created the story out of whole cloth, but at this point it no longer matters. I have told and retold it many times and, by now, I half believe it.

In fact, this story oversimplifies what are really much more interesting differences between Judaism and Christianity. It is deceptive to imply, as the story does, that what divides Jews and Christians on redemption comes down to the simple question of the Messiah coming for the first or the second time. On the other hand, the story reflects a significant truth. We Jews and Christians *have* made a lot of noise over the centuries, drawing boundaries in the wrong places and reducing subtle dialectics that exist in both faiths to dichotomies that allegedly divide one from the other. When our traditions have tried to paint pictures of the other, they have hardly been at their best. We have spent considerable energies in the effort to defend or to define ourselves. In this essay, I, as a Jew, will look at Christian views of redemption with a different goal: to understand, and, perhaps, to learn.

Mordecai Kaplan (1881–1983) used to say that it is hell to live without hope. He would then add that it is the purpose of religion to save men and women from hell. That, it seems, is the core meaning of redemption in both the Jewish and Christian traditions. We are instructed to live our lives informed by a master story that speaks of redemption in the past (the exodus from Egypt, the resurrection of Jesus), of glimpses of redemption in the present moment, and, finally, of the hope that the future will bring the long awaited consummation of history. Redemption, in both our faiths, is past, present, and, most of all, future.

For both Jews and Christians, it is our task to figure out how to relate ourselves appropriately to the current, flawed, reality while waiting for that final redemption. In other words, we need to live with integrity "between the times." In both Judaism and Christianity, a variety of models toward that end have been proposed and lived out over the centuries.

Christian Views of Redemption

The Christian tradition contains many views on how to live in a world whose redemption is not yet complete, on what to do—in the words of the title of a book on Jewish socialism—while Messiah tarries. In *Christ and Culture*, a classic work of modern Christian theology, H. Richard Niebuhr, a twentieth-century Protestant theologian, argues that there are five characteristic Christian responses to the problem of living in the world as we find it: Christ against Culture, Christ of Culture, Christ above Culture, Christ and Culture in Paradox, and Christ the Transformer of Culture.

Christian Dualism

The motif represented most typically by the Apostle Paul and Martin Luther, "Christ and Culture in Paradox," is the version of Christian faith that most Jews have in mind when they speak about the differences between Judaism and Christianity, which is not surprising since Jewish thinkers, coming to Christianity in the modern period, read Paul through the eyes of Luther and both through the eyes of latter-day German scholars. In Niebuhr's description of Paul and Luther one hears the very motifs toward which Jews have been so reactive, particularly the strong sense of sin.

Unfortunately, in many Jewish readings, one gets the impression that what Niebuhr describes as "Christ and Culture in Paradox" is *the* Christian view of redemption. But we should recall that this is only one of the five models Niebuhr presents, one with which Niebuhr, along with many other Christians, past and present, would take strong issue.

For Christians who fit this model, and only for such Christians, the very heart of the matter lies in the sinfulness of human beings and the grace of God, which is not, as in some other readings of Christianity, mediated through human acts. Grace is entirely God's; human beings are, without God, entirely lost. Here both the extent and thoroughness of human sin are stressed as nowhere else in Christianity, and this stress has important consequences for understanding redemption. Amid such sin, human reason is not of much help. Paul and Luther in their own lives discovered that obeying the law was not a redemptive path—not for Jews, not for themselves, not for anyone. This revelation is not gloomy, however, because it comes hand in hand with the news that in Christ there is total forgiveness and grace. As Karl Barth explains it, upon awakening in the hospital, clearly on the mend, we realize we have been in a terrible accident; so it is that the Christian learns simultaneously of the bad news of sin and the good news of grace.

In this view, redemption is very much a matter of God's unilateral action rather than some kind of partnership. Because all goodness resides in God, the goodness of redemption will come from one direction. Human culture and society are irreparably flawed, irredeemable except by God. How are we to live in the corrupted world of human sinfulness in the interim? Paul is probably not a very good place to look for answers to that question since he believed that the interim would be quite short. On the other hand, Martin Luther created in his thought a delicate balance of joy and terror, of personal ethics and political concern, which—unfortunately—in some of the less attractive versions his followers turned into the ethical quietism that some Jews associate with the "Christian" view of redemption. As Niebuhr suggests, when the temporal world is seen as sinful and dying, there is an enormous risk that one will take an extremely conservative view of societal institutions as bulwarks against chaos or—even more likely— lose interest in the political arena entirely.

Søren Kierkegaard represents an extreme example of the dualistic tendency within Christianity to divide the eternal good grace of God from the sinful temporal world. In his famous essay on the sacrifice of Isaac, he suggests that radical faith and rational ethics can be at odds with one another and that, in this story, Abraham rightly chooses the former over the latter. This reading of Genesis is roundly condemned by a host of Jewish writers who are eager to explain that in the Jewish view there can be no such severing between God's redemptive plan and our understanding of what ethics requires. But Jews should understand that Kierkegaard represents only one particular strain of Christianity, and a rather exaggerated version at that. Mainstream Christianity rejected the Gnostic idea that the created world is inherently evil and declared it a heresy.

Despite Jewish polemical stereotyping of Christianity as world denying, Christianity has definitively rejected this idea. Christianity insists that the same God who created the world will redeem it through Christ. It thus commits itself to the notion that the created order is good, even though it has become corrupted. Thus the most extreme forms of dualism are simply not good Christian theology. It will not be surprising, then, to learn that in Niebuhr's view there are other ways to look at this issue. It is worth exploring two of the additional paths that Niebuhr describes.

Christian Counterculturalism

One additional path Niebuhr explores, he calls "Christ against Culture." At least some of the early Christians took the position that, given what they now knew because of Jesus, the only way to live in this flawed world was not to live in it at all. Loyalty to the vision of the future redemption required absenting oneself as much as possible from the present corrupt reality and creating, on the fringes of society, a new order here on earth. In our time, the Mennonites and Amish exemplify this position; in the history of Christianity the most obvious representative is the monastic movement.

Benedict of Nursia, a sixth-century Italian Christian, wrote the famous "Rule for Monks" ("The Rule of St. Benedict"), which is still used throughout the world to guide the day-to-day life of the thousands of cloistered men and women who live by its rule. Countless others are inspired by it. Although Jews typically picture Christian theologians as obsessed with details of creed—and indeed, many of them are fairly thorough on those points—Benedict sounds more like a rabbi in his fascination with making everyday life into a holy enterprise. What interests Benedict is community, how people can live together in a spiritual way. He knows it is not easy for human beings to get along with one another; still, he offers complete rules on how to work with our human nature to the best advantage.

What do these rules have to do with redemption? At the current time, the redeemed world and the one we live in are utterly unlike each other. But by building monasteries, Benedict hoped to create outposts of the kingdom of God on earth. Furthermore, those who participate in these communities have a chance at a "foretaste" of redemption. Clearly, retreat from society is a decidedly minor theme in Jewish history, yet in some ways the entire enterprise of Jewish communal life, particularly when it was carried on apart from the general culture, is not unlike Benedict's strategy. If we can not transform all of society into a new heaven and a new earth, at the very least we can provide the heavenly city with a foothold.

In Benedict, as in Judaism, the heavenly city depends upon people obeying the command of law, treating each other in ways that are dictated to maximize the community's effectiveness. In both cases, the essence of the community is prayer and scripture study. For Benedict, unlike the popular Jewish misconception of Christianity, redemption is not "pie in the sky when you die." Benedict writes that one should "seek the kingdom of God, so that you may deserve to see him." Amazingly, it is the life lived in humility, obedience, and love that turns out to be the very path to God. Just as Jewish liturgy praises God for giving us the law, so Benedict writes, "What can be sweeter to us, dear brethren, than this voice of the Lord inviting us? Behold, in his loving kindness, the Lord shows us the way of life." It is in response to God's love and God's promise that the monk joyfully takes on the duties and constrictions of monastic life.

Meeting God Halfway

Creating a mini-messianic world in which to retreat was only one possible path within historic Christianity. Another strategy is the one
Niebuhr calls "Christ the Transformer of Culture." This is the last of
the five of Niebuhr's motifs and clearly the one he favors. In this version of Christianity, according to Niebuhr, there is a good balance between the recognition of the sinfulness of humanity and human culture and a commitment to try to change it. Not willing either to
abandon culture or—as in other versions—deify it, the transformer-
of-culture Christians never forget that God who created the world is
also the one who will ultimately redeem it.

An example of this view is the thinking of John Calvin (1509–1564),
followed by that of John Wesley (1703–1791) and a host of
other Christian thinkers, including Jonathan Edwards (1703–1758),
colonial America's greatest theologian. As Niebuhr explains it, the
"transformer-of-culture" model, while acknowledging the fall, never
denies the glory of creation and human nature that is still evident. It
holds that human beings are called to do their part, through human
efforts and activity in history, to bring about God's sovereign reign. In
other words, the world as we know it can and will be transformed. In
this vision, the redemption that is anticipated is more than just the
saving of individual souls in some private mystical encounter or
through the afterlife. The full realization of the kingdom of God will
be universal, social, and political.

In the 1960s, a young German Protestant theologian, Jürgen Moltmann, published a book entitled *Theology of Hope*. Closely linked with
Moltmann's thought was the emergence of "political theology,"
which, like liberation theology in its various forms (Latin American,
feminist, Black), has emphasized the political dimension of redemption. Moltmann sees the meaning of the cross and resurrection of Jesus as the guarantor of hope. Moltmann's theology pays serious attention to eschatology, which many New Testament scholars think was a
major theme of Jesus' ministry and of the early church. For Moltmann, the church is defined as "the world open to the future," and the
Christian is a "worker helping to build the kingdom."

Moltmann's "messianic theology" is designed to have direct relevance not merely to social service but to social action. He is heavily
influenced by Marxist utopianism and believes in the future redemption, but he asserts that it is an illusion to think we can achieve these

dreams without God; he speaks of the impossibility of "transcending without transcendence." Moltmann writes that theology should be "biblically founded, eschatologically oriented, and politically responsible." For Moltmann, the present world is clearly out of joint, but the church should not abandon "the strength of its faith in creation."

Central to Moltmann's theology is the scriptural theme of promise. The primary way we know God is not through a present epiphany of the eternal that exists in some heavenly realm. Rather, God's presence is in the form of God's promise concerning the future, a promise that presumes that history is linear, that it is moving forward, and that we are called to move and act within it. Christian faith is a form of hopefulness. God is neither within us (immanent) nor above us (transcendent) but rather "in front of us." The Christian faith is an initiative toward the transformation of the world. We must set out to meet God's future, and it will "meet us halfway."

Moltmann's understanding that God's kingdom of glory, the final consummation of human history, will come with human and divine effort is a notion that Jews can easily recognize. In Moltmann, Jews also find themes that are less familiar. Moltmann strongly stresses the suffering of God. According to Moltmann, in the life and death of Jesus, God chose to enter history and to suffer its vulnerability and defeats. But even this idea resonates powerfully with the Jewish teaching that we can know God, even the God who promises redemption, not only in times of wonder and glory, but also in times of pain and despair. The comfort of such a notion—"If I make my bed in Sheol, You are there" (Ps.138:9)—is palpable.

What I Have Learned from Christians

As a Jew, what do I learn from encounters with these various Christian views of redemption? First, I recall how varied and complex a tradition Christianity is and how difficult it is to make generalizations. Each type of Christianity holds teachings and challenges.

By Paul, I am reminded to maintain a healthy skepticism about all human projects. As I understand it, Paul's criticism of the law was neither a critique specifically of Judaism—as it has been traditionally misunderstood by both Jews and Christians—nor only a meditation on the role of the Gentiles—as the new paradigm thinkers such as Krister Stendahl, E. P. Sanders, and Clark Williamson have suggested. Rather, it was most likely a critique of all human projects and presumptions, the law being the one with which Paul was most familiar. For this reason, the greatest of Christian thinkers through the centuries have used Paul to launch scathing criticisms of the Christianity of their own day; they know that men and women are, indeed, foolish and that the systems they create, be they Jewish law or church law, especially when they are taken as ultimate, are likely to be deeply flawed.

Similarly, our human plans for redemption, although surely to be pursued with all our vigor, are frail attempts at perfecting the world. Paul's warning concerning human foolishness is especially apt when it comes to secular messianisms of all kinds. The fall of the Soviet Union and the disenchantment with communism throughout the world should be strong reminders of this same lesson. "We have this treasure in earthen vessels, to show us that the transcendent power belongs to God and not to us" (2 Cor. 4:7). Our plans for redeeming the world are earthen vessels. The claim that the Messiah will be a supernatural being is a claim precisely that we should be wary of human plans and projects of all sorts. What I especially love about Paul is that he noticed that religion (in his case it was Jewish religion, for that was the one he knew) was also an earthen vessel. That sounds right to me.

At the same time, from Benedict, the Mennonites, and other Christian critics of culture, I am reminded of how we sometimes need to step back from the culture in which we live and not identify ourselves too fully with it. As a liberal Jew, living in two civilizations, often very comfortably, I have to be mindful not simply to identify the best of my Jewish tradition with the best of my American culture and assume a too easy and comfortable alliance between them. The Christians who simply set up alternative worlds remind me that I may need to be more conscious of the way I live and of the boundaries I build with the world.

Moltmann and many political and liberation theologians remind me of the necessity to link theology to "helping bring the Messiah," a theme that is underemphasized in many Jewish writings, despite the claim that we are an activist religion. In modern Jewish history, alas, there has been a split in which secular and political versions of Judaism, such as socialism at the turn of the century, have largely taken up the messianic/eschatological energies of the tradition, whereas the religious movements, even while giving lip service to Judaism as a religion of action, have busied themselves primarily with tradition, ritual, community building—everything but a serious look at how we can "meet the Messiah half way."

Encountering Christian views of redemption, I am struck by how reassuring and encouraging it must be to have the personal foretaste of redemption available for the individual of faith. For Christians, although redemption is yet to come, there is one sense in which redemption is already here. All Christians who experience grace already experience redemption in a way, on an individual existential level, even while still looking forward to the more universal, historical redemption to come. In Judaism, we have stressed the communal nature of redemption and the "not yet" quality of its futurity. In my judgment, many Jews have underemphasized the idea that at least a taste of redemption is already here. The idea surfaces in the notion that the Sabbath is the foretaste of the Messianic Time, but many Jews do not put sufficient weight on this concept and spend more time speaking of past and future than of the present.

I also learn from Christianity an appreciation for the imagery of Messiah as a person. Growing up as a liberal Jew in mid-twentieth-century America, I heard a great deal more about redemption, a world full of peace and justice that was coming soon, than I heard about the Messiah, an individual who would be connected with that final consummation of history. This stress on redemption and not on the Messiah was not surprising—and not only because the Reform and Reconstructionist prayer books had substituted the word *geulah* (redemption) for the word *goel* (redeemer). Long before these modern liturgical changes, Jews had become wary of putting too much faith in one individual and had opted, except at junctures in history such as the disastrous Shabbatai Zvi episode, for a more wary approach. I remember learning in Sunday School the talmudic dictum that if you are going to plant a tree and someone says that the Messiah has arrived, you should first plant the tree and then check out the reports. That statement always struck me as indicative of the salty and sane view of the world I admired in Jewish tradition. Yet there were glimpses in Jewish tradition of more.

At the great feast celebrating redemption past, present, and future, the Passover seder, we did not dare be so bold as to talk specifically about the Messiah. Rather, one step removed, we peeked out the door into the dark night looking for the one who would announce the Messiah, listening for Elijah. That bit of distancing allowed us to play more freely with an image that captures the heart: a human being who is somehow tied to our redemption. Like many Jewish children, I adored the Elijah moment at the seder and waited all year to feel the shock of cool air as I opened the door, sure that Elijah's white cloak brushed my dress—ever so barely—as he whisked past, headed for the table to take his sip of wine.

The rest of the year, however, it was visions of peace and justice, not of a Messiah who was a human being in a human body. When I first studied Christianity, and especially Paul, Jesus as Messiah was the part of the tradition that seemed compelling. I realize that the idea is Jewish in its origins. I realize, as well, the many pitfalls of such a concept, not the least of which is that a Messiah with a human body needs to be either a man or a woman, and, our traditions being what they have been, the Messiah has turned out to be male. Accepting the problematics, I still find myself drawn to the idea that redemption will be tied up with the coming of a human being who is more than a human being.

In an essay published in 1956, Steven Schwartzchild speculates about why contemporary Jews have turned their backs on the concept of a personal Messiah and thus reconceived redemption as an abstract matter. He points out that during the Christian Middle Ages, Joseph Albo recommended against belief in a personal Messiah, specifically because the "others make out of it a basic principle with which to refute the Torah of Moses." In other words, if we were to grant that there could be a person who was the Messiah, we would have a harder time refuting Christian claims that this person had indeed come in the form of Jesus of Nazareth.

If, as it appears, a reaction to Christian claims has caused Jews to back away from the notion of a redeemer who comes in human form, then we are in a position to revisit that issue today, when relations between the two faiths, at least in certain circles, have moved beyond the realm of polemics and disputation. When I encounter the idea of the Messiah as person as it is held by the Christians I know, what I find is an authentic Jewish idea that has great power to move me. I do not share the view that the Redeemer has come, but I am intrigued with the power of the idea that the Redeemer will come as a person and that redemption is thus not merely a time.

I close with the question: What *will* redemption finally be like? In the world of Jewish–Christian dialogue, heated debates often center upon the ending of Romans 11, where Paul discusses that very question. When I read that passage, I cannot help but hear it the way it was first interpreted for me by my teacher Father Gerard Sloyan. Paul's working assumption is that redemption will be wonderful, beyond our imagining. Would Jews have to convert to faith in Jesus before they could be saved? Paul never says. This is frustrating to the scholars. Why could not Paul have made himself clearer? The answer, Sloyan taught me many years ago, was that Paul did not know. He believed in God's mercy, and he trusted God to figure it out. That is why he quoted Isaiah, "For who has known the mind of the Lord or who has been his counselor?" Paul concludes this part of his letter by saying, "from God and through God and to God are all things" (Rom. 12:36).

A Christian View of Redemption

CLARK WILLIAMSON

In his essay on Paul's understanding of redemption, Menachem Kellner argues that because Paul asked the wrong question—"What must I believe in order to be gifted with grace?"—he got the wrong answer. Not only is this individualistic question at a far remove from what the Jewish people must do, but its wrong answer views redemption as "wholly other-worldly, divorced from good works, and focused entirely on truth." Further, because of his doctrine of original sin, Paul's understanding of redemption requires that grace be available only to those "happy enough to recognize it and receive it." Unlike the Mishnah, Paul cannot say, "All Israelites have a share in the world to come."

From my point of view, as a Christian theologian committed to rethinking Christianity after the Shoah and to changing Christian attitudes and practices toward Jews and Judaism, Kellner's views reflect the results of a tragic history of conflict, separation, and lack of conversation between Jews and Christians, a history for which the church bears by far the greater burden of accountability. Seldom have either Jews or Christians been able to understand each other except as exam-

ples of bad religion. The Christian stereotype of Judaism as arid, legalistic, grace-less, and devoid of faith is familiar. Kellner's views are
the other side of the stereotype: Christianity is individualistic, other-
worldly, unconcerned with doing good works, focused entirely on
truth, and exclusivist with regard to salvation. One can find Christians
who live the stereotype. But there is no basis for it in Paul, and Christian theology rejects it as inauthentic.

Consider that Paul asserts exactly what Kellner concludes he cannot:
"And so all Israel will be saved" (Rom. 11:26). Several things about this
statement are worth noting. First, it is closely parallel to the later mish-
naic version of the same claim.[1] Second, Paul says this because, not in
spite of, his firm belief in God's constancy, *chesed*, what Christians understand by "grace" when Christians speak properly: "the gifts and the
calling of God are irrevocable" (Rom. 11:29). These gifts include
God's free election of the people Israel and the Torah (Rom. 9:4–5).
Third, Paul's whole argument is intended to counter the rise of early
displacement theology among his Gentile followers in Rome (that Romans was addressed predominantly to Gentile followers of Jesus is
made clear in chapter one, vv. 6 and 13). Just as in his earlier letters,
Paul was concerned with relations between Jews and Gentiles within
one congregation of Jesus-followers, so in Romans he is primarily concerned with a new issue: the relations between those, primarily Gentiles, who are Jesus-followers and Jews who are not. In both cases, his
understanding of redemption is both social and this-worldly, which is
not to deny that he also understands redemption in ultimate terms.

Faith as Trust and Freedom

How, then, do Christians understand redemption when they express
themselves appropriately? First, for Christians faith is neither primarily nor only a matter of believing certain things about God. Faith as
fundamentally or merely belief about God is an idea that finds no justification in the scriptures. There is a distinction, but not a separation,
to be made between "believing in" a person and believing certain
things "about" a person. Faith in God is a matter of radical trust in
God's *chesed*, God's trustworthiness. To rely utterly on God's steadfast
love as disclosed in the Torah and the prophets and in Jesus Christ is
to believe "in" God. Analogously, to rely on, to trust, one's spouse is to
believe in that person. Yet such radical trust unmistakably assumes
that God is indeed the God who, without any regard for our faithful-

ness, loves each and all of God's creatures and therefore us as well. If we do not believe that God is ultimately trustworthy, does it make sense to place our ultimate trust in God's love? Faith, hence, is primarily radical trust, a matter of believing in God, not of believing something about God. It is distinguishable but inseparable from its entailed assumption that God is indeed a God of *chesed*. As Paul puts it: "But God proves his love for us in that while we still were sinners, Christ died for us" (Rom. 5:8). God's gracious gift precedes and evokes the response of faith; it does not depend on our prior trust or belief, any more than God's redemption of Israel from slavery in Egypt depended on Israel's prior faith in God.

Second, for Christians redemption has several meanings. In one meaning it points to *a past event or events* where redemption has already occurred. In another sense, it is a present event, insofar as people appropriate and are transformed by the meaning of the past event(s) of redemption. In a third sense, redemption lies in the future; it refers to the liberation of the entire created order from its "bondage to decay" (Rom. 8:18–25).

Third, redemption has two dimensions. In each of its meanings, redemption always refers to the two sides of freedom—freedom from and freedom for. As we have been graciously *freed from* bondage to every earthly pharaoh, so we have become *free for* the task of setting others free from the bondages that enslave them. Faith is existence in this dual freedom.

Because faith is trust in God as the one ultimate source of the meaning and value of our lives, faith is freedom from anything or anyone other than God deciding the ultimate meaning of our lives. According ultimate importance to anything less than the One who is ultimate is idolatry. God's boundless love embraces all our lives and makes us safe in spite of and in the face of the undeniable reality of our own death and the perishing of everything finite. We are freed, even, from the "fear of death." For precisely the same reason, faith is existence in freedom in the positive sense of *freedom for*—freedom for the neighbor and for the stranger, freedom for all of those whom God loves. We who are friends of the One who is Friend of all are, thereby, also friends of all our neighbors on the planet. Freedom in this second sense is not only trust in God's love but also loyalty to God and therefore to all those to whom God is loyal.

One might express this two-dimensional Christian understanding of redemption this way: God loves us into freedom and frees us into loving our neighbors. To live in faith *is* to do the works of love. To Gentiles wishing to undergo circumcision, Paul said: "In Christ Jesus neither circumcision nor uncircumcision counts for anything; the only thing that counts is faith working through love" (Gal. 5:6). The life of faith is both a liberated and a liberating life, both grace and ethics. Grace is the melody, ethics the lyrics, of Christian life.

Redemption and Reconciliation

The root meaning of the concept of redemption is *buying back*. It entails a situation in which a group or a person is in some kind of captivity, as were the Israelites in Egypt. Redemption does not make important sense apart from the myriad ways in which human beings manage to enslave, oppress, threaten, confine, and bring calamity and ruin upon one another. It is precisely this meaning that plays the greatest role in the scriptures that the church and the people Israel share. Primarily, the writers of the Torah use the term "redemption" as the appropriate word to describe the great liberation of the Israelite people from the bondage of their Egyptian oppressors: "It was because the LORD loved you and kept the oath that he swore to your ancestors, that the LORD has brought you out with a mighty hand, and redeemed you from the house of slavery, from the hand of Pharaoh king of Egypt" (Deut. 7:8).

The next great crisis in the history of biblical Israel after the enslavement in Egypt was exile in Babylon. The message was proclaimed that the God who liberated Israel from Egypt would act again. "In overflowing wrath for a moment I hid my face from you, but with everlasting love I will have compassion on you, says the LORD, your Redeemer" (Is. 54:8). The writers of the New Testament confidently assume and claim that the same God—the God of Israel—still works in, through, and by means of Jesus Christ to liberate human beings from any and all kinds of enslavements. Matthew's Gospel quotes Hosea's comment about Israel and applies it to the infant Jesus and his family's return from Egypt whence they had fled in fear of a murderous king (Matthew 2, the story of Jesus' infancy, retells Exodus 2, the story of Moses' infancy): "Out of Egypt I have called my son" (Mt. 2:15/Hos. 11:1). The God who redeems Israel is again at work through Jesus.

So, redemption is, in one sense, in the past. God (YHVH) redeemed Israel from slavery in Egypt and from exile in Babylon. But clearly, however real redemption is, it is far from complete. Slavery is not eradicated from the face of the earth, and therefore it is the mission of Israel and the church to witness and work on behalf of God's liberating intent for all human beings.

For Christians, God working through Christ "reconciled us to himself . . . and has given us the ministry of reconciliation" (2 Cor. 5:18). Here we see redemption as reconciliation, the overcoming of estrangement, both as something having been accomplished ("God reconciled us to himself") and as something that remains a task: both as a ministry to others and as an ongoing relationship with God: "We entreat you on behalf of Christ, be reconciled to God" (2 Cor. 5:20). Reconciliation is both a gracious gift—something that has already happened—and a command, something that we must do. This character of redemption/salvation is reflected in the literary structure of Paul's letters. Each letter opens with a long section in the indicative mood, proclaiming that here is what God has done for you. This section is followed by another in the imperative mood, announcing, again, what we have been given and then telling us what to do with the gift. The pattern should be familiar to Jewish readers. It is the pattern of the Torah, which opens with a long story about all that God has done for Israel, which includes the creation of a world in which Israel might live, before God gets around to giving commandments. And even then, God begins with a recitation of God's gracious, redemptive activity on Israel's behalf: "I am the LORD your God, who brought you out of the land of Egypt, out of the house of slavery; you shall have no other gods before me" (Ex. 20:2–3). The grace/command, indicative/imperative structure of Paul's thought is precisely that of the scriptures of Israel and also, according to Christian scholars who have taken the trouble to look, that of the early rabbis.[2]

Jewish readers may wonder why these matters are so complex for Paul. Why worry about being reconciled with God? After all, one has only to turn or, better, turn again (*shuv*) to God, and God will forgive and accept the sinner. But Paul was writing to Gentiles who had yet to turn to God in the first place. Paul predominantly identifies his readers as Gentiles. Consider his audience in the letter to the Galatians: "Formerly, when you did not know God, you were enslaved to beings that by nature are not gods" (Gal. 4:8). He is not addressing Jews; thus it is that he called himself the "Apostle to the Gentiles."

Reconciliation Between Jews and Gentiles

What this matter of Jews and Gentiles in Paul's communities has to do with his understanding of redemption/justification/reconciliation is terribly important. He always brings up the topic of justification in the context of a discussion of a social conflict in one of his congregations. Paul is concerned to "set right" these relationships. "Justification" is a gerund, a verbal noun. It means "right-setting." God is a "right-setting" God, a God who wants to set right our relationships with each other and with God. Two aspects of the "law" and how they affect the Gentile members of his congregation consistently concern Paul: circumcision and the dietary laws. Paul wants Gentile members of the congregation to participate on an equal basis without taking upon themselves these ritual "boundary markers." Paul's negative statements about "the law," please note, always have to do with membership requirements. His affirmative statements about "the law" all occur when questions of moral behavior are under discussion.[3] His discussions of justification are always attempts to effect reconciliation between members of the community and/or between different communities. Redemption always has a social aspect for Paul; we are all "members one of another" (Rom. 12:5).[4] In Galatians, immediately after he discusses the problems generated within the community by an insistence on circumcision and the dietary laws, he proclaims that justification is through faith in Christ and not "by the works of the law" (2:15). His concern is with one of the deepest themes of biblical faith—namely, that ritual insistence not obstruct the blessing of Abraham from getting to Gentiles, in this case, through the church's witness to Jesus Christ (Gal. 3:14).

Abraham is primarily important to Paul because of God's promise to Abraham that "in you all the families of the earth shall be blessed" (Gen. 12:3); "all the nations of the earth shall be blessed in him" (Gen. 18:18). God's blessing of well-being in all its aspects (peace, justice, long life, freedom from want and hunger, freedom from and for one another in love, etc.) was not to be showered upon Israel alone. Blessing/well-being is a gift from God to God's creatures, and as a gift it is to be shared. Paul is tapping into the bedrock of biblical faith with his insistence that the blessings of God were promised to both Abraham and the Gentiles, not to either one at the expense of the other.

Hence, part of the meaning of redemption for Paul and his school was that the "hostility" between Jews and Gentiles be overcome. Paul's student, in the letter to the Ephesians, reminds his Gentile readers that before they were confronted with the gospel of Christ they were "strangers" to Israel, to the covenants, and "without God in the world" (2:13). The writer of Ephesians proclaims that in Christ the divisions have been overcome, peace and reconciliation have been effected, and Gentiles are now "also members [not the only members] of the household of God" (2:19). Yet, he has to remind the Ephesians that this lack of division is part of redemption. Reconciliation remains the largest unaccomplished task in the Christian vision of redemption.

Redemption has taken place in the past, is a present task, and remains a future hope for which we are called both to pray and to work. Paul claimed that "the sufferings of this present time are not worth comparing with the glory about to be revealed to us" (Rom. 8:18). He may have thought that the complete redemption of the world would happen soon. We know a time, a post-Auschwitz, post-Hiroshima time, a genocidal dark ages, that gives new meaning to Paul's expression "the sufferings of this present time." Christians and Jews have a mutual obligation to work and witness against all forms of injustice and oppression that hold our fellow human beings in bondage. We need also to pray that God will bring *shalom* to Jerusalem and all Israel and all humanity, speedily and soon. And we need to learn how to talk with one another.

12

SIN AND

REPENTANCE

"Turn Us to You and We Shall Return": Original Sin, Atonement, and Redemption in Jewish Terms

STEVEN KEPNES

Therefore just as sin came into the world through one man, and death came through sin, and so death came to all because all have sinned . . . Yet death exercised dominion from Adam to Moses, even over those whose sins were not like the transgression of Adam. But the free gift is not like the trespass. For if the many died through the one man's trespass, much more surely have the grace of God and the free gift in the grace of the one man, Jesus Christ, abounded for the many. (Rom. 5:12–15)

This quote from Paul is a pivotal text in the development of the Christian doctrines of "original sin" and "atonement." Adam's sin of disobedience in the garden brought death and the "condemnation" (Rom. 5:16) of all humans, which placed them in a condition or state of sin. This condition prohibited them from "doing the good" (Rom. 7:19) and required Jesus' crucifixion as a free gift to bring "atonement" (Rom. 3:25) and "eternal life" (Rom. 5:21). Sin for Christianity always seems to be more than a single immoral act of an individual. The sinner, as we see Jesus facing him in the Gospels, is often plagued by sickness, by "evil" or "unclean spirits," even by the devil (Mt. 6–7). Sinners are blinded; they are unable to see their sinfulness and the opportunity of the kingdom of heaven that is being offered them. The antidote for sin requires being healed or saved; it is not merely a matter of giving restitution for wrong and doing good deeds. Redemption requires the grace of divine intervention, and even, as Paul suggests, the monumental event of divine self-sacrifice in Jesus' crucifixion.

Jews usually think that Judaism lacks parallels to these Christian notions of sin as an evil condition and of atonement and redemption as divine gifts. Humans are not mired in a "state" of sin; they naturally can choose to do the good (Deut. 30:14), which is not far off from them (Deut. 30:11). They therefore are in no need of an atoning redeemer. The rabbis of the first six centuries of the common era who developed rabbinic Judaism address sin not so much as a condition or state but as a transgression of the elaborate system of ritual, civil, criminal, and ethical *mitsvot* or commandments laid down in the written Torah and developed in the Talmud and its commentaries.[1] This system is based on the principle that humans receive commandments and freely obey or disobey them. When they obey they are rewarded, and when they disobey they are punished. If humans suffered from a state of sin that limited their free will, the entire system of *mitsvot* would be compromised. As the great medieval Jewish philosopher Maimonides (1135–1204) shows in his "laws of repentance," sin and repentance are matters that are handled within the domain of human free choice and require minimal divine intervention. "Man is given the option of taking the path of goodness . . . or of taking the path of evil."[2] "The choice now is up to us. 'Let us seek our path and investigate it and return unto the Lord' (Lam. 3:40)."[3]

The simple Jewish view is that Christianity begins with a world plagued by sin and ends with Christ as savior; Judaism begins with a world as "very good" (Gen. 1:31) and ends with Torah as its complement and Shabbat as its completion (Gen. R. on Gen. 2:12). Lacking a notion of original sin means that sin, atonement, and repentance are not the central concerns for Jews that they are for Christians.

There is of course truth to these simple, stereotypical formulations of the differences between Christianity and Judaism. But a deeper probing of biblical, rabbinic, and modern Jewish thought reveals significant affinities between Christian and Jewish notions of sin, atonement, and repentance that can make Christian doctrines more easily understood in Jewish terms. Indeed, although sin, atonement, and repentance are notions that hold different weight and status in Christianity than they do in Judaism, there is no doubt that they find parallels in Judaism. Jews should be able to understand Christian sin, atonement, and repentance because these notions are also Jewish terms.

Original Sin and Exile

Let us return to Paul and to Adam's disobedience. Judaism agrees with Paul's assertion that Adam (and Eve's) disobedience brought death with it. God did not fulfill his promise—"if you eat of the fruit . . . you shall surely die" (2:17)—immediately. But Jewish interpreters point out that Adam and Eve did eventually die, and therefore the rabbis understand God's words to mean that after Adam disobeys, humans become mortal and are subject to death (Genesis R. 17:8). The Adam and Eve story establishes the fundamental principle: sin results in punishment. It suggests that the appropriate punishment for grave sin, such as intentional disobedience of God's command, is death.

In addition, the disobedience of Adam and Eve results in their expulsion from the garden and establishes the conditions of human life, which begins with the pain of childbirth, is sustained through toil, and, as the book of Genesis starkly reveals, is plagued by shame, envy, deceit, robbery, violence, and murder. The Torah speaks of "visiting the iniquity of the parents upon the children" (Ex. 34:7), a point displayed clearly early in the first story after the expulsion from the garden, when Adam's first son Cain murders his brother Abel simply out of envy. If Jews do not want to use Augustine's phrase "original sin" to describe the conditions in which human life naturally transpires after Adam, they can be referred to the words of Genesis 4:7—"Sin crouches at the door"—or Genesis 8:21: "The devisings (*yetser*) of man's heart are evil from his youth.[4]' Judaism also has a Hebrew term that, like "original sin," is suggestive of a state or condition that limits the human ability to be in free contact with God. This term is *galut*, exile.

The contemporary Jewish philosopher Arnold Eisen tells us that exile is a "theme that stamps all the five books of Moses" and "has been intertwined with Jewish reflection ever after."[5] The notion of *galut* marks all rabbinic Judaism, since the rabbis constructed Judaism after and out of the destruction of the Temple and the dispersion of the Jews from Jerusalem. In significant ways, rabbinic Judaism is a Judaism of exiles marked by the trauma of the destruction of the Temple in 70 C.E. and a consistent longing for return to Jerusalem and Jewish political control over the land of Israel. Eisen suggests that exile is not only a central concept for Judaism but a term that describes an existential reality of life with which Jews can identify far more easily than with paradise. The term *galut* is used most extensively by the prophets to describe the Babylonian exile but has multiple levels of meaning that begin with Adam's alienation from the very ground *(adamah)* from which he was taken. Not only is Adam alienated from that ground, but the ground itself is cursed because of Adam (Gen. 3:17). This scene recalls Paul's pronouncement that "sin has come into the world" through Adam's sin. Humans are alienated from innocence and perfection, from each other and from God. *Galut* thus means a deep sense of homelessness in a world that is not quite right. *Galut*, in its deeper spiritual meaning, is not only about longing for the physical return of the Jewish people to the land of Israel, it is about the longing for final redemption and for return to the Edenic state of harmony between human and human, between humans and the world, and between humans and God.

The concept of exile has affinities with original sin because both are states or conditions that affect the whole person, the human community, and the world, and because both require divine help to be rectified. Like original sin, *galut* cannot be overcome by human will alone; exile will end only when God intervenes to make it end. There are certainly differences between the notions of original sin and *galut*. *Galut* usually is tied to the Jewish people and addresses the physical distance of the Jews from the land of Israel and the political domination of Israel by non-Jewish nations. Original sin and its antidote, salvation, tend to be articulated more in terms of the individual than the community, and they carry a stronger moral tone than does *galut* for Jews. But our task here is not so much to provide direct correlates between Christian and Jewish terms as it is to use terms familiar to Jews and Judaism as lenses through which to view Christianity. As with any lens, there is necessarily some distortion of the reality toward which it opens, yet, hopefully, there is also a new and clarified ability to see.

The notion of *galut* can help Jews, and perhaps Christians as well, understand that original sin is not primarily an issue of Adam's or Eve's disobedience. Rather, it refers to the reality that we are born into a world that lacks moral and spiritual wholeness. Original sin and exile are terms that convey the vast potential for evil in humans (Gen. R. on Gen. 1:26). The terms are also meant to convey the sense of spiritual longing within us that drives us to want to overcome the distance between us and others, between us and our ideals, between us and God.

The original nature of sin and exile means that overcoming the distance is an endless task that occurs on multiple levels and follows many turns, so that every success opens to a new level of moral and religious challenge. For contemporary Jews, the nature of this task has been made clear by the success of the Zionist movement in returning the Jews to the land of Israel. Even though the establishment of the state of Israel has brought an end to the suffering of many Jewish communities in exile, the state of Israel cannot be confused with ultimate redemption. Similarly, Christians cannot say that being baptized in Christ eradicates all sin and brings about salvation and the kingdom of heaven on earth. Rather baptism and acceptance of Christ are only the first steps for Christians in a lifelong struggle to walk in the footsteps of their savior and await his return.

Christ's Atonement in Jewish Terms

"Behold the Lamb of God who takes away the sin of the world." (Jn. 1:29)

How can Jews understand the Christian proposition that Jesus Christ's crucifixion is an atonement for the original sin of Adam that brings salvation to Christians and restores a condition of harmony for the world?

Jews can gain insight into Christ's atoning crucifixion by recalling the contexts of the biblical notions of purity and impurity and the sacrificial system of the priests, the rituals of the sanctuary, and the Temple. Jews can understand Christ's atonement as a liturgical event with some parallels to the Jewish liturgy of the High Holidays, particularly Yom Kippur—the Day of Atonement. In referring to Jesus as "the lamb who takes away sin" John invites his readers to make a connection between Christ and the slaughtering of lambs for the purpose of the expiation of sin, something we find throughout the Torah. Let us follow John's lead.

Sin Offerings and Impurity

The book of Leviticus delineates and systematizes the ways in which animal sacrifice brings expiation for sin to the individual and community. Chapters four through six enumerate the reasons why a person brings a *chatat*, a sin offering, to the altar for sacrifice. A sin offering is for sins that are committed unintentionally, or through lying or failing to testify in court when viewing a crime, or by taking a vow or coming into contact with things considered impure such as a dead person. These sins, I would argue, all suggest a state of mind or state of being rather than occasional transgressions. They are sins that compose an odd category. Crimes of lying and failing to testify suggest a weakness of character. Contact with impurity can happen with or without one's intent and could simply be the result of bad fortune. Nevertheless, one's social and physical condition is altered. This category of the *chatat* refers to crimes that are less serious than the willful harming of others, yet also more serious because they affect one's condition in the world, one's state of mind or character. They render one "impure."

The Levitical laws of purity and impurity may help Jews and others understand the connection that Jesus often makes between impurity and sin. And it may help Jews and others to understand the connection that Jesus often makes between "impurity" and "unclean spirits"—between sin and evil. Concern with purity is a consistent preoccupation in biblical Israelite religion and in rabbinic Judaism. As Jews, Jesus and his disciples would have shared these concerns. It is interesting to think about the condition of original sin itself as the condition of being *tameh*, "impure." Both are states of being that affect the whole person and render persons unfit to participate fully in society and religious life, and both are conditions changed through rituals of sacrifice and bathing in a *mikvah*, a ritual bath. Jesus' crucifixion can be understood as a great sin offering, and the Christian ritual of baptism as a *mikvah*! Cast in these terms, Jesus' self-sacrifice and Christian baptism provide purification from the state of impurity that could not be overcome through an act of the human will alone.

Yom Kippur

Christians will be quick to assert that the sins for which Jesus died must go beyond the narrow category circumscribed by the *chatat* or sin offering in the opening chapters of Leviticus. Indeed, and I suggest that we look further in Leviticus to examine how a larger compass of sins was expiated. Chapter 16 describes the festival of Yom Kippur, the Day of Atonement. This full day of "afflicting the soul" included fasting and the sacrifice of two goats for "all sins" of the people. One goat was sacrificed at the altar "to make atonement" (16:16) for the children of Israel, and the other, called the "scapegoat" in the King James Bible, was sent to die in the wilderness. The following passage from Leviticus is recited in traditional Yom Kippur morning services to this day. "Aaron shall lay both his hands upon the head of the live goat and confess over it *all the iniquities and transgressions of the Is-raelites, whatever their sins*, putting them on the head of the goat; and it shall be sent off to the wilderness. . . . The goat shall carry on it all their iniquities to an inaccessible region" (Lev. 16:21–22).[6]

The Yom Kippur context should enable Jews to understand what Paul means when he says: "We were reconciled to God by the death of his Son . . . by whom we have now received atonement" (Rom. 5:10–11). In the context of Leviticus 16, Jesus' crucifixion is not only a sin offering to render Christians ritually pure, but also the sending off of a scapegoat that atones for all the sins of Christians, be they ritual or moral, intentional or unintentional.

The Akedah

The story of the binding of Isaac, the *Akedah*, is a central feature of the Rosh Hashanah liturgy. The parallels between the *Akedah* and the Gospel story are easy to make, and John assumes them in referring to Jesus as lamb. The church father Origen (185–255) has interpreted the lamb that Abraham sacrificed instead of his "only son" Isaac as a Christian "prefiguration" of God's sacrifice of his "only begotten son" Jesus (Genesis Homily, 8). The rabbinic interpreters give multiple reasons for God's command to Abraham to sacrifice Isaac, but one reason that clearly resonates with the theme of the High Holidays is that Abraham's willingness to sacrifice Isaac is an act of merit and atonement upon which the Jewish people could count as expiation for

their sins. This understanding also underlies the interpretation offered by a seventh-century Jewish *Targum* on the *Akedah* that has
many earlier parallels in rabbinic literature.

> I beseech you by the mercy that is before you. O Lord: it is revealed be-
> fore you that there was no insincerity in my heart, but I sought to per-
> form your decree with joy; so, when the descendants of Isaac my son
> shall come to the time of distress, remember them, hear their supplica-
> tions, and deliver them, and generations to come will say, "In this moun-
> tain Abraham bound Isaac, his son, and there the Presence of the Lord
> was revealed to him." (*Targum Pseudo-Jonathan* on Gen. 14)

Here, Jews will intercede with the crucial difference between the
two central cases of sacrifice in Judaism and Christianity. Abraham did
not finally sacrifice Isaac, whereas Jesus was actually sacrificed. Indeed, it could be said that the point of the *Akedah* is explicitly to dis-
courage the practice of child sacrifice. The mainstream rabbinic view
of the *Akedah* is that Abraham's willingness to sacrifice Isaac was, itself, the act of merit that bestowed upon the Jewish people expiation
for their sins. Yet there have always been minority views that Abraham, who returned from Mount Moriah without Isaac (Gen. 22:19),
actually did sacrifice him.[7] These positions make the actual sacrifice of
Isaac the basis of the atonement for sin.

Liturgy and Sacrifice

The idea of animal and, worse, child sacrifice may seem to us moderns
to be the height of sin and totally lacking in expiatory and atoning
power. Yet we cannot understand Jewish and Christian symbols and
rituals without some understanding of the sacrificial system. For example, the sacrificial system is important in helping to explain the
central ritual event of Christianity, the Eucharist, in which the body
and blood of Christ are imbibed by Christians through the eating of a
wafer and the drinking of wine or grape juice (Mt. 26:26). We see in
Leviticus that many of the offerings that were brought for sacrifice,
after they were ritually roasted, were eaten by the priests, and some,
like the peace offering, were eaten by those who brought the sacrifice
as well. Eating of the sacrifice has the effect of physically and directly
taking its healing and purifying power into one's body.

The Atonement liturgies of the High Holidays in Judaism and the Eucharist in Christianity are great communal acts of catharsis and healing. Sacrifice, *korban*, whose Hebrew root means "to be close," may be understood as a means to overcome distance between humans and God. The human longing for release from the sense of being broken and morally flawed that the terms original sin, impurity, and exile are meant to convey cannot be quenched by material goods, by power, or land. This spiritual longing is met through liturgies in which we retell the stories of expiation and symbolically reenact atoning sacrifices that render us whole. In the liturgical moment, we achieve the wholeness that we lack in life and that we hope will be realized in the future. Thus the rabbis say that their festivals give them a "glimpse into the messianic age." Franz Rosenzweig (1886–1929) said that in and through our liturgy Jews touch "eternity."[8] To understand Christian salvation in Jewish terms is to see that in the eucharistic liturgy Christians also glimpse the age to come and touch eternity.

Turn Us to You: Repentance as Will or Gift

God has given even to the Gentiles the repentance that leads to life. (Acts 11:18)

God says to Israel: My Sons, open for me an aperture of Repentance as narrow as the eye of a needle and I will open for you gates through which wagons and coaches can pass. (Song R. 5:2, 2)

Despite its great importance to Judaism, repentance appears to be of relatively minor import to Christianity. This point can be illustrated by the fact that the *Encyclopedia Judaica* devotes six full columns to the term, whereas the *New Catholic Encyclopedia* devotes one scant paragraph and points us to different terms—"conversion" and "penance"—for further clarification. Clearly Christianity lacks a direct correlate to the Hebrew term for repentance, *teshuvah*, and reflection on the first sentence of the *Encyclopedia Judaica* entry reveals why. "Repentance," the entry says, "is a prerequisite for divine forgiveness: God will not pardon man unconditionally but waits for him to repent." This fact gives rise to elaborate laws that provide guidance and strategies for Jews to "do *teshuvah*." But for Christianity the notion that humans and not God initiate repentance contradicts the fundamental Pauline assertion that forgiveness is a free "unconditional" gift of grace by God to humans through Christ. This point returns us to the stereotypical polarity between Jews and Christians on the efficacy of the human will. Certainly we must say that there is a different emphasis on the importance of the will in the two religions. Yet if we refuse to end with this polarity and search further, we will find resonance for each position in the other religion.

If repentance was only a gift in Christianity, then the call to repent ("The Kingdom of God is at hand: repent you and believe the Gospel"—Mk. 1:15) would be rendered nonsensical. Indeed, none of Jesus' ministry—his healings, parables, sermons, and miraculous demonstrations, whose persuasive power is so palatable—would make sense. Obviously Jesus is making an attempt to get people to make a decision to turn from their old ways toward the new life that he is offering. If this turning is a matter of belief, then here, too, we can speak of a dimension of will in coming to believe that Jesus is the Christ, the Messiah. The Gospel of Luke and the Acts of the Apostles are full of directives to repent and turn to God (e.g., Acts 3:19). And it is clear that even as they stress that salvation from sin is a free gift from Christ, the Pauline Epistles contain argument upon argument constructed to persuade Jew and Gentile alike to follow Christ.

At the same time, Judaism is equally full of signs that repentance is not only a matter of the will and that one who sins will require divine assistance to turn back to the life of Torah. Whenever Jews place the Torah back in the ark after reading it in synagogue, they sing the verse from Lamentations 5:21: *hashivenu YHVH elecha ve-nashuva* (Turn us to you and we shall return). One could argue that all of Jewish prayer is structured to infuse individual Jews and the community as a whole with spiritual energy from God, thus enabling them to live a life that is in tune with the commandments and ideals of the Torah. If we could will ourselves to do good, why bother to pray at all? Once a year, the day of Yom Kippur itself cleanses the Jew from sin and gives him or her a "clean slate."

However, the Yom Kippur rituals together with the admonitions and guidance provided for Jews to repent suggest that *teshuvah* is neither purely a matter of will nor a gift but involves both. Analysis of the Hebrew word *teshuvah* gives us a clue to the dynamic process involved in repentance. *Teshuvah* must be translated by multiple words: turn, return, answer, respond. Repentance is at once an active and willful turning of the Jew to Torah and God and a return to that which was already there previously as a given gift. If repentance is conceived as an answer, then it must be a response to a previous question. If *teshuvah* is a response, then the initiative came from outside me. Abraham Joshua Heschel suggests that repentance is my response to God who is in search of me.[9]

The foregoing discussion should be enough to reveal the artificial quality of the supposed dichotomy between a "Jewish" notion of repentance as willed by humans and a "Christian" notion of repentance as a gift that comes by the grace of God. Both religions consider repentance to be both a willed human act and a divine gift. Martin Buber conveys the dynamic combination of willing and receiving that is involved in repentance through his discussion of the encounter with the *Thou:* "The Thou encounters me by grace; it cannot be found by seeking. . . . The Thou encounters me, but I enter into a direct relationship to it. Thus the relationship is election and electing, active and passive at once.[10]

Both Judaism and Christianity use the terms sin, atonement, and repentance to address the different phases in the human relationship to the "eternal Thou" or God. At times we know that it is our own acts of stupidity, envy, greed, and desire that wrack us with guilt, shake our confidence in our own goodness, and render us with a feeling of spiritlessness and distance from God. At other times we are blamed for wrongs we did not commit but suffer grave consequences nevertheless. Here life seems to be full of sinful injustice and is plagued by what the psalmist has called "the generation of the lie" (Ps. 12). Then the long struggle for justice and goodness ensues and in fits and starts is disappointed and met. Capturing the ebb and flow of human failing and redemption in religious terms and working to tip the world to the side of the good are goals that Christianity and Judaism share. Sin, original sin, exile, atonement, scapegoat, repentance, purity—these are terms that attempt to express the long and dynamic processes of human spiritual and moral degradation and renewal and the struggles of humans with, against, and for the divine. Jews and Christians can agree that something about the given situation in which humans find themselves is lacking. For Jews, the Torah fills that lack and provides them with the direction, ideals, and spirit that lead them both forward and back to a hoped for state of harmony and wholeness; for Christians, Christ provides the same resources. In the middle time of now,

Jews and Christians are supported by rituals and liturgies of purification and atonement that render the future redemption present and sustain the world in hope.

Conclusion: Redemption Through Liturgy at the Turn of the Twenty-First Century

I have tried to convey the powerful human realities, desires, and hopes that lie behind the terms sin, atonement, and repentance. The sense that there is a flaw within humanity and the world and that humans and the world are in need of healing, salvation, and redemption runs deep through Judaism and Christianity. The twentieth century saw a variety of secular movements of redemption that played upon the human desire for atonement and purity. These movements often adapted Jewish and Christian structures of redemption into horrible nationalistic ideologies that identified minority groups as scapegoats and proposed to cleanse and purify the nation through the sacrifice of massive numbers of people in genocide and war. As a new millennium begins, we can be sure to see both secular and religious calls for atonement and repentance, defined in a variety of religious, moral, economic, ecological, and medical ways. These varied diagnoses of sin and prescriptions for cures should serve to further underscore the power of the human desire for salvation and the impossibility of eradicating that desire. But that desire alone is not enough, as the events of the twentieth century proved. Although the ultimate stage upon which redemption much be worked out is that of human history, Judaism and Christianity have always said that that process is properly left in the hands of God. Here, I would make a plea for liturgy as the most productive vehicle for channeling the human desire for salvation into a life-affirming and healing spirit for individual communities and for the world. It is fitting that at the end of a modern period that has witnessed countless failed secular messianisms predicated on a rejection of Jewish and Christian rituals, both Jews and Christians are doing their own forms of *teshuvah* and are returning to their unique liturgies of atonement and repentance to sustain them until the Messiah comes (back).

Exile and Return in a World of Injustice:
A Response to Steven Kepnes

LAURIE ZOLOTH

Understanding sin and redemption requires thinking about why there is sin in the world, who is to blame, and how sinners are to be redeemed and forgiven. In this essay, I reinforce and also extend Steven Kepnes's efforts to uncover parallels between Christian and Jewish beliefs about sin and death, death and exile, and home after exile. Kepnes draws parallels between Christian notions of sin as individual alienation and Jewish notions of sin as corporate exile, and he suggests that sin and exile are redeemed through prayer. I agree, but I want to suggest that both traditions also share a deeper understanding of sin as injustice and of redemption as acts of righteousness. Because space is limited, I will make a series of connected arguments on the problem of Jewish and Christian conceptions of faith and action, revelation and witness.

Moral Seeing

Consider these two divergent texts:

> See! I am setting before you today: Blessing and curse. . . . I call heaven and earth to witness against you this day: I have put before you life and death, blessing and curse. Choose life—if you and your offspring would live—by loving the Lord your God, heeding his commandments, and holding close to Him. (Deut. 11:26–29; 30:19–20)

> In this way it is written that the Christ would suffer and rise from among the dead on the third day, and on the basis of his name repentance for forgiveness of sins would be preached in all the nations—starting out

from Jerusalem. You are to be witnesses of these things. And look! (Luke 24:46–49)

Here are two narratives about good and evil, one Jewish, one Christian. In the first, the Jews are assembled at the very gates to the long-promised land, and Moses speaks to them, opening with a single word: See! *Re'eh!* Behold! It is a call to attention that begins, surprisingly, in the second person singular—a call to each person individually—before it turns to address the people in the second person plural—"I have put before [all of] you life and death." Moses is speaking to the people of an imagined future that they will encounter in a land unseen, in a place and time that is theoretical. This radical choice for the good is set before them on this very day, *ha-yom*, even though the actual events that will require difficult moral decisions are yet ahead.

Moral choice will require *paying attention* to "seeing" not only to the commanded laws but also to the community that surrounds each of the individuals in Moses' audience. The first moral activity they face is "seeing" their relation to those who make up the community around them. The horror and evil of Epyptian slavery is interrupted by the radical liberation of the Exodus. Because of the Exodus, the people traveled from the narrow place of Egypt, where there were no choices, into the wide, chancy, place of freedom, where terrible failure is always also possible. To begin life in the Promised Land, the moral order that permits justice must first be established, a task that requires the ability to discern and choose between good and evil, to find the path to justice.

This ability to choose the path to a world based on justice will shape the understanding of sin and redemption for the next centuries of Jewish thought. A choice for the good will mean living this commanded life, living against sinful desires, always in the name of justice. Receiving the laws and commands of the Torah is the culmination of Israel's redemption from slavery. But no individual alone receives the Torah. As Emmanuel Levinas phrases it, the redemptive moment within revelation is the "seeing of the other's hearing," which means, "seeing that the Law is given to the whole community."[1] For Jews, unshackling the history of enslavement means being bound in a new kind of obedience to the freely chosen law: in biblical Hebrew, the word *avadim* can mean both "slaves" and "worshipers."

The Christian text is taken from the Gospel of Luke and tells about the moment just after Jesus has risen as Christ, has eaten with the disciples, and has instructed them again about the meaning of the Torah ("then he opened up their minds to grasp fully the meaning of [the Hebrew] Scriptures"). Jesus calls his followers to witness (to "see" each other and to "see" the world) "these things"—the words and events of that day and of his time among them. This story is obviously different from Deuteronomy's account of Israel's Exodus. Nonetheless, one is struck by the similarity of concept, construction, and language.

In both stories, humans are offered a choice for the expiation of sin and for redemption. In both, what is at stake, this very day, is *seeing* the necessity for both faith and action, and this seeing involves seeing the other person's seeing of the call to faith. For both Jews and Christians, the "moral seeing" that is needed to live a good life requires public acts of communal faith, witness, and promise: giving witness to promises made in public by your neighbor.

Sin and Death

For Jews, sin is a kind of error *(chet)*, a deviation from a set of commanded acts rooted in justice toward the vulnerable. Our text from Deuteronomy portrays a world fraught with evil, in which curses present irresistible temptations and blessings are faintly heard. In such a world, how could people actually make clear choices against evil? With the confusion of the passage to a new land, far from the purity of the desert and the column of fire, the temptation to choose evil is immense; indeed, it threatens to unwrite the collective human project. Thus Moses tells the people that sin will bring death and that the Torah—the law and the structure of justice—will bring life; indeed, the observance of Torah law is inherently redemptive. At the banks of the Jordan, at this very moment of decision and of mutual election in the Torah, what is at stake is the capacity and obligation of even a fallen, vulnerable and failed human person to be a just moral agent.

For Christians, sin lies in nature of the individual: limited and creaturely.[2] Created by a loving God but driven to evil by satanic desire,[3] the fallen human creature repeatedly fails. Jesus is the second chance. God enters the human story as human to stand in for the word/law of Torah and to bear the weight, by his blood and body, of redemption. Human persons are born into fate, time, and history, but always they have an opportunity for redemption, for a similar new birth with new possibilities. Kepnes emphases Christian theologies that describe sin as alienation: an alienation so profound that its bearers appear in the

Gospel texts as sickened by their sin: blinded, deafened, or plague-ridden. For these theologies, one must actually be reborn from this blinded and lost self into a new life, and this is possible only if one has sincere faith in the sacrifice of Jesus and in the good news of the resurrection, and only if one has the courage to understand that such deep faith will allow one to emulate the life of Christ and his disciples. Other Christian approaches extend the theologies of alienation into theologies of social justice, as we will see. First, however, let us consider the relationship between the notions of sin, death, and exile.

Death and Exile

Kepnes allows us to interpret the Christian notion of alienation within the terms of the Jewish notion of exile. The exile from the Garden of Eden is an exile into mortality, labor, and estrangement. Let me add, however, that there is also a deeper exile, the exile of Cain. The first death in the Bible is the result of murder: an act of injustice. Cain is the embodiment of death in the world because he brought about the first death—that of his brother. In this way, Cain's own life becomes an exile. This is not the exile of a people from its land, nor the exile of alienated individuals from themselves; it is the exile of the murderer from all others who would be oppressed by his injustice.

We live in the world after Cain, which is this world of injustice. If we are going to understand Christian and Jewish notions of redemption, we must do so in a way that responds to the conditions of brokenness that we share. It is not enough to speak, in Jewish terms, of returning home from a corporate exile, or, in Christian terms, of returning back to the self from which we have been alienated. We must speak of returning to a just world. This is to speak of return from sin as repair of the world, *tikkun olam*. Return, in this sense, entails reconstructing relationships of power among human beings, and not only repairing relations between humans and God. Humans are not only exiled wanderers, in flight from their lives with God; they can also be oppressors, tempted to undo the lives of the vulnerable.

Home After Exile

For Jews and for Christians, tangible good works can repair the breach of exile. Justice restored is sin redeemed. To understand this in

Jewish terms, consider the symbolic meanings of the holiday of Yom Kippur. In the time of the Temple, this day marked a complex ritual in which the sins of the community were symbolically "placed" on the head of a real goat who was sent away into the wilderness to die (Lev. 16:8, 10). (Christians share in the theology of this ritual when Jesus is portrayed as the goat that is sent to Azazel to carry away the sins of the people.) But after the Temple was destroyed, Jews, like the Christian fellowship, faced a crisis. How can one atone for sin if there is no sacrifice, no goat to carry the sins away, and no prayer liturgy to perform? The rabbis struggled with this crisis by replacing the ritual of animal sacrifice with a new liturgy of atonement. In the rabbinic liturgy of Yom Kippur, after reciting the list of sins for which it takes responsibility, the congregation responds with a query: What mitigates the stern decree, this life in an unjust world? The answer is: *"teshuvah, tzedakah, tefillah"* (repentance, charity, prayer).

Johanan b. Zakkai argued that giving charity, *tzedakah*, would restore the world ruptured by Roman occupation and war: the demand for justice for the poor is a way to restore justice and to repair sin in the days after the Temple sacrifices are ended. Only with charity, *tzedakah*, can justice, *tzedek*, begin. In the language of the prayers, one can return or repent *(teshuvah)* only if one first hears the call of the other person from out of her oppression. In this critical way, the emerging answer to sin is the sacrifice of the self—a serious tithing of self: work, attention, time, and income.

Justice is the way to think and act our way to a redeemed world. In redemptive action, we link the response of God at the very moment of expulsion and exile to how it is that we are to heal the exile. Because of exile, we must work the land and wrest food from it; to repair the exile, we must understand that the harvest is also claimed by the poor, and rightly so. The temptation, which crouches at the door at the moment of abundance, is to think that what you have belongs to you personally, that the stuff that you possess is in fact who you are. The first temptation of sin, as Cain (whose name means "the acquirer") discovered, is always the sin of injustice.

But if redemption *is* justice, and atonement (self-) sacrifice, then the rabbinic structure of *tzedakah* allows the very punishment of the expulsion (work) to be restorative. God answers evil only through human acts. To know "where you are," to struggle out of exile, to return home is to answer a God who speaks in the voice of the most desper-

ate and the most vulnerable. To be redeemed from the sins of the
world is to answer this voice, as Adam, Eve, and Cain could not.

For both Jews and Christians redemption begins with the one who
says "I am here; I see," and in saying so accepts the necessary burden
of the work of justice.

The Turn to Liberation

Let me now turn my attention to a distinctive question—how should
Jews understand recent developments in Christian theology? Understanding how charity repairs injustice allows Jews to understand more
fully the critical, new Catholic and Protestant accounts of sin and redemption. The rabbis's insistence on the link between repentance and
charity, *teshuvah* and *tzedakah*—the Jewish answer to sin—is parallel in
structure and meaning to this Christian liberation theology, which is
not well known among Jews.

For Gustavo Gutierrez, writing out of the Catholic tradition, the
tragically sinful situation of humankind is rooted in our inability to
see what is sacred in each one of our neighbors. The sin of sins is the
oppression of the poor by the powerful, the act of Cain. The human
condition is rooted in a sinfulness for which the sacrifice of Jesus offers expiation. However, this is possible only if the story of Jesus is understood as a "situated narrative about an actual and particular
person-as-God." Gutierrez notes that Jesus is found *with the poor* and
crucified on the garbage heaps outside the city. A Christian who seeks
salvation must, therefore, read the texts, history, and practices of
Christianity with a similar "preferential option for the poor." Like a
Jewish reading of liberation/salvation, this Catholic reading insists
that personal liberation is linked to the political liberation of humankind. The problem of sin is profoundly and thoroughly social:

> Misery and social injustice reveal a "sinful situation" a sin-tergration of
> brotherhood and communion; by freeing us from sin, Jesus attacks the
> roots of an unjust order. . . .
>
> Sin appears as the fundamental alienation, the root of a situation of
> injustice and exploitation. It cannot be encountered in itself, but only in
> concrete situations, in particular alienation. Sin demands a radical liber-
> ation, which in turn necessarily implies a political liberation. . . . This
> radical liberation is the gift which Christ offers us. . . . This is why the

Christian life is a Passover, a transition from sin to grace, from death to life, from injustice to justice, from the subhuman to the human. Christ introduces us by the gift of his Spirit into communion with God and with all men. More precisely, it is *because* he introduces us into this communion, into a continuous search for its fullness, that he conquers sin—which is the negation of love—and all its consequences.[4]

Justice, here, as in our Jewish sources, is given collectively and must be expressed communally.[5]

Catholic liberation theologians are not alone in understanding sin and redemption as social. For the Lutheran Ted Peters, the question of sin and redemption is entirely about an existential state of social alienation. Following Paul Tillich, Peters notes that the social relationships of injustice create a state of sin. Actions in the world either express or resist this sinfulness:

What is the "state of sin?" It is the condition in which we find ourselves estranged from God. Our relationship with God is broken, and this fundamental break causes other breaks, such as alienation from other people and even from ourselves. The broken relationship with God, who is the source of all life, is what subjects us to death and to anxiety over the prospect of nonbeing. In this situation of estrangement, we act. And an act that expresses this estrangement is an act of sin.[6]

An act of estrangement is an act of sin, but the reverse is true as well. We can return from sin by undoing oppression through righteous acts of resistance to a world of injustice. Jews can understand such a text in the light of both the prophetic tradition of rebuking oppressors in the name of justice, and the talmudic requirement to heal the unredeemed world. In Peters's writing, the sin of creation dooms us not only to mortality but also to a spiritual death—to existential aloneness. Then redemption is action against this estrangement. Jews can understand this clearly in light of the paradoxical call to love even the stranger. We see that the stranger is the estranged in the midst of the community, is the sinning self lost in exile, unless and until he or she attends to the moral needs of the other person.

In the liberation theologies of theologians like Gutierrez and Peters, we can see a shared concern with social evil and collective redemption. In these theologies, sin and redemption are placed in the context of the idea that to be faithful to Jesus is to act in his name. To be faithful, then, is to be reborn as someone who is on the side of the enslaved and not on the side of the oppressors, and who is prepared to work at changing the world in concrete, daily terms: an end as meaningful for the ethics of Judaism as it is for Christianity.

Redemption, Prayer, and Justice

Prayer and the response of concrete acts of justice are linked. To live ethically, to live as if the problem of good and evil is one's central problem, is both to hear an *appeal* and to make one—to *invoke;* it is to *pray.* To answer calls, and to call out truth—both are critical acts in a world of injustice. In Christian liberation texts based on Jewish prophetic traditions, and in rabbinic traditions of social action on behalf of the vulnerable, no one is alone, neither in the speech that is prayer nor in acts of justice, repair, and charity. Moving from exile back to home, from sin to redemption, from slavery to oppression, begins with the understanding that justice is constitutive of all faith; it is the work that is done on behalf of the exiled world.

Theologians in both the Jewish and Christian traditions speak of the deep link between a life of faith and the responsibility to attend to the problem of evil, to the fragility of goodness in a world of injustice. Seeing sin as injustice and righteous actions as redemption may, therefore, enable Jews to gain purchase on Christianity's complex notions of sin. Furthermore, it may allow contemporary Jews and Christians to explore together how text, tradition, and religious citizenship create possibilities for a conversation about morality.

The Lamb of God and the Sin of the World

MIROSLAV VOLF

Paul's Conversion and the Christian Doctrine of Salvation

At the time I received Professor Kepnes's text I was working on a project that involved a study of Paul's life-changing encounter with Jesus Christ on the road to Damascus. This event decisively shaped his religious thought, which in turn had an enormous impact on Christian theology, most notably on the understanding of salvation. Here is how Paul himself described it:

> For I want you to know, brothers and sisters, that the gospel that was proclaimed by me is not of human origin; for I did not receive it from a human source, nor was I taught it, but I received it through a revelation of Jesus Christ. You have heard, no doubt, of my earlier life in Judaism. I was violently persecuting the church of God and was trying to destroy it. I advanced in Judaism beyond many among my people of the same age, for I was far more zealous for the tradition of my ancestors. But when God, who had called me through his grace, was pleased to reveal his Son to me, so that I might proclaim him among the Gentiles, I did not confer with any human being. (Gal. 1:11–16)

Let me isolate three key elements implied in the story of Paul's religious transformation. First, his violent persecution was clearly identified as a wrongdoing, and yet justice was not carried out but unmistakably transcended. And both of these things happened in the single act of offering grace: God did not punish Saul for his wrongful persecution but instead sought to make a friend from an enemy. Second, it was precisely this act of grace that changed the direction of Saul's, now Paul's, life. Saul neither sought the change nor was pressured into it. The change was the result of the reconciliation offered. Third, Paul was persecuting the church out of the purest of religious motives (zeal for God and the Law), but in the encounter with the risen Christ he discovered that he was God's enemy. He believed he was at his very best, but he was—or so he came to believe—profoundly ungodly, and yet blind to the fact of it.

From these three elements in the story of Paul's conversion one can extrapolate three pillars of the later Christian doctrine of salvation: the unconditionality of God's grace, the indispensability of grace for repentance, and the captivity of all to sin. None of the three pillars are *as such* foreign to Judaism, notwithstanding the fact that an impetus for their development in the Christian tradition came in part from an event that contributed significantly to Christianity's parting of ways with Judaism. By showing, at least implicitly, these links between Judaism and Christianity Professor Kepnes's essay makes a major contribution to Jewish–Christian dialogue. Of course, differences in how Judaism and Christianity understand these themes are undeniable. These differences reside primarily in the weight assigned to the themes in each tradition, in the degree of radicality with which they are understood, and above all in the particular way in which they are related or not related to the death of Jesus Christ and to the sending of the Spirit.

Sin

"Exile" is the image Professor Kepnes uses to describe the human predicament. Human beings find themselves "east of Eden" and in a "Babylonian captivity." The image is good, provided that at the heart of the "homeland" from which they are exiled lies communion with God. Sin is an irreducibly theocentric notion that cannot be translated without loss into psychological, sociological, or cosmological terms. Whatever else sin may be formally (e.g., homelessness or disharmony), it is "ungodliness" in the sense of turning away from God. Being turned away from God is a condition that affects "the whole person, the human community, and the world." The metaphor of "exile" captures this condition well. What is less clear from the metaphor is that sin is not simply a condition that human beings suffer passively. Affected by it, they act, and by acting they make their own small or large contributions to keeping themselves and others in exile. Sin is a corporate condition we inherit ("original sin"), and sin is an act we personally commit ("actual sin"); the one makes the other worse, and both shape human identities.

Exile describes the world in which we live, and it describes us who live in it. Not that the world is a terrestrial hell with devilish little creatures as its warring masters. The world is a good creation of God and a proper home of human beings; and human beings share in and contribute to that goodness, their undeniable propensity toward evil notwithstanding. Much of what we do is good, even highly admirable. But if a person's heart is a land of exile, then the incontestable good that we do is infested with an inescapable evil. Looked at from one angle—but from one angle only!—our best clothes are "like a filthy cloth," as the prophet Isaiah puts it (64:6). Moreover, often we are incapable of doing the good we want but instead do the evil we do not want. Sometimes we are even happy to want and do what we want even when we know that what we want is evil.

With the claim that the stain of evil mars all our deeds and that our wills are weak and sometimes outright perverted—a claim that, though not made by Professor Kepnes, is loosely in line with what he said about sin as exile—we have come close to the Christian notions about captivity to sin. We are not quite there yet, however. For at the heart of the captivity to sin lies not the inescapable moral underperformance of human beings that accompanies their equally undeniable moral excellence, but the inability to turn to God on one's own, indeed even to properly recognize one's sin *as* sin and therefore oneself as a sinner. Given the state of captivity to sin, our "exile will end only when God intervenes to make it end," as Professor Kepnes states.

Atonement

In his discussion of Yom Kippur—the Day of Atonement—and Jewish conceptions of repentance or *teshuvah*, Professor Kepnes speaks of being actually cleansed "from sin" and given "a clean slate" through ritual and liturgy. It is in relation to the need for erasing sin as sin that Professor Kepnes looks at the Christian theology of Christ's death. He is right to do so, since the Christian tradition, at least in its western form, has placed a great deal of emphasis precisely there. Yet one should not forget other aspects of Christ's work, such as Christ as the example or Christ as the conqueror over evil. Christian soteriology gets its proper balance only if these other aspects are also given their proper due.

The most important lens that Professor Kepnes offers for reading the Christian notion of atonement—a notion that itself owes much to the sacrificial system as described in the Pentateuch—is Abraham's binding of Isaac. Yet this powerful and formative story, which has important echoes in Pauline accounts of the death of Christ, occludes as well as illumines what is going on in the Christian theology of Christ's death. For the story of the binding of Isaac operates with two separate human agents, one who sacrifices and the other who is (unknowingly or willingly) sacrificed. In the story of Christ's death, the two primary agents—Jesus Christ himself and the One he called "Father"—are not strictly separate and the action must be understood as the deed of God. The thought is expressed in a rudimentary way by the Apostle Paul: "God was in Christ reconciling the world to himself" (2 Cor. 5:19). Atonement, in the most fundamental sense, is an *event in the life of God* for the sake of the world. It is God taking upon himself, in the person of Jesus Christ, the sins of the world and thereby erasing them. He who "knew no sin" was made sin "so that in him we might become the righteousness of God" (2 Cor. 5:21).

How precisely atonement is to be understood as an event in the life of God, how God's taking upon himself the sins of the world takes place, and why some such atonement is necessary is the stuff out of which the intricate debates about the Trinity and atonement in Christian theology are made. But the consequences of placing the atonement in the life of God are clear. It implies a rejection of both a religiously crude notion that God's anger must be placated before God can love a sinner and a morally dubious notion that an innocent third person can be legitimately punished by God for the guilty sinner. Moreover, to make atonement an event in the life of God is to underscore that nothing can undo it and that the thought of its repetition is unthinkable.

If one wanted to understand in Jewish terms what drives the Christian understanding of atonement, I think it would be useful to look at one Jewish notion of election.[1] Israel is irrevocably elect and immutably loved by God; no failure on Israel's part can change this. God will not deal with Israel only in the light of Israel's failure, but will deal with Israel's failure in the light of God's irrevocable commitment to Israel. At the root of the Christian understanding of atonement lies a universalized and radicalized version of Israel's election. Because God, being the God of all reality, loves the world with that same immutable love with which God loves Israel, God has dealt with the history of the world's failure by taking the world's sins once and for all upon himself and thereby unconditionally reconciling the world to himself.

Even though for Christians reconciliation is in an important sense a done deed, it is in another sense not complete. In the very text in which the Apostle Paul boldly states that "God was in Christ reconciling the world to himself," he goes on to link to that divine work his own "ministry of reconciliation" and to plead with his readers to "be reconciled to God" (2 Cor. 5:19–20). The world *was* reconciled to God by God but it still *needs to be* reconciled; the accomplished reconciliation still awaits completion! The completed reconciliation is in fact a threshold of the age to come. Once that threshold is crossed, all will have stepped into a world in which each enjoys the other in communion with God and therefore all will take part in the dance of love freely given and freely received.

Repentance

Repentance in the broad sense—as one of the ways in which to express the whole of the subjective appropriation of salvation—is the consequence of the distinction between reconciliation accomplished (past) and reconciliation completed (future). However one relates these paradoxical notions, repentance, as a process that involves the relation of human beings to God and their own multifaceted relation to one another, is an indispensable structural element of that same reconciliation as experienced in the present.

For Christians, the rituals of baptism and Eucharist are normally the place where repentance and the transformation of human beings take place. Professor Kepnes is right to stress their significance. However, we should not forget that rituals are religiously ambiguous, as the prophets of old well knew. "Liturgy" can too easily become a religious substitute for turning away from evil and living a life of righteousness, a divinely mandated way of avoiding the very repentance that is supposed to take place through it. Over the centuries, Christians have not heard with sufficient attentiveness the prophetic critique of liturgy.

To lodge repentance between reconciliation accomplished and reconciliation still to be completed means to place it in the context of God's unconditional grace. It is quite correct to say, with Abraham Heschel, that repentance is my response to God who is in search for me. But Christians claim more, significantly more. In his search of me, God has gone to such lengths as to be able to tell me: "The sins that weigh you down have already been 'taken away!'"

The fact that the sin of the world *has been taken away* has two important consequences, one for how the problem of sin is understood and the other for how it is dealt with. First, if the sin of the world has been "taken away," then what is held against transgressors is ultimately not the sins they have committed but the failure to accept their sins as sins—as forgiven sins—and the consequent unwillingness to turn away from them. Second, what makes repentance possible is again God's unconditional grace. Repentance, of course, presupposes an accusation: you have gone astray and you need to return. Much depends on how the accusation is made. To accuse sinners apart from offering them grace is to drive them down the road of self-justification and denial. To accuse them *by offering them grace*—and grace does accuse, as everyone who has been "forgiven" for what she has not done will know!—is to invite them to self-knowledge and release.

What Christians believe about the unconditionality of grace is shaped in decisive ways by the dual fact that sins are always already forgiven and that repentance is nevertheless essential. Consider, first, a particular *pattern of relations* between forgiveness, repentance, and reconciliation that follows from this dual fact. Repentance is a consequence of forgiveness, not its prerequisite. And it is a consequence whose absence amounts to a refusal to be reconciled with God and therefore is itself a form of sin. The unconditionality of grace *includes repentance as an essential element of reconciliation with God.* Consider, second, the nature of agency through which repentance takes place (human will in relation to divine action)—an issue distinct from the pattern of relations between forgiveness, repentance, and reconciliation. The second issue concerns the ability—or rather, given human captivity to sin, the inability—of human beings to do what is necessary (repentance). Here the unconditionality of grace means that repentance itself must be seen as a gift of God.

But how should one understand that divine giving? Repentance is one of the most difficult things for human beings to do. There are no assurances that even reconciliation accomplished and the consequent call to repentance will lead to it. One of the most notable features of sin is that it unfailingly refuses to be sin. And often for those who are "good" the recognition of sin is even more difficult than for those who are "evil." When repentance happens, it seems to have its source somewhere beyond our own selves. Hence the Jews do wisely when they pray, "Turn us to you, and we shall return." Hence Christians do well when they, more radically, think of repentance as the work of God's Spirit. A "knock" on the door of the heart by the unconditional grace coming from outside needs a "nudge" of the Spirit to open it from inside. That universal and incessant "nudging" of the Spirit to say "yes" to unconditional and indiscriminate grace is the form that both the divine gift of repentance and the divine "waiting" for humans to receive the gift take in the Christian tradition. Can we reject the gift and make God wait? It is hard to deny the obvious! In the end, we are left with hope (*not* with certainty) that all will be reconciled to the God of infinite love who has reconciled the world to himself.

A Puzzlement

Let me conclude. It is pleasing to read such a sympathetic treatment of one's tradition as Professor Kepnes has offered here. And yet pleasure is mixed with puzzlement. My guess would be that even a Jew who uses the "terms familiar to . . . Judaism as lens to view Christianity through" would see some things that are incompatible with Judaism and to which she would have to say a resolute "no" (say, the notion of atonement that understands the death of Christ on the cross as an event in the life of God). Other things would elicit an uncomprehending "why?" even when all the reasons that Christians give for their position have been noted (say, why does repentance not suffice such that the Son of God must take the sins of the world away?). Still other things might call for something like, "But this is not quite right!" (say, are the best clothes of *all* people, even when looked from one angle only, really like filthy cloth?). None of these kinds of reactions are found in Professor Kepnes's text. I wonder why? I would hope that his response would be that everything has its time. There is a time to look for affinities, parallels, and resonances of one religious system in another—an endeavor that aims at better understanding and more congenial practicing of our faith. But there is a time to pose hard questions of truth and adequacy—an endeavor that aims at mutual enrichment and, ultimately, even at agreement. For my own good as a Christian thinker and for the good of my tradition, I need to hear Jewish thinkers ask such hard questions.[2]

13

IMAGE OF
GOD

The Image:
Religious Anthropology in
Judaism and Christianity

TIKVA FRYMER-KENSKY

When Jews think about Christianity, they are often struck by ideas and images fundamentally different from Jewish traditions. Icons, statues, incense, crucifixes, and even crosses create a physical environment radically different from Jewish worship; notions of trinity and incarnation form a mental universe equally bizarre to traditional Jewish concepts. It is with some degree of relief that Jews often turn to Christian ideas of humanity and society, finding common ground with Christianity precisely on the common ground of earth and human beings. The nature of human beings and of the human relationship with God affords at least a common theological language with which to think about the issues of human existence, the language of *tselem elohim* and *imago dei:* the image of God.

The Image of God: A History

The "Image" in the Hebrew Bible

This language of the "image of God" has its source in the Hebrew Bible, in the first chapter of Genesis "God created humanity in his own image; in the image of God he created him" (1:27). Genesis 1 does not spell out the implications of the "image"; possibly there is a connection here with God's blessing, with fertility, and with "dominion" over the earth. In Mesopotamia and Egypt, kings erected statues of themselves at the farthest reaches of their empires to represent their dominion. In Akkadian, the word for statue is *tsalmu*, the same as Hebrew *tselem* (image). Furthermore, Assyrian texts describe the king himself as *tsalam ili*, "image of the god," the representative of God on earth. In the same way, says Genesis, humans are to act for God on this earth, administrating and performing other acts of "dominion."

Genesis 5:1–3 develops the concept of "image" further as it begins the genealogies with a recapitulation that God created humanity in God's likeness *(demut elohim)*; the passage then specifies that "God created them male and female, blessed them and called them 'Adam.'" The next verse makes the meaning of the term "likeness" clear, for Adam "begat in his image as his likeness" and called his name "Seth." God created us to be like God, and even though God is beyond gender, it is the nexus of male and female that is the likeness and creates the likeness. As we create children, we take on the God-like role of creator. Moreover, we create children who look like us, and we, and they, look like God. The use of the word *demut* in these two sentences makes the physicality of our likeness to God apparent.

A completely different aspect of the concept of "image of God" emerges in the more legally oriented passage of Genesis 9:1–8, the re-institution of humanity after the flood. Here a fundamental difference between humanity and the animals is reinforced: human beings can kill and eat animals (with some restrictions), but no one, not even an animal, can kill a human. Whoever kills a human being forfeits his life, because "in the image of God he made humanity." Here, the concept of "image" determines not how we should act, but how others should act toward us. Each human is to be treated as the representative of God. In this way, the concept of "image of God" creates a sense of the inviolability and sacredness of human life.

These Genesis passages form the basis for a religious anthropology that concentrates on the divine aspects of human form and function.

Both the New Testament and early Jewish sources found this concept of *tselem* very attractive, maybe because the Greco-Roman world knew images and statues, surrounded as it was by rules concerning the treatment of the statues of Roman emperors. In this cultural milieu, it was perhaps inevitable that the relationship of humanity and God, described already in the Hebrew Bible as one of image to source, should be explored in terms of the image of God.

The Rabbinic and New Testament "Image"

The rabbis of this period emphasize the connection between humanity and God. To them, our physical resemblance is a sign of a connection so deep that injury to a human being injures God. They understand the deep paradox underlying Genesis 9, which proclaims the sanctity of human life even as it announces that this sanctity will be safeguarded by the death of a human being. Rabbi Meir tells a parable about a king whose twin brother was an outlaw. The king crucified him, but as he was hanging on the cross the passersby saw (they thought) that the king had been hung.[1] The implication is clear: what is done to human beings reflects on God. In the same spirit, Rabbi Akiba declared that "whoever sheds blood cancels the image,"[2] a sentiment expressed also by the Mechilta, which relates a parable about a king who enters a state, puts up statues and impresses coins, only to have the statues broken and the coins invalidated: "so too, one who spills blood is one who lessens the king's image."[3] This way of thinking about human beings had great legal implications; as Rabbi Akiba and Rabbi Tarphon declared, "if we were in the Sanhedrin, no one would ever be killed" (M. Mak. 1:10).

The rabbinic notion of image is concrete: it relates to people's looks, to their face and form, which are like God's, and not to some concept of mind, soul, spirit, or intellect. The bodily resemblance leads Hillel to declare that we have an obligation to care for our body as the image of God.[4] Moreover, since each individual person is the image of God, we have an obligation to maximize the image of God both by creating more people and by not killing people: "whoever does not engage in procreation has diminished the divine image"; "whoever spills blood cancels the image."[5] Acts that "lessen the divine image" and that harm the image have a major impact on God in the world and, in a more mystical sense, on the very self of God.[6]

The physical resemblance between humans and God is also a factor in New Testament teaching, particularly in relationship to the appearance of Jesus, who was a perfect representation of God. John reports Jesus' response to Philip's request to see the father: "Anyone who has seen me has seen the father" (Jn. 14:8–9). Similarly, some of the Epistles stress that Christ is the "image of the invisible God" (Col. 1:15; cf. 2 Cor. 4:4), "the radiance of God's glory and the exact representation of his being" (Heb. 1:3). Jesus may be the most perfect image (a position that some Jewish sources ascribe to Jacob),[7] but all of the rest of us are also in the image of God. Like the Jewish sources, James, asking how we can praise God and also curse men who have been made in God's likeness, understands that the "image" concept should determine how we treat each other (Jam. 3:9). This practical consequence of seeing people in God's image is also expressed by "Pseudo-Clementine," an author writing in the first half of the second century who was possibly Jewish–Christian. Clementine picks up Genesis's idea of dominion, declaring that the purpose for which humans are "impressed as with the greatest seal in his form" is so that he will rule over all and all will serve him." Moreover, declares Clementine, "whoever wants to worship Him will honor His image."[8]

Paul introduces a new element into the concept of the image, a dynamic and relative sense: "we are being transformed into his likeness with ever-increasing glory" (2 Cor. 3:18). The new self of the faithful is being renewed in the image. When the rabbis talk about "lessening the image," they are referring to the quantity of humans in the world, for all of us are the image. Paul, on the other hand, speaks about quality, for each of us can be more the image.

Original Sin and the Fall of the "Image"

Becoming more of the image can also mean that we can be less of the image. Christian sources speak often about "the Fall" of Adam and Eve, a fall that damaged the very nature of humanity. There are some similar Jewish traditions, clustered around the idea of *adam ha-rishon*, the first Adam,[9] but these traditions are nowhere near as common as the Christian discussion of "the Fall" or "original sin." The second-century theologian Irenaeus distinguished between the "image" and the "likeness." The likeness was lost in the Fall, but the image remained, and the likeness was restored when God became his image at the incarnation. For a long time, Christian writers incorporated the notion of the Fall of humanity into their concept of humans as an essential part of the idea of the image of God. Humanity was born in the full image and likeness. After the Fall, in some way this image was lessened, disfigured, or destroyed, and humans could no longer be full images of God. God's redemption, which began with the incarnation, served to remedy this flaw in humanity, and it is belief in this redemption, expressed concretely through baptism, that enables people to be restored in God's eyes.

"The Fall" and "original sin" are difficult concepts for Jews. Even though Jewish tradition speaks of Adam's sin and punishment, the idea that we are still somehow involved in this very ancient sin and punishment offends basic Jewish ideas of justice. One of the stories basic to Jewish spiritual formation, Abraham's argument with God over the fate of Sodom, rejects the notion of collective punishment: "God forbid that you should do such a thing, to kill the righteous with the wicked, that the righteous should be like the wicked" (Gen. 18:25). Punishing anybody but the perpetrator offends Abraham's (and our) sense of justice: "God forbid, should the judge of the world not do justice?" (Gen. 18:25) Jews also find the "verticality," the transgenerational nature, of the punishment problematic. It is true that the Ten Commandments contain God's promise to "visit the sins of the fathers upon the sons," but this punishment does not carry past the third or fourth generation; only the good deeds are to resonate to thousands of generations. The Hebrew Bible ultimately rejects even the idea that God can punish to the fourth generation, as the prophet Ezekiel proclaims a new moral order after the Babylonian exile in which God would not punish any child for the sin of the parents (Ezek. 18). Given this clear teaching of individual responsibility, it is hard for Jews to follow language that speaks of a sin or punishment inherited from Adam.

Jewish eyes also have problems with the remedy for this sin. Rabbinic tradition concentrates on commandments that have to be performed, actions of both moral and ritual valence. These commandments describe the life that one is to live in order to please God. One of the earliest Jewish traditions, attributed to Antiochos of Socho, declares, "Do not be like servants who serve their master expecting to receive a reward; be rather like servants who serve their master unconditionally, with no thought of reward" (M. Avot 1:3). Despite this ideal, the rabbis developed an elaborate conception of reward and punishment and, in fact, declared belief in reward and punishment to be one of the core essential beliefs. A doctrine that considers human beings to be incapable of right action and makes salvation dependent upon a specific belief in the salvific life and death of Jesus seems to go against the very basis of the Jewish system of *mitsvot*.

On closer examination, of course, the difference between the Christian and Jewish notions of salvation is not that enormous. A recurrent motif of the High Holiday liturgy proclaims the importance of remembering the virtues of the patriarchs, and above all Abraham's willingness to sacrifice Isaac. The merit of this act accrues to all future Jews, and is a "trump card" that they play in the drama of sin, repentance, and atonement. If Abraham's act can reverberate throughout the eons, one can understand that Jesus' sacrifice can have a transformative impact. Nor is the requirement of belief entirely unknown in Judaism. The Mishnah speaks of those who "have no share in the world to come": those who do not believe that the resurrection is a biblical doctrine, and those who say that the Torah was not revealed (M. Sanh. 11:1). The legend of Elisha ben Abuya underscores the importance of such beliefs for rabbinic Judaism.

Elisha was one of the four great sages who took a mystical voyage to heaven. While he was there, he saw the angel Metatron sitting and writing the merits of Israel in a book. Elisha was surprised to see Metatron sitting, since he knew that angels do not get tired and therefore should not need to sit. As a result, Elisha deduced that *perhaps* there might be two powers in heaven. This momentary loss of total faith in the absolute unity of God was enough to remove him entirely from the Jewish system. He became "the other" *(aher)*, and even God, when calling for his "wandering children" to return, adds, "except for *aher*."[10]

The Jerusalem Talmud's version of the "otherizing" of Elisha ben Abuya also indicates the extreme importance of certain essentials of rabbinic belief. The Jerusalem Talmud relates two stories in which Elisha lost faith that God rewards actions with their just rewards or punishments. In one story, Elisha saw a boy fall out of a tree as he was in the act of performing the mitzvah of returning a fallen egg to its nest. If God rewarded good and punished evil, certainly the boy would not have died while performing a righteous act! In the other story, Elisha saw the tongue of a great martyred Torah sage and no longer believed that the great righteous act of Torah study had just rewards.

Once Elisha lost his faith he stepped outside the Jewish system. And even though he remained physically in the Jewish community and continued to teach Rabbi Meir,[11] he was no longer part of the community in his own eyes, in the eyes of the community, or (according to the stories) in the eyes of God. Belief, then, at least in certain key precepts, was as crucial as the performance of the commandments. The Christian idea that belief in the savior is necessary for salvation should not seem so strange in the light of these Jewish traditions.[12] On the other hand, the notion of the advent and pervasiveness of original sin, so important in Paul and classical Christianity, finds little counterpart in Jewish thought.

The Philosophical "Image"

Another key difference between Christian and Jewish ideas developed as Christianity adopted the language of Greek philosophy. The New Testament, like the Hebrew Bible, considered the human being indivisible: a person was an indissoluble mix of body, mind, soul, and spirit. The image and likeness of God, therefore, referred to the whole package. The use of the metaphor of the impressions on a coin to express the idea of the image underscores the physical likeness of humans to God, and it is the body that bears this physical likeness. A tradition about Hillel makes the bodily nature of the image explicit. Hillel declared that he performed God's commandment in the act of going to the bathroom or bathhouse, for he was rendering his obligation to the body in the image (Avot de Rabbi Natan B 30). As Christianity became more hellenized, it began to adopt the Greek mind/body dichotomy, distinguishing between the "lower" and "higher" aspects of a human being. In this vein, Irenaeus locates the image of God in human rationality and freedom of will.[13] The "likeness" of God was the "robe of sanctity" the Holy Spirit gave Adam. This spirit was lost in the Fall and restored in redemption. In effect, Irenaeus sees the human being as triune, made up of body, soul, and spirit. The image is the rational soul, possessed by all; the likeness, possessed only by believers, is the spirit, a kind of added gift. The body does not figure in to this mode of thought at all.

The body undergoes an even greater fall in Gregory of Nyssa, who holds that only when one has ridded oneself of creaturely passions can one behold the image of the divine nature "in their own inner beauty." Rather than use the metaphor of impressing coins, he chooses the sculptor's technique of "lost wax," *cire perdu:* "For God has stamped the image of the good properties of his own essence in your makeup, as when a sculptor carves in wax the image of a sculpture he intends to cast."[14] Sin, which is congenital, overlays this image, and since our lives are permeated with passion, the image is permeated with evil. To Gregory, the cure lies in the precepts that the Lord taught, as in the Sermon on the Mount. The divine image is stamped on a virtuous life, the demonic on the sinful one, and one must strive to become pure by virtuous life so that the divine image can be formed in us by pure conduct. The divine image is thus an inner potential that we must attain.

The concern with governing the passions that was so prevalent in the Greco-Roman world is part of the reason that the body was eclipsed in classical Christian conceptions of the image of God. A quintessentially Greek notion, this concern also takes root in Judaism—for instance in the classic formulation "who is a hero: the one who conquers his urges"[15] and in the valorization of Joseph "the righteous" *(ha-tsadik)* for his resistance to the temptation of Potiphar's wife (Gen. 39). The worries about temptation, particularly sexual temptation, permeate Hellenistic Judaism and play their role in the elimination of women from Jewish public life.

The Anthropomorphic Dilemma

In Judaism, there is even a further reason for the interiorization and decorporalization of the "image and likeness of God." A physical understanding of "the image" limits God to the human form. The many powerful metaphors of God in human form—as a young warrior, an old sage, a loving mother—can create a mental "graven image" that can easily become idolatrous in its restriction of God to the human body. Religious unease with the depictions of God as human (what we call "anthropomorphisms") develops early in Jewish tradition, and the targums (the various Aramaic translations of the Bible) employ numerous circumlocutions to eradicate the human language with which God is depicted in the Hebrew Bible.

In Christianity, the presence of God on earth, incarnate in human flesh and form, would seem to finesse the anthropomorphic dilemma, for the incarnate God, who is the exact representation of God, provides a template in whose image the rest of humanity can be described. But the problem is only deflected, not eliminated. A corporeal sense of "image" could be understood to mean that this human-form existence constitutes the totality of the divine essence. Moreover, the historical Jesus was a male. Even more specifically, Jesus was a young, circumcised male. Might one deduce that humans of different ages, skin tones, gender, or foreskin are somehow less in the image of God? Christianity quickly made it clear that the age, skin tone, and foreskin of Jesus were historical circumstances, not essential parts of the image of God. Christianity, however, has had a harder time ridding itself of the notion that gender is more significant than age, and that women are somewhat less the divine image than men.

Perhaps because of this inherent problem of anthropomorphism and limitation in image language, the divine-like aspect of humanity has sometimes been expressed in other language, in terms, for instance, of the presence of sparks of divinity or of the Spirit (the *Shechinah*) within human beings. Another solution has been to interiorize the meaning of "image," as Gregory does, or to intellectualize it, to define the image of God in humanity as the human intellect. This interpretation ultimately derives from Greek philosophers, notably Plato and Aristotle, whose idea of God was intellect and who believed that the human intellect was the divine element in humans. Such conceptions came into both Judaism and Christianity with the growth of the philosophical traditions, espoused in Judaism by Maimonides (1135–1204) and in Christianity by Thomas Aquinas (c. 1225–1274). To Aquinas, the image was the intellect. All humans have a natural aptitude for understanding and knowing God; those who know God ("the just") have the image "by conformity of grace"; those who know and love God perfectly ("the blessed") have the image "by likeness of glory." In these different manifestations, the image can be faint, dim, or disfigured—or bright and beautiful. Maimonides shares both the identification of the image as intellect and its limitation to a few individuals, for only those people whose intellect is in its most perfect state are really the image of God.

A less philosophically driven but no less noncorporeal seat of the image is the "soul." Perhaps in reaction to the changing sense of "intellect" from the Renaissance on, John Calvin (1509–1564) speaks of the image in the soul, although the body still has some sparks, and at the final restoration the image will be restored to the body. More recent Christian thinkers have gotten away from ontological descriptions of the image. Karl Barth (1886–1968) defines humanity's relational quality, which he calls its "existence in confrontation," as the image of God. An individual's ability to have an I-thou relationship with others and with God is the essential meaning of "image of God." Furthermore, the creation of humanity as "male and female" allows for an I-thou confrontation between man and woman, and for the same kind of confrontation between man and God. Emil Brunner (1889–1966) argues on similar grounds that the "image" resides in relationship and responsibility and expresses the notion of a creature who can respond to a call of love with responsive love.[16]

Alongside these different interpretations of the image of God have come different understandings of the Christian concepts of "the Fall" and "original sin," so important to Paul and early Christian thinkers, so essential to Augustine, and so strange to Jewish ways of thinking. Aquinas places far less emphasis on the loss of the image in a fall than many earlier writers. Nevertheless, he, too, believes that human beings were deprived of something at the Fall: "the gift of supernatural grace" that helps us control our passions. To Irenaeus, it was the likeness-bearing spirit that was lost[17] By contrast, the Fall was far more significant to John Calvin, who considered fallen humanity to be depraved and afflicted with a perverted nature, a pessimistic view of humanity also held by Martin Luther. Calvin held that there are some remaining traces *(notas)* of the image of God, but it is frightfully deformed, and both reason and will have been weakened.

"Fall" language has become far less pervasive in modern Christian discourse. For more modern thinkers like Barth and Brunner, the Fall has ceased to be a historic fact. Human beings are the image of God, it is their nature. The image is essentially fixed, inherent, and cannot be lost.

The Image of God: An Evaluation

The image of God means many things to different Christians, as it does to different Jews. In more metaphysical circles, it depicts the relationship of the persons of the Trinity. In more mystical circles, it can point to an essential connection between humanity and God. In Jewish tradition it has sometimes been used to support the imperative for procreation to make more images. Today it is most often used to say something about human beings, though what exactly the image is used to say varies widely. At rock bottom, however, the notion that humans are created in the image of God forms the basis of a religious anthropology that stresses the God-like aspects of human existence. Even in the past, when the concept of "the image" was invoked in connection with the Fall in order to state that the image had been obscured, deprived, or depraved, it nevertheless expressed a belief that beyond all that, humans still have something special, that before matters deteriorated, humanity was God-like, and what we had once, we can have again.

We can no more pin down the exact nature of this God-like quality than we can pin down the nature of God. Often, the two depend on each other. Those who would define God as the World Intellect define the "image" as intellect; those who would define God as "love" locate the image in the human capacity to love; those who would define God as process or relationship define the image in the same way. Whatever God is, as God's image, humans share in the divine.

Three Important Aspects of the "Image"

The first appearance of image talk, in Genesis, has three key features that demonstrate the value of the concept of "image" despite its elusiveness and indeterminacy. First, humans are created through joint activity, as God interrupts the pattern of the creative word to state "we will make in our image." The use of the plural "we" indicates intentionality and cooperation in the creation of humanity, regardless of whether the "we" implies cooperation between the persons of the Trinity (as many Christians have suggested), among all the elements of the divine world (as some Jewish thinkers have said), or between God and the world (as other Jewish thinkers have offered). Whatever the precise interpretation, the plural nature of the creation of humanity applies both to the creator ("we") and to the creature ("he created them male and female"). Social relationship is an indispensable part of both human nature and human purpose, and there can be no utterly single human being.

The second aspect of the image that emerges from Genesis is that humans are given dominion over the rest of creation. Dominion is also part of human nature and purpose, for as the representative, or avatar, of God on earth, humanity cannot *not* be in charge. Whether we define our "dominion" as the right of conquest or the demand of stewardship, whether we embrace control or run from it, humans have power in and over the world. Everything we have done, from the day we invented our first tool, has modified and changed our environment. Humans have a major impact on the world. Deuteronomy expresses some of this human impact as it declares the dependence of fertility on God's reaction to human action (Deut. 11:13–17). Genesis 1 expresses our impact on the world by noting our God-like agency and dominion. Human dominion is part of the created order; we cannot escape it and should not ignore it or try to deny it. The language of the "image of God" can enable us to embrace the responsibility. It is not hubris to acknowledge that we have such power. On the contrary, admitting it and accepting it as our nature can help us assume responsibility and accountability for this undeniable facet of human existence.

A third aspect of the "image of God" emerges from the socially and legally oriented passage of Genesis 9, which expresses some of the fundamental aspects of humans living in society. This passage extends the God-like nature of human action depicted in Genesis 1. Genesis 1 alluded to the human impact on the earth; Genesis 9 speaks explicitly of human control of animals. This text grants humanity the right of life-or-death over animals. The primacy of human over animal life was already implicit in God's clothing Adam and Eve in animal skins, but Genesis 9 gives a stamp of approval to humanity's right to kill animals and also acknowledges humanity's carnivorous nature. It permits humanity's violence toward animals even as it sets controls by declaring blood inviolate. Genesis 9 also makes it clear that nobody, animals or humans, can kill a human being. Turning from the subject to the object of action (from what the image does to how the image should be treated), this command extends the implications of the concept of "image." Humans may be God-like in their right to kill animals, but not in their right to kill each other.

The Universality of the "Image"

An essential part of the "image of God" is that it is shared among all humans. Each human being lives among other humans, who are also the "image of God." Each human being has the right to be treated as a stand-in for God in all circumstances. Legal formulations, from Genesis 9 through rabbinic writings, have concerned themselves with the necessity of making this right concrete in a way that assures that human beings, God's representatives, are treated in a godly fashion. Human beings should not be murdered, says Genesis 9; they should not be executed, say Rabbi Akiba and Rabbi Tarphon; they should not be cursed, says James. Even Calvin, who emphasized the depraved and deformed nature of the fallen human being, nevertheless admonished people to look at the image of God in all humans, to look beyond their worthlessness and to see the image of God.

The essential importance of "image of God" is that it stands alone and eternal, independent of any qualities a human being might possess. Nobody can be more of the image of God than anyone else. There can be no moral qualification: no matter what kind of a life someone has led, no matter how much evil that person may manifest, he or she is no less an image of God than the greatest saint, and cannot be treated as any less God's image. There can also be no qualification or distinction among individual human beings according to class, race, gender, or age, and there can be no distinction between people on the basis of personal merit. The "image of God" is a universal quality of human beings, not limited to a few just or wise people.

There can also be no distinction among nations or other organizations. No group or nation is more the "image of God" than any other. It doesn't matter whether people are believers or nonbelievers in Christ and Christianity, whether people are part of Israel or the nations, whether people consider themselves the image of God or even deny that there is God or that there is any special worth to humanity. Nobody is "other" to the image of God, and no one can be treated in ways that do not recognize this divine quality. The "image of God" is an essential aspect of human nature, shared by all, and the treatment of all human beings must be mindful of this "imagehood." All people, without fail, are equally to be treated as one would treat God.

In practical terms, "imagehood" means that human beings can have dominion only over the earth and over animals. No person can have full dominion over another human being. This imperative has often been ignored in the past, as the subordination of individuals and of nations was claimed as the right of the powerful. But the idea of humanity as "image of God" makes no sense if it does not limit the ability of one human or one group of humans to exert their will over another. This is a bedrock concept in Judaism and Christianity.

Today, in an age of increasing respect for a diversity of cultures and social organization, this "image of God" view of human beings should set limits to how much we embrace and respect other mores. All human life is sacred. The genuine need for all of us to respect each other's culture should not induce us to accept the right of men to murder their wives, sisters, or daughters, as is done with horrifying frequency in Jordan, Saudi Arabia, Iran, and Afghanistan, to name only a few of the places in which such murders are culturally approved and even applauded. No amount of pluralism and tolerance should stop us from protesting the killing of widows or the more frequent burning of brides for dowries (as is happening in India) or the exposure of infant daughters (as in China). No ideas of social diversity and no euphemisms of "female circumcision" should make us ignore the suffering of women because of genital mutilation in parts of Africa. No belief in cultural autonomy should let us close our eyes to the use of genocide and mass rape as instruments of war or to the ongoing traffic in and possession of slaves. It is not cultural imperialism or Eurocentrism to protest such behaviors. Our concept of humanity as the image of God demands that we consider the worth of individual humans and act accordingly. There can be no distinctions between "lesser" or "greater" images of God, autonomous or subordinate, for if we begin to make such distinctions, then the notion of image becomes a meaningless bit of self-congratulation. It is our duty to recognize and respect the image of God in all people, whether they themselves accept such a concept or not.

From Image to Imitation

Acknowledging human dominion and its limits is not by itself adequate for a full religious anthropology. The concept of the "image of God" does not refer only to God's power and dominion. There are other aspects of God that the image of God should share. Human "images" have a responsibility to behave in God-like ways, to walk in God's path and imitate God's actions. *Imitatio dei*, the "imitation of God," is an integral part of *imago dei*, God's image; imitation enables the image actively to "image" God. Paul states this bluntly, exhorting the people to be imitators of God (Eph. 5:1) and to "be imitators of me as I am of Christ" (1 Cor. 11:1). He also has a specific example of what form such imitation should take: "forgive one another as God forgave and live a life of love as Christ loves us" (Eph. 5:2). This idea of *imitatio dei* is formulated just as bluntly by Abba Saul in the Mechilta: "Resemble Him! Just as He is gracious and merciful, so you should be gracious and merciful" (*Mechilta* Shirata 3 on Ex 15:2b). The Sifre to Deuteronomy also elaborates on this idea in a comment on the injunction "to go in his ways":

> As God is merciful, so you too be merciful. The Holy Blessed One is called "gracious," so you too be gracious . . . and give freely. God is called "righteous," so you too be righteous, God is called "devoted," you too be devoted, for thus it is written "all you call by my name will es-

cape" (Joel 3:5) and "all who are called by my name, I have created for my glory" (Is. 43:7).[18]

It is noteworthy that the idea of "imitation of God" always refers to those qualities of God that human beings most fervently desire. No one in either Jewish or Christian tradition has ever used the concept of "imitation of God" to counsel people to get angry and punish others, or to counsel people to insist that their commands be obeyed. "Imitation of God" never prescribes behavior that takes advantage of power and dominion. On the contrary, "imitation of God" always involves self-control, self-abnegation, and love of others. "Imitation of God" enumerates as God's behaviors those behaviors that we hold morally superior and beneficial to humanity, like love, forgiveness, and compassion.

In Genesis Rabbah, Rabbi Simlai finds textual proof that God performs many of the key "acts of loving-kindness" that rabbinic Judaism recommends:

> We have found that the Holy Blessed one blesses bridegrooms and adorns brides and visits the sick and buries the dead. Blesses bridegrooms, from "God blessed them" (Gen. 1:28), adorns brides ("God built upon his side," Gen. 2:22), visits the sick ("God appeared to him by the terebinth of Mamreh," Gen. 18:1), and buries the dead ("God buried him in the ravine," Deut. 32:6). R. Shmuel bar Nahman said, "even consoles the dead, for it is written 'God appeared to Jacob when he came from Padan-Aram and blessed him'" (Gen. 35:9).[19]

As historically conscious contemporary thinkers, we recognize that the rabbis project onto God the human traits that they consider most desirable, so that these traits can be reflected back as divine exemplars, as warrants and mandates for humans to act in this way. By projecting these traits onto God, Rabbi Simlai provides a divine template to encourage humans to behave in this way. The most elaborate Jewish expression of this concept of *imitatio dei* is by Moses Cordovero (1522–1570) in *Tomer Devorah*, in which he derives the requirements for compassion, tolerance, kindness, and right action from the attributes of God listed in Micah 7:18–20.

The notion of imitation of God seems circular, for our description of the Godly nature and behaviors that we are to imitate conforms to the pattern of behavior that we wish to encourage. Nevertheless, ascribing these patterns to God has great persuasive power, enabling those doing the describing to convince others that they should follow these patterns of behavior. We are imagining the God we are trying to image, and we seek to be the image of the God we imagine. Possibly, this circular rhetoric has far less persuasive impact upon those who understand the mechanism of projection involved here. Nevertheless, the concept of "imitating" or "imaging" God retains its importance, for believing that one is following in God's way enriches the experience of performing ethical actions. To the sense of rightness that the deed itself inspires, the notion of "imitation of God" adds a dimension of sacredness to the ethical act. Being mindful of the divine precedent makes one aware of acting as God's representative or image, increases one's awareness of the presence of God, and, traditional language would add, increases God's presence. Even after we become aware that we have no incontrovertible way of knowing that God acts in these ways, a philosophy of "the image of God actively imaging God" creates an awareness and presence of God. *Tomer Devorah* suggests that such active imaging has an even greater impact, for the performance of the actions has a theurgic effect, that is, it brings forth these behaviors in God.

Jews can appreciate the fact that the actions of the historical Jesus provide Christians with an accessible role model. From a Jewish perspective, the imitation of Christ, *Imitatio Christi*, is understandable, and Paul could be sure that his audience would understand him when he told them to imitate him as he imitated Christ. The somewhat controversial Christian question about right action—What would Jesus do? (WWJD)—brings the imitation of God down to earth in the simplest, most dramatically visible way, presenting an unadulterated role model whose behavior is wholly good (unlike the behavior of the characters of the Hebrew Bible). For many, WWJD is a two-edged sword, both simplifying matters for pedagogical and dramatic purposes and oversimplifying them, and in doing the latter, forgetting the transcendent qualities of Jesus and the special purpose of his life. Of course, not even the most literal proponents of WWJD would want the imitators of Christ to publicly humiliate their mothers or to call down the punitive power of the state against them, both things that Jesus did.

Much of the Christian discourse on these topics seems quite familiar to Jews, especially those Christian discussions that have moved beyond the concept of original sin and its impact. Even notions of the

Fall can be appreciated when they are taken as a metaphor for the deficiencies of the "fallen universe." The concepts of "image of God" and "imitation of God," particularly in their modern manifestations, present a sense of human nature, purpose, and destiny that can provide common ground for mutual understanding and mission. They provide a basis for understanding and appreciating the closeness of Judaism and Christianity, a basis that does not at the same time serve to "otherize" nonmonotheist religions. Unfortunately, this shared philosophy of the "image of God" is not often recognized. Christians speak of the image of God and the imitation of God as if these were uniquely Christian developments that derived directly from Genesis 1; Jews often speak of *tselem elohim* as an exclusively Jewish way of appreciating the dignity and sacredness of human life. It is important to realize the significance of these concepts in both Judaism and Christianity and the fact that the development of these concepts often took place with mutual cross-fertilization. Embracing a joint religious humanism should enable us to continue to enrich each other in an increasingly open and mutually inclusive way.

Tselem: Toward an Anthropopathic Theology of Image

DAVID R. BLUMENTHAL

The Problem: God's Image and God-Language

"If we are created in God's image *(tselem)*, what is God like?" Theologians and psychologists alike ask this question, but their answers couldn't be more different.

Secular psychologists, together with secular philosophers, say that we humans create God in our own image. They maintain that we confront the unforgiving reality of the universe and society and slowly realize that we simply cannot control the world in which we live. This impotence leaves us feeling angry. To compensate, we evolve a fantasy in which there is a good and powerful figure who rights the wrongs we cannot correct, who makes love triumph over hate, peace over war, and right over might. We are in dire need of this powerful and good figure because He (for some, She) brings lived reality back into balance, restoring our sense of proportion and, hence, our faith in the world and in ourselves. The name of Freud is most prominently associated with this analysis, but he is not the only psychologist or philosopher to have argued that God is a fantasy.[1]

By contrast, theologians say that it is we humans who are created in God's image, not the other way around. We do not create God; God creates us, as indeed the Genesis passages indicate.

Some theologians say that our personal and physical characteristics are the image of God in us—an approach that I shall call "anthropopathic," preferring this word, which suggests "having characteristics of the human personality," over "anthropomorphic," which suggests "having actual human form and shape." Anthropopathic theologians argue that it is not we who project ourselves onto God, but God Who projects Godself onto humanity. Put differently: Since personhood is the core of our being and since we are created in God's image, God must also have personhood. In anthropopathic theology, God has a Face and a real Personal Presence or Personality. To put it formally: Personhood, with its expression as face, presence, and personality, is God's, and we have that capacity because God has created us in God's image. This view has serious legal implications, not the least of which is that murder is an unforgivable offense and, even more, that it impossible to use execution as a punishment for any bodily or monetary crime. This view is also at the core of the disagreement over whether the death penalty is a fit punishment even for murder.

How do anthropopathic theologians arrive at a view of God's image so different from philosophers and psychologists like Freud? For anthropopathic theologians, there are two methods for answering the question about the relationship between God and God's image. First, we can examine Scripture to see how God describes Godself. To do this, we admit that Scripture represents the way God wishes to communicate with us and, hence, we induce from scriptural language what it is that God says God is. Second, we can find something deeply personal about ourselves as humanity and draw an analogy backward to

God. To do this, we examine human nature and choose certain human qualities. We then reason backward to say that God must possess these characteristics since we are in God's image. Either method is theologically acceptable, the one recognizing God's communication to us and the other following the inner logic of "in the image of." The results will be much the same.

There are, however, other theologians who wish to avoid anthropomorphism as much as possible. They look not to our personal and physical characteristics but to one or more of our inner capacities for the image of God in us: intelligence, spirituality, and/or morality. For this group, then, it is not personality or face but mind, soul, or spirit that is the aspect of God in us. Indeed, since intelligence, spirituality, and morality are core to our being and since we are created in God's image, God must also have these qualities. To put it formally: Intelligence, spirituality, and/or morality are God's, and we have those capacities because God has created us in God's image.

The issue of God's gender illustrates the conflict over God-language nicely: Do we refer to God as He or as She or in some more neutral way such as The Radiant One? Secular psychologists and philosophers say that gendered language is clearly a projection, that is, an attempt on our part to imagine into being a figure that is strong and kind, powerful and loving. Given the male–female stereotypes of our culture, the need for a strong and powerful figure leads toward a preference for He, whereas the need for a kind and loving figure leads toward a preference for She. To achieve both, according to these thinkers, one needs either two entities who participate in the divine or a single entity with both capacities. Thus, many Christians understand Jesus as an intercessory, loving figure contrasted with the sterner figure of God; and in Catholic tradition, Mary represents a further extension of the loving figure in intercession with the more demanding Father-Son. Jews, by contrast, say that the one God is both loving and just. Either way, for the secularists, God Godself is neither He nor She, if there is a God at all.

There are some psychologists and philosophers who say that one can best refer to God as the Power or Force or Energy behind the universe. Such designations are rooted in what Freud called the "oceanic feeling" for what lies beyond physical reality as we know it. This view is close to many eastern understandings of the divine. These psychologists and philosophers favor neutral, nongendered terminology for God.

Theologians who tend toward de-anthropomorphization and certain abstract mystical conceptions of God agree with the psychologists and philosophers who acknowledge God as the Power behind and beyond the universe. They, too, favor neutral, nongendered terminology for God. In contemporary Jewish practice, this neutrality is well illustrated by the series of prayer books published recently by the Reconstructionist movement in American Judaism.[2] These books use a stunning series of words for God, most of which catch the ineffable yet transcendent quality of holy being, without implying gender or, for the most part, personhood: The Faithful One, The Radiant One, The Eternal One, The Abundant One, The Veiled One, and so on.

However, theologians who favor anthropopathic language must, in some way, opt for He and/or She, for gender is quintessentially human. Maleness and femaleness are part of our being. Since we are created in the image of God, God, too, must have gender. "How does one write a liturgy that accommodates both human genders?" you may ask. This is a serious question for anthropopathic theologians. Some alternate exclusive male-gendered with exclusive female-gendered liturgy. Others use inclusive language, alternating gender by paragraph or by sentence and adding references to matriarchs as well as patriarchs. Still others use single-gendered liturgy but think double-gendered. No matter what the practical solution, the option for gendered language is rooted in the theology of image in its anthropopathic sense.

Positive Anthropopathic Attributes

My own inclination, rooted in the biblical and rabbinic tradition, and following Abraham Joshua Heschel's "theology of pathos," is toward the anthropopathic approach.[3] So, I must ask the questions: "If we are created in God's image, what is God like? What personality characteristics does God have, reasoning from those that humans have, and judging from the way God describes Godself in Scripture?" I would say God has the following six positive personal characteristics.[4]

First, God must be fair.   In American English, the word "just" is too strong, for it conjures up the stereotype of a God of law who punishes severely, except insofar as God's mercy overrules the strict requirement of the law. It conjures up, too, the person compulsively pursuing the letter of the law, ignoring the spirit thereof. "Fairness" has just the right connotation in American English. God must act fairly, appropriately punishing the wicked, including ourselves, and appropriately rewarding the faithful, including our enemies. Traditional texts support the teaching of God's fairness, and hence, God's commitment to moral dialogue. For morality is an integral part of all personality; it is integral to the being of God and, then, to God's creation.

Second, God addresses, and can be addressed by, humankind. Although God is totally autonomous, God is in contact with humanity. God can be angered, or pleased, by what humans do. Ultimately, this means that God can be induced by human words and behavior to change God's mind, to reverse a decision, to alter a judgment. This insight is sometimes formulated as "the efficacy of prayer" or "original repentance."

Because creation is morally neutral, there is no "natural moral law." Hence, God addressed humankind to give it guidance. God's presence continues to draw humanity onto the path God wishes. Furthermore, God's guidance causes humans anguish, joy, guilt, and satisfaction.

This com-munication, this mutual addressing of one another, is central to the dialogic nature of creation-revelation-piety. It constitutes the interrelatedness of humankind and God.

Third, God is powerful but not perfect. God makes mistakes and admits it, as after the flood of Noah (Gen. 8:21–2). God can be seduced by Satan, as in the prologue of Job. God is unnecessarily short-tempered with the Jewish people,[5] and God repents.[6] Some argue that all such incidents are just a testing of humankind, but that does not seem to be the simpler meaning of the texts. Zoharic and Lurianic mysticism, too, left room for God's imperfection.[7]

God, however, does have power. God's power is absolute, but God cannot use it absolutely. For, having created a being also capable of moral judgment, God must limit God's own power so as to empower the being God created. Humankind, too, thus has power, though not as much as God. Power is dialectical. It is the interrelatedness of God's and humankind's expectations.

Fourth, God is loving. There are many ways to love. There is erotic love, virtuous love, and parental love. Love can be unilateral or dialogic. Sometimes love is sacrificial; sometimes it is commanding, imperial. Love can be open, articulated clearly; love can be hidden. Love is a glance into another's eyes, the embrace of a child, the gratitude of an elderly person not forgotten. Love is the affirmation of the other, given and received in wholeness. And forgiveness. Love is the presence of moral truth and goodness. Love is commitment to lead a life dedicated to truth and goodness. It is stubborn perseverance on the way, no matter what the temptation. Love does not tolerate injustice; it impels one to action. Love frustrates; it causes deep anger. How does one love one's parent without superimposing that image on the child? How does one love one's child who rebels forcefully? Love is exclusive, dedicated to special persons in special ways. And love is in-clusive, reaching from one to an-other, seeking to embrace the stranger. Love is not monolithic. It cannot be rationalized into a co-herent whole, into a system or a single theology. Love is much more complex than its metaphors.

God loves all humanity, and individual human beings, in all these ways—just as human beings love others and seek to be loved in all these ways. Human beings touch the text of God's love and of human love. We enter it. We read it and ponder it. And it touches us, perme-ates us, puzzles and pains us, gives us life and demands death. Love, in all its complexity, makes us blossom and become that which we are destined to be.

Fifth, God gets angry.   There is anger that is righteous indignation in the face of moral iniquity. This is God's anger spoken by the prophets and the prophets' anger spoken on behalf of God: "Shall one steal, kill, fornicate, swear falsely, make offerings to Baal, and follow other gods whom you do not even know; and then come and stand before Me, in this house upon which My Name is called, and say 'We are saved,' only to go and do again those abominations?!" (Jer. 7:9–10).

There is also an anger that flows from bitterness. God creates hu-mankind, and humanity turns rotten, "the instincts of the heart of hu-manity being evil from its earliest days" (Gen. 8:21). God brings the Jewish people out of Egypt with signs and wonders, and they rebel again and again, and God punishes them.[8] The people also get angry. Rooted in the mutuality of covenant,[9] they experience righteous in-dignation toward God.[10] They also respond in bitterness.[11]

There is nothing wrong with these kinds of anger. If one loves pas-sionately, zealously, one expects great things. God loves humanity, and humanity loves God. The anger of righteous indignation and the anger of bitterness and vengeance have their place.

Sixth, God chooses; God is partisan. No one likes to hear this, but God chooses and, having chosen, God jealously guards that which is God's; and God demands loyalty from those whom God chooses.

God chose to create the world. It is God's possession. For exactly that reason, no one may abuse it or lay absolute claim to it. God chose the Jewish people. They, too, in their flesh, are God's possession; they belong to God. For exactly that reason, no one may abuse them or lay claim to absolute authority over them. God chose the holy land. God resides in it. God's people reside in it. For exactly that reason, no one may abuse the land or the people's right to it. The people must respect God's land because the land is theirs, from God.

The election of the Jews was always a scandal. How could a universal God elect one people from among the myriads of creation? But, if God has personality, of course God has preferences. Personality means having a character and a history, and character and history mean having preferences. One need not always act on one's preferences. And one must always carefully consider one's preferences and the consequences of acting on them. But preference is the core of personality. Therefore, the scandal of particularity is the core of anthropopathic theology.[12]

In addition to these six anthropopathic attributes, God's personality, like ours, contains holiness, sacredness.[13]

Negative Anthropopathic Attributes

But does God's personality not also have "negative" characteristics? Reasoning from the human image and judging from God's own language about Godself in Scripture, one can argue that God indeed does have negative characteristics. We are hesitant, suspicious, selfish, impulsive, impatient, demanding, and rigid. Sometimes, we are even punitive and irrational. As noted above, God makes mistakes and admits it. God also gets angry at God's stiff-necked people and acts punitively against them. Further, God's preference for God's people is irrational.

In the period after the shoah,[14] Jews have asked themselves, "How can God have allowed the shoah to happen?" The usual answers to this question are as follows:[15] (1) God did not let it happen but gave humans free will, and humans caused it; this answer denies God's providential action in history during the shoah. (2) God was in eclipse or hiding God's Face; this answer is a good metaphor, but it dodges the question. (3) God's ways are not our ways, and hence we cannot know why God allowed the shoah; this answer, too, evades the question. And so on. It seems to me better to assert the shoah for what it was, to affirm God's ongoing presence in history, and then to seek an answer as best we can. I have, therefore, argued that the shoah was an act of abuse, that is, that it was a punitive action against the Jews that they did not deserve. Abuse is punishment that does not fit the crime. The Jewish people, I and most others maintain, did not deserve the shoah; hence, it was an act of abuse. God is not the only abuser, to be sure; humans effectuated the shoah. But God is co-responsible and, hence, an Abuser. This means that God's personality also has this irrational, one might even say evil, side to it.[16] The study of the history of God's action and inaction in our time support this conclusion; Scripture, too, has many passages in this vein.[17]

What is the proper response to the abusive dimension of God's personality? Drawing on the long tradition of protest, I have argued that challenging God, protesting God's wrong behavior, is the proper response. Basing myself on ample precedent within the Jewish tradition, I have called for thinking the truth and praying the truth to God. This approach, rooted as it is in the moral mutuality of covenant, is, to my mind, the only redeeming move left to us.[18]

This move, however, is not enough; we must also take constructive steps to resist evil and to bind ourselves to community:[19] To have faith in God in a post-holocaust, abuse-sensitive world, we must: (1) acknowledge the awful truth of God's abusing behavior; (2) adopt a theology of protest and sustained suspicion; and (3) develop the religious affections of distrust and unrelenting challenge. And yet we will also: (4) engage the process of re-new-ed spiritual healing with all that entails of confrontation, mourning, and empowerment; (5) resist all evil mightily, supporting resistance to abuse wherever it is found; (6) open ourselves to the good side of God, painful though that is; and (7) we will turn to address God, face to Face, presence to Presence.

Healing from the shoah, like all healing from abuse, is a very complicated process.[20]

Taking *Tselem* Seriously

I will not pretend to be happy with this theology, though I do think that my own faith is deeper for it.[21] Resistance comes from many directions.[22] If we are to take the image of God seriously, however, we must learn to think of the "negative" as well as the "positive" dimensions of God's being. That is what "image" means. We must, it seems to me, consider that most persons reach the point of realizing that their parents are (or were) not perfect, perhaps that they are (or were) not even really good, really loving. Some touch this realization and shy away from it as quickly as possible. Most come to it and go on to consider in what ways their parents are (or were) also good. This is called "maturity," "growing up." The same is true of our relationship with God. Human beings do not need to have a perfect God. Rather, humans need to have a realistic view of, and appreciation for, God. Then, and only then, can human beings arrange their patterns of relatedness to God. One can accept the good and the evil, praising where fitting and protesting where appropriate. One can alternate between love and challenge, between acceptance and protest. Just as having a mature understanding of one's parents enables one to become a more mature person, so having a mature understanding of God enables one to become a more mature servant.[23]

The Doctrine of the Incarnation

When I teach Introduction to Judaism, I include early Christian thinking, and I have always found that the doctrine of the incarnation is not hard to explain, once one acknowledges the anthropopathic nature of God. If we are created in God's image, as Scripture says, then nothing human is alien to God. The idea that God might want to actually em-body God's image is only a few steps beyond the idea that God revealed God's will in some concrete way, or beyond the concept of God manifesting Godself in a vision or theophany.

One way to better understand the anthropopathic dimension of God's being, then, is to contemplate the idea of the incarnation of God as taught in Christianity. I often ask the following question of Christians and Jews: "What did God learn when, according to Christianity, God became incarnate? What quintessentially human experiences enlarged God's mind and heart when God became a human body and lived among us?" There is no correct answer to this question; still, some responses are intriguing.

God learned about sin and temptation. Prior to being incarnated, God probably had only an intellectual understanding of just how deep the feeling of sin goes. God probably underestimated the compulsive power of sin, for sin is just that—a compulsive need to do that which we know is wrong. Sin arises from rebellion and from addiction. God learned about this when God became human.

God also learned about fear. The divine fears nothing, but humans fear many things. We fear pain. We fear loneliness. Sometimes we fear things of which we are not even conscious. And we fear death, the stoppage of all life and connection. God did not know these things until God took on a body and came among us.

Finally, God knows two kinds of love: grace that is unconditional and not related to our deeds, and compassion that is linked to what we do. (Mercy, which is a forgiving of our sins and sinfulness, is motivated by compassion and/or by grace.) But God's love in all its forms is infinite. When God became incarnate, God learned the limits of love. God learned how hard it is to love even those who love us, much less those who hate us. God learned that humans are sometimes justifiably motivated by justice or even hate, and that we often have things to do other than love one another.

The doctrine of the incarnation is, thus, not beyond the Jewish theological imagination. It can be seen as an extension of the anthropopathic understanding of God. Thinking about it could help Jews, and Christians, understand the theology of the image of God in which we are created.

However, Jews cannot accept the doctrine of the incarnation for several reasons: First, it is too anthropomorphic. It is one thing to say that God has anthropopathic qualities, characteristics that we think of as human, and quite another to say that God has (or had) an actual body. The biblical, rabbinic, and mystical traditions resist this anthropomorphization of God even though they accept bodily terms as metaphorically descriptive of God. The prohibition against imaging God extends, in all these Jewish traditions, to giving God a real body, though not to giving God a mind-bound body.

Second, the doctrine of the incarnation is inescapably linked to other Christian doctrines: to the suffering of the incarnate God, to his death on the cross, and to the atoning power of that death for those who participate in it through faith. Jewish tradition, in the main, rejects the doctrine of redemption through suffering and, again in its mainstream, rejects the idea of vicarious atonement. Furthermore, Judaism rejects the fact of the specific incarnation of God in Jesus of Nazareth because of the unfulfilled messianic claims made on his behalf by Christian tradition.

Finally, the bloody history of Christian–Jewish relations over two millennia does not allow the traditional Jew to identify with a doctrine that is specifically Christian, even if it were otherwise true. Christianity has simply been too cruel to Jews and Judaism, even if, in very recent times, some Christians have taken a different attitude toward us. "How can one sing the songs of the Lord on alien soil?" It would be a betrayal of all our ancestors to do so. It would render the death of thousands of martyrs an act of futility. Rather: "Good fences make good neighbors."

All this having been said, Christians and Jews have much to learn from one another in taking *tselem* seriously—not only ethically but also spiritually and intellectually. Exploring together the positive and negative attributes of God using all we know of Scripture and of human nature will enrich our knowledge of ourselves and of the God in Whose image we are created.

The Image of God in Christian Faith: Vocation, Dignity, and Redemption

WILLIAM SCHWEIKER

In her essay on "The Image," Tikva Frymer-Kensky helpfully isolates features of Jewish and Christian ideas about human existence. She observes that Jews and Christians often discover each other's worship and faith difficult to comprehend. Crosses, icons, and the doctrine of the trinity disorient (maybe offend) Jews; Torah scrolls, the "Western Wall," and legal traditions are difficult (maybe impossible) for Christians to grasp. Of course, as a Christian, I frequently find the piety of fellow Christians confusing. There is little room in my Protestant sensibilities for Roman Catholic veneration of the Virgin Mary or Eastern Orthodox icons. And even within Protestantism, there are forms of faith—fundamentalist or charismatic—that are strange, even vicious, to me. I recognize these as fellow Christians, yet certain beliefs and practices do not resonate. I suspect that the same diversity is found among Jews. Understanding others is difficult, indeed. Difficult too is the task of explaining one's own piety.

Although understanding is hard to attain, Professor Frymer-Kensky is absolutely right that convictions about the sanctity of human life provide common ground for Jews and Christians in their many forms. The crucial insight of these traditions is this: faith in the living God enables an apprehension of inviolable worth that enlivens passionate responsibility for the created world and all people. The image of God, in other words, signifies human dignity, moral calling, and our truest good. Given this, I heartily endorse a religious humanism aimed at respecting and enhancing the integrity of life. The intellectual task is to specify this common agenda in a way consistent with the faith and life of distinct communities and traditions—a task including the criticism of all malice.

In what follows I seek to unfold a Christian conception of the image of God and its contribution to a religiously humanistic outlook. I want to show how beliefs about creation back an idea of "the image" in vocation, how Christians think about "soul" as the image, and, finally, how redemption and the redeemer relate to the image of God. Christians, like Jews, have a nuanced understanding of the "image" that touches all human existence: our actions, the depths of the self, and the religious and moral need for reconciliation with the living God as the ultimate good. That said, I want to begin with basic questions important for thinking about human existence.

Basic Questions

The image of God entails an account of human existence and dignity. What kind of anthropology is embedded in that idea? Christians and Jews believe that what it means to be human is intrinsically related to the divine. Convictions about who God is and God's relation to the world are the core of self-understanding. Christians have a complex idea of the divine—both in terms of God's activity (creature, redeemer, sustainer, even slayer) and in terms of divine being (God is triune)—and this idea influences Christian conceptions of the religious anthropology contained in the notion of the image of God.

Augustine, in his *Confessions*, was the first to argue that when considering human beings, one needs to address two questions: "Who am

I?" and "What am I?" The first question is directed by persons at themselves and is answered by an account of one's deeds and of the relations one has with others. I shape and express my identity through stories and accounts I give of my actions and encounters. These stories and accounts do not, however, provide a complete answer to the question "Who am I?" For Christians, one's identity is most decisively shaped in response to Jesus' question: "Who do you say I am?" (Mt. 16:15). A "Christian" is a follower of Christ; my identity is ascribed to me in relation to a response of faith. This is in fact the meaning of baptism. "Who I am," religiously speaking, is enacted by a confessional response to the Christ in the whole of life.

If we ask, following the psalmist, "What is man that thou are mindful of him?" (Ps. 8:4) then reference is made not to *who* humans are, but to *what* they are, or to who "made" them. As Tikva Frymer-Kensky notes "the notion that humans are created in the image of God forms the basis of a religious anthropology that stresses the God-like aspects of human existence." And further, "All people, without fail, are equally to be treated as one would treat God." To be sure, contemporary people usually assume that religious ideas (God, image) are projections aimed at furthering social or psychological purposes. That judgment ought not to blind us to a truth. For Christians as well as Jews the ascription of identity ("who" I am) is set within wider claims about "what" human beings are in relation to the deity. The confession that Jesus is the Christ is intelligible only given convictions about the living, sovereign, creating God. I share a common humanity and dignity with all other persons, but I do so with a distinctly Christian self-understanding of who I am.

The relation between being (what I am) and identity (who I am) is important for a viable Christian humanism. It enables one to affirm shared humanity with respect to distinctively Christian beliefs. Let me now turn to the themes of vocation, dignity, and redemption in order to unfold a Christian account of the image of God and its meaning for today.

Vocation: Dominion and Service

Christians look to scripture for insight into God's will and way and thus into the meaning and purpose of existence. The texts that have dominated thought about the *imago dei* have been the creation accounts in Genesis 1–2. The difficulty, as Michael Welker argues, is that each account bespeaks problems and possibilities. In Genesis 1, the image seems keyed to the domination and subduing of the earth. This view relies on ancient conceptions of kingship and divine mandates that may in our age back ecological crises.[1] Yet despite themes of domination, the same account surprisingly accords equality between the sexes. Genesis 1 is an aid to thinking beyond patriarchal accounts of the human. Theologians like Karl Barth and Jürgen Moltmann fasten on relationality (male/female) as basic to the *imago dei*.[2] Sexual difference is to correspond to the divine image. Genesis 1 is a boon for human relations but a bust for nature.

If we turn to Genesis 2, again as Welker notes, the inverse is the case. In the so-called "J" account, "woman" is taken from the rib of man, and yet Adam and Eve are given the mandate to till *(abd)* and keep *(smr)* the garden. This picture of service aids in thinking about the vocation of humans in relation to the natural world, but it has been roundly criticized as endorsing sexism. Feminist theologians like Rosemary Radford Reuther bemoan the painful legacy of this text, which has been used to cast women as derivative males.[3] Again, the text is a boon and bust for understanding the image of God, and yet, oddly enough, for the very opposite reason as Genesis 1. In Genesis 2 nature is cared for but women are subjected! Could it be that Christians and Jews cannot untangle coherently the question of human embodied relations from responsibility for the natural world? Are these traditions morally at cross-purposes with each other?

We need to be honest—even repentant—about this problem. For much of Christian history the vocation of man has been defined in terms of the mandate to subdue the earth and to be the head of woman. This legacy extends beyond Genesis into the New Testament (cf., Eph. 5:22–23; Col. 3:18; 1 Pet. 3:1). Of course, Christians note that these passages speak of the husband's loving duty to his wife. There is also a tradition within Christianity of stewardship of God's gifts, including nature. Nevertheless, as usually interpreted, the image of God has a paradoxical meaning that cuts through embodied existence and ecological relations. Clearly, this paradoxical image as we find it in Genesis 1–2 manifests in a pointed way the myriad forms of human fault and sin. But does the image say anything else?

It is important to take another look at the texts bracketing preconceptions of "rule" and "subdue." When one does so, it becomes clear that the "image of God" in Genesis and also in the New Testament articulates a picture of human existence in terms of the differentiated activity of God. God's acts of commanding dominion and creating sexual difference are linked in these accounts to blessing. God blesses an engendered humanity (Gen. 1:27), and this blessing—also pronounced on the Sabbath (Gen. 2:3)!—is manifest in Genesis 1:28 in terms of fecundity ("Be fruitful and multiply") and "dominion" ("replenish the earth and subdue it"). In bringing forth life and tending to life, human beings—as male and female—imitate God's primal blessing on existence, the endorsement of its "goodness." The reality they care for and help to create is complex—light and dark (cosmic), time sequences ("days"), fish and foul (sentient beings), vegetation (what bears seed). Man and woman subdue the earth, but they have "dominion" over other living beings. This suggests tilling and also caring lordship for creatures, a vision close to Genesis 2:15. As part of God's creation, all living things have worth ("And God saw that it was good"), but human beings have a special calling or responsibility and thus dignity. To be the image of God is in part to imitate God's activity as creator and sovereign who blesses—not destroys or exploits—created reality.

This idea seems to be the force of Jesus' teaching as well. Matthew 5:45 (part of the so-called Sermon on the Mount) speaks about how God acts in the universe by continual creation. God dispenses justice and mercy throughout creation: the sun and the rain are given to all, the righteous and the unrighteous alike. Christians link a belief about God's action in creation with the redemption of evil by goodness. The moral task of life, one's vocation as the very image of God, is to imitate God's action in creation (dominion but also blessing, to all). For Christians, this vocation finds focus in the imitation of Christ, an idea far richer than popular beliefs about WWJD (What would Jesus do?)! To imitate the dominion and blessing of God by following Christ is an answer to the forms of fault and sin that beset the earth and human life.

Let me now shift from activity and vocation to the human self, the "soul." Here, too, the human relation to the divine is revealed. But this is a point at which classical Hellenistic philosophy, and not only the biblical text, has informed Christian faith.

Dignity: Soul and Trinity

Christians look to scripture to understand the image of God. Yet we also hold beliefs about the human person as a "place" where God's image is manifest. This belief undergirds the respect owed all people. But the image of God has never been a matter of reading off empirical data about Homo sapiens. As Frymer-Kensky notes, even among Jews who insist on the corporeal nature of the "image" there is the need to avoid idolatry. What she calls the "decorporalization of the image" in Christian faith is due not only to Greek philosophy; it is also consistent with monotheistic belief and human dignity. God is not reducible to our "image" of deity. Human dignity defined in relation to the one Holy God is never to be equated with physical, political, or economic utility. Christians make this point by insisting that the internal complexity of the self resonates with the being of God as creator, sustainer, and redeemer, that is, as "triune."

Traditionally, the term "soul" designates the human capacity of thought and self-directed action. The soul is human nature (what I am) in activity and self-awareness (who I am). The idea of the soul has been the subject of debates among Christians in ways important for the *imago dei*. One debate is whether the soul is eternal or whether it is created good but finite; the other is whether the image of the triune God has a vestige in the human or not. These debates represent the creative and unique tension between biblical and philosophical outlooks in Christian conviction, and to understand the image of God we have to understand the biblical *and* Hellenistic, hence cross-cultural, character of Christian convictions about dignity.[4]

Recall some of the convictions about human beings that we find in Genesis 2–3: (1) with the breath of life, the human being becomes a "living soul"; (2) "Adam"—as undifferentiated humanity—is given the power to "name" other living creatures, or, in other words, human beings inhabit earth in and through cultural, meaning systems; (3) created finite and without knowledge of good and evil, the "fall" of humanity is a fall into self-knowledge ("and they saw they were naked") and a banishment from unending life (Gen 3:22). Christian claims about dignity that develop from these convictions are similar to claims about vocation: humans are created good (a living soul), empowered to participate in God's ongoing creative activity (to name other beings), and, due to sin, in need of redemption. "Original sin," while it might offend a Jewish sense of justice, is really meant to denote the ubiquity of human fault that strikes to the core of our created goodness and unique dignity. The human heart seems incapable of redeeming itself.

Some of the same troubles we encountered with vocation also befuddle this account of the image. The "fall" has too often been blamed on Eve—that is, on women—and the perpetuation of human sin is too often linked to sexual transmission (so-called "original sin"), which further subjugates woman to man (Gen. 3:16). The distinctly human activity of naming, or cultural production, has led to the widely held anthropocentric belief that somehow only human beings have intrinsic worth.

Biblically speaking, the center of personality is the "heart" and not an eternal soul whose goodness is unerring. The human being becomes a living "soul" (Gen. 2:7) when a divine source of life is breathed into dust. The soul comes directly from God (Gen. 24:14). When the human dies, the soul is "dead" (Num. 23:10, 24:14). Jesus, in the Sermon on the Mount, also rejects Greek ideas about an eternal soul (Mt. 6:21–23). The soul is part of creation; it can fail or become dark and thus is not the unerring inner light of Greek thought. The soul is also not, as it was for the Stoics, refined matter and part of the great world-reason. For Jesus the "soul" is not immortal; it is not, as it was for Plato and others, trapped in the prison of the body.

Jesus' views of the soul are continued in St. Paul's writings. Paul does distinguish flesh (Greek: *sarx*) and spirit *(pneuma)*, but this distinction is not the Platonic contrast of body and soul. Rather, for Paul the contrast is between the whole person, as flesh and spirit, and the person who is alienated from God, and thus not whole. The goal is not to release an eternal soul to eternity but to overcome alienation between oneself and God. For Christians who accept this strictly biblical account of "soul," the problem of "death" is really about spiritual death. One can be alive physically but spiritually dead. Salvation is about a spiritual renewal and the perfection of creation.

Despite this biblical understanding of a finite soul, many Christians hold to the idea of an eternal soul. From Origen in ancient Alexandria to Gregory of Nyssa and Augustine and even to recent thinkers, the "soul" *(pysche)* has been described as "spirit" *(nous)* and mind *(mens)* that participates in divine wisdom. This idea had wide currency in Hellenistic culture. Plato, for example, understands the soul as a mixture of reason *(logoistikon)*, heart *(thumeides)*, and desire *(epithumatikon)*, that is, as a mixture of the changeable and the unchangeable. Ancient theologians give this tripartite conception a distinctly Christian cast. For Augustine, human beings are creatures of loves or desires, and the soul is composed of memory, understanding, and will. In Christian fashion the soul is thus an image of the divine Trinity, the so-called *vestigum trinitatis*. This view might suggest that one need look only within the self to discover God. Concerned with a slide into anthropomorphism, some Christians reject the idea of an imprint of the Trinity in the soul. However, those who insist on the *vestigum trinitatis* see it as a bulwark of human worth and dignity. Every human being bears the image of the living God in the depth of her or his existence.

Whether Christians conceive of the soul as a finite "heart" or as something eternal, the idea has practical force. Christians, like Jews, worry more about the denial of God in actual life, about living as if justice, love, and righteousness do not matter, than about verbal or speculative denials of God. Practical atheism is genuine sin and also a denial of our very humanity. Ideas about the soul help us avoid this sin by situating human existence inescapably before God.

Christians understand the image as dignity in terms of the triune being of God. The idea of a triune God is no doubt the most opaque of Christian beliefs. For a Christian, the one, holy God is livingly complex: God's very being is relational and is the source of "what I am," that is, a being created with inviolable dignity. The confession of the triune God shapes Christian self-understanding. It also clarifies the human dilemma, Christianly defined. As finite and relational creatures, we can fall away from or rebel against the divine in whose image we exist; the light can go dark; the heart can betray its maker and redeemer. We can deny God in our actions and relations. This fall happens when the sustaining relations of life are demeaned and destroyed. In this way the "image" is distorted, and terribly so.

Cast in these terms, redemption, to which I turn next, is an internal revolution or reformation of the person, healing the complexity of relations that constitute life. As Paul puts it, "be transformed by the renewal of your mind (*nous!*) so that you might prove what is good, acceptable, and perfect" (Rom. 12:2). The renewal of the person is the ground for action imitative of the divine. The conception of the image of God as triune moves in a pattern of thought, a logic of faith, from being to activity (dignity to service), just as the image as vocation traces the connection the other way, from activity to being (imitation to image).

Redemption: Dignity and Service in Christ

Christians conceive of the image in terms of God's activity in creation; since God is just, that activity is paradigmatically redemptive. Caring dominion and the fecundity of creation are thus to be set within the act of divine blessing. The implications of this outlook for sexual and ecological relations are far reaching indeed. Frymer-Kensky has noted some of them; I agree with her judgments but would add that for Christians the image also implies the dignity of the human person as a sign of the triune or relational being of God. Christians believe that the fullness of human life can never be achieved if we deny this link between human dignity and God's being, that is, if we deny the source and constitutive nature of the relations that sustain us; and yet, this denial is a fact of our world.

Human beings are created good, able to participate responsibly in God's life, and yet due to sin are in need of redemption. Redemption is new life that overcomes the spiritual death that besets human existence. Redemption is not the polishing up of a soiled eternal soul; it is not the success of the ultimate social justice program. Redemption is the triumph of life over death. For Christians, this triumph has a name: Jesus Christ. In this very specific sense one can, following St. Paul, speak of Christ as the "image of the invisible God" (Col. 1:15; 2 Cor. 4:4). Christ is the second Adam. In him the invisible being and the creative, just, and merciful activity of God are manifest in ways consistent with the created image of God.

In Christ's actions of healing and feeding, divine love (abundant care) is manifest amid a violent, unjust world. Jesus beckons one to participate responsibly in God's reign now, to take up anew the vocation instituted in creation. Christians labor to do so through the church. But Christians are called not only to take up this vocation but also to confess that the resurrection is the vindication of Jesus' action, the triumph of a new life in which God overcomes evil through goodness. When Christians confess that Jesus is the Christ, they understand that they are to enact the *imitatio Dei* in and through the *imitatio Christi*.[5] To imitate Christ is to respond to the dignity of persons despite their brokenness and vulnerability.

This account of the "image of God" bridges shared convictions among Jews and Christians (God as one, holy, just, creative) as well as expresses distinctly Christian beliefs (God as triune; Jesus as Christ). It is of course with respect to Christ that matters of identity enter most forcefully. Questions of personal identity and of how that identity "images" God are bound for any Christian to a confessional response that Jesus is the Christ. Of course, beliefs about Christ and redemption are fantastically complex. They cannot be addressed fully in

a short essay. But we can at least say this much: as teacher and redeemer, Christ is confessed by all Christians to be the forerunner of
new life, the source of new creation. Christian self-understanding,
resting as it does on the call to imitate Christ, is then a distinctive way
of being human before the God of all reality. This is the profound humanism of Christian faith.

The Image Today

The idea of the "image" speaks powerfully to contemporary concerns.
Currently, personal and social existence, and so too the sad legacy of
Christian relations to Jews, continues to be driven by consumption
not blessing, by the violation of persons not the celebration of their
dignity, by the machination of death not the fostering of life. Written
into the very fabric of existence is both a hunger for and a denial of
life. Enlivened by the sanctity of human existence, faithful people
everywhere, especially Jews and Christians, have a mission to expose
this paradox and to bless, dignify, and transform life. By living that
mission maybe we can enact the image of God in distinctive ways.

EPILOGUE:
CONCLUDING VISIONS

Where do we go from here? The editors invited George Lindbeck, one of the foremost Christian theologians devoted to fostering Jewish–Christian dialogue, to offer his response to this volume. Professor Lindbeck's insights, with which this epilogue begins, serve as the stimulus for our own thoughts about the promises and challenges of this new era of Jewish–Christian relations.

What of the Future?
A Christian Response

GEORGE LINDBECK

In parts of this book, Christians display new attitudes toward Judaism. What is the future of these attitudes? Will they spread and endure, or will they weaken and perhaps disappear as guilt-inducing memories such as those of the Holocaust fade away? Isn't anti-Judaism part of Christianity's DNA, undetachable from what have historically been the major sources of its vitality and identity? These are questions that call for a Christian response.

A Proposal

The answers I propose depend on whether supersessionism, the belief that the church replaces Israel, can be eliminated even as the understanding of the church as Israel is regained. Both developments are necessary. Eliminating supersessionism severs the taproot of Christian anti-Judaism, but if that is all that happens, modern Christianity becomes even more detached than it already is from the Old Testament portion of its heritage. That heritage can flourish without anti-Judaism, so my argument goes, only if the premodern understanding of the church as in some sense Israel is retrieved and joined with the long-forgotten New Testament conviction that the covenant with the Jews has never been revoked.

The anti-supersessionist part of this proposal is familiar. Almost everyone agrees that the understanding of the church as the replacement of Israel is the major ecclesiological source of Christian anti-Judaism. Roman Catholic authorities, among others, have now publicly declared that the covenant with Israel has not been revoked and that the Jews remain God's chosen people (though, needless to say, not exclusively such). The general impression is that this declaration implies that the church cannot be Israel, for that would be supersessionist. The opposite proposal is so unfamiliar and so little discussed that I must make it tentatively. I shall perhaps sound more confident than I am when I suggest that, stripped of its supersessionism, the understanding of the church as Israel can and should be recovered, together with the reading of what Christians call the Old Testament as genuinely and centrally the church's book (which does not deny that the same text, read as Tanach, is also Judaism's property).

Expropriating Israel

The fundamental obstacle to this proposal is the deeply embedded conviction that the linkage between the church as Israel and supersessionism is unbreakable. This link is assumed even by those who know that it was not true for Paul, the earliest and, many would say, the most authoritative of New Testament writers. For Paul, as has been noted more than once in this book, Gentile Christians are wild olive branches grafted into the olive tree that is Israel; and of unbelieving Jewry, Paul says, "The gifts and call of God are irrevocable" (Rom. 11:29). Paul did not espouse supersessionism. Yet, so the argument goes, there are indications of supersessionism in other New Testament writings, most notoriously in Matthew 21:43, which says, in contrast to the other versions of the parable of the wicked tenants, that the vineyard will be given to another *ethnos* (people). Almost all Christians, from the immediate post-New Testament period until around the middle of this century, have taken such passages to be definitive statements of supersessionism. Early on, Christianity was thought of as such a complete replacement of Judaism that, more or less simultaneously with the expulsion of Jesus-believing Jews from the synagogue, Jews as well as Gentiles who were Christian were forbidden by the "great church" (as it has come to be called) to engage in distinctively Jewish practices. Jewish Christians thus lost their group identity and become indistinguishable from their Gentile fellow believers. That the first Christians had remained Torah-observant was explained away, in a blatant instance of Gentile special pleading, as a temporary permission that had been rescinded.

On this view, the church, and the church alone, is Israel. Old Testament promises and prophecies are fulfilled not only in Jesus (an assertion essential to mainstream Christian identity), but also in the church—and in such a way that it replaces Israel. The church is the "New" Israel (an expression not found in the New Testament) and has become the sole heir to the entirety of Israel's heritage. Since Christ came, Israel's prophecies, promises, prerogatives, and scriptures do not belong to unbelieving Jews but only to Christians. Because Jews are no longer the people of the Bible, they cannot read it rightly. The Oral Torah and its midrashic, talmudic, and other rabbinic elaborations are thus condemned unseen and a priori as not simply false but as deliberately misleading. Rabbinic Judaism was for some Christians an illegitimate option worse than paganism or even atheism. The latter options could be honest errors, but the former was a deliberately deceitful simulacrum of the truth. It is as if Esau (the Jews) pretended not to have sold his birthright and sought to steal it back from Jacob (the Christians), who had rightfully dispossessed him. Expropriation, as this might be called, is not the only kind of supersessionism, but it is the one linked to the church as Israel.

The conceptual linkage, however, is one of possibility, not necessity. If Paul is right, then, as we have seen, thinking of the church as Israel does not require the exclusive claim that after Christ only the church is Israel. Ascribing Israelhood to the church, in other words, is a necessary but not a sufficient condition for expropriation; it is thus logically possible to retrieve Israelhood for Christians without denying it to the Jews. The counterargument, however, is that what is logically possible may, in the course of time, become historically necessary. Because Christian claims to Israelhood have been supersessionist almost from the start, it seems evident to many that Israelhood without supersession is not now available in practice. Before taking this consideration into account, however, we need to look at the converse relation, supersession without Israelhood, which has been the normal situation for the last several hundred years.

Discarding Israel

In the modern period, emphasis on the church as Israel disappeared, partly as a result of the sixteenth-century controversies over how and when the church was founded. The papacy could best be defended, Roman Catholics believed, by placing the church's origins in Jesus' statement to Peter, "On this rock I will build my church" (Mt. 16:18). The various Protestant groups countered in terms of their own ecclesial self-interest by claiming that the beginnings of the church were in Jesus' baptism, in the call of the apostles, or in Pentecost. An unintended consequence of these debates was that the resultant pictures of the church were marked by discontinuity rather than continuity with Israel.[1] In addition, as a consequence of the Enlightenment attention shifted from the church and Israel as bodies of people to Judaism and Christianity conceived of as religions that individuals believed in and/or practiced.

In time, these shifts of attention brought on by the Reformation and the Enlightenment gave way to the now prevailing theologies of replacement, which do more than neglect the church as Israel: they discard it. Liturgy and hymnody abound with scriptural, especially psalmic, references to Israel, Jerusalem, and Zion, and these references, as in the past, are applied to the church, but they have become dead metaphors devoid of the powerful typological realism they once possessed. The notion of fulfillment continues to be realistically affirmed, but with a radically different meaning. Fulfillment is no longer conceptualized in terms of the biblical narratives of God keeping and confirming promises and prophecies to persons and groups, but in terms of the impersonal patterns of evolutionary progress according to which one religion provides the conditions for the emergence of a better and higher one. Fulfillment now applies to religions, not peoples.

The less objectionable versions of this outlook could be said to liken Judaism to a flourishing vineyard that, although climactically fulfilled in the best of its harvests (that is, in Christianity), has retained enough fertility to bear new fruit down through the millennia, though of a less succulent kind. More commonly, however, the condescension implicit in these patterns of thought has been less benign. Judaism has been construed in terms of the progressivist axiom that the good becomes a drag on the best once it gives birth to the better. For Arnold Toynbee, to take a typical though not theological example, rabbinic Judaism seems to resemble the remains of a burned-out booster rocket whose role was to launch a space ship toward the stars. The nadir of such views was reached by the *deutsche Christen*, fellow travelers of the Nazis, for whom the Jews and their religion were a cancer in the flesh of the future.

All of these modern supersessionisms, from the least offensive to the most vicious, vehemently repudiate the Israel-likeness of the church. They grant that Christianity originated in Judaism but hold that it has mutated into a radically new reality. Countries, to be sure, have been thought of as Israel in modern times. Christians—ranging from British Israelites to Dutch, Swedes, and Poles, and, outside Europe, from South African Boers to Americans—have represented their nations, but not the church, as somehow Israel-like.

The Covenant Unrevoked

The discarding of ecclesial Israelhood has not diminished supersessionism. Perhaps, then, the retrieval of the premodern understanding of the church as Israel will accomplish what modern, progressivist theologies have not. And yet the horrors of premodern theologies of replacement were no less than those of modern progressivist ones (except for those perpetrated by Nazism, which, in any case, was a Manichaean dualism rather than a Christian supersessionist heresy: instead of viewing the Jews as a once helpful but now discarded stepping stone to higher goods, the Nazis regarded them as *ab initio* evil). Eleventh-century Rhineland massacres at the time of the First Crusade may have been perpetrated, as standard histories put it, by ecclesiastically disapproved wild bands of illiterate peasants stirred to fury by false rumors that it was Jews who had betrayed Jerusalem (which the peasants had set out to rescue) to the Turks, but even if such accounts are true, the church's ecclesiology was responsible. The massacres took place in a culture saturated iconographically as well as verbally from the highest to the lowest levels with the idea that the church alone is Israel. Given this history, even toying with the retrieval of the idea that the church is Israel—minus the "alone"—is indecent unless there are good reasons for believing that it will not again be misused to deny the Jews their birthright, as it always has been in post-New Testament times.

Historical criticism is a main source of assurance that the idea will not be so misused. Even conservative Vatican church leaders, not to mention Protestant ones, are persuaded, sometimes reluctantly, by the consensus in modern biblical, historical, and theological studies that the New Testament taken as a whole does not teach supersessionism. The emotions that have motivated the rejection of supersessionism in our day may well have come mostly from horror at the Holocaust, but this rejection would not have been possible without historical-critical ground-clearing.

This consensus can be expected to survive as long as modern modes of critical inquiry persist. Critical interpreters disagree endlessly on what the Bible affirms about the church with or without Israel, but they join unanimously in the negative judgment that, taken as a whole, the Bible does not teach supersessionism in either its premodern or modern form. This scholarly consensus allows Christians to recover their historic belief in God's election of the Jews and to reject replacement theology: the covenant with Israel has not been revoked, which means that the church's effort to identify itself with Israel need not lead to supersessionism. Not only individuals but whole communions are beginning to affirm that the covenant with Israel remains in force and extends to contemporary Jews and Judaism. To the degree this trend continues, it becomes safe, so to speak, to affirm that the church is also Israel. Breaking the tie with supersessionism makes the church's effort to identify itself with Israel into an innocent rather than menacing enterprise.

Appropriation: Sharing Israelhood

Innocence, however, is not a sufficient reason for embarking on this difficult undertaking; the effort will have to benefit Christians, and not simply be harmless to Jews. To see what Christians gain, recall the general benefits of taking the church as Israel that I have described earlier in this book. First, if the church is Israel, then the whole Old

Testament is as essential as the New for Christian communal self-understanding. Thus the church cannot be thought of in modern fashion as a religious instance of a limited liability corporation formed by individuals freely contracting together for the furtherance of their personal projects. On the contrary, the church is a people that God has gathered out of many nations to bear corporate witness along with Israel to the promise made to Abraham and Sarah that their seed would bless all humankind. Second, such an Old Testament understanding of the church challenges the Christian tendency to polarize collectivism and individualism, this-worldliness and other-worldliness, extramural concern for humanity as a whole and intramural attention to the elect community. Finally, and most decisively, the Old Testament emphasis on Israel's unconditional corporate election is vital in the struggle against Christian claims that Israel's election was merely conditional, was abrogated, and was replaced by the church's own election. Such are the general benefits of understanding the church as Israel; now let me turn to specific contemporary examples.

The use of the Old Testament, on which Christianity's vitality has in large part depended, tends to go awry when something other than the church is thought of as Israel. Admittedly, sometimes associating Israel with something other than the church has good, but ultimately limited, consequences, as when the social gospelers identified themselves with the Hebrew prophets or when blacks in the United States and liberation movements in Latin America appropriated the Exodus story. More often, however, such appropriations of Israelhood end up being simply disastrous, as when it is predicated of "Christendom," or of a "Christian" nation, or, worst of all, of a race, as in the case of the apartheid Boers in South Africa.

One odd but currently urgent example of this peril is supplied by the fundamentalist "dispensationalists," as they are called, found mainly but not entirely in North America. They interpret the Old Testament not with the typological imaginativeness still found in black preaching, for example, but in an intensely modern, literalistic fashion. They repudiate for themselves every trace of Israelhood, even of the emptily metaphorical kind, and insist that all Jews and only Jews are Israel, the sole visible corporate body elected by God to be his chosen people both in the past and present. In this scenario, the mainline Christian churches have no role because the true church is invisible, and it is the Jews who in the last days, after their conversion to Christ, will reign on a higher level than even Gentile believers in the visible messianic kingdom. Dispensationalists are often, though not always, Zionist in politics, but they are always supersessionists who have expropriated the Old Testament for their Christian purposes. The picture of the future they have concocted seems mad to all Jews and most Christians, and yet attracts millions. The Old Testament read without a church-as-Israel outlook is a dangerous book.

A second contemporary example of a problem related to disassociating the church from Israel is an inversion of the triumphalism from which Christianity has historically suffered. In some circles, self-flagellation has acquired the aura of a virtue. Talk of what is wrong with Christianity is acceptable and praiseworthy, whereas the positive aspects of Christianity are passed over in silence. These attacks on real evils such as the church's long-standing Eurocentrism, patriarchalism, anti-Semitism, and general oppressiveness regularly lose their effectiveness because of the holier-than-thou lovelessness with which they are made. Judgment is rendered in terms of alien standards rather than indigenous or scriptural ones, and the alienation of both critics and the criticized from historic communities of faith (or, to use the ordinary phrase, from "organized religion") is a common consequence.

In the face of such criticisms of Christianity, Christians need to be reminded that biblical denunciations of God's people in both Testaments were voiced, unlike most contemporary ones, by prophets unshakably committed to the community. To understand the church as Israel is to recover such critical voices. The prophets constituted a loyal opposition, not an adversarial one. As watchmen, they did not desert their God-appointed posts but continued to plead at the risk of their lives with those who were deaf or opposed to their warnings. In contrast, so it seems to this observer, contemporary Christian protesters tend to disengage from their opponents, and they thereby lapse readily into communal self-abuse. What Christians need is an Israel-like sense of common peoplehood sufficient to sustain the loyal oppositions that make possible the persistence through time of those continuing and often bitter arguments without which otherwise divided communities do not survive.

One final example of what Christians can gain from understanding the church as Israel in nonsupersessionist terms is that it frees them to hear God speak not only through Old Testament Israelites, but also through postbiblical Jews; this freedom follows from the belief that the covenant with Israel has not been revoked. The Jews remain God's chosen people and are thus a primary source for Christian understandings of God's intentions. With the passing of Christendom that is now taking place it is increasingly important for the churches to turn for instruction to Judaism. Jews learned much about faithful survival in hostile societies during the long *galut*; Christians need comparable lessons now that they are themselves becoming a world-wide diaspora and are seeking, via the ecumenical movement, to end their own dispersion by creating an institutionally decentralized common universe of discourse and, it is hoped, witness.

Of course the church cannot and should not resemble rabbinic Judaism any more than the latter resembles the Judaism of the First or Second Temple, but some of the strategies that the rabbis devised, not least the hermeneutical ones, are instructive for post-Christendom churches. Consider, for example, the talmudic practice of juxtaposing contrary opinions as authoritative instead of blandly harmonizing or brutally rejecting one or another as Christians have usually done. More comprehensively, the roles of the two Torahs and of rabbinic commentaries in Judaism are not without value for resolving church-dividing Christian differences over the interrelationships of the two Testaments and church tradition.[2] How much Christians will learn from such Jewish community-building practices is an open question, but to the extent that they learn to learn, contempt for Judaism will be enduringly banished from Christianity. Yet would such a development be good for Jews? In closing, let me consider that question.

Naysayers could argue that the more Israel-like and the less anti-Judaic the church is, the greater the assimilationist threat it poses. Dissimilarity spiced with a bit of hostility, some will say, contributes more to the survival of Judaism than does resemblance and friendliness. A very different scenario, however, is also plausible. The major challenge to minority identity is no longer from established Enlightenment and Christian majorities but from a pervasive pluralistic consumerism destructive of all enduring traditions and communities. Christians no less than Jews are engulfed by this assimilationist wave, and the best resistance Christians can offer is the reappropriation without expropriation of the church's roots in Israel and Israel's scriptures. For this task, Christians need the help of the original proprietors, and both parties will find that both the distinctiveness and the depth of their respective roots in the shared sacred text are increased rather than diminished by their collaboration. There is no danger of syncretism here, since each tradition is rooted in this shared text in its own particular way. Sibling-like quarrels are the greater danger, and

Jews and Christians will need God's grace to carry on the conversations that have now begun. They must do so for the sake of the communities of faith they are called to serve, and they can do so because they share a common hope for the coming of the Messiah round whom all their disagreements circle and in whom all their divisions will be overcome. It is this second scenario that faith calls Christians to prefer, but without forgetting assimilationist dangers. Whether this is also the future for which Jews should strive is for them to decide.

What of the Future?
A Jewish Response

TIKVA FRYMER-KENSKY, DAVID NOVAK,
PETER OCHS, DAVID FOX SANDMEL,
AND MICHAEL A. SIGNER

Beyond Supersessionism

MICHAEL SIGNER: During the past fifty years, after serious soul searching, many Christians have concluded that their supersessionist attitudes toward Jews and Judaism have led them away from the deepest demands of their faith. For more than thirty years since the Second Vatican Council (1965), many Christians from all over the world have reached out in friendship to the Jewish people. Pope John Paul II has reiterated, in many speeches, that God's covenant with the Jewish people continues and that Jews have an abiding relationship with the Land of Israel. Pope John Paul has called upon Christians to engage in *teshuvah*—he used the Hebrew word for "repentance"—for the harsh treatment that Jews have received at the hands of Christians during the past two millennia. Other Christian groups have expressed similar initiatives toward friendship and dialogue with Jews.

Why the Change?

DAVID SANDMEL: The Shoah, as an event with significance both for Jewish–Christian relations and for humanity, has provided a moral imperative for Jews and Christians to move beyond traditional antagonisms. It has made intercommunal dialogue a necessity; we must talk to our neighbors. That Jews and Christians are talking to one another and learning from each other is not new. What *is* new is that we actively seek each other out for shared goals: tolerance and respect, certainly, but also a deepening of our own religious experience and self-understanding. More than an intellectual endeavor, this dialogue might also lay the foundation for a new kind of creative cooperation between traditions within the changing religious environment of contemporary society.

DAVID NOVAK: The world that Jews and Christians now inhabit is neither Jewish nor Christian. For that reason, Jews and Christians interested in surviving in this world need to become more genuinely religious for the sake of their own identity. The changes in Jewish–Christian relations must also be seen against the background of a more startling fact: in the latter half of this past century, the political power of Jews had grown at the same time that the political power of Christians has shrunk. The political power of Christians has diminished insofar as our society and culture, which formerly were considered "Christian," no longer look to Christianity for their justification in any significant way. This diminished power has come as a great shock to many Christians, and it largely explains why Christians cannot relate to Jews as they have done in the past.

Despite the Holocaust, Jewish power in the secular world has grown enormously. The Jewish people survived the Holocaust with a greater determination to be more active and less vulnerable in this world. Jews have become not only equal but also leading citizens in Western democracies. And, of course, the reestablishment of the State of Israel has given Jews a political presence in the world they have not had since biblical times. Many Jews have looked to the increasing secularity of the world as the source of their newly won power. Jews of this mind set are usually anti-Christian since they regard Christians as the prime group wanting our return to the Ghetto—or worse.

An increasing number of Jews, however, now realize that looking to secularity as the source of our success means making it our god. But since secularity has no need for Judaism, it has no need for what makes Jews Jewish in the first place. As such, it is a recipe for our disappearance—either with a bang or a whimper. An awareness of the dangers of secularity has caused more and more Jews to turn inward to the religious content of the Jewish tradition to justify their continued identity. And, although some of these returning Jews look at Christianity and Christians as an ancient foe, others are beginning to realize that Christians are facing challenges similar to those facing us, and for the same reasons. In this age of secularism, *both* Christians and Jews must learn how to sing the song of the Lord God of Israel in the new exile *(galut)* in the strange land of contemporary society. Our relationship is therefore more than "interreligious" in the usual sense of that term. For better or for worse, we have never really been without each other. And, now, we need each other in new and surprising ways.

The New Jewish–Christian Dialogue

DAVID NOVAK: Because of the long history of Christian power over Jews, the new Jewish–Christian dialogue had to be initiated by Christians. This Christian initiative has been good for Jews and for Judaism, just as it has been good for Christians and Christianity. The initiative has been good for both Jews and Christians because it has lessened Christian participation in anti-Semitism. Anti-Semitism is bad for Jews because it harms us politically and even physically; anti-Semitism is bad for Christians because it is immoral and thus spiritually destructive. This Christian initiative has been good for both Judaism and Christianity because it has renewed the Jewish roots of Christianity. Forgetting these roots has been bad for Christians because it has led them to be tempted by various idolatries; it has been bad for Jews because it has obscured our unique historical relationship with Christianity. So far this new dialogue has taken place largely between Christian and Jewish scholars. Jewish scholars, nurturing long and close contact with Christian scholars during the course of their scholarly work, are eager and qualified to engage in this religious and theological exchange. Nothing less than such an exchange will serve the needs of Jews to recover their Jewish identity in a secular world; and nothing less is worthy of the intellectual depth of the Jewish tradition.

DAVID SANDMEL: But I am also keenly aware—and continually reminded—that this new dialogue is taking place among a relatively small group of Jews and Christians. Traditional mistrust and misunderstanding are still very much alive within each community. As important as this pioneering theological exploration is—and I believe it is very important—expanding the circle of dialogue is equally important. This expansion will not be easy, for our traditional wariness of Christians and Christianity and our current struggle to preserve both Jewish numbers and Jewish vitality make it difficult to appreciate the value of expending limited communal resources on an endeavor that engages people we have feared and avoided for so long. More "intrafaith" dialogue among Jews should lead to increased understanding that dialogue with Christianity is "good for the Jews."

Christians who have rejected supersessionism and are anxious for a deep exchange may be frustrated with the pace of the dialogue and surprised that Jews they encounter do not share—and, indeed, feel threatened by—their enthusiasm. This frustration is another indication of the newness of the endeavor. Although individuals within both communities may have achieved a new understanding and can address one another with mutuality and integrity, this is not the norm in either community. As long as the old antagonisms persist—and in both communities they are the rule, not the exception—those who see the promise of moving forward into this uncharted territory must have the patience and the commitment to bring the rest of their respective community along.

TIKVA FRYMER-KENSKY: Serious dialogue has been growing, involving many religiously committed Jews from all walks of Judaism. Today, when our ethical imperative towards *tikkun olam* impels us to remove inequality wherever possible and inequity based on inequality everywhere else, both Jews and Christians experience the tension between past and future that is so important to each religion's life. Responsible change demands that we magnify our perspectives. Internally, this magnification requires that we carefully study the many resources of the past: biblical texts independent of the rabbinic voice, the kabbalistic texts, and the remnants of folk tradition. Externally, serious engagement with Christianity gives us yet another perspective, not quite our own and yet not so far away that it is an Other of contrasts. Sometimes, this close engagement helps illuminate our mutual dilemmas. For example, to those of us involved in reforming the gender system of Judaism, it is illuminating to discover that rabbinic ideas about what men and women should be are often quite different from either Christian or contemporary ideas about gender. Exploring Judaism and Christianity together brings home the extent to which our religions have been influenced by cultural conventions and thus enables us to be flexible and dynamic in our own approach.

PETER OCHS: Dialogue can also enrich those not seeking change. About fifteen years ago, I heard Michael Wyschogrod, the Orthodox Jewish theologian, participate in a Jewish–Christian dialogue. Professor Wyschogrod gave a wonderful talk about ways in which their overlapping, biblical faiths make religious Jews and Christians closer, and about how his observance of the commandments (*mitzvot*) enrich his dialogue with Christians. In the question-and-answer period, a secular colleague protested that Professor Wyschogrod's orthodoxy was in fact an obstacle to dialogue, as were comparable Christian orthodoxies: these "outdated" faiths, he argued, draw people farther apart, not closer, by making them loyal to competing systems of belief and practice. "Your complaint," Professor Wyschogrod answered (as I recall, with some paraphrasing), "reminds me of the folktale of the bee that couldn't fly. Observing this robust creature with tiny wings, the doctors and scientists of the insect world, armed with their measuring sticks and compasses and all sorts of equations, concluded that 'this bee can't fly.' But, of course, it could fly, more powerfully than most of the others. The proof was in the flying! So, too, in this case. The most profound and mutually caring dialogues I have engaged in were between orthodox Catholics and Jews (meeting in conjunction with Vatican-sponsored events) and between Orthodox Jewish scholars and Christian Barthians. These dialogues succeeded, where many liberal efforts fail, because there is no effort in these cases for the two sides to become one and because each side saw in the other a witness to God, rather than to some concepts about God, even though these were different witnesses to God. True dialogue is dialogue that respects difference and is animated by it."

TIKVA FRYMER-KENSKY: Dialogue between Jews and Christians makes sense, for we share significant things. As monotheists, we see the world as a dialogue between God and humanity. Both our religions are "religious humanisms" that embrace the significance of human beings as "the image of God" and that seek to understand who and what we are supposed to be. We are biblically based religions that "triangulate" our lived experience with a sacred scripture and with a long tradition. We have much to learn by looking at how we each have lived over our long histories. Jews have excelled at communal text study and the practice of everyday law. Christians have, over hundreds of years, achieved great sophistication in theological reflection. Stimulated by the other, we can all increase the scope of our own understanding.

PETER OCHS: Here is one example. Several years ago, a group of Jewish, Christian, and Muslim scholars founded the Society for Scriptural Reasoning, dedicated to integrating the academic *and* the practical dimensions of this kind of dialogue. After sharing essays during the year through a common Website, forty to fifty scholars gather annually to study scriptural texts together in a setting that is both religious and academic. One of the society's goals is academic: to deepen each participant's own tradition of scriptural study, to deepen familiarity with the other biblical traditions, and to share insights on contemporary scholarship. Another goal is both academic and practical. Although acts of religious intolerance often make international headlines, most folks are not aware of how much religious Muslims, Jews, and Christians suffer from the antireligious prejudices of modern secular society. The secular university is often an oppressive place for academics who consider the biblical traditions as worthy of broad scholarly study as the Greco-Roman and modern European traditions. One of the society's goals is to work against this prejudice by fostering a pluralistic environment in which religious Jews, Christians, and Muslims study of all aspects of the humanities. In the future, this mode of study may stand as a model for a more tolerant university, where generations of students will learn to study our traditions of religious wisdom and ethics with the respect and care they now devote primarily and often exclusively to nonbiblical traditions.[1]

TIKVA FRYMER-KENSKY: Sometimes dialogue with a close sister can shed a transformative light on our own tradition. Jewish writers are used to contrasting the Jewish system of "obligation" with the "rights" approach of the Western legal tradition, stressing that "obligation" has a communal thrust and an important sense of moral commitment. Dialogue with Christianity may bring us to stress also the "privilege " of having the opportunity to do something. This is not a radically new idea, for rabbinic thought considers it a privilege to be obligated to perform commandments. But since Christianity does not have the language of commandments and does not often speak of "obligations," it uses other language to explain its moral demands, sometimes stressing the privilege of having the opportunity to do something or the "principle" of such deeds laid down by God's own actions. For example, on the relations of humans to ecology, Jews stress that we are obligated to protect the earth. Christians may state that we are privileged to care for the world according to the principle of hospitality, for we are guests on God's earth. On one level, the difference in language is irrelevant: either way, humans are to care for the earth. But linguistic variety shows us another facet of our mandate, giving us a fuller sense of the nature of "commandment" and enriching our view of the relationship between humanity, God, and the earth.

DAVID NOVAK: I think Jewish–Christian relations in this new century will grow in breadth and depth if Jews and Christians accept the truth that neither community can or should control the secular realm and, thus, the other. Christians cannot and should not regain a world they have lost, and Jews cannot and should not try to gain a world we have never had. As Jews and Christians are able to say more and more "I am a stranger on earth, do not hide for me Your commandments" (Ps. 119:19), they find how much they need each other to be able to keep these commandments here and now. In the presently unredeemed world, we are all strangers. Those who recognize this fact and accept its responsibilities will thereby become less strange to each other.

MICHAEL SIGNER: Serious interreligious dialogue is not assimilation. When Christians and Jews engage in dialogue, they come together to discuss how their particular religions and its practices enrich their experience of life. They describe the rituals in church and synagogue that sustain them in moments of trial and that transmit their heritage from one generation to another. In dialogue we search for common ground that is based on our difference.

In the coming years, Jews and Christians should engage in a mutual search for respect, justice, and love. We should begin this dialogue with a different framework than previous conversations. Both communities should face each other with the idea that we are groups of people who have spent our histories trying to live by the words, deeds, and message of the Hebrew Bible. Each community has found its unique way to live out that message. Over the centuries, both communities have enjoyed the teaching of brilliant minds and the actions of ordinary people. We need to share these experiences and teachings with one another. We should admit from the very beginning that there are elements in each tradition that the other side can never fully comprehend. We should enjoy the fact that we are different from one another. We should understand that the sweetness of agreement and the disappointment of disagreement are part of a relationship of caring about one another and the world that the Creator has put in our trust. There is no compromise in this encounter because there is no victory for one community or the other. There is only life together. It will be a life of "yes" and "no," of community and alienation, and of continued searching. The comfort and joy of our common and separate searches will provide the continuing motivation for our changed framework. We need not know everything that awaits us on the road ahead. The mystery of surprise will surely bring greater joy than the pessimism that growth and understanding are beyond our grasp.

PETER OCHS: Together we can celebrate what is most sacred, precious, and singular in our scriptural faiths. Such dialogue will benefit us and the world around us. Jews are about to discover how much that world needs us, how much the secular world needs to rehear the Teachings that we carry with us as a blessing to the nations and how much Christians and Muslims have to gain from studying those Teachings with us. Discovering that need, Jews are bound to rediscover their place among the nations. With the self-respect and sense of responsibility that comes from this rediscovery, Jews are also bound to reexperience the majesty and preciousness of their own religious heritage. We will find that the social and political influence of this heritage grows even stronger when we work closely with like-minded Christians on issues of shared concern. And we should be warmed to see how this shared work deepens and sweetens the religious lives of both dialogue partners.

NOTES

Chapter One

1. See D. Novak, *Jewish-Christian Dialogue* (New York, 1989), 14ff.
2. See B. Ned. 11a and parallels.
3. A good model for this is the concept of "mediation" *(pesharah)* in Jewish civil law. *Pesharah* is advocated (see B. Sanh. 6b–7a) when the full exercise of an individual claim in a property dispute would result in one side becoming the winner and the other the loser, thus resulting in a further rupture of the peace of the community in which both parties participate. To avoid this result, each party is to be persuaded (but not forced) to bracket his or her full claim with all its dissonance in favor of a partial claim in order to not further impede what the two parties have and should have in common.
4. See D. Novak, *The Election of Israel* (Cambridge, 1995), 40ff.
5. See Maimonides, *Guide of the Perplexed*, 2.33, on Ex. 20:3; also, Rom. 1:18–23.
6. Ps. 81:10.
7. See Lev. 10:1; R. Judah Halevi, *Kuzari*, 1.97; also, M. Halbertal and A. Margalit, *Idolatry*, trans. N. Goldblum (Cambridge, Mass., 1992), 186ff.
8. See R. Abraham Gumbiner, *Magen Avraham* on *Shulhan Aruch*: Orah Hayyim, 128.37 based on B. Sanh. 74a on Lev. 22:32.
9. See Novak, *The Election of Israel*, 177ff.
10. See B. Kid. 70b, and Rashi, s.v. *kashin gerim.*
11. See, e.g., *Pesiqta Rabbati*, chap. 35 on Zech. 2:15, ed. Friedmann, p. 161a, and chap. 40 on Lev. 23:24, p. 167b; *Tanhuma*: Tsav on Lev. 8:1, ed. Buber, p. 9b; Maimonides, *Teshuvot ha-Rambam*, 1, no. 149, ed. Blau (Jerusalem, 1960), pp. 284ff. Cf. B. Yev. 109a and Tos., s.v. "ra'ah."
12. See C. H. Dodd, *The Apostolic Preaching* (New York, 1960), 93ff.
13. See Is. 66:22.
14. See B. Ber. 34b; 1 Cor. 2:9.

Chapter Three

Christian Theology After the Shoah

1. See the so-called *Epistle of Barnabas* (ca. 132 C.E.); Justin Martyr's *Dialogue with Trypho* (ca. 150 C.E.); Melito of Sardis's *Homily on the Passover* (ca. 160–170 C.E.); Irenaeus of Lyon's *Against Heresies* (ca. 170 C.E.); and Tertullian's *Against the Jews* (ca.

190 C.E.). These second-century writings establish the standard supersessionist narrative within the Christian tradition.

2. See Augustine's typological reading of the Cain and Abel story in his *Reply to Faustus the Manichean* (Bk. 12).

3. *Reflections and Suggestions for the Application of Directives of Nostra Aetate* (December 1969); *Guidelines and Suggestions for Implementing the Conciliar Declaration Nostra Aetate* (January 1975); *We Remember: A Reflection on the Shoah* (March 1998).

4. "As Baptist Christians we are the inheritors of and transmitters of . . . a theology which has usurped for the Church the biblical promises and prerogatives given by God to the Jews; a theology which ignores nineteen centuries of Jewish development by viewing contemporary Jews as modern versions of their first century coreligionists; a theology which views the Jewish people and Jewish nationhood merely as pieces in an eschatological chess game; a theology which has valued conversion over dialogue, invective over understanding, and prejudice over knowledge; a theology which does not acknowledge the vibrancy, vitality, and efficacy of the Jewish faith." Issued by the Alliance of Baptists on March 4, 1995, at the Vienna Baptist Church in Virginia.

5. The views formulated by Hermann Gunkel extend through nineteenth-century scholarship, and they stretch from F. C. Baur to Rudolf Bultmann. E. P. Sanders examines and critiques this legacy in twentieth-century New Testament studies in the first chapter of *Jesus and Judaism* (Philadelphia: Fortress, 1985), 1–58.

6. The contemporary studies of Krister Stendahl, E. P. Sanders, W. D. Davies, Lloyd Gaston, Raymond Brown, Daniel Harrington, John Gager, James Dunn, and Martin Hengel build upon earlier scholarship by James Parkes, Trevor Herford, and George Foote Moore, which in turn drew upon a rich, albeit neglected, tradition of Christian Hebraists from the Victorines through John Lightfoot.

7. See Daniel Boyarin, *A Radical Jew* (Berkeley: University of California Press, 1994); W. D. Davies, *Paul and Rabbinic Judaism* (Philadelphia: Fortress Press, 1948); Lloyd Gaston, *Paul and the Torah* (Vancouver: University of British Columbia Press, 1987); E. P. Sanders, *Paul and Palestinian Judaism* (Philadelphia: Fortress Press, 1977); Alan F. Segal, *Paul the Convert* (New Haven: Yale University Press, 1990).

8. See Luke Timothy Johnson, "The New Testament's Anti-Jewish Slander and the Conventions of Ancient Polemic," *Journal of Biblical Literature* 108, no. 3 (1989): 419–441; and Anthony J. Saldarini, "Delegitimation of Leaders in Matthew 23," *The Catholic Quarterly* 54, no. 4 (October 1992): 659–680.

9. Martin Hengel and C. K. Barrett, *Conflicts and Challenges in Early Christianity* (Harrisburg: Trinity Press International, 1999), 26.

Chapter Four

The God of Jews and Christians

1. See Max Kadushin, *Worship and Ethics* (Evanston: Northwestern University Press, 1964), 63–96.

2. B. Shab. 88a-b.

3. B. Ber. 61b.

4. Peretz Markish, "The Mound," trans. Leonard Wolf, in *The Penguin Book of Modern Yiddish Verse*, collected by Irving Howe, Ruth Wisse, and Chone Schmeruk (New York: Penguin Books, 1987), 314–326.

5. Deut. R. 4:2.

6. David Weiss Halivni, *The Book and the Sword: A Life of Learning in the Shadow of Destruction* (Boulder, Colo.: Westview Press, 1998), frontispiece.

7. See Eugene Borowitz, *Renewing the Covenant: A Theology for the Postmodern Jew* (Philadelphia: Jewish Publication Society, 1991), chap. 2.

8. Ex. R. on Ex. 3.

9. Moses Maimonides, *The Guide of the Perplexed*, trans. Shlomo Pines (Chicago: University Press of Chicago, 1963), bk. 1, chap. 63.

10. Moses Nahmanides, *Commentary on Exodus 3:13*.

11. Ex. R. 30:24. Cited in Michael Fishbane, *The Garments of Torah: Essays in Biblical Hermeneutics* (Bloomington: Indiana University Press, 1989), 27–28.

12. See the discussion of the "Mourners of Zion" in Michael Fishbane, *The Exegetical Imagination: On Jewish Thought and Theology* (Cambridge: Harvard University Press, 1998), 77ff.

13. The Kabbalah of Isaac Luria.

14. Stanley Hauerwas, "In Defense of Cultural Christianity: Reflections on Going to Church," in *Sanctify Them in the Truth: Holiness Exemplified* (Nashville: Abingdon, 1998), 157–193. All the quotations from Hauerwas in what follows are taken from this essay.

15. Here Hauerwas is commenting on, and sometimes quoting from (thus the quotation marks within this block quote), Reverend Allred's sermon on the readings for the day, which were 1 Samuel and 1 Peter.

16. See David Novak's discussion of the "Noahide laws," the rabbinic effort to identify what conduct would be expected, within rabbinic jurisdiction, of persons from any faith whatsoever: David Novak, *The Image of the Non-Jew in Judaism* (New York and Toronto, E. Mellen Press, 1983).

17. This distinction is not a Christian one. Christian theology often stands, in fact, on the claim that what Jewish thinkers might call "philosophic" or "prophetic" truth is the most public truth for all the world to know. I suggest, nevertheless, that the Christian effort to make such claims public is itself a stumbling block to Jewish understanding; for the sake of Jewish understanding, we should therefore begin by rereading Christian claims in terms of a Jewish distinction.

18. Robert Jenson, *The Triune God: Systematic Theology*, Vol. 1 (Oxford: Oxford University Press, 1997), 63.

19. Jewish thinkers are often uncomfortable with Christian tendencies to read Scripture as a full disclosure of God's way of being. Jenson writes in the form of this tradition (stating what "God is") but in order to say something different: we know only as much about God as is displayed in God's acts, and among these acts are the biblical narratives. Jenson also writes of God's hiddenness *in* the very world that discloses His being.

20. Passover Haggadah.

21. Robert Jenson, "The Hidden and Triune God," unpublished lecture, 7.

22. Jenson, "Hidden," 3.

23. Jenson, *Triune God*, 126.

24. Articulating his biblical Judaism in the terms of Hellenistic philosophy, Philo reasoned, in fact, that for God to offer us his word (*logos* in Greek, referring at once to word and thought), God must "beget" the word. In Philo's Judaism, "giving birth" is a trope both for the production of speech and for rational implication. This is not the source, per se, of Trinitarian language, but Philo's theology provides Jewish thinkers a means of discussing Trinitarian notions with Christian theologians.

25. Jenson, "Hidden," 7.

26. Ibid., 8.

27. Ibid., 9.

28. T. Pes. IV.13.

29. B. Suk. 28a.

30. David Weiss Halivni, *Revelation Restored: Divine Writ and Critical Responses* (Boulder, Colo.: Westview Press, 1997), 3–4.

31. These include the "postliberal" theologians such as Hans Frei, George Lindbeck, Stanley Hauerwas, and their students; related interpreters of Karl Barth, such as Peter von der Osten-Sacken and Friedrich Marquardt; and a complementary but different variety of Anglican postcritical theologians, such as Daniel Hardy, David Ford, and their colleagues.

A Jewish View of the Christian God

1. Hasdai Crescas, *The Refutation of Christian Principles*, trans., with intro. and notes, Daniel J. Lasker (Albany: State University of New York Press, 1992), 25.

2. The translation here is taken from Jacob Katz, *Exclusiveness and Tolerance: Jewish–Gentile Relations in Medieval and Modern Times* (New York: Schocken, 1969), 35. The emphasis is mine.

3. Ibid., 36.

4. Ibid., 121, 136.

5. Ibid., 115. The emphasis is once more mine.

6. Quoted in Harvey Falk, "Rabbi Jacob Emden's Views on Christianity," *Journal of Ecumenical Studies* 19, 1 (1982): 106.

7. Ibid., 110.

8. See Isserles's remarks in *Shulchan Aruch, Orah Hayyim*, 156:1.

9. Marcus Horovitz, *Matte Levi, Yoreh Deah*, 28.

Chapter Five

Searching the Scriptures: Jews, Christians, and the Book

1. David Weiss Halivini, *Peshat and Derash: Plain and Applied Meaning in Rabbinic Exegesis* (Oxford: Oxford University Press, 1991). See also Peter Ochs, *The Return to Scripture in Judaism and Christianity* (New York: Paulist Press, 1993).

The Writings and Reception of Philo of Alexandria

1. Philo sometimes expresses his indebtedness to the ancient "traditions of the fathers" (*Life of Moses* 1:4; *Hypothetica* 7:6).

2. See, for example, *On the Migration of Abraham*, 44–45, 89–90.

3. I am indebted to Paul Franks, Michael Signer, and Gregory Sterling for their incisive comments and helpful suggestions.

Chapter Six

Mitsvah

1. See Rom. 3:20; Gal. 2:15–16 and 3:10–12.

2. See Maimonides, *Mishneh Torah*, AZ 1.3–4. For Maimonides' seemingly changed view of Christianity, however, see D. Novak, *Jewish–Christian Dialogue* (New York, 1989), 57ff.

3. See M. Avot 2.15–16. For the notion of the acceptance of the Torah as a complete act of faith, which transcends the always partial performance of the specific commandments themselves, see Nahmanides, *Commentary on the Torah:* Deut. 27:26 (which is also a polemic against Gal. 3:10, which itself is based on the Septuagint version of Deut. 27:26); also, B. Shab. 88a on Ex. 24:7. Even the celebrated rabbinic text that states "the Torah is not in heaven" (B. BM 59b on Deut. 30:12) means only that the law of God here and now is interpreted by human reason, not by divine oracle. It does not mean God's work in history for the sake of the redemptive end of history has been superseded. See D. Novak, *Jewish Social Ethics* (New York, 1992), 17ff.

4. See Maimonides, *Guide of the Perplexed*, 3.54 on Jer. 9:22–23.

5. See R. Judah Halevi, *Kuzari*, 1.25.

6. See *Targum Jonathan ben Uzziel:* Gen. 4:8.

7. See D. Novak, *The Image of the Non-Jew in Judaism* (New York and Toronto, 1983), chap. 1.

8. See B. Sanh. 57a.

9. See ibid., 74a and parallels.

10. *Mishneh Torah:* Melachim, 8.11.

11. See Clark M. Williamson, *A Guest in the House of Israel* (Louisville, Ky., 1993), 129f.

12. For the influential efforts of R. Menahem ha-Meiri in the fourteenth century to distinguish between "idolaters" mentioned in the Talmud and contemporary Christians and Muslims, see Novak, *The Image of the Non-Jew in Judaism*, 351ff.

13. See TJ Ned. 9.4/41c on Gen. 5:1.

14. To answer the Barthian charge that asserting general revelation ties one to "natural theology" and all that it presupposes and entails, see D. Novak, *Natural Law in Judaism* (New York, 1998), 142ff. For a Christian answer, see Oliver O'Donovan, *Resurrection and Moral Order* (Grand Rapids, Mich., 1986), 86f.

15. See Maimonides, *Guide of the Perplexed*, 2.40.

16. See Mt. 22:36–40; Acts 15:28–29; Rom. 1:18–32.

17. See Thomas Aquinas, *Summa Theologiae*, 2/1, q. 98, a. 5.

18. See T. Ber. 1.12–13 on Jer. 23:7–8. Regarding the *renewed* covenant, see 1 Sam. 11:14–15; Jer. 31:30–33.

19. See B. Nid. 61b on Ps. 88:6.

20. *Mishneh Torah:* Melachim, 8.9–10; 11.1; 12.3–5.

21. See Thomas Aquinas, *Summa Theologiae*, 2/1, q. 100, a. 8.

22. TJ Ber. 1.8/3c on M. Tam. 5.1.

23. See T. Sot. 8.6 on Deut. 27:3.

24. This is best expressed by the talmudic principle, "One is to be raised *(ma'alin ba-kodesh)* not lowered in holiness" (B. Yom. 12b and 73a).

25. For the most impressive contemporary attempt to present a nonsupersessionist Christian theology, see Paul van Buren, *A Theology of the Jewish–Christian Reality*, vol. 1 (San Francisco, 1987); and most recently, R. K. Soulen, *The God of Israel and Christian Theology* (Minneapolis, 1996), and Scott Bader-Saye, *Church and Israel After Christendom* (Boulder, Colo., 1999). Van Buren, Soulen, and Bader-Saye make a convincing case only against the more radical type of Christian supersessionism. But that is all Jews can really ask Christians to do as Christians. It certainly makes a new form of dialogue possible from the Christian side.

26. See Ludwig Wittgenstein, *Philosophical Investigations*, 2d ed., trans. G. E. M. Anscombe (New York, 1958), 1.18.

27. Cf. Oliver O'Donovan, *The Desire of the Nations* (Cambridge, 1996), 224ff.

28. For the political significance of a logic of "overlapping," see John Rawls, *Political Liberalism* (New York, 1993), 35ff.

29. See Reinhold Niebuhr, *The Nature and Destiny of Man* (New York, 1941), 1:150ff.

30. See Novak, *Natural Law in Judaism*, 164ff.

31. See D. Novak, "Religious Communities, Secular Society, and Sexuality: One Jewish Opinion," in *Sexual Orientation and Human Rights in American Religious Discourse*, ed. S. M. Olyan and M. C. Nussbaum (New York, 1998), 17ff.

32. See Ibn Ezra, *Commentary on the Torah*: Deut. 21:13.

33. See M. Yom. 8.9.

Another Jewish View of Ethics, Christian and Jewish

1. For example, Rom. 3:21–31 (esp. 3:28); 4:1–8, 13–17 (esp. 4:13).

2. For example, Lev. 26; Deut. 11:13–17; 28.

3. Zech. 13:2–4; B. Sanh. 11a; Num. R. 14:4.

4. Among many examples, see Is. 1:16–28; 5:7, 20–23; 10:1–4; Jer. 5:28; 7:4–7; 9:1–8; Amos 2:6–8; 4:1; 5:7–14.

5. Mic. 6:8; Ps. 34:13–15.

6. B. Shab. 31a.

7. Jewish history records the existence of a Jewish supreme court in Israel known as the Sanhedrin (from the first century C.E., and possibly earlier, to 361 C.E.), of regional rabbinic synods in central and western Europe during the twelfth through fourteenth centuries, and of the Committee of Four Lands in eastern Europe from 1550 to 1750. Today, in England, France, and Israel, there is an office of the Chief Rabbinate.

8. Lev. 24:10–16; Num. 15:32–36; 27:1–11.

9. See Deut. 13 and 18 for two different criteria to distinguish true from false prophets, neither of which works very well, and so Jeremiah, in particular, complains of the prevalence of false prophets; see, for example, Jer. 14:14ff; 23:14–22; 27:9–17.

10. Deuteronomy 17:8–13; the citation is from verse 11.

11. B. BB 12a. For a description of the process by which, and the reasons for which, prophecy was replaced by interpretation and the ongoing, oral tradition, see Elliot N. Dorff and Arthur Rosett, *A Living Tree: The Roots and Growth of Jewish Law* (Albany: State University of New York Press, 1988), chap. 5.

12. Of course, what I say below of Jewish law applies to the features and advantages of any legal system, including American law. However, Jewish law's claim to divine origin makes it a distinctly "religious" legal system, and that makes it different from American law in some significant ways. For a full discussion of the ways in which Jewish law, as a religious system, is both similar to and different from secular legal systems like American law, see Elliot N. Dorff, "Judaism as a Religious Legal System," *Hastings Law Journal* 29, no. 6 (July 1978): 1331–1360.

13. I have described my own approach to interfaith dialogue at some length in an essay entitled "A Jewish Theology of Jewish Relations to Other Peoples," first published in *People of God, Peoples of God: A Jewish–Christian Conversation in Asia*, ed. Hans Ucko (Geneva: World Council of Churches, 1996), 46–66, and reprinted in *Contemporary Jewish Theology: A Reader*, ed. Elliot N. Dorff and Louis E. Newman (New York: Oxford, 1999), 263–277.

Christian Ethics in Jewish Terms

1. See, for example, Will Willimon's and my book, *Resident Aliens* (Nashville: Abingdon Press, 1989). Critical responses to this perspective are unending, but for one that has achieved canonical status, see James Gustafson, "The Sectarian Temptation: Reflections on Theology, the Church, and the University," *Proceedings of the Catholic Theological Society* 40 (1985): 83–94. For my response, see Hauerwas, *Christian Existence Today: Essays on Church, World, and Living in Between* (Grand Rapids: Baker Books, 1995), 1–24. For a definitive analysis as well as critique of the epithet "sectarian," see Philip Kenneson, *Beyond Sectarianism: Re-Imagining Church and World* (Harrisburg, Pa.: Trinity Press International, 1999).

2. Karl Barth, *Church Dogmatics* II/2 (Edinburgh: T&T Clark, 1957), 509.

3. For a recent attempt to provide a commentary on the Ten Commandments in accordance with Luther's claim, see Will Willimon and Stanley Hauerwas, *The Truth About God: The Ten Commandments in Christian Life* (Nashville: Abingdon Press, 1999).

4. Bruce Marshall, "Christ and the Cultures: The Jewish People and Christian Theology," in *The Cambridge Companion to Christian Doctrine*, ed. Colin Gunton (Cambridge: Cambridge University Press, 1997), 92–93. I am deeply indebted to Marshall's article. Equally important for my understanding of the continuity of Israel and the church is George Lindbeck's series of articles on this issue. See, for example, his "The Church," in *Keeping the Faith: Essays to Mark the Centenary of Lux Mundi*, ed. Geoffrey Wainwright (Philadelphia: Fortress Press, 1988), 179–208.

5. St. Thomas Aquinas's account of natural law is often interpreted in a manner quite similar to Novak's understanding of natural law, that is, as an attempt to articulate the minimal requirements to sustain human community as well as the basic principles from which specific obligations can be derived. The problem with such accounts of Aquinas's "ethics" is that the natural law is abstracted from his account of the virtues, with the result that the theological account crucial to understanding

Aquinas's view of the natural law is ignored. Aquinas did not use the notion of natural law to provide a morality in common to all humans but to provide an exegetical principle for discerning those aspects of the Old Testament law still incumbent on Christians. For an account of Aquinas's understanding of natural law along the lines I am suggesting, see John Bowlin's *Contingency and Fortune in Aquinas's Ethics* (Cambridge: Cambridge University Press, 1999), 93-137.

Chapter Seven

Israel, Judaism, and Christianity

1. The Hebrew word *yehudi* in its various forms appears twenty-four times outside the Book of Esther, where it is used regularly. Though most often translated into English as "Jew," in context the best translation may be "Judean."

2. In the Orthodox prayer book, the same benediction is found in a negative formulation: "who has not made me a Gentile."

3. Sanh. 22a.

4. Thus a Jew-by-choice is given a Hebrew name reflecting the family relationship—X the son/daughter of Abraham and Sara.

5. Paul uses the plural "covenants," probably a reference to successive covenants with Abraham as well as to the covenant at Sinai. It should be remembered that what we have of Paul's writings is a collection of occasional letters, not an organized, worked-out theology. All interpretations of Paul are, by necessity, constructions.

6. Cf. Gal. 3:7, 9, 14, 29; 6:19.

7. See, for but one example, Mt. 22:33–41.

8. Much of Christian anti-Semitism can be traced to the view that the Jews ("carnal Israel") had rejected Jesus, indeed had crucified him. See Chapter 2 for a further discussion of this topic.

9. The term "anti-Semitism" is problematic. It is important to differentiate between religiously based and racially based prejudice against Jews. Some consider only the latter to be "anti-Semitism." Nonetheless, although it is important to distinguish different types of "Jew-hatred," it seems to me that the term "anti-Semitism," despite its shortcomings, is now understood to encompass both "religious" and "racial" Jew-hatred. It is also important to stress that although Christian anti-Semitism made the Shoah possible, "Nazism was not a Christian phenomenon," to quote "A Jewish Statement on Christians and Christianity," which appears at the beginning of this volume.

10. See Peter Ochs, "Jewish and Christian Theology," in *The Modern Theologians: An Introduction to Christian Theology in the Twentieth Century*, 2d ed., ed. David Ford (Cambridge: Cambridge University Press, 1987), 607. Ochs's article provides a good synopsis of this trend in contemporary Christian theology.

11. For more on this resolution and its implications, see Denise Dombkowski Hopkins, "God's Continuing Covenant with the Jews and the Christian Reading of the Bible," in *Prism: A Theological Forum for the UCC* 3, no. 2 (fall 1988): 60–75.

12. Hans Küng, *The Church*, trans. Ray and Rosaleen Oekenden (London: Burns and Oates, 1967), 138.

13. Ibid., 148.

14. Kendall Soulen, *The God of Israel and Christian Theology* (Minneapolis: Fortress Press, 1996), 3.

15. Ibid., 110.

16. Ibid., 176.

17. Scott Bader-Saye, *Church and Israel After Christendom: The Politics of Election* (Boulder, Colo.: Westview Press, 1999), 148.

Israel and the Church

1. Karl Barth, "Verheissung, Zeit, Erfüllung," *Zwischen den Zeiten* 9 (1931): 460.

2. At the end of his essay, Rabbi Greenberg briefly entertains the possibility that Christians and Jews are more closely connected than is suggested by the notion of "parallel covenants." In particular, he asks whether Christians might be "part of a single covenant alongside Jewry." It seems to me this latter (undeveloped) view is the more nearly correct one.

3. The teaching of supersessionism was never—thank God—explicitly defined by an ecumenical council of the church. This was not because Christians harbored strong doubts on the matter, but rather because the view was so widely held that doctrinal definition was superfluous. Be that as it may, the absence of doctrinal definition gives the contemporary church great latitude as it rethinks its relation to the Jewish people today.

4. Examples of such church statements can be found in Helga Croner, comp., *Stepping Stones to Further Jewish–Christian Relations* (New York: Paulist Press, 1977); *More Stepping Stones to Jewish-Christian Relations* (New York: Paulist Press, 1985); and Allan Brockway et al., *The Theology of the Churches and the Jewish People: Statements by the World Council of Churches and Its Member Churches* (Geneva: WCC Publications, 1988).

5. Michael Wyschogrod makes this point in his remarkable book, *The Body of Faith: God in the People Israel* (San Francisco: Harper and Row, 1989). See also Irving Greenberg, "New Revelations and New Patterns in the Relationship of Judaism and Christianity," *The Journal of Ecumenical Studies* 16 (1979): 249–267, esp. 258.

Chapter Eight

Jewish and Christian Liturgy

1. The Talmud (R.H. 17b) designates prayer as *seder tefillah* (order of prayer). By the ninth century, the order was canonized in a book known as *Seder Rav Amram*, "The Order According to Rav Amram," and the tenth century saw the promulgation of *Siddur Saadiah*, "The Order According to Saadiah." For some time, *seder* and *siddur* were used interchangeably. Now, however, *Siddur* is the designation for the daily and Sabbath prayers, and *Seder* refers to the Passover eve ritual, the prayers for which are in a separate book called the *Haggadah*, "The telling [of the tale of the Exodus]." Another term, *Machzor* (cycle), was once used interchangeably with *Siddur* and *Seder*, as in *Machzor Vitry*, the "Annual Cycle of Prayers from Vitry [in France]." Eventually, it became common to bind the daily and Sabbath liturgy separately from the liturgy for

the various holidays. The former became known as a *Siddur,* and each holiday liturgy was called *Machzor.* Christian liturgy, too, has its characteristic set of books, compiled, however, earlier than the Jewish ones. Popes Leo the Great (390–461) and Gelasius I (492–496) are said to have put together the earliest liturgical volumes, though there is some question as to what they actually accomplished, since in their final form the books are more properly dated to the sixth or seventh century. Under Pope Gregory the Great (540–604) and his successors, various canonical collections emerged with differentiating titles according to the ritual participant who would be using them. A *sacramentary* gave the presiding priest or bishop the prayers that varied from holiday to holiday (Christians prefer the word "feast"). The *apostolus* and the *evangelium* provided the order of scriptural readings, the former giving the Epistle and the latter the Gospel; together they formed a *lectionary.* An *antiphonary* provided the music for choral singing, and a *cantatorium* gave the musical settings for the soloist who led the responsorial chants in the service. Books called *ordines* provided instructions for the service leader who directed the worship, as a sort of master of ceremonies. Nowadays, different churches have their own versions of prayer books. Eastern Orthodoxy still follows the ancient practice of a set of books divided according to the role of the participants. Western churches distinguish worship books as Jews do, according to content. The Roman Catholic worship book that contains the mass, for instance, and which combines, in effect, the content of all of the volumes listed above, is called a *missal,* the first version of which developed between the tenth and the thirteenth centuries. The parallel book giving the liturgy of the hours is called a *breviary.* Protestants use various words for their books—Methodists, for instance, use a *Hymnal,* the current version of which contains not just hymns but also prayers for all occasions.

2. As with other technical terms, however, "celebrate" develops its own Christian theological significance. Thus Edward J. Kilmartin, S.J., in *Christian Liturgy: Theology and Practice* (Kansas City: Sheed and Ward, 1988), describes human celebration in general, for instance, as "a primordial phenomenon of human life" like love itself—known only in the experience thereof, and "not to be brought back to another category and explained through it." Liturgical celebration in particular thus becomes "the expansion of consciousness" without which liturgy does not occur, since true liturgy is the "exercise of the life of faith under the aspect of being together 'in the name of Jesus' for the realization of communion, the sharing and receiving, between God, community and individual in a coordinated system of ministerial services" (112–113).

3. 1 Corinthians 11:23–26.

4. Clifford Geertz, *The Interpretation of Cultures* (New York: Basic Books, 1973), 19.

5. On which, see Blake Leyerle's summary, "Meal Customs in the Greco-Roman World," and Joseph Tabory, "Towards a History of the Paschal Meal," in Paul F. Bradshaw and Lawrence A. Hoffman, eds., *Passover and Easter: Origin and History to Modern Times,* vol. 5 of *Two Liturgical Traditions* (Notre Dame: University of Notre Dame Press, 1999), 29–61, 62–80.

6. For references and discussion, see Lawrence A. Hoffman, "A Symbol of Salvation in the Passover Seder," *Worship* 53, 6 (1969): 519–537; reprinted in Paul F. Bradshaw and Lawrence A. Hoffman, eds., *Passover and Easter: The Symbolic Structuring of Sacred Seasons,* vol. 6 of *Two Liturgical Traditions* (Notre Dame: University of Notre Dame Press, 1999), 109–125.

7. For references and discussion, see Lawrence A. Hoffman, "Wine, Blood, and Salvation in Rabbinic Judaism," in *Covenant of Blood: Circumcision and Gender in Rabbinic Judaism* (Chicago: University of Chicago Press, 1996), 96–110.

8. T.J. Pes. 10:3.

9. For citation and discussion, see Hoffman, *Covenant of Blood*, p. 99.

10. Gordon W. Lathrop, *Holy Things: A Liturgical Theology* (Minneapolis: Fortress Press, 1993), 139–140.

11. Joseph A. Jungmann, *The Mass: An Historical, Theological and Pastoral Survey*, trans. Julian Fernandes, S.J. (Collegeville, Minn.: Liturgical Press, 1976), 112.

12. Alexander Schmemann, *Introduction to Liturgical Theology*, trans. Asheleigh E. Moorhouse (Crestwood, N.Y.: St. Vladimir's Seminary Press, 1986), 101–102.

13. Peter E. Fink, S.J., *The New Dictionary of Sacramental Worship* (Collegeville, Minn.: Liturgical Press, 1990), 45.

14. Translation taken from Theodor Klauser, *A Short History of the Western Liturgy* (Oxford: Oxford University Press, 1979), 17. See pp. 16–17 for the entire eucharistic prayer of which the single-line *anamnesis* is just a part.

15. Traditionally, this debate often takes the form of arguing for or against the doctrine of transubstantiation, that is, the change in essence of the bread and wine. Jews are apt to misunderstand the dogma, since its classical formulation depends on neo-Aristotelian categories of thought as formulated by Thomas Aquinas. Catholic thought did not maintain that some magical change in outward shape took place. Rather, the Thomists differentiated between substance and accidents, substance being the invisible essence of a thing and accidents being the way we perceive it. The bread and wine remain bread and wine insofar as their accidents are concerned, but the substance is invisibly altered to become the real presence of Christ. Reformation theology frequently took issue with this doctrine of real presence, and with Vatican II, the doctrine was expanded to say that Christ is present not just in the consecrated bread and wine, but also in the liturgy of the word, in the presiding priest, and in the entire assembly gathered together.

16. For detailed treatment of *zecher* and *zikaron*, see Lawrence A. Hoffman, "Does God Remember? Memory in Jewish Liturgy," in Michael Signer, ed., *Memory in Judaism and Christianity* (Notre Dame: University of Notre Dame Press, forthcoming).

17. Josef A. Jungmann, S.J., *The Early Liturgy to the Time of Gregory the Great*, trans. Francis A. Brunner, C.S.S.R. (Notre Dame: University of Notre Dame Press, 1959). This book was published just prior to Vatican II, so it is theologically dated but provides a classic statement in a popular vein.

18. The best example is from the morning *Yotser*, the blessing immediately after the call to prayer, where we hear that the angels open their mouths: *u-mevar'chim u-meshabechim u-mefa'arim u-ma'aritsim u-makdishim u-mamlichim*. Precise translation is difficult, but the image is clearly that of the heavenly hosts praising and acclaiming God the Ruler of all. The notion of thanksgiving is noticeably absent. Other instances put the verb in apposition to *lehallel* and *lekales*—clearly verbs of praise. The Hebrew for "thanksgiving" is a variation of the root *y.d.h.*, usually occurring liturgically as *hodu* (Give thanks!) or *modim* (We give thanks). The imperative *hodu* occurs regularly in Psalms and again in a psalm-like litany in the final chapter of the Hebrew Ben Sirah, usually dated at either 280 B.C.E. or 180 B.C.E. But interestingly enough, rabbinic liturgy rarely uses it. A survey of Jewish liturgy does turn up the regular use of *modim*,

but even *modim*, liturgically, does not mean "to give thanks," so much as it means "to acknowledge."

Liturgy and Sensory Experience

1. Synagogue decorative styles have consistently been strongly influenced by the artistic values of the dominant surrounding cultures. In many cases, it is demonstrable that the same artisans have built synagogues and churches with only minor modifications in decorative content. For recent scholarship on the early synagogue, see Dan Urman and Paul V. M. Flesher, eds., *Ancient Synagogues: Historical Analysis and Archaeological Discovery*, 2 vols. (Leiden, the Netherlands: E. J. Brill, 1995). On European synagogues, the most comprehensive work is Carol Herselle Krinsky's *Synagogues of Europe: Architecture, History, Meaning* (New York: The Architectural History Foundation and the MIT Press, 1985).

2. For a detailed discussion of this dynamic, see my *To Worship God Properly: Tensions Between Liturgical Custom and Halakhah in Judaism* (Cincinnati: Hebrew Union College Press, 1998), 5–14. The traditional liturgy creates a "virtual" incense offering through the daily ritual recitation of the talmudic discussion of the formulation of the incense, *Pitom Haketoret* (B. Ker. 6a).

3. W. Jardine Grisbrooke, "Incense," in *The New Westminster Dictionary of Liturgy and Worship*, ed. J. G. Davies (Philadelphia: Westminster Press, 1986), 265–266.

4. Of course, the "high" points of the liturgical calendar when incense might most naturally add to the worship experience are also those where halachah restricts the use of fire.

5. For a history of the debates over the organ, see Meir Benayahu, "Daat Ḥokhmei Italiyah al Haneginah Be-ugav Batefillah" (The opinion of the Italian rabbis about playing the organ during services), *Asupot* 1 (1987): 265–305. Note that although the aesthetic issues motivating the changes may be merged, the objections to instrumental music on the Sabbath and to public singing by women have quite different sources.

6. For a summary of the place of music in the church, see, for example, J. Gelineau, S.J., "Music and Singing in the Liturgy," in *The Study of Liturgy*, rev. ed., ed. Cheslyn Jones, Geoffrey Wainwright, Edward Yarnold, S.J., and Paul Bradshaw (New York: Oxford University Press, 1992), 493–507. Note that the use of instruments in liturgical music is primarily a phenomenon of the western church. Note, too, that in the church as in Judaism, the primary value of liturgical music is to carry the words of the liturgy. However, because church liturgies tend to have far fewer prescribed words than their Jewish counterparts (and because the church lacks kabbalistic concerns about the precision of language), there is room for much more musical elaboration, some of which obscures the text's verbal element.

7. B. Ber. 6a; Mek. Yitro 11.

8. While the Jerusalem Temple stood, it was understood to be God's place of indwelling on Earth. Its destruction was a primary source of this existential crisis in Judaism. On the impact of this crisis on Jewish liturgical life, see my *To Worship God Properly*, 1–14.

9. See John Meyendorff, "Christ as Savior in the East," in *Christian Spirituality: Origins to the Twelfth Century*, ed. Bernard McGinn, John Meyendorff, and Jean

Leclerq (New York: Crossroad, 1993), esp. the section titled "Christ's Humanity: The Meaning of Icons," 242–243; see also Leonid Ouspensky, "Icon and Art," in the same volume, 382–394. Concerns about idolatry have indeed caused significant controversy at various points in the history of Christianity and led to a removal of most imagery from many post-Reformation churches.

10. For a summary of the medieval debates about the status of Christianity, see David Novak, "The Status of Christianity in Medieval European Halakhah," in *Jewish-Christian Dialogue: A Jewish Justification* (New York: Oxford University Press, 1989), 42–56. Note that the motivation for this stance seems to have been economic necessity. Halachah prohibits participation in anything that might cause even a Gentile to perform an idolatrous act, such as swearing by a divinity other than God. As business transactions commonly required such oaths, Jewish welfare required that these not be considered idolatrous. This understanding probably did not really affect Jews' attitude toward the Christian liturgical world. See, too, Jacob Katz, *Exclusiveness and Tolerance: Jewish-Gentile Relations in Medieval and Modern Times* (New York: Schocken, 1961; reprint 1973), 24–36.

11. This is an understudied topic, both because it was somewhat embarrassing to modern sensibilities and because it is part of popular custom and not particularly important to the "high culture" of rabbinic learning. But it is easy to document, particularly in the newly emerging studies of women's spirituality. See, for instance, the various collections of Yiddish supplicatory prayers *(techines)* studied by Chava Weissler in her various publications and published in translation by Tracy Guren Klirs, *The Merit of Our Mothers* (Cincinnati: Hebrew Union College Press, 1992). See, too, for an anthropological study of the customs of Jewish women from Kurdistan and Yemen, Susan Starr Sered, *Women as Ritual Experts: The Religious Lives of Elderly Jewish Women in Jerusalem* (New York: Oxford University Press, 1992).

12. Of course the cross/crucifix is a ritual object that extends well beyond the limits of strictly liturgical use. However, it is fair to claim that its primary meanings for Christians are grounded in its liturgical setting.

13. See Mary Boys, "The Cross: Should a Symbol Betrayed Be Reclaimed?" *Cross Currents* 44, 1 (1994): 5–27.

14. However, note that a standard explanation of the symbolism of the cross is that it is a sign of victory over sin, but also, by easy extension, over the unsaved world. From Constantine on, the cross was a military standard as well as a sign of the central mystery of Christianity. See, for example, the entries under "Cross" in the *New Catholic Encyclopedia* and *The Encyclopedia of Religion*, and in books such as Heather Child and Dorothy Colles, *Christian Symbols: Ancient and Modern* (London: G. Bell and Sons, 1971), 10–42. For a contemporary attempt to reinterpret this symbol, see, for example, Paul M. van Buren, *A Theology of the Jewish-Christian Reality, Part 3: Christ in Context* (Lanham, Md.: University Press of America, 1995), 160–182.

15. Gershom Scholem, "Magen David," in *Encyclopedia Judaica* (CD-ROM edition).

16. I develop these ideas in detail in my book in progress, *Celebrating Torah*. Elements of it are forthcoming in an article, "Sinai, Zion, and God in the Synagogue: Celebrating Torah in Ashkenaz," in *Liturgy and the Life of the Synagogue*, ed. Steven Fine and Ruth Langer (Durham, N.C.: Duke University Press, forthcoming).

Christian Worship

1. Not all Christians hold this belief about the Eucharist, however. One of the divisions within Christianity since the Reformation is rooted in the fact that some Christian bodies consider the bread and wine "symbolic," that is, they signify the sacrifice of Christ but do not re-present it. In these traditions, the Holy Communion (as it is more frequently called) is understood as a memorial of the sacrifice of Christ, which took place centuries ago.

Chapter Nine

On the Suffering of God's Chosen

1. This, of course, is just a brief overview of the views of retributive suffering in the Hebrew Bible. See also Isaiah 3:16–26, as well as Ezekiel 3:17. See also 2 Kings:17 for a similar response to suffering in the context of the destruction of the two Israelite kingdoms.

2. For a good overview of the issues, see H. H. Rowley, *The Servant of the Lord and Other Essays on the Old Testament* (London: Lutterworth Press, 1952).

3. See, in particular, 44:21: "Remember these things, O Jacob. For you, O Israel, are My servant: I fashioned you, you are My servant—O Israel never forget me!" See also 41:8, 44:2, and 49:3.

4. *Mekhilta de-Rabbi Ishmael* (par. 10, pp. 239–41); repeated in *Sifrei Deuteronomy* (para. 32, pp. 55–58); *Sifrei Devarim*, 311, ed. L. Finkelstein (1939; reprint, New York: Jewish Theological Seminary, 1962), 351. I am indebted to David Kraemer's discussion of this text in chapter six of his *Responses to Suffering in Classical Rabbinic Literature* (New York: Oxford University Press, 1995), esp. 81–84.

5. Strands of the early rabbinic tradition in fact suggest that suffering is a sign of God's love for the people of Israel:

"When Abraham, our father, had not yet come into the world, the Holy One, Blessed be He, judged the world—as if it could be—with a strict [cruel, severe, merciless] measure.

[Thus] the people of the [generation of the] flood sinned [and God] scattered them like sparks upon the water. The people of the [generation of the] tower [of Babel] sinned [and God] scattered them from one end of the earth to the other. The people of Sodom sinned [and God] flooded them with brimstone and fire.

But when Abraham came to the world, he had merit to receive suffering and they [sufferings] began coming slowly. As it is said, 'There was a famine in the land, and Abram went down to Egypt' (Gen. 12:10). And if you should say, Why do sufferings come? Because of the love of Israel: 'He fixed the boundaries of peoples/In relation to Israel's numbers'" (Deut. 32:8 [Sifrei 311]). See Kraemer's discussion of this text, in *Responses to Suffering in Classical Rabbinic Literature*, 88.

6. Jon D. Levenson, *The Death and Resurrection of the Beloved Son* (New Haven: Yale University Press, 1993), esp. 201.

7. As cited in Shalom Spiegel, *The Last Trial* (New York: Behman House, 1967), 148–149.

8. As quoted in Robert Chazan, *Daggers of Faith: Thirteenth-Century Christian Missionizing and Jewish Response* (Berkeley: University of California Press, 1989), 66.

9. *The Kuzari: In Defense of the Despised Faith*, trans. N. Daniel Korobkin (New Jersey and Jerusalem: Jason Aronson Inc., 1998).

10. Ibid., 2:35, pp. 90–92.

11. Thomas Aquinas, *The Literal Exposition on Job: A Scriptural Commentary Concerning Providence*, trans. Anthony Damico and Martin Yaffe (Atlanta: Scholars Press, 1989), 146. As quoted in Eleonore Stump, "Aquinas on the Sufferings of Job," in *Reasoned Faith: Essays in Philosophical Theology in Honor of Norman Kretzmann*, ed. Eleonore Stump (Ithaca: Cornell University Press, 1993), 342.

12. Ibid., 345.

13. Ibid., 353.

14. Maimonides' philosophy would usually be the obvious one to compare with Aquinas's. On the question of suffering, however, Maimonides is quite different from Aquinas and Halevi. He ascribes human suffering almost entirely to the human inability to comprehend God properly. Here as elsewhere, Maimonides has a highly intellectual approach to God. For a good introduction to and overview of the problem of suffering in Maimonides' thought, see Oliver Leaman, *Evil and Suffering in Jewish Philosophy* (Cambridge: Cambridge University Press, 1995), 64–101.

15. For an excellent general work on the Reform movement in Europe, see Michael A. Meyer, *Response to Modernity: A History of the Reform Movement in Judaism* (New York: Oxford University Press, 1988). For an extremely helpful overview of Reform interpretations of chosenness as they transferred to the American context, see Arnold Eisen's *The Chosen People in America: A Study in Religious Ideology* (Bloomington: Indiana University Press, 1983). For a recent criticism of liberal accounts of Jewish chosenness, see David Novak, *The Election of Israel: The Idea of the Chosen People* (Cambridge: Cambridge University Press, 1995).

16. Abraham Geiger, "The Essence of Religion," in *Abraham Geiger and Liberal Judaism*, ed. Max Wiener (Philadelphia: The Jewish Publication Society of America, 1962), 182.

17. Hermann Cohen, *Religion of Reason out of the Sources of Judaism*, trans. Simon Kaplan (New York: Frederick Ungar Publishing Co., 1971), 268.

18. Ibid., 263.

19. See, for example, David Novak's comments in *Natural Law in Judaism* (New York: Cambridge University Press, 1998), 31. Novak cites B. Kiddushin 30b in support of his view.

20. Richard Rubenstein, *After Auschwitz: Radical Theology and Contemporary Judaism* (New York: Bobbs-Merril, 1966), 153.

21. Among those who argue that the Holocaust presents a complete paradigm shift for Jewish thought are Arthur Cohen, Emil Fackenheim, and Eli Wiesel. For recent discussions of post-Holocaust thought, see Leaman, *Evil and Suffering in Jewish Philosophy*, 185–219, and Zachary Braiterman, *(God) After Auschwitz* (Princeton: Princeton University Press, 1998).

22. Eliezer Berkovits, *Faith After the Holocaust* (New York: Ktav, 1973), 136.

23. Simone Weil, *Gravity and Grace* (London: Routledge, 1995), 73.

24. *The Simone Weil Reader*, ed. George A. Panichas (Wakefield, R.I.: Moyer Bell Limited, 1994), 462.

25. C. S. Lewis, *The Problem of Pain: How Human Suffering Raises Almost Intolerable Intellectual Problems* (New York: Macmillan, 1962).

26. Emmanuel Levinas, "Useless Suffering," in *The Provocation of Levinas: Re-thinking the Other*, ed. Robert Bernasconi and David Wood (London: Routledge, 1988), 156–167.

27. Ibid., 166.

28. See Kraemer's *Responses to Suffering in Classical Rabbinic Literature* for an exceptionally clear, helpful, and provocative presentation of rabbinic responses to suffering.

29. *The Tosefta: According to Codex Vienna*. 5 vols., ed. S. Lieberman (New York: Jewish Theological Seminary of America, 1955–1988), 3:25, p. 79.

30. See for example Gustavo Gutierrez's theological articulation of this position in *On Job: God-Talk and the Suffering of the Innocent* (Maryknoll, N.Y.: Orbis Books, 1987).

31. Pope John Paul II, *Crossing the Threshold of Hope* (New York: Alfred A. Knopf, 1994).

Suspicions of Suffering

1. Emmanuel Levinas, *Otherwise Than Being or Beyond Essence*, trans. Alphonso Lingis (The Hague: Martinus Nijhoff, 1981), 111.

2. Rosemary Ruether, *Faith and Fratricide: The Theological Roots of Anti-Semitism* (New York: Seabury Press, 1974), 230.

The Meaning and Value of Suffering

1. The position that there is an original, intrinsically evil nature in the world, co-eternal and coexistent with God, is the position of the Manichees, followers of the Persian syncretist Mani (216–277), who had spread through the Roman Empire by the time of Augustine. Augustine spent nine years as a Manichee himself before his conversion to Catholic Christianity. The Manichees taught that human beings have an intrinsically evil nature as part of their makeup. The body and all that is associated with it is evil, and the urges that come from it are the source of sin. It is this position, imputing an intrinsically evil nature as the cause of human sin, that Augustine's doctrine of original sin was meant to oppose. Original sin is the result of free will, not the work of an intrinsically evil nature within us, and it results in the weakening of human nature, which remains, nevertheless, good.

2. Citations from Simone Weil are taken from the collection of essays, Simone Weil, *Waiting for God*, trans. Emma Craufurd, intro. Leslie A. Fiedler (New York: Harper & Row, 1951).

Chapter Ten

Judaism and Incarnation

1. Consider, for example, G. Parrinder, *Avatar and Incarnation* (London, 1970).

2. Hans Joachim Schoeps, *The Jewish-Christian Argument: A History of Theologies in Conflict* (New York, 1963), 23.

3. See M. Wyschogrod, *The Body of Faith: Judaism as Corporeal Election* (New York, 1983), xv, 11, 113, 138, 212–213. Cf. p. 95, where the author rejects what he refers to as the "materialization" of God in kabbalistic sources. On the classification of the Christian doctrine of incarnation as idolatry from a Judaic perspective, see S. S. Schwarzschild, "De Idololatria," in *Proceedings of the Academy for Jewish Philosophy*, ed. D. Novak and N. M. Samuelson (Lanham, 1992), 223–225.

4. M. Wyschogrod, "A Jewish Perspective on Incarnation," *Modern Theology* 12 (1996): 195–209.

5. See, for example. M. Goulder, "The Two Roots of the Christian Myth," and F. Young, "Two Roots of a Tangled Mass?" in *The Myth of God Incarnate*, ed. J. Hick (Philadelphia, 1977), 64–86; 87–121.

6. J. Neusner, *The Incarnation of God: The Character of Divinity in Formative Judaism* (Philadelphia, 1988), 6.

7. See G. G. Stroumsa, "The Incorporeality of God: Context and Implications of Origen's Position," *Religion* 13 (1983): 345–358; D. L. Paulsen, "Early Christian Belief in a Corporeal Deity: Origen and Augustine as Reluctant Witness," *Harvard Theological Review* 83 (1990): 105–116; J. Pelikan, *Christianity and Classical Culture: The Metamorphosis of Natural Theology in the Christian Encounter with Hellenism* (New Haven and London, 1993), 40–73; E. A. Clark, *The Origenist Controversy: The Cultural Construction of an Early Christian Debate* (Princeton, 1992), 43–84.

8. This is the gist of my criticism of Neusner's monograph, *The Incarnation of God*, in *Jewish Quarterly Review* 81 (1990): 219–222.

9. A similar position is taken by D. Stern, "*Imitatio Hominis*: Anthropomorphism and the Character(s) of God in Rabbinic Literature," *Prooftexts* 12 (1992): 151–174.

10. K. Rudolph, *Gnosis: The Nature and History of Gnosticism*, trans. R. M. Wilson (San Francisco, 1983), 157.

11. E. R. Wolfson, *Through a Speculum That Shines: Vision and Imagination in Medieval Jewish Mysticism* (Princeton, 1994), 8–9, 35–41, 144–148, 152–153, 204–234, 306–317.

12. My formulation here has been enhanced by the discussion in J. M. Trau, "Modalism Revisited: Persons and Symbols," in *Negation and Theology*, ed. R. P. Scharlemann (Charlottesville, 1992), 56–71.

13. See H. Eilberg-Schwartz, "The Problem of the Body for the People of the Book," in *People of the Body: Jews and Judaism from an Embodied Perspective*, ed. H. Eilberg-Schwartz (Albany, 1992), 17–46; and idem, *God's Phallus and Other Problems for Men and Monotheism* (Boston, 1994).

14. J. Glen Taylor, "The Two Earliest Known Representations of Yahweh," in *Ascribe to the Lord: Biblical and Other Studies in Memory of Peter C. Craigie*, ed. L. Eslinger and G. Taylor (Sheffield, 1988), 557–566. See T. N. D. Mettinger, *In Search of God: The Meaning and Message of the Everlasting Names* (Philadelphia, 1988), 123–157.

15. T. N. D. Mettinger, "The Veto on Images and the Aniconic God in Ancient Israel," in *Religious Symbols and Their Functions*, ed. H. Biezas (Uppsala, 1979), 27, cited by Taylor, "Two Earliest Known Representations," 561 n. 11.

16. Neusner, *Incarnation of God*, 4: "The incarnation of God forms a commonplace for Judaisms from the formation of Scripture forward. For the Priestly author—not to mention authorship of JE, as well as the prophetic visionaries who saw God enthroned, riding horses or chariots, and the like—invited precisely that exercise of re-

markable imagination. . . . The history of how diverse Judaisms imagined God contains more than a single, uniform chapter about God portrayed as a human being (ordinarily, a man)."

17. On the depiction of the God of Israel as king, see Mettinger, *In Search of God* (Philadelphia, 1988), pp. 92–122.

18. See Mettinger, *In Search of God*, pp. 1–74; A. LaCocque, "The Revelation of Revelations," in A. LaCocque and P. Ricoeur, *Thinking Biblically: Exegetical and Hermeneutical Studies*, trans. D. Pellauer (Chicago, 1998), 307–329.

19. An echo of the Deuteronomic notion of the in-dwelling of the name in the temple is evident in Jubilees 32:10, 49:20–21. In 36:7, the name is described as that "which created heaven and earth and everything together." One may surmise that in this pre-Christian Jewish source we have evidence for the hypostatic understanding of the name. See J. Fossum, *The Name of God and the Angel of the Lord: Samaritan and Jewish Concepts of Intermediation and the Origin of Gnosticism* (Tübingen, 1985), 255–256.

20. Ibid., 86–87.

21. See W. G. Heidt, *Angelology of the Old Testament* (Washington, D.C., 1949), 69–99; A. Rofé, *The Belief in Angels in the Bible and in Early Israel* (Jerusalem, 1979), 236–238 (in Hebrew).

22. See E. R. Wolfson, "The Secret of the Garment in Nahmanides," *Da'at* 24 (1990): 25–49 (English section); idem, "God, the Demiurge, and the Intellect: On the Usage of the Word *Kol* in Abraham ibn Ezra," *Revue des études juives* 149 (1990): 77–111; idem, *Through a Speculum That Shines*, 63–64, 223–228, 255–263. See also D. Abrams, "The Boundaries of Divine Ontology: The Inclusion and Exclusion of Metatron in the Godhead," *Harvard Theological Review* 87 (1994): 291–321.

23. For a recent analysis of this theme with citation of many of the relevant scholarly discussions, see N. Deutsch, *Guardians of the Gate: Angelic Vice Regency in Late Antiquity* (Leiden, 1999), 27–47.

24. See J. Daniélou, "Trinité et angélologie dans la théologie judéo-chrétienne," *Recherches science religieuse* 45 (1957): 5–41; idem, *The Origins of Latin Christianity* (London, 1977), 149–152. The angelic role of Jesus in Christological theology as the form of God's body (or the theophany of the preexistent Logos) and the function of Metatron in Jewish esotericism has been discussed by a number of scholars; for example, A. F. Segal, *Two Powers in Heaven: Early Rabbinic Reports about Christianity and Gnosticism* (Leiden, 1977), 220–234; and G. G. Stroumsa, "Form(s) of God: Some Notes on Metatron and Christ," *Harvard Theological Review* 76 (1983): 269–288. See also, C. Gieschen, *Angelomorphic Christology: Antecedents and Early Evidence* (Leiden, 1998).

25. Gen. R. 97:3.

26. Ex. R. 32:9.

27. Ex. R. 2:5. I have translated the version of the text presented in *Midrash Shemot Rabbah, Chapters I–XIV*, ed. A. Shinan (Jerusalem, 1984), 111.

28. The variant readings are cited by Shinan, ibid., 112.

29. B. Hag. 14a.

30. On the general religious and intellectual climate of this town in the early rabbinic period, see S. S. Miller, *Studies in the History and Traditions of Sepphoris* (Leiden, 1984).

31. R. Hayward, *Divine Name and Presence: The Memra* (Totowa, 1981), 132–136. In a number of passages in rabbinic literature, R. Jonathan is depicted as interacting with heretics *(minim)* who seem to be Jewish Christians. See R. Travers Herford, *Christianity in Talmud and Midrash* (London, 1903), 215–217, 253–255, 301–302, 319–320. R. Samuel ben Nahman was also involved in statements directed against Christians who are referred to as *minim*. See M. Simon, *Verus Israel: A Study of the Relations Between Christians and Jews in the Roman Empire (A.D. 135–425)*, trans. H. McKeating (London, 1996), 190.

32. For a similar polemical strategy of reading on the part of the rabbis, see E. E. Urbach, "The Homiletical Interpretations of the Sages and the Expositions of Origen on Canticles, and the Jewish-Christian Disputation," *Scripta Hierosolymitana* 22 (1971): 247–275.

33. A hypostatic notion of angels is implied in another teaching of R. Jonathan, reported by R. Samuel ben Nahman, in Gen. R. 8:8, pp. 61–62. According to the reading of Gen. 1:26 attributed to R. Jonathan, the plural form of the verse "Let us make Adam in our image and in our likeness" refers to God and the angels creating man together.

34. See M. Idel, *Kabbalah: New Perspectives* (New Haven, 1988), 38–39, 113–122, 128–136, 156–172; idem, *Golem: Jewish Magical and Mystical Traditions on the Artificial Anthropoid* (Albany, 1990), 27–43; D. Boyarin, *Intertextuality and the Reading of Midrash* (Bloomington, 1990); idem, *Carnal Israel: Reading Sex in Talmudic Culture* (Berkeley, 1993); M. Fishbane, "Some Forms of Divine Appearance in Ancient Jewish Thought," in *From Ancient Israel to Modern Judaism: Intellect in Quest of Understanding: Essays in Honor of Marvin Fox*, ed. J. Neusner, E. S. Frerichs, and N. M. Sarna (Atlanta, 1989), 2:261–270; idem, "The 'Measures' of God's Glory in the Ancient Midrash," in *Messiah and Christos: Studies in the Jewish Origins of Christianity Presented to David Flusser on the Occasion of His Seventy-Fifth Birthday*, ed. I. Gruenwald, S. Shaked, and G. G. Stroumsa (Tübingen, 1992), 53–74; idem, "The Well of Living Water: A Biblical Motif and its Ancient Transformation," in *Sha'arei Talmon: Studies in the Bible, Qumran, and the Ancient Near East Presented to Shemaryahu Talmon*, ed. M. Fishbane and E. Tov (Winona Lake, 1992), 3–16; idem, "Arm of the Lord: Biblical Myth, Rabbinic Midrash, and the Mystery of History," in *Language, Theology, and the Bible: Essays in Honour of James Barr*, ed. S. E. Balentine and J. Barton (Oxford, 1994), 271–292; E. R. Wolfson, "Images of God's Feet: Some Observations on the Divine Body in Judaism," in Eilberg-Schwartz, *People of the Body*, 143–181; Y. Liebes, *Studies in Jewish Myth and Jewish Messianism*, trans. B. Stein (Albany, 1993), 1–64; M. Bar-Ilan, "The Hand of God: A Chapter in Rabbinic Anthropomorphism," in *Rashi 1040–1990: Hommage à Ephraim E. Urbach*, ed. G. Sed-Rajna (Paris, 1993), 321–335; A. Goshen-Gottstein, "The Body as Image of God in Rabbinic Literature," *Harvard Theological Review* 87 (1994): 171–195; D. Aaron, "Shedding Light on God's Body in Rabbinic Midrashim: Reflections on the Theory of a Luminous Adam," *Harvard Theological Review* 90 (1997): 299–314. Cf. also the study of Stern cited in n. 9 and that of Eilberg-Schwartz in n. 13.

35. An important source that articulates the rabbinic belief is *Sifre on Deuteronomy*, ed. L. Finkelstein (New York, 1969), sec. 41, 87–88; see also S. D. Fraade, *From Tradition to Commentary: Torah and Its Interpretation in the Midrash Sifre to Deuteronomy* (Albany, 1991), 89–92.

36. J. Neusner, *Torah: From Scroll to Symbol in Formative Judaism* (Philadelphia, 1985), 4.

37. Neusner, *Incarnation of God*, 188–192.

38. For discussion of this motif, see E. R. Wolfson, *Circle in the Square: Studies in the Use of Gender in Kabbalistic Symbolism* (Albany, 1995), 1–28.

39. *Midrash Tanhuma*, Vayelech, 2.

40. M. Avot 3:6. It is of interest to consider the utilization of this dictum in B. Ber. 6a. In that context, the divine presence is said to dwell with ten men who pray together, with three men who sit to render judgment, and with two who are occupied with Torah. That study of Torah is the most important expression of religious devotion is underscored by the fact that the passage concludes with the assurance that the presence is found even with the man who studies alone.

41. As noted by M. Kadushin, *The Rabbinic Mind* (New York, 1952), 214.

42. See G. Scholem, *On the Kabbalah and Its Symbolism*, trans. R. Manheim (New York, 1965), 37–44; idem, "The Name of God and the Linguistic Theory of the Kabbala," *Diogenes* 79 (1972): 77–80, and *Diogenes* 80 (1972): 178–179; I. Tishby, *The Wisdom of the Zohar*, trans. D. Goldstein (Oxford, 1989), 283–284, 292–295, 1079–1082; and M. Idel, "The Concept of Torah in Hekhalot Literature and Its Metamophosis in Kabbalah," *Jerusalem Studies in Jewish Thought* 1 (1981): 49–58 (in Hebrew).

43. B. Ber. 21a.

44. For a review of some of the relevant scholarly literature on this facet of ancient Jewish esotericism, see M. S. Cohen, *The Shi'ur Qomah: Liturgy and Theurgy in Pre-Kabbalistic Jewish Mysticism* (Lanham, 1983), 13–41.

45. This is the position taken, for example, by J. Dan, *Jewish Mysticism*, 3 vols. (Northvale, 1999), 3: 142.

46. The relationship between mythical image and philosophical concept that I am presuming is in line with the thesis presented by H. Jonas, "Myth and Mysticism: A Study of Objectification and Interiorization in Religious Thought," *The Journal of Religion* 49 (1969): 315–329.

47. B. Ber. 55a.

48. See Scholem, "Name of God," 71; idem, *On the Kabbalah*, 166–167. For references to the primary sources, see Wolfson, *Circle in the Square*, 159 n. 23. See also Fossum, *Name of God*, 241–256 and, on the demiurgic role of the name of God in Samaritan hymns, 76–84.

49. My translation is based on the text established by I. Gruenwald, "A Preliminary Critical Edition of *Sefer Yezira*," *Israel Oriental Studies* 1 (1971): 147–148 (§§ 18–19).

50. An intelligent account of various ways to explain the 231 gates in later kabbalistic literature is found in A. Kaplan, *Sefer Yetzirah: The Book of Creation in Theory and Practice* (York Beach, 1990), 109–124.

51. Gruenwald, "Preliminary Edition," 150 (§ 22).

52. My interpretation of the passage in *Sefer Yetsirah* concurs with that of Idel, *Golem*, 13.

53. B. Ber. 5b.

54. Kadushin, *Rabbinic Mind*, 213.

55. E. R. Wolfson, "Iconic Visualization and the Imaginal Body of God: The Role of Intention in the Rabbinic Conception of Prayer," *Modern Theology* 12 (1996): 137–162.

56. B. Sanh. 22a.

57. See E. R. Wolfson, "Sacred Space and Mental Iconography: *Imago Templi* and Contemplation in Rhineland Jewish Pietism," in *Ki Baruch Hu: Ancient Near Eastern, Biblical, and Judaic Studies in Honor of Baruch A. Levine*, ed. R. Chazan, W. Hallo, and L. H. Schiffman (Winona Lake, 1999), 593–634.

58. The literal translation of *otiyot* should be "letters," but it is clear from the context that here this term signifies an occurrence of the divine name. I have translated the word according to its idiomatic usage.

59. Immediately prior to the dictum of R. Eleazar one finds the following statement attributed to R. Ami: "Great is knowledge because it is placed in between two names, as it says, 'For the Lord is an all-knowing God'(1 Sam. 2:2)." In B. Sanh. 92a, this teaching is attributed to R. Eleazar. See Wolfson, *Through a Speculum That Shines*, 293.

60. This phrase is based on Neh. 8:8.

61. *Derash Mosheh* (Cracow, 1589), 15a.

62. TJ Ber. 5:1, 8d.

63. G. Bachelard, *The Poetics of Space*, trans. M. Jolas, foreword by E. Gilson (Boston, 1969), 89.

The Christian Doctrine of the Incarnation

1. Michael Fishbane, *Garments of Torah: Essays in Biblical Hermeneutics* (Bloomington: Indiana University Press, 1989), 35.

2. Translation from *The Complete Art Scroll Siddur*, trans. Rabbi Nosson Scherman (Brooklyn: Mesorah Publications, 1988).

3. Michael Wyschogrod, *The Body of Faith: God and the People Israel* (New Jersey: Jason Aaronson Inc., 1996), 176.

4. Many Jewish feminists, among them Susan Shapiro and Judith Plaskow, have challenged efforts to highlight the import of circumcision, insofar as it suggests that only men bear the mark of the covenant with God. Still, a recognition of God's commandment that we embody God's Torah may invite a new appreciation for the meeting between Torah and our bodies, male and female both. For such a Jewish ethics of the body, see Rachel Adler, "Justice and Peace Shall Kiss: An Ethics of Sexuality and Relationship," in *Engendering Judaism* (Philadelphia: Jewish Publication Society, 1998), chap. 4.

5. This is not to suggest that rabbinic Judaism was devoid of political interest and influence. For a valuable discussion of the political theory of rabbinic Judaism, see David Biale's *Power and Powerlessness in Jewish History* (New York: Schocken Books, 1986).

6. Based on T. BM 59b. See Eliezer Berkovitz, *Not in Heaven: The Nature and Function of Halakha* (New York: Ktav Publishing House, 1983), 47–48.

7. David Weiss Halivni's theory of the maculate Torah, discussed in his *Revelation Restored* (Boulder, Colo.: Westview Press, 1997), further nuances this notion of the embodiment of the Word of God, suggesting that in the process of God's giving the Torah to the Jews and the Jews' embodiment of it, the text comes to be flawed or maculate. For the purposes of this discussion, one might expand upon Halivni's view and

say that in this sense, the body of the Jewish people becomes simultaneously the cause for the fallibility of the text and the place for its subsequent repair. As such, the body of the Jewish people can be an analogue to the body of Jesus Christ, at once the place of human death and fallibility, and subsequently, as risen body, the place where triumph over fallibility is possible.

8. The concept of the community of scholars as the visible presentation of God's presence with us has received new attention from such noteworthy Jewish scholars as Robert Gibbs, Peter Ochs, and Steven Kepnes. Gibbs argues that rabbinic Judaism's dialogical practice affords the opportunity to recognize the *trace* of God present in the other person who studies or embodies the text together with me. Following Levinas, Gibbs rejects the notion that the other person is the *presence* of God; rather the other is only a *trace* of the God whose immediate presence is no longer with us. Nonetheless, Gibbs's thought is an extension of the notion that one who embodies God's Torah becomes a sign or a testimony to God's presence on earth. For more, see Steven Kepnes, Peter Ochs, and Robert Gibbs, *Reasoning After Revelation* (Boulder, Colo.: Westview Press, 1998).

9. Graham Ward, *Barth, Derrida, and the Language of Theology* (Cambridge: Cambridge University Press, 1995), 16.

10. Wyschogrod, *Body of Faith*, 24–25.

11. Additionally, although one may argue, as Michael Wyschogrod does, that the Jewish God humanizes himself in his involvement with the Jews of the Bible, God's humanity is not identical to the community of Jews who embody God's Word. See Wyschogrod, *Body of Faith*.

Embodiment and Incarnation

1. *The Inclusive Language Lectionary: Readings for Year A* (Atlanta: Cooperative Publishing Association/John Knox Press; New York: Pilgrim Press; Philadelphia: Westminster Press, 1983).

2. See Lisa Sowle Cahill, *Sex, Gender, and Christian Ethics* (Cambridge: Cambridge University Press, 1996); Christine E. Gudorf, *Body, Sex, and Pleasure: Reconstructing Christian Sexual Ethics* (Cleveland: Pilgrim Press, 1994).

3. For a discussion of God in female terms, see Elizabeth A. Johnson, *She Who Is: The Mystery of God in Feminist Theological Discourse* (New York: Crossroad, 1992).

4. *The Catechism of the Catholic Church* (Mahwah, N.J.: Paulist Press, 1994), p. 173, § 665.

5. Karl Rahner, S.J., *Mary, Mother of the Lord: Theological Meditations*, trans. W. J. O'Hara (New York: Herder and Herder, 1963).

Chapter Eleven

How Ought a Jew View
Christian Beliefs About Redemption?

1. Rom. 1:17; 3:21ff; 4:1–3, 9, 13; 5:1, 6ff, 18ff; 8:1; 9:16; 10:9; 11:5–6, 20.

2. B. Mak. 23b–24a. R. Nahman's comment here is noteworthy. The Talmud had said that the prophet Amos had reduced all of the 613 commandments to one: "For

thus saith the Lord unto the house of Israel, Seek ye Me and live." R. Nahman demurred, concerned that the verse might be interpreted to mean that only those who correctly fulfilled every single one of the 613 commandments are true God-seekers, and only they will live. This, as is well known, is the picture of Judaism presented by the Apostle Paul. Paul replaced observance of the commandments with correct faith. R. Nahman's comment may be part of an anti-Christian polemic, an attempt to undermine Paul's portrait of Judaism as a tradition bound narrowly to "the law."

3. Since many righteous people suffer and do not live long in the world as we know it, the verse must be promising life in the world to come.

4. Originally presented (in Arabic) in his commentary to Mishnah Sanhedrin 10. For an annotated English translation, see Menachem Kellner, *Must a Jew Believe Anything?* (London: Littman Library of Jewish Civilization, 1999), 142–152.

5. Moses Maimonides, *Guide of the Perplexed* I.34; in the translation of Shlomo Pines (Chicago: University of Chicago Press, 1963), 76–77. See further, I.5 (p. 28), I.62 (p. 152), II.36 (pp. 369, 371, 372), III.27 (p. 510), and III.54 (p. 635).

6. On Maimonides' messianic doctrine, see Aviezer Ravitzky, "'To the Utmost of Human Capacity': Maimonides on the Days of the Messiah," in *Perspectives on Maimonides*, ed. Joel Kraemer (London: Littman Library of Jewish Civilization, 1991): 221–256.

7. "Laws of Kings," XI.4. I cite the translation of A. M. Hershman, *The Book of Judges* (New Haven: Yale University Press, 1949), p. xxiii, with occasional emendations. See Leah Naomi Goldfeld, "Laws of Kings, Their Wars, and the King Messiah," *Sinai* 91 (1983): 69–79 (in Hebrew) on the passage here. As Goldfeld notes, it is hard to know who had a greater interest in censoring the passage: Christians, for whom it is offensive because of the way in which it "demotes" their messianic role, or Jews, who might see it as dangerous for that reason, or offensive because of the way it "promotes" the messianic role of Christianity and Islam.

8. "Laws of Kings," XII.1.

9. The Jewish tradition is so unequivocal on its acceptance of this teaching that when studied or recited, each chapter of the "Ethics of the Fathers" is customarily prefaced by the passage here quoted.

A Christian View of Redemption

1. See David Satran, "Paul Among the Rabbis and the Fathers," *The Princeton Seminary Bulletin*, Supplementary Issue, no. 1 (1999), 105.

2. See the work of E. P. Sanders, *Paul and Palestinian Judaism* (London: SCM Press, 1977).

3. See the discussion in Clark Williamson, *A Guest in the House of Israel* (Louisville: Westminster/John Knox Press, 1993), 94–98. See also Alan Segal, *Paul the Convert* (New Haven: Yale University Press, 1990), 169.

4. Krister Stendahl argues that the individualistic interpretation of Paul arose after and because of Augustine of Hippo in the fifth century; see "The Apostle Paul and the Introspective Conscience of the West," in *Paul Among Jews and Gentiles* (Philadelphia: Fortress Press, 1976), 78–96.

Chapter Twelve

Original Sin, Atonement, and Redemption

1. Adin Steinsalz, "Sin," in *Contemporary Jewish Religious Thought*, ed. A. Cohen and P. Mendes-Flohr (New York: Charles Scribner's Sons, 1987).

2. Moses Maimonides, *Mishneh Torah*, "The Book of Knowledge—Laws of Repentance," chap. 5:3.

3. Ibid., chap. 5:2.

4. For Augustine on original sin, see his *Confessions*, Book 5. Ephraim Urbach argues that the rabbis viewed Adam's disobedience as causing a "deterioration in [human] nature." See his extended discussion in *The Sages* (Jerusalem: Magnes Press, 1979), 422ff.

5. Arnold Eisen, "Exile," in *Contemporary Jewish Religious Thought*, 220.

6. Emphasis mine.

7. See Shalom Spiegel, *The Last Trial* (New York: Behrman House, 1979).

8. Franz Rosenzweig, *The Star of Redemption*, trans. W. Hallo (Boston: Beacon Press, 1972), pt. 3.

9. Abraham Joshua Heschel, *God in Search of Man* (Philadelphia: Jewish Publication Society, 1955).

10. Martin Buber, *I and Thou*, trans. R. G. Smith (New York: Scriber's Sons, 1958), 62.

Exile and Return in a World of Injustice

1. Emmanuel Levinas, *Difficult Freedom: Essays on Judaism*, trans. Sean Hand (Baltimore: Johns Hopkins University Press, 1990).

2. Reinhold Niebuhr, *The Essential Reinhold Niebuhr* (New Haven: Yale University Press, 1986), 3–21.

3. Elaine Pagels, *Adam, Eve, and the Serpent* (New York: Vintage Books, 1988), 3–32.

4. Gustavo Gutierrez, *A Theology of Liberation* (Maryknoll, N.Y.: Orbis Books, 1985), 152; 175–176.

5. For Roman Catholics, communion after Vatican II is to be understood in all of this fullness and duality, both as taking in the sacrifice of Christ, by the incarnate ritual of blood and flesh, and as accepting the fellowship of the others with whom one stands in congregation. I am indebted to Professor Michael Mendiola for his reflection on this point.

6. Ted Peters, *Sin: Radical Evil in Soul and Society* (Grand Rapids Mich.: William B. Erdman Publishing Company, 1994), 23.

The Lamb of God and the Sin of the World

1. As advocated, say, by Michael Wyschogrod, though this view of election is certainly not uncontested.

2. Ivica Novakovic, research assistant extraordinaire, thought along with me about the form and the matter of this text. The text was composed while I was enjoying the outstanding hospitality of the Center for Theological Inquiry, Princeton, New Jersey. Judy Gundry-Volf, Robert Jenson, Julianna Reno, Rusty R. Reno, and Kendall Soulen—all in one way or another related to the Center for Theological Inquiry—read a previous version of this text and offered valuable comments.

Chapter Thirteen

Religious Anthropology in Judaism and Christianity

1. T. Sanh. 9:7 and cf. B. Sanh. 46b. Many of the rabbinic sources have been collected and analyzed by Yair Loberbaum in his 1997 Hebrew University Ph.D. dissertation *Imago Dei: Rabbinic Literature, Maimonides and Nahmanides.*

2. T. Yev 8 (end).

3. Mek. bahodesh 8.

4. ARN B 30.

5. Gen. R. 34, 20 (see also B. Yev. 64a); T. Yev. 8 (end).

6. M. Sanh. 6:5.

7. Gen. R. 68:2.

8. Pseudo-Clementine, homily 17 22, 6.

9. See Gen. R. 11:2, 12:6.

10. This is the version in B. Hag. 15a-b. The legend of Elisha ben Abuya is first found in the Tosefta and has a long development in Jewish sources.

11. Elisha's relationship with R. Meir is mentioned in a number of sources, including B. Hag. 15a.

12. TJ Hag. 2:1 77b-c.

13. Irenaeus, *Against Heresies.* See the discussion in Anthony A. Hoekema, *Created in God's Image* (Grand Rapids, Mich.: Eerdmans, 1986), 33–42.

14. Gregory of Nyssa, *Sermon on the Sixth Beatitude*, trans. Joseph E. Trigg, in J. Patout Burns, *Theological Anthropology* (Philadelphia: Fortress Press, 1981), 29–38.

15. Ben Zoma in M. Avot 4:1.

16. For a discussion of Calvin, Barth, and Brunner, see Hoekema, *Created in God's Image*, 44–49, 49–52, and 52–58, respectively.

17. See Hoekema, *Created in God's Image*, 36–42.

18. Sifrei Deuteronomy Ekev 49.

19. Gen. R. 8, 13.

Toward an Anthropopathic Theology of Image

1. S. Freud, *The Future of an Illusion* (available in many editions).

2. *Kol Haneshamah*, 4 vols. (Wyncote, Penn.: The Reconstructionist Press, 1992).

3. A. J. Heschel, *The Prophets* (various editions).

4. For a fuller explication of these personalist attributes, see D. Blumenthal, *Facing the Abusing God: A Theology of Protest* (Louisville, Ky.: Westminster/John Knox, 1993), chap. 2.

5. E.g., Ex. 32:7–14; Num. 14:11–20.

6. Gen. 6:6; Ex. 32:14; 1 Sam. 15:11, 35; 2 Sam. 24:16.

7. D. Blumenthal, *Understanding Jewish Mysticism*, vol. 1 (New York: KTAV Publishing, 1993), chap. 2.

8. See H. Fisch, *Poetry with a Purpose: Biblical Poetics and Interpretation* (Bloomington: Indiana University Press, 1988/1990); see my review in *Midstream* (August-September 1992): 41–43.

9. There is a general covenant with all humanity, through Adam and Noah, and a specific covenant with the Jewish people, through Sinai. Both are grounds for the appeal to God's fairness.

10. See, for example, Ps. 88:15, 19; Ps. 44:21–24; Lam. 5:20. As I show in *Facing* and will mention below, if there is a post-shoah Jewish theology, it is this theology of anger and protest, of righteous indignation, rooted in the intertext of the covenant, in mutual expectations and obligations. See also, D. Blumenthal, *The Place of Faith and Grace in Judaism* (Austin, Tex.: The Center for Judaic-Christian Studies, 1985); idem, "Mercy," in *Contemporary Jewish Religious Thought*, ed. A. Cohen and P. Mendes-Flohr (New York: Scribners, 1987), 589–595; E. Wiesel, *The Trial of God* (New York: Schocken Books, 1979); and A. Laytner, *Arguing with God* (Northvale, N.J.: Jason Aronson, 1990); see my review in *Modern Judaism* 12, no. 1 (February 1992): 105–110.

11. See, for example, Ps. 79:6 and Ps. 137:9.

12. See M. Wyschogrod, *The Body of Faith: Judaism as Corporeal Election* (New York: Seabury, 1983); see my review in *Association for Jewish Studies Review* 11: 116–121; and D. Hartman, *A Living Covenant* (New York: Free Press, 1985); see my review in *Association for Jewish Studies Review* 12: 298–305. One can even read the book of Genesis as an essay in chosenness and rejection.

13. *Facing*, chap. 3.

14. The word "shoah" is preferable to "holocaust" because the latter connotes a whole-burned sacrifice, certainly not a meaning to be signaled here. The former has the merit of being a Hebrew term and, hence, allows the Jewish people to name its own disaster.

15. For a fuller discussion, see D. Blumenthal, "Theodicy: Dissonance in Theory and Praxis," *Concilium* 1 (1998): 95–98; also available on my Website (it is capital-sensitive): <http://www.emory.edu/UDR/BLUMENTHAL>.

16. It may even be the case that God has an unconscious.

17. *Facing*, 240–246.

18. *Facing*, chaps. 17–18.

19. *Facing*, 259, modified slightly.

20. See "Theodicy," 100–103.

21. "My Faith is Deeper Now," *Jewish Spectator* (Spring): 40–43.

22. See "Theodicy," 98.

23. Note, this paragraph is adapted from "Theodicy," 103–104. To be sure, there are those who would argue the contrary: The fascination with evil results from a desire to undermine the legitimacy of the good God. Not resolving the theodical problem but holding onto it is itself a desire to keep the problem alive and, hence, to avoid

total submission to the omnibenevolent God. I hear the argument but am not persuaded. Contending with God requires very deep faith and, in the final analysis, is rooted in a mature, loving relationship. See "My Faith is Deeper Now."

The Image of God in Christian Faith

1. See Michael Welker, *Creation and Reality*, trans. John Hoffmeyer (Minneapolis: Fortress Press, 1999). On the supposed connection between Genesis and the ecological problem, see Lynn White, "The Historical Roots of Our Ecological Crisis," *Science* 155 (1967).

2. Jürgen Moltmann, *God in Creation: A New Theology of Creation and the Spirit of God*, trans. M. Kohl (San Francisco: Harper & Rowe, 1985), 215ff.

3. See Rosemary Radford Reuther, *Sexism and God-Talk: Toward a Feminist Theology* (Boston: Beacon Press, 1983).

4. There are also debates in Christian thought about when and how a person becomes a living soul. Some hold to "creationism," which means that God creates each and every human soul at the moment of conception; others believe that an eternal soul enters the body at the time of conception. Although important for issues in medical ethics, I cannot explore this distinction here.

5. On Jesus' ministry, and thus on what it might mean to imitate Christ, see John Dominic Crossan, *Jesus: A Revolutionary Biography* (San Francisco: HarperSanFrancisco, 1994). On the *imitatio Dei*, see William Schweiker, *Mimetic Reflections: A Study in Hermeneutics, Theology, and Ethics* (New York: Fordham University Press, 1990). Also see Paul Tillich, *Systematic Theology*, 3 vols. (Chicago: University of Chicago Press, 1967); and James Gustafson, *Christ and the Moral Life* (Chicago: University of Chicago Press, 1979).

Epilogue

What of the Future?
A Christian Response

1. Only in the work of John Calvin and in Calvinism did talk of "the church in the Old Testament" survive as a standard practice, but little of this talk continued into the Enlightenment, except in isolated pockets such as New England.

2. For an account of the role of the two Torahs and of rabbinic commentaries in Judaism, see David Weiss Halivni, *Revelation Restored: Divine Writ and Critical Responses* (Boulder, Colo.: Westview Press, 1997).

What of the Future?
A Jewish Response

3. The work of the society began as a Jewish–Anglican dialogue among the Cambridge University theologians Daniel Hardy and David Ford and the Jewish thinkers Elliot Wolfson and Peter Ochs. The society has since expanded to include among its

leaders many of the authors who have written essays for this volume. In some ways, the work of the society has been anticipated by the intense program of Catholic-Protestant-Jewish theological study that is promoted by the Catholic theologians Richard Neuhaus and Avery Dulles. Numerous people involved in that program have contributed to this book: Robert Wilken, Stanley Hauerwas, George Lindbeck, David Novak, Peter Ochs, and Shalom Carmy (our editorial consultant).

GLOSSARY

This glossary presents brief, and therefore general, definitions of key terms that appear throughout the essays in this book. For more information, and for terms not included here, the reader should consult one or more of the following references: the *Encyclopedia Judaica*, the *Anchor Bible Dictionary*, and the *Encyclopedia of Religion*. Another useful resource is the glossary initiated by Robert Kraft (expanded and refined by others) for the University of Pennsylvania course "Religions of the West"; it can be found on the World Wide Web at http://ccat.sas.upenn.edu/~rs2/glossopt.html.

Apocrypha   From the Greek meaning "to hide" or "to uncover." Refers to certain Jewish books written in the Hellenistic-Roman period that came to be included in the Greek translation of Jewish scriptures (and thus in the Eastern Christian biblical canon) and in the Roman Catholic canon (as "deuterocanonical") but not in the Jewish or Protestant biblical canons.

Apostle   Greek for "ambassador, legate." In early Christian circles, it was used to refer especially to the earliest missionaries sent out to preach the gospel message concerning Jesus; traditionally twelve of Jesus' close associates came to be called "the 12 Apostles" (also "the 12 disciples"). Paul considered himself an apostle of Jesus Christ, although he had not been an associate of Jesus during his life.

Augustine (354–430 C.E.)   One of the foremost philosophers and theologians of early Christianity. He had a profound influence on the subsequent development of Western thought and culture and first gave shape to the themes and defined the problems that have characterized the Western tradition of Christian theology.

B.C.E. (before the common era)   An attempt to use a neutral designation for the period traditionally labeled "B.C." (before Christ) by Christians. Thus 586 B.C.E. is identical to 586 B.C.

Baptism   In earliest Christianity, the rite of ritual immersion in water that initiated a person (usually an "adult") into the Christian church. Later, pouring or sprinkling with water, as well as the practice of baptizing infants, came into use in some churches.

Bar Kochba, Simon   Jewish leader of a failed revolt against Rome (132–135 C.E.).

Ben (Hebrew) or Bar (Aramaic)   "Son," used frequently in "patronymics" (naming by identity of father); Akiba ben Joseph means Akiba son of Joseph.

C.E. (common era)   An attempt to use a neutral designation for the period traditionally labeled "A.D." (in Latin, *anno domini*, or "year of the Lord") by Christians. Thus 1992 C.E. is identical to 1992 A.D.

Church Fathers   Term used to describe the writers of early Christian literature (excluding the New Testament itself) whose works, written between the first and the sixth century, were considered correct and appropriate ("orthodox") by the church.

Church   The designation traditionally used for a specifically Christian assembly or body of people, and thus also for the building or location in which the assembled people meet. By extension it is also used for a specific organized denomination within Christianity (e.g., Roman Catholic Church, Methodist Church, etc.).

Communion   A term used especially in Protestant Christian circles for the sacrament (see below) of receiving bread and wine as the body and blood of Christ (or as symbols thereof), also known as the Lord's Supper or the Eucharist (see below).

Dead Sea Scrolls   A collection of Jewish religious manuscripts written between the third century B.C.E. and 70 C.E. that were discovered near the Dead Sea. They provide insight into Second Temple Judaism and subsequent rabbinic Judaism, as well as into the religious world in which Jesus and his early followers lived.

Docetism   The belief that the divine Christ could not suffer pain and death, and that he only seemed (Greek, *dokeo*) to do so. Docetism came to be regarded as a heresy, since it is incompatible with incarnation (see below).

Eschatology   Refers in general to what is expected to take place in the "last times" (from the inquirer's perspective), and thus to the study of the ultimate destiny or purpose of humankind and the world, how and when the end will occur, and what the end or last period of history or existence will be like.

Eucharist   The Christian sacrament of receiving bread (usually unleavened) and wine as the body and blood of Christ (or as symbols thereof). This term is more often used for the sacrament in the Roman Catholic and Eastern Orthodox churches, whereas "communion" or "Lord's Supper" is the term more common in the Protestant traditions.

Gemara (Aramaic, "completion")   See "Talmud."

Gnosticism   A form of mysticism found in Judaism, Christianity, and paganism in the Roman world. Although Gnosticism took many forms, it generally distinguished the Supreme Divine Being (usually seen as good) from the demiurge (usually seen as evil), a secondary power responsible for creation and involved in the material world. Dualism, the belief that the world is ruled by two opposing powers, was common to most forms of Gnosticism. Both rabbinic Judaism and classical Christianity were opposed to Gnosticism and viewed it as heretical.

Gospel (literally, "good news")   In the New Testament, it refers to four separate accounts of the life, death, and resurrection of Jesus Christ. In addition to the four canonical Gospels, there are other "lives of Jesus" from the same time period that were not included in the canon of the New Testament; these are sometimes referred to as noncanonical Gospels.

Grace   In Christian thought, unmerited divine assistance on one's spiritual path; often conceived as a special blessing received in an intense experience, but also may include a sense of special direction in one's life.

Haggadah (Hebrew, "telling")   Liturgical manual used in the Jewish Passover Seder. The term also sometimes refers to homiletic and legend-like portions of rabbinic literature, more properly known as *aggadah*.

Halachah (Hebrew, "the way")   Law established or custom ratified by authoritative rabbinic jurists and teachers. Colloquially, if something is deemed halachic, it is considered proper and normative behavior.

Immaculate Conception   The belief that Mary, the mother of Jesus, was free from original sin (see below) from the moment of her conception in her mother's womb. Often confused with Virgin Birth (see below).

Incarnation   A term in Christianity applied to the "becoming flesh" (human birth) of Jesus Christ.

Kingdom of God   The state of the world in which God's will is fulfilled, expected to be brought into being at the end of time. In Judaism this occurs with the coming of the Messiah; in Christianity it occurs when Christ returns.

Lent   In the Christian liturgical calendar, the period of forty days beginning with "Ash Wednesday" (so called because penitents mark their heads with ashes) and ending with Easter, the celebration of Jesus' resurrection.

Maimonides, Moses (1134–1205)   Premier medieval Jewish philosopher and legal expert also known as RaMBaM (acronym for Rabbi Moses ben Maimon).

Marcion   A second-century Christian who was considered heretical by his opponents because of certain dualistic and gnostic (see above) ideas. Marcion denied the sacred nature of the "Old Testament," viewing it as the book of an evil creator God.

Messiah   From the Hebrew meaning "anointed one" (in Greek, *christos*). Ancient priests and kings (and sometimes prophets) of Israel were anointed with oil. In early Judaism, the term came to mean a royal descendant of the dynasty of David who would restore the united kingdom of Israel and Judah and usher in an age of peace, justice, and plenty: the redeemer figure. The concept developed in many directions over the centuries. The messianic age was believed by some Jews to be a time of perfection of human institutions; others believed it to be a time of radical new beginnings, a new heaven and earth, after divine judgment and destruction. The title "Christos" came to be applied to Jesus of Nazareth by his followers, who were soon called "Christians" in Greek and Latin usage.

Midrash (Hebrew, "interpretation")   A general term for rabbinic interpretation of Scripture, as well as for specific collections of rabbinic literature.

Mishnah (Hebrew, "teaching")   An authorized compilation of rabbinic law, promulgated c. 210 C.E. by Rabbi Judah Ha-Nasi. See "Talmud."

Mitsvah (Hebrew, "commandment"), pl. mitzvot   A ritual or ethical duty or act of obedience to God's will. According to rabbinic Jewish tradition, there are 613 religious commandments referred to in the Torah (and elaborated upon by the rabbinic sages). In general, a mitsvah refers to any act of religious duty or obligation; more colloquially, a mitsvah refers to a "good deed."

Noahide Laws   According to rabbinic interpretation, seven laws were given to Noah (see Genesis 9) and were incumbent upon all humanity. A Gentile who followed the Noahide Laws was considered righteous (see Sanh. 105a).

Oral Torah   In traditional Jewish pharisaic/rabbinic thought, God revealed instructions for living through the Written Torah (Tanach) and through a parallel process of orally transmitted traditions. The Oral Torah was later written down as the Mishnah, Midrash, Tosefta, and the Talmuds (see entries above and below).

Origen (c. 185–251 C.E.)   One of the leading church fathers (see above).

Original Sin   In classical Christian thought, the term refers to the fundamental state of sinfulness and guilt inherited from the first man, Adam, that infects all of humanity but can be removed through depending on Christ and the grace he provides (e.g., in baptism).

Passion of Christ A technical term in Christian circles for Jesus' suffering and crucifixion.

Pentecost In Judaism, refers to the festival that occurs fifty days after Passover, known in Hebrew as Shavuot. In Christianity, it refers to the seventh Sunday after Easter, which commemorates the appearance of the Holy Spirit in Acts 2:1.

Philo Judaeus ("Philo the Jew") of Alexandria Greek speaking (and writing) prolific Jewish author in the first century C.E. Provides extensive evidence for Jewish thought in the Greco-Roman ("Hellenistic") world outside of Palestine. Philo's works were not preserved by the Jewish tradition but rather in Christianity, where they were influential in early Christian theology.

R. or Rabbi (Hebrew, "my master") An authorized teacher of the classical Jewish tradition (see oral law) after the fall of the Second Temple in 70 C.E. The role of the rabbi has changed considerably throughout the centuries. Traditionally, rabbis serve as the legal and spiritual guides of their congregations and communities. The title is conferred after considerable study of traditional Jewish sources. This conferral and its responsibilities are central to the chain of tradition in Judaism.

Rashi Acronym of Rabbi Shlomo Yitzhaki (1040–1105), who wrote classical commentaries on both the Tanach and the Talmud (see below).

Sacrament Especially in classical Christianity, a formal religious rite (e.g., baptism, Eucharist; see above) regarded as sacred for its ability to convey divine blessing; in some traditions (especially Protestant), it is regarded as not effective in itself but as a sign or symbol of spiritual reality or truth.

Shema Title of the fundamental, monotheistic statement of Judaism, found in Deuteronomy 6:4 ("Hear, O Israel, the Lord is God, the Lord alone" *(shema Yisrael adonai elohenu adonai echad)*. This statement avers the unity of God and is recited daily in the liturgy (along with Deut. 6:5–9, 11.13–21; Num. 15.37–41, and other passages) and customarily before sleep at night. This proclamation also climaxes special liturgies (like Yom Kippur) and is central to the confession before death and to the ritual of martyrdom. The Shema is inscribed on the mezuzah and the tefillin (phylacteries). In public services, it is recited in unison.

Shoah (Hebrew, "destruction") The term used for the destruction of European Jewry by the Nazis during World War II. The English term "holocaust" comes from the Greek meaning "wholly burnt," which is itself a translation of a Hebrew term, *olah*, found in the Tanach, referring to a sacrifice that was completely burnt. When applying the word "holocaust" to the Nazi destruction of European Jewry, the images of sacrifice and of being wholly burnt are troubling to Jews, who are increasingly using the term "Shoah," as are Christians who are sensitive to these same concerns.

Siddur The standard daily Jewish prayer book.

Talmud (Hebrew, "study" or "learning") Rabbinic Judaism produced two Talmuds: the one known as "Babylonian" is the most famous in the Western world and was completed around the fifth century C.E.; the other, known as the "Palestinian" or "Jerusalem" Talmud, was edited perhaps in the early fourth century C.E. Both have as their common core the Mishnah (see above), a collection of early rabbinic law, to which the *amoraim* (teachers) of the respective locales added commentary and discussion (*gemara*). Gemara has also become a colloquial, generic term for the Talmud and its study, popularly applied to the Jewish Talmud as a whole, to discussions by rabbinic teachers on Mishnah, and to decisions reached in these discussions.

Tanach A relatively modern acronym for the Jewish Bible, made up of the names of its three parts: Torah (Pentateuch or Law), Nevi'im (Prophets), and Ketuvim (Writings)—thus TNK, pronounced TaNaCh.

Targum Generally used to designate Aramaic translations of the Jewish scriptures.

Tosefta (Aramaic, "additional") Early rabbinic work containing supplements to the Mishnah, called *beraita* (extraneous material) in the Talmud.

Virgin Birth The belief that Mary, the mother of Jesus, was a virgin when Jesus was conceived and born. Often confused with Immaculate Conception (see above).

SELECTED
BIBLIOGRAPHY

There is an enormous wealth of material on Judaism, Christianity, and Jewish–Christian relation, both in print and on the World Wide Web. Basic information can be found in the *Anchor Bible Dictionary*, the *Encyclopedia Judaica*, and the *Encyclopedia of Religion* (edited by Mircea Eliade). The internet sites listed below provide access to many good resources. The bibliography that follows refers to works specifically on the relation between Jews and Christians. A useful bibliography, prepared by Jeffrey S. Siker, is found on pages 242–248 of *Jews and Christians: Exploring the Past, Present, and Future*, edited by James Charlesworth (see below).

Internet Resources

Institute for Christian & Jewish Studies (http://www.icjs.edu): The site for materials related to this book and the greater project of which it is part, as well as information about Jewish–Christian relations and an excellent list of related links.

Jewish Christian Relations (http://jcrelations.com): A substantial source of information about Jewish–Christian relations, with numerous links.

Internet Resources for the Study of Judaism and Christianity (http://ccat.sas.upenn.edu/rs/resources.html): This site, prepared by Dr. Jay Treat of the University of Pennsylvania, is a particularly rich set of links to academic sites that deal with a broad array of topics in the study of Judaism and Christianity.

Books

Allen, Ronald, and Clark M. Williamson. *Interpreting Difficult Texts: Anti-Judaism and Christian Preaching*. Philadelphia: Trinity Press International, 1989.

Beck, Norman A. *Mature Christianity in the Twenty-First Century*. New York: Crossroad, 1994.

Boadt, Lawrence, Helga Croner, and Leon Klenicki, eds. *Biblical Studies: Meeting Ground of Jews and Christians*. New York: Paulist Press, 1980.

Boys, Mary C. *Has God Only One Blessing? Judaism as a Source of Christian Self-Understanding*. New York: Paulist Press, 2000.

Braybrooke, Marcus. *Time to Meet: Toward a Deeper Relationship Between Jews and Christians*. Philadelphia: Trinity Press International, 1990.

Burrell, David, and Yehezkel Landau, eds. *Voices from Jerusalem: Jews and Christians Reflect on the Holy Land*. New York: Paulist Press, 1992.

Charlesworth, James, ed. *Jews and Christians: Exploring the Past, Present, and Future*. New York: Crossroad, 1990.

———. *Overcoming Fear Between Jews and Christians*. New York: Crossroad, 1992.

Cohen, Jeremy. *Living Letters of the Law: Ideas of the Jew in Medieval Christianity*. The S. Mark Taper Foundation Imprint in Jewish Studies. Berkeley: University of California Press, 1999.

Cohen, Martin A., and Helga Croner. *Christian Mission, Jewish Mission*. New York: Paulist Press, 1982.

Cohn-Sherbok, Dan. *A Dictionary of Judaism and Christianity*. Philadelphia: Trinity Press International, 1991.

Croner, Helga, and Leon Klenicki, eds. *Issues in the Jewish–Christian Dialogue: Jewish Perspectives on Covenant, Mission, and Witness*. New York: Paulist Press, 1979.

Cunningham, Philip A. *Education for Shalom*. Philadelphia: Liturgical Press, 1995.

Cunningham, Philip A., and Arthur F. Starr. *Sharing Shalom: A Process for Local Interfaith Dialogue Between Christians and Jews*. New York: Paulist Press, 1998.

Davies, W. D. *Christian Engagements with Judaism*. Harrisburg: Trinity Press International, 1999.

Dawe, Donald G., and Aurelia T. Fule. *Christians and Jews Together: Voices from the Conversation*. Louisville: Theology and Worship Ministry Unit, Presbyterian Church, U.S.A., 1991.

Eakin, Frank E., Jr. *What Price Prejudice? Christian Anti-Semitism in America*. New York: Paulist Press, 1998.

Fisher, Eugene J. *Faith Without Prejudice: Rebuilding Christian Attitudes Toward Judaism*. Rev. and exp. ed. New York: Crossroad, 1993.

Fisher, Eugene J., ed. *Interwoven Destinies: Jews and Christians Throughout the Ages*. New York: Paulist Press, 1993.

———. *Visions of the Other: Jewish and Christian Theologians Assess the Dialogue*. New York: Paulist Press, 1994.

Fisher, Eugene J., and Leon Klenicki, eds. *In Our Time: The Flowering of Jewish–Catholic Dialogue*. With an annotated bibliography by Eugene J. Fisher. New York: Paulist Press, 1990.

———. *Spiritual Pilgrimage: Texts on Jews and Judaism, 1979–1995*. New York: Crossroad, 1995.

Flannery, Edward H. *The Anguish of the Jews: Twenty-Three Centuries of Anti-Semitism*. New York: Paulist Press, 1985.

Goldberg, Michael. *Jews and Christians: Getting Our Stories Straight*. Nashville: Abingdon Press, 1985.

Huck, Gabe, and Leon Klenicki, eds. *Spirituality and Prayer: Jewish and Christian Understandings*. New York: Paulist Press, 1983.

Interreligious Council of San Diego. *Bridging Our Faiths*. New York: Paulist Press, 1997.

Kee, Howard Clark, and Irvin J. Borowsky. *Removing Anti-Judaism from the Pulpit*. Philadelphia: American Interfaith Institute; New York: Continuum, 1996.

Kenny, Anthony. *Catholics, Jews, and the State of Israel*. New York: Paulist Press, 1993.

Klenicki, Leon, ed. *Toward a Theological Encounter: Jewish Understandings of Christianity.* New York: Paulist Press, 1991.

Klenicki, Leon, and Geoffrey Wigoder, eds. *A Dictionary of the Jewish–Christian Dialogue.* New York: Paulist Press, 1995.

Klenicki, Leon, and Michael Wyschogrod, eds. *Understanding Scripture: Explorations of Jewish and Christian Traditions of Interpretation.* New York: Paulist Press, 1987.

Lodahl, Michael E. *Shekhinah Spirit: Divine Presence in Jewish and Christian Religion.* New York: Paulist Press, 1992.

Novak, David. *Jewish–Christian Dialogue: A Jewish Justification.* New York: Oxford University Press, 1989.

Ochs, Peter, ed. *The Return of Scripture in Judaism and Christianity: Essays in Postcritical Scriptural Interpretation.* New York: Paulist Press, 1993.

O'Hare, Padraic. *The Enduring Covenant: The Education of Christians and the End of Anti-Semitism.* Valley Forge: Trinity Press International, 1997.

Pawlikowski, John T. *Christ in the Light of the Christian–Jewish Dialogue.* New York: Paulist Press, 1982.

Pawlikowski, John T., and Hayim Goren Perelmuter, eds. *Reinterpreting Revelation and Tradition: Jews and Christians in Conversation.* Franklin, Wis.: Sheed and Ward, 2000.

Rothschild, Fritz A., ed. *Jewish Perspectives on Christianity: Leo Baeck, Martin Buber, Franz Rosenzweig, Will Herberg, and Abraham Joshua Heschel.* New York: Continuum, 1990.

Sandmel, Samuel. *We Jews and Jesus.* New York: Oxford University Press, 1965.

———. *We Jews and You Christians: An Inquiry into Attitudes.* Philadelphia: Lippincott, 1967.

———. *A Jewish Understanding of the New Testament.* Augmented ed. New York: KTAV Publishing House, 1974.

———. *Anti-Semitism in the New Testament?* Philadelphia: Fortress Press, 1978.

Saperstein, Marc. *Moments of Crisis in Jewish–Christian Relations.* Philadelphia: Trinity Press International, 1989.

Shermis, Michael, and Arthur E. Zannoni. *Introduction to Jewish–Christian Relations.* New York: Paulist Press, 1991.

Soulen, R. Kendall. *The God of Israel and Christian Theology.* Minneapolis: Fortress Press, 1996.

Stimulus Foundation. *More Stepping Stones to Jewish–Christian Relations.* Compiled by Helga Croner. New York: Paulist Press, 1985.

Thoma, Clemens. *A Christian Theology of Judaism.* New York: Paulist Press, 1980.

van Buren, Paul M. *A Christian Theology of the People Israel: A Theology of the Jewish–Christian Reality.* New York: Seabury Press, 1983.

———. *Discerning the Way: A Theology of the Jewish–Christian Reality, Part 2.* New York: Seabury Press, 1980.

———. *A Theology of the Jewish–Christian Reality, Part 3.* San Francisco: Harper and Row Publishers, 1988.

Williamson, Clark M. *A Guest in the House of Israel: Post-Holocaust Church Theology.* Louisville: Westminster/John Knox Press, 1993.

———. *Way of Blessing, Way of Life: A Christian Theology.* St. Louis: Chalice Press, 1999.

ABOUT THE EDITORS
AND CONTRIBUTORS

Editors

Tikva Frymer-Kensky is Professor of Hebrew Bible at the Divinity School of University of Chicago. Her most recent books are *In the Wake of the Goddesses: Women, Culture, and the Biblical Transformation of Pagan Myth* (New York: Free Press, 1992) and *Motherprayer: The Pregnant Woman's Spiritual Companion* (New York: Riverhead Books, 1995).

David Novak holds the J. Richard and Dorothy Shiff Chair of Jewish Studies at the University of Toronto and serves as Director of the Jewish Studies Programme. Professor Novak's latest book is *Natural Law in Judaism* (Cambridge University Press, 1998). His next book, *Covenantal Rights*, will be published by Princeton University Press in 2000.

Peter Ochs is the Edgar M. Bronfman Professor of Modern Judaic Studies at the University of Virginia and cofounder of the Society for Scriptural Reasoning and the Society for Textual Reasoning. He is the author of *Peirce, Pragmatism and the Logic of Scripture* (Cambridge, N.Y.: Cambridge University Press, 1998) and the editor of *Reviewing the Covenant: Eugene Borowitz and the Postmodern Renewal of Jewish Theology* (Albany: State University of New York Press, 2000).

David Fox Sandmel is the Jewish Scholar at the Institute for Christian & Jewish Studies in Baltimore. He directs the National Jewish Scholars Project, which includes the publication of this book and the Jewish Statement on Christians and Christianity. He is also editing the study guide and designing the program of outreach and dissemination that will be built on these resources.

Michael A. Signer is the Abrams Professor of Jewish Thought and Culture at the University of Notre Dame. Among his recent publications are a critical edition of Andrew of St. Victor's *Expositionem in Ezechielem Prophetam* (1991) and *Humanity at the Limit: The Impact of the Holocaust Experience on Jews and Christians* (Bloomington: Indiana University Press, 2000).

Contributors

Leora Batnitzky teaches at Princeton University and is the author of *Idolatry and Representation: The Philosophy of Franz Rosenzweig Reconsidered* (Princeton, N.J.: Princeton University Press, 2000). She is currently at work on a book with the working title

Jewish Philosophy and the Crisis of Historicism, which focuses on the philosophies of Emmanuel Levinas and Leo Strauss.

David R. Blumenthal is Jay and Leslie Cohen Professor of Judaic Studies at Emory University. His publications include the two-volume *Understanding Jewish Mysticism* (New York: KTAV, 1978, 1982). His newest book is *The Banality of Good and Evil: Moral Lessons from the Shoah and Jewish Tradition* (Washington, D.C.: Georgetown University Press, 1999).

John C. Cavadini is Chair of the Department of Theology and Associate Professor of Historical Theology at the University of Notre Dame. His publications include *The Last Christology of the West: Adoptionism in Spain and Gaul, 785–820* (Philadelphia: University of Pennsylvania Press, 1993) and *Miracles in Jewish and Christian Antiquity: Imagining Truth* (Notre Dame, Ind.: University of Notre Dame Press, 1999).

Robert Chazan is the Scheuer Professor of Jewish Studies at New York University and President of American Academy for Jewish Research. In 1999 he received the Career Achievement Award in Jewish History from the National Foundation for Jewish Culture. He is the author of *Jewish Suffering: The Interplay of Medieval Christian and Jewish Perspectives* (Kalamazoo, Mich.: Medieval Institute Publications, 1998) and *God, Humanity, and History: The Hebrew First-Crusade Narratives* (Berkeley: University of California Press, 2000).

Elliot N. Dorff is Rector and Professor of Philosophy at the University of Judaism and has appeared before President Clinton's National Bioethics Advisory. He is the author of *Matters of Life and Death: A Jewish Approach to Modern Medical Ethics* (Philadelphia: Jewish Publication Society, 1998) and *Knowing God: Jewish Journeys to the Unknown* (Northvale, N.J.: Jason Aronson, 1992).

David Ellenson is the I.H. and Anna Grancell Professor of Jewish Religious Thought at Hebrew Union College-Jewish Institute of Religion in Los Angeles. He is the author of *Between Tradition and Culture: The Dialectics of Modern Jewish Religion and Identity* (Atlanta, Ga.: Scholars Press, 1994) and *Tradition in Transition: Orthodoxy, Halakhah, and the Boundaries of Modern Jewish Identity* (Lanham, Md.; University Press of America, 1989).

Nancy Fuchs-Kreimer teaches at the Reconstructionist Rabbinical College in Wyncote, Pennsylvania, and has served as Director of Kaplan Institute for Adult Jewish Studies and Editor of *Raayonot*, the Reconstructionist Rabbinical Association Journal. She is the author of *Our Share of Night, Our Share of Morning: Parenting as a Spiritual Journey* (San Francisco: HarperSanFrancisco, 1996) and her articles have appeared in *Journal of Ecumenical Studies, Religious Education, Cross Currents, Lilith, The Reconstructionist*, and other periodicals.

Irving Greenberg is the President of the Jewish Life Institute and Chair of the United States Holocaust Memorial Council. Among his publications are *The Jewish Way* (New York: Summit Books, 1988) and *Living in the Image of God* (New York: Jason Aronson, 1998).

Robert Gibbs teaches in the Department of Philosophy at the University of Toronto. Recent publications include *Correlations in Rosenzweig and Levinas*, (Princeton, N.J.: Princeton University Press, 1992) and *Why Ethics?: Signs of Responsibility* (Princeton, N.J.: University Press, 2000).

Stanley Hauerwas teaches theological ethics at Duke University. He is the author of *The Peaceable Kingdom, A Community of Character*, and (with Will Willimon) *Resi-*

dent Aliens: Life in the Christian Colony (Nashville, Tenn.: Abingdon Press, 1989). His most recent book is *Sanctifying Them for the Truth: Holiness Exemplified* (Nashville, Tenn.: Abingdon Press, 1999). Dr. Hauerwas has been named to the prestigious Gifford Lectures at the University of St Andrews, Scotland, for the year 2000–2001.

Lawrence A. Hoffman is Professor of Liturgy at Hebrew Union College-Jewish Institute of Religion, New York, and Director of the Synagogue 2000 Initiative for synagogue spirituality. Recent books include *The Art of Public Prayer: Not for Clergy Only* (Woodstock, Vt.: Jewish Lights Pub., 1999) *and Covenant of Blood: Circumcision and Gender in Rabbinic Judaism* (Chicago: University of Chicago Press, 1995).

Menachem Kellner is Sir Isaac and Lady Edith Wolfson Professor of Jewish Religious Thought at the University of Haifa. His publications include *Must a Jew Believe Anything?* (Portland, Ore.: Littman Library of Jewish Civilization, 1999) and a translation of *Gersonides' Commentary on Song of Songs* (New Haven, Ct.: Yale University Press, 1998).

Steven Kepnes is Director of Jewish Studies and Associate Professor of Religion at Colgate University. Recent books include *Interpreting Judaism in a Postmodern Age* (ed., New York: New York University Press, 1996) and *Reasoning After Revelation: Dialogues in Postmodern Jewish Philosophy* (co-author, Boulder, Colo.: Westview Press, 1998). Kepnes is co-director of the Society for Textual Reasoning and co-editor of the Journal of Textual Reasoning.

Ruth Langer is Assistant Professor of Jewish Studies at Boston College and the author of *To Worship God Properly: Tensions Between Liturgical Custom and Halakhah in Judaism* (Cincinnati: Hebrew Union College Press, 1998) and "From Study of Scripture to a Reenactment of Sinai" in Worship (1998).

Christopher M. Leighton has served as the Executive Director of the Institute for Christian & Jewish Studies in Baltimore, Md., since its inception in 1987. In addition to his work at the ICJS, he is an adjunct professor at the Johns Hopkins University. He co-edited *About Genesis: A Resource Guide* for the Bill Moyers series.

George Lindbeck, is Pitkin Prof Emeritus of Historical Theology and Religious Studies at Yale University and author of *The Nature of Doctrine: Religion and Theology in a Postliberal Age* (Philadelphia: Westminster Press, 1984) and *Theology and Dialogue: Essays in Conversation with George Lindbeck* (edited by Bruce D. Marshall. Notre Dame, Ind.: University of Notre Dame Press, 1990).

Hindy Najman is University of Notre Dame is Assistant Professor of Theology, with a primary specialization in Second Temple Judaism and early Rabbinics. Her forthcoming book is entitled *Sacred Writing and Sacred Reading: Invoking Mosaic Torah in Second Temple Judaism* (Leiden, the Netherlands: E.J. Brill, 2001).

Randi Rashkover is Assistant Professor of Jewish Studies at the Cleveland College of Jewish Studies. She is the Assistant Editor of *Cross Currents* and serves on the editorial board of *Textual Reasoning.*

Susan A. Ross is Associate Professor of Theology at Loyola University of Chicago and the author of *Broken and Whole: Essays on Religion and the Body*, co-edited with Maureen A. Tilley (Lanham, Md.: University Press of America, 1995) and *Extravagant Affections: A Feminist Sacramental Theology* (New York: Continuum, 1998).

William Schweiker is Associate Professor of Theological Ethics, The Divinity School at the University of Chicago. His works include *Responsibility and Christian*

Ethics (New York: Cambridge University Press, 1995) and *Power, Value, and Conviction: Theological Ethics in the Postmodern Age* (Cleveland, Ohio: Pilgrim Press, 1998).

R. Kendall Soulen, Wesley Theological Seminary is associate professor of Systematic Theology at Wesley Theological Seminary in Washington, D.C., and author of *The God of Israel and Christian Theology* (Minneapolis: Fortress Press, 1996).

David Tracy is the Andrew Thomas Greeley and Grace McNichols Greeley Distinguished Service Professor of Catholic Studies at The Divinity School of the University of Chicago (Gregorian University). His publications include *The Analogical Imagination: Christian Theology and the Culture of Pluralism* (New York: Crossroad, 1981) and *On Naming the Present: Reflections on God, Hermeneutics, and Church* (Maryknoll, N.Y.: Orbis Books, 1994).

Miroslav Volf is Professor of Systematic Theology at Yale University. Professor Volf has written nine books, most recently *After Our Likeness: The Church as the Image of the Trinity* (Grand Rapids, Mich.: William B. Eerdmans, 1998) and *A Spacious Heart: Essays on Identity and Togetherness* (Valley Forge, Pa.: Trinity Press International 1997).

Robert Louis Wilken is the William R. Kenan, Jr. Professor of Christianity at the University of Virginia. Among his publications are *The Christians as the Romans Saw Them* (New Haven, Ct.: Yale University Press, 1986), *The Land Called Holy: Palestine in Christian History and Thought* (New Haven: Yale University Press, 1992), and *Remembering the Christian Past* (Grand Rapids, Mich.: W.B. Eerdmans, 1995).

Clark Williamson is Dean, Vice-President for Academic Affairs, and Indiana Professor of Christian Thought at Christian Theological Seminary. His most recent books are *Way of Blessing, Way of Life: A Christian Theology* (St. Louis: Chalice Press, 1999), *The Vital Church*, with Ron Allen (St. Louis: Chalice Press, 1998), and *Adventures of the Spirit: A Guide to Worship from the Perspective of Process Theology*, with Ron Allen (Lanham, Md.: University Press of America, 1997).

Elliot R. Wolfson is the Judge Abraham Lieberman Professor of Hebrew Studies and Director of Religious Studies at New York University. Recent books include *Hermeneutics, Theosophy, and Theory and the Prophetic Kabbalah of Abraham Abulafia* (Los Angeles: Cherub Press, 1999) and *Rending the Veil: Concealment and Secrecy in the History of Religions* (New York: Seven Bridges Press, 1999). Professor Wolfson received the National Jewish Book Award for Excellence in Scholarship, for *Through a Speculum That Shines* (Princeton, N.J.: Princeton University Press, 1994).

Laurie Zoloth is Associate Professor and Director of Jewish Studies at San Francisco State University. She also is the clinical ethicist and co-founder, The Ethics Practice in Berkeley. Recent publications include, *Health Care and the Ethics of Encounter: A Jewish Discussion of Social Justice* (Chapel Hill, N. C.; London: University of North Carolina Press, 1999) and "The Ethics of Encounter: Community and Conscience in Health Care Reform" (1997) and "Heroic Measures: The Ethics of the Ordinary World" (1997).

INDEX